Talk Talk

Other books by Allan Vorda

Face to Face: Interviews with Contemporary Novelists
(Rice University Press)

Psychedelic Psounds: Interviews from A to Z
with 60s Psychedelic and Garage Bands
(Borderline Productions/U.K.)

Talk Talk: Interviews with Writers

Allan Vorda

Fort Worth, Texas

Library of Congress Cataloging-in-Publication Data

Names: Vorda, Allan, 1948- compiler, interviewer. | Haber, Mark, 1972- writer of foreword.
Title: Talk talk : interviews with writers / Allan Vorda.
Description: Fort Worth : TCU Press, [2022] | Foreword by Mark Haber. | Summary: "Talk Talk: Interviews with Writers covers thirty-five years of interviews with writers including Max Apple, Greg Bear, Jamaica Kincaid, Ron Hansen, Kazuo Ishiguro, Jennifer Egan, Madison Smartt Bell, Elizabeth Crook, Robert Stone, and many others. Conducted at the time the writer's latest book was published, each interview displays the kind of depth and fascinating detail that can only be achieved when the interviewer comes equipped with a deep, broad knowledge of his subject's work. The resulting conversations range over a spectrum of contemporary and classic fiction and poetry, revealing much about the writers' impulses, backgrounds, and sources of inspiration. Talk Talk will not only help lay readers gain insight into the works of these important writers but will become a valuable resource for scholars and students"-- Provided by publisher.
Identifiers: LCCN 2021048311 (print) | LCCN 2021048312 (ebook) | ISBN 9780875657929 (paperback) | ISBN 9780875658063 (ebook)
Subjects: LCSH: Novelists, American--20th century--Interviews. | Novelists,
American--21st century--Interviews. | Novelists--20th century--Interviews. | Novelists--21st century--Interviews. | Literature and society. | Fiction--Authorship. | LCGFT: Interviews.
Classification: LCC PS371 .V673 2022 (print) | LCC PS371 (ebook) | DDC 813/.5409--dc23/eng/20220401
LC record available at https://lccn.loc.gov/2021048311
LC ebook record available at https://lccn.loc.gov/2021048312

Design by Bill Brammer
Front Cover Concept: Allan Vorda and Melanie Savoie

TCU Box 298300
Fort Worth, Texas 76129
To order books: 1.800.826.8911

These interviews first appeared in the following publications:

Rain Taxi: Paolo Bacigalupi, Madison Smartt Bell, Elizabeth Crook, Kim Echlin, Jennifer Egan, Aminatta Forna, Mark Haber, Valeria Luiselli, Emily St. John Mandel, Benjamin Moser, Steven Pinker, Richard Powers, Samanta Schweblin, Dan Simmons, and Neal Stephenson.

Interviews conducted for later novels were with Cristina García, Ron Hansen, and Richard Powers.

Sonora Review: Paula Byrne, Annabel Lyon, Ron Hansen, and James Romm.

Michigan Quarterly Review: Max Apple.

Mississippi Review: Kazuo Ishiguro, Jamaica Kincaid, and Robert Stone.

Literary Review: Hubert Selby Jr.

Extrapolation: Greg Bear.

Face to Face: Interviews with Contemporary Novelists (Rice University Press): Cristina García and Marilynne Robinson.

Dedicated to Le-My Nguyen Vorda
Words cannot express what we have shared.

“The orange blossom would have scarcely withered on the grave,” as a poet might have said. But I am no poet. I am only a very conscientious recorder.

—VLADIMIR NABOKOV, *Lolita*

CONTENTS

Foreword

Interviews about the craft of writing can sometimes feel academic, even specialized, and yet, when a great interview happens something clicks, something ineffable but true, and the reader knows it. The right questions are posed and the answers reveal hidden depths, unseeded notions, ideas the author perhaps never even considered. The magic of an interview is the art of the spontaneous, the uncontrived push and pull of any great conversation, and yet, what comes across as a natural act requires knowledge and research, an extensive understanding of the author and their work.

Spanning several decades, Allan Vorda's interviews—including countless genres and an enviable roster of writers—contain this magic. From American writers like Richard Powers and Marilynne Robinson, to the newer voices of Latin American literature like Samanta Schweblin and Valeria Luiselli, to the science fiction of Neal Stephenson and Greg Bear, Vorda's interviews combine a deep understanding of the writer's craft and the author's work, seamlessly meshed with the breathing room to discuss literally *anything.* From the impulse to write itself, to the act of memoir. From Jamaica Kincaid discussing the origin of her name to Jennifer Egan's "epiphany" to become a writer while backpacking in Europe, this is a book awash with both anecdote and wisdom.

Reading these interviews, one sees the landscape of the time; an interview from 1990, for example, can't help but reflect the trends and ideas in writing, the books winning awards, as well as the larger backdrop of culture, both of the United States and the rest of the world. Vorda's deep understanding of the writers that he's interviewing comes alive on every page—a respect for the craft as well as the human experience behind that craft. In addition, the sheer joy of reading an interview with a writer one has not yet read (which happened to me in several cases) is just as rewarding. Read as a whole, this book is a great introduction to writers who may be new to even the best-read reader.

There are a great many discussions about the American landscape and culture; there are opinions about research, academia, and the joys of reading for pleasure. There are opinions by writers about *other* writers in the book. There are remarkable revelations, as when Nobel Prize winner Kazuo Ishiguro discusses *The Remains of the Day* as being a pastiche, not a book based in reality but a book *more English than English.* Every interview displays a deep generousness: on ideas, art, and the belief that literature is a shared experience; and although often writing (and reading) feels like an isolated practice, it truly isn't (speaking of generousness, what book of interviews contains Hubert Selby Jr. discussing *Last Exit to Brooklyn,* and, by simply turning the page, Samanta Schweblin discussing the environmental catastrophe of *Fever Dream*?). This generousness is evident in the works of these writers and is displayed in full in these wonderful conversations.

Vorda's interviews offer an expansive look at internationally celebrated writers and their writing over the course of decades. Each conversation constitutes its own world while simultaneously speaking to the other world, to both the past and the present, both the historical writer and the writers of the fantastic, to the *inner* life of the writer and the *outer* world in which we all must participate. The singular habits of writers, their superstitions, and their challenges are also discussed. At no moment is the writer's art better illustrated, perhaps, than in the interview with Robert Stone, from 1990, in which Stone says: *"a writer is an illusionist, a performer. You don't expect an actor to be as crazy as his performance, and writing is a performance. It is art. It is storytelling."* The interviews in these pages demonstrate the logic (and irreverence) of an often inscrutable craft.

There is also some regional pride in these pages: Allan Vorda, a Texan, conducted the majority of these interviews at hotels both in Houston and near Rice University prior to Rice-related author events. Texas natives like Elizabeth Crook and Ben Moser, winner of the 2020 Pulitzer Prize, are interviewed, and both Houston and Texas often emerge as a subject. Another reminder that literature is both provincial *and* universal, an act both shared and solitary, and Texas, no different than Austria or South Africa or Brazil, is part of that dialogue.

In short, this book is an embarrassment of riches, and I implore the reader to dig in: find a writer you love and relish the intelligence and humanity of the dialogue; next perhaps read an author whose name may be new because both interviews, I assure you, will be equally rewarding, and you'll likely find yourself quickly searching for their books.

Mark Haber
Houston, TX
September 2020

Author's Preface

I love reading interviews. This passion began when I was in graduate school pursuing my master's in English. After reading the work of a writer, we would often discuss the writer in a seminar and write a paper. If I was able to find an interview with a writer I was researching, I found it instrumental in helping me understand what the author was writing.

I am not sure when the first literary interview was conducted, but it was *The Paris Review* which made it a staple for their publications. Their interviews were later compiled in *Writers at Work.* George Plimpton and Peter Matthiessen, the cofounders of *The Paris Review,* were responsible for starting this practice with their magazine in 1953.

The first interview *The Paris Review* published was conducted by P. N. Furbank and F. J. H. Haskel with E. M. Forster. This was an important interview, since Forster had not written a novel since 1924. (One critic, speaking of the grand total of the five novels Forster had written, stated that Forster's reputation increased with each novel he didn't write.) The process involved Furbank asking a question and Haskel scribbling down Forster's response as fast as he could. The process of the interview has come a long way since 1953.

My own experiences are somewhat similar and have evolved as the years have passed. My first interview was conducted with the British singer Eric Burdon in 1982. He was playing in a club called the Rock Saloon in Houston, and I had written a few music reviews for a local underground newspaper called *Public News.* I walked into the club with a notepad and a tape recorder and said I would like to interview Eric Burdon. Despite my having no credentials, the person at the desk told me to go backstage. It is pretty shocking, in retrospect, that I was able to pull this off. Once backstage I sat down with Burdon and attempted to start the interview, only to find I had difficulty with my tape recorder. I couldn't get it to work! I finally gave up and scribbled down Burdon's comments just like Haskel did for *The Paris Review*. Once I got home, I realized this tape recorder required not just the "record" button to be engaged, but both the "play" and "record" button at the same time. This taught me a valuable lesson: always be prepared when conducting an interview.

The first interview I conducted with a writer was with Ron Hansen, who was a classmate of mine at Creighton Prep High School and at Creighton University. I knew Ron only from seeing him in the hallways at Prep, as we never were in the same classes and never really spoke to one another. Since he had just published his second novel, I sent a letter during 1985 asking if he would like to do an interview; he graciously agreed, and I sent him a list of questions. When I returned with my wife from a vacation to the Virgin Islands, there was a letter neatly typed from Ron with all of his eloquent answers. One of his answers discussed that he wrote his fiction in a notebook using a pencil. One can see how much interviews have changed since this first interview of mine.

The first in-person interview I conducted with a writer was with Max Apple in 1987. This interview involved an incredible amount of luck. I had just read Apple's *The Oranging of America*, which I thoroughly enjoyed, and wondered if I could interview him. Since he had received his PhD in English from the University of Michigan, I called the well-regarded *Michigan Quarterly Review* to see if they would be interested in an interview with Apple. Ordinarily the answer would not be positive, but *MQR* was doing a special double issue on Contemporary American Fiction and said they would love to have an interview with one of their graduates. I then met Apple in his office at Rice University, and this time I was well prepared with my tape recorder.

I think doing an interview in person with a recorder is by far the best method. Often while running down a list of prepared questions, the writer occasionally will say something that evokes a totally new question. It is like going up a tree and then going off onto different branches where the interviewer can explore something totally unexpected. This has happened countless times and has added exponentially to the interview process. All of my early interviews in person were conducted with a tape recorder, but in the last decade or so it has changed to using digital recorders. Typically, I use two digital recorders in case there is a problem, such as with the battery or something else.

The downside to using a tape or digital recorder? The unbelievably tedious amount of time to transcribe! This also involves a great deal of going back and forth on the recorder trying to correctly write down what the writer has said. Quite often some words are hard to understand, and a decent portion might have to be edited due to long, run-on sentences that are inherent to colloquial speech.

With the advent of computers and email, conducting interviews has eliminated the time-consuming process of transcribing. The advantage for the writer is that they can think and respond exactly as they want to. Of course, the downside is this precludes asking questions and going off on tangents, which is only possible with interviews that are done in person.

Naturally, there have been some interesting stories that have occurred during these interviews. One involves Kazuo Ishiguro, who was in town for the Houston International Festival in 1990. His third novel, *The Remains of the Day,* had just won the Booker Prize. Even so, he was relatively unknown to readers in America. When I called him at his hotel for our pre-arranged interview, I asked him if he would like me to drive downtown to his hotel. Kazuo's response was something like, "God, no, get me out of here, as I have been trapped here for three days!" Kazuo had just concluded a book reading at the Downtown Central Library, and I asked him how it went. Kazuo said, "It was held in a room in the basement and one person showed up!" We ended up driving to my house in Sugar Land and proceeded to have one of the most engaging interviews I have ever done. Needless to say, twenty-eight years later he won the Nobel Prize for Literature.

I also want to give the perspective of the writer when the interview is done in person. These writers are often jumping from one city to another, meeting new people, giving readings, doing their post-reading Q&A sessions, and signing books. Then the next day off to another city. One can imagine how exhausting this can be for the writer.

The reason I bring this up is to relate my interview with the brilliant psychologist and thinker Steven Pinker. The interview was to be conducted at the lavish ZaZa Hotel near Rice University and the Medical Center. My son (an engineer who helped prepare questions for Pinker's book *Enlightenment Now*) and I arrived and inquired at the registration desk if Pinker could see us. We were told Pinker had not checked in. Just then my son noticed Pinker by his distinctive white curls, just as the author walked through the doorway. Pinker apologized, as his plane had just arrived from Miami, and asked if we could give him ten minutes so he could unpack. Ten minutes later we were in his room and proceeded with the interview, which lasted around ninety minutes. Answering questions off the cuff, Pinker was unbelievably eloquent, despite his jet lag. I was duly impressed. Then he said he had to meet someone at 3:00 p.m., have a dinner, and then give his reading before flying to the next city on his schedule. I have gained a lot of respect for writers who handle these interviews with such aplomb.

Once the interview has been conducted, a great deal of editing occurs. When finally edited, it is sent to the publisher, who then does their own editing. Then back to me for my approval before sending it to the writer, who has the final say. All in all, it is a lot of work, but it is also immensely rewarding when the interview is eventually published.

When I started doing interviews with writers in the 1980s, I had no idea I would be doing interviews for nearly forty years, pretty much as a hobby, while I ran my own company selling Controlled Environment Rooms for university research. Looking back on the entire process reminds me of how Max Apple concluded our interview. He was talking about the process of writing and, in a slightly humorous reference to the Howard Johnson motel chain for his book *The Oranging of America*, Apple said: "I hope to learn to do this better and better. That is the work of my life. My writings are my motels. My hope is to have a chain." I guess that is how I feel about my interviews.

The Interviews

Max Apple. Courtesy of Talya Fishman.

A Continuing Act of Wonder: An Interview with Max Apple

Max Apple was born in 1941 to a Jewish family in Grand Rapids, Michigan. He attended the University of Michigan, where he received his BA and PhD. He took a job teaching creative writing at Rice University, where he taught for twenty-nine years, holding the Fox Chair in English. In 1976 he published his first book to great critical acclaim: a collection of short stories titled *The Oranging of America*. Some of his subsequent publications include the novels *Zip* (1978) and *The Propheteers* (1987), the latter being a satirical take on Walt Disney and Disneyland. Apple also wrote screenplays for *Smokey Bites the Dust, The Air Up There,* and *Roommates,* based on the biography of the same name, which was about his grandfather. Upon retiring from

Rice University, he moved to Philadelphia, where he has taught at the University of Pennsylvania.

The following interview took place on the morning of February 19, 1987, in his third-floor office at Rice University. There were towers of books, arranged apparently deliberately around the room, causing one to wonder if he might be moving in or out of the office. The taping took place with us facing each other across a small wooden table. The interview was as congenial and jovial as one could imagine, almost like we were characters in *The Oranging of America*. Max Apple was one of the most pleasant people I have ever interviewed.

Allan Vorda: *The Propheteers*, your second novel, has just been released. When one first starts reading it, it's like seeing an old friend, because the first chapter is essentially the short story "The Oranging of America." Yet there is a sense of mistrust on the reader's part that this has been ground already covered. By using former characters and themes, do you feel you have opened yourself for criticism such as John Barth received for his epistolary novel *LETTERS*?

Max Apple: Yes, I worried about that, and I thought of just leaving that out because a lot of people had read it. On the other hand, even if people had read it before, it is still the starting ground, because you need to know who Howard Johnson is. That was in my mind when I originally wrote the story: I wanted to continue. I ended it many years ago with him about to meet the Disneys. It's just life got in the way of finishing it. I did worry about it, I do worry about it, and I think it's a legitimate criticism. I just have to ask the reader's trust, assuming some readers will have read it, that their curiosity will equal mine to see what happens.

AV: Later on, you also incorporate the short story "Walt and Will" (from *Free Agents*) for chapters seventeen and eighteen. By now the reader can see you are weaving an intricate fabric utilizing American characters of almost mythic proportions. Did it coalesce as early as when you wrote "Walt and Will" (originally titled "Disneyad")?

MA: We're talking editorial decisions. In my mind this was a book I started which used to be called *The Disneyad,* but it was published as *The Propheteers.* It's a product of nine years' work—not consecutive, since I left it for many years—but "Walt and Will" is part of the novel. "The Oranging of America" was a story which I continued. I didn't see "Walt and Will" as a separate story. My editor did, and he encouraged me to use that in *Free Agents.* I thought I didn't want to use it, because to me it was part of the novel. It was his feeling that it wouldn't make any difference. Your question suggests to me my own feeling that it probably does. Why would anyone want to read it again? I had to find a place for "Walt and Will" because that was a crucial part of the novel. To have that follow right after "The Oranging of America," which for me would have been two previously published pieces in a row, was not the way I wanted it. I found a spot for "Walt and Will," but there again it occurred to me not to use it. Both those sections were too important so I had to trust that, statically being kind of old stuff, it wouldn't upset the flow of the novel.

I was trying to write a novel, and I want to say this because I think a lot of reviews have not gotten this, that if I could have kept my original title, *The Disneyad,* which the lawyers didn't let me keep, then maybe it would have been apparent. I was trying to write a mock epic. Behind *The Disneyad* and *The Iliad* and *The Aeneid,* and another mock epic, *The Dunciad,* which was so important to me. Just as every reader or listener of Homer knew that there was a Troy that had fallen and knew all Priam's sons, so I'm counting on my readers to be familiar with Walt Disney and Disney World in Orlando. Of course, there's a big difference between Troy and Disney World—that's part of what the novel is about, part of its Kafkaesque and modernist comedy.

AV: Since you couldn't use the title *The Disneyad,* did you consider variations on the original title, and how did you coin a new word with the title *The Propheteers?*

MA: A lawyer for Harper & Row insisted on the change for not using *The Disneyad*, and I'm sure he was correct. The content of the book is protected by the First Amendment. You can use the name Walt Disney in the text, but the book jacket and title are considered advertising. Using the name Disney might be construed as infringement of what the Disney people own.

I couldn't think of any other title since I was so wedded to *The Disneyad*. I was in Buenos Aires at the time when I got the call that I needed a new title. My children and I walked the streets, but we couldn't think of one. Ted Solotaroff, my editor, came up with the new title. I'm very satisfied with it, but all those years I had the book in mind, it was *The Disneyad* to me and it always will be.

AV: Most of the relationships your characters have seem fanciful. For example, Margery Post meets James Merriweather and quickly marries him. Then she meets Clarence Birdseye and runs off with him after a chance meeting in the Russian countryside. Other fanciful relationships can be seen in such stories as "Vegetable Love" and "Carbo-loading." Why is your world so fanciful?

MA: That's not fanciful. It's called reality, biology, or other things. These are things that happen on the whole to everyone. I'm not much interested in describing a conventional courtship. I like the short cuts. It's not the fanciful I'm looking for in daily life, but also to squeeze everything together.

For example, I wanted to set it up that Margery Post probably would have fallen in love with just about anybody. She has this guy with black teeth making passes at her in the middle of an absolute wilderness. She has a husband who is more interested in his gout and his black maids than he could ever be in her. She has a father who was interested in the next world and not this world. Then she has Birdseye, who puts a freezing berry into her mouth and tells her she is the second person to taste a berry over a year old. I think he said "it was as stiff as a hard-on." When you hear a line like that from a strange guy in the middle of nowhere, it doesn't seem to me that it's unlikely at all they would make love. It is just about inevitable. I think that's the way it is in the world.

AV: It seems you're fond of fanciful ways of saying something abstract.

MA: Fanciful isn't the word. Maybe the word is epiphany, but I don't see it as quite that either. I read an interview with García Márquez a few years ago, and someone asked him a similar question. I'm not comparing myself to García Márquez, but he said that he needed to render reality through surreal images in order to be faithful to its eerie strangeness. In one particular episode, every time the woman touches a glass, the glass turns blue. That was the way he found for saying "falling in love," for defamiliarizing it, as the critics say.

In my short story "Vegetable Love," the man and the waitress put on their running shoes and go off to Mexico. It means that his quest is for nothing less extravagant than the meaning of life. But if I put it like that, who would want to read it? Who would want to write it? So I find a dramatic or metaphorical way of talking about things that matter most to people. Poets get away with these tropes all the time. Really, twentieth-century fiction owes a lot to the narrative stock-in-trade of poets and makers of fairy tales and folklore.

AV: Walt Disney's character is ironic since he makes everyone happy, but he is quite often depressed. Was this intentionally done?

MA: Very much. I have no idea what Walt was really like. If Walt Disney was really like that, his whole family and the world have my sympathy. I'm sure he wasn't. That's exactly the way I wanted him to be. I wanted him to be in great despair.

AV: Is C. W. Post, who is cast as a Nazirite, a metaphor for religion which many people now see as old-fashioned?

MA: I think it's been old-fashioned since Samson's time. But there are still Philistines.

AV: Margery Post and Bones Jones both come to realize their unhappiness with life is because they don't have kids and consequently don't understand children.

MA: I think you're reading in a lot of my feelings about the world and that I've lived very close to my children these last few years especially. To me, that pretty much wraps up what the essence of life is. If I have characters who seem arid and who think they have missed the world, then I guess they have if they haven't had children.

AV: The use of popular culture in contemporary fiction is a fascinating subject. Your novel contains some household names as characters: Howard Johnson, Walt Disney, Clarence Birdseye, C. W. Post, and Margery Post Merriweather. Why did you select these historical figures, and did you research their lives for accuracy?

MA: No, I didn't research them. I didn't even know Margery Post had met Birdseye. I like the names. I always liked the name Birdseye, and that little trademark has been in my mind since I was a kid. The disclaimer at the beginning of the novel, where I said that I was mostly acquainted with these people from my breakfast table, is the truth. I grew up in Grand Rapids, which is down the road from Battle Creek, and one of the earliest trips I took was to a cereal factory. People like the Posts and Kelloggs have been in my mind since childhood. Obviously, they are recognizable symbols of American success, and for that reason I can use them, as names or ciphers, not as realistic historical figures. I wanted to suggest that what motivates people who become household words is something more complicated than money.

If I called them John Smith or Allan Vorda or Max Apple, I would have to treat them more realistically, perhaps write about them as people who do want to earn more money. I don't believe anybody does anything for money. I know that sounds perfectly crazy. I mean everyday people, men and women who go to work in the morning to a store or factory, work for money. But someone who has ninety motels—why do they want ninety-one or ninety-two or ninety-three? Or if someone has Disneyland—why do they want Disney World? I'm just trying to imagine what it would be like because I think all of us know why we work. We work for a paycheck every week or every two weeks, but if I had one hundred million dollars, I'd still work.

Why does a writer with three books want another one? It's the same thing. Why does someone who has drawn a series of cartoons want to draw another one? What is the blank page or open celluloid? Those are life-and-death questions. I can't just state them boldly, theologically, or religiously. There is no way to do it. The novel becomes a vision of what life is. Now maybe I've romanticized it, sentimentalized it. Maybe these moguls are awful people. No doubt some of them are. I read the paper too, and unfortunately, I've met some of them.

I was looking for a vision that is generous. I honestly believed from the few things I know about Post or Kellogg that they still held an idea of making money for the sake of stewardship. C. W. Post believed very seriously that the world would be better if animals weren't killed. For me, this makes C. W. Post a much more interesting character. He's not a case study in how to get rich or what money is. That is what most popular fiction, what little I've read, is about—rich people and how they got rich. You know, the page-turning best sellers by people like Judith Krantz.

I wanted to write another version of this fundamental American story. I was interested in the concept of money, but in a different way. I was interested in why C. W. Post didn't want his money. Why money doesn't mean anything to him or to Howard Johnson or, finally, Walt Disney. When I was creating Walt Disney, I was trying to make a portrait of the artist. I think Disney was a great artist. You know Whitman's remark that "money is a form of poetry"? What if getting rich is not the sordid thing it's depicted to be in so many American novels? Or say that wealth might serve a writer now as Priam's wealth served Homer, as an opportunity to investigate the whole national character, its sweetness, its pathos, and its existential terrors. Maybe that's what more formula writers ought to be doing in their novels? I'm just asking.

AV: Or one might be rich and inherit it like Margery Post, yet even she's not totally happy.

MA: No, she's not. My sympathies with her are very great because this is a woman who has had virtually everything, but she has never been loved nor been able to. One of the saddest episodes in the book is when she's talking to the lawyer when she goes through Orlando looking at children. She describes children climbing trees, and the lawyer says to her, "They're playing." This is what's missing, because she doesn't know what playing is. She might be the richest woman in the world with mansions and all sorts of sophistication, but she doesn't know what play is, and play is at the heart of life.

AV: Is Katherine Woodson, a minor figure who makes a late appearance in the novel, modeled after anyone?

MA: No.

AV: What was the reason for her appearance?

MA: I wanted Margery to be jealous of someone. Katherine Woodson is a woman who is beautiful and young. She's doing things, and Margery hates her. It is just realism, because here is a woman who has basically taken over her house, and Margery doesn't like anyone very much.

AV: What prompted that whole sequence of bizarre, almost hallucinogenic scenes with Walt Disney: cat-got-his-tongue in mental animation, the nurse moving her eyeballs, and the needle as Mr. Shovel?

MA: To me that's the core of the novel. I can't explain it, but that's the absolute center.

AV: The ending of *The Propheteers* is somewhat demonic, where Walt is mildly electrocuting the Disney children who wait to return for more electrical shock treatment. "As awful as it looked," you write, "as awful as it was, he was giving them what they wanted." Can you elaborate on this unconventional ending?

MA: I think the quote is all I can say. I wanted the end to be both a surprise and inevitable. That is, here we have the world as it is. I've shown in the novel that Walt Disney, who's depressed and brooding on death, is an artist who can't help but wonder what happens when he erases a line, thereby raising existential and metaphysical issues. He is not a happy man. So we wonder: what is the magic of Walt Disney? Like any artist, he works in loneliness. He works in that dreamy, dark undercurrent that produces both great joy and inexplicable despair. Margery Post, by contrast, works in a straightforward way. Money can do this; power can do this. I'll hire the lawyers. She understands the world, she thinks. So when there is a confrontation, I wanted it to be a confrontation between the artist and the world.

AV: It also deals with your other theme: art versus life.

MA: Yes. I can't make it any bolder than that. What I'm saying is the end is exactly what I wanted: to see not only the triumph of Disney, but it's a comment about where art comes from. That this dreamy, depressed, hardly-being-able-to-get-along-in-the-world person can and does rise to do what nobody else can do. It may be somewhat awful, yet it's exactly what the world wants and deserves.

AV: I really thought that made it.

MA: I didn't know that I had it. I kept writing. I finished it, but I didn't have the end that I wanted. I kept writing it even after I sent it in because I had to get the ending just right.

AV: Another theme or motif I would like to review is the use of fruits and color. The first one that comes to mind, other than the apple which you never seem to make an issue, is the color orange associated with Howard Johnson in your story "The Oranging of America." There is also the metaphor utilizing the orange-topped cryonic U-Haul freezer attached to his car for his secretary, Milly. What caused this inspiration?

MA: I don't know. That's all unconscious. The apple stuff doesn't mean anything to me other than you have to take your name into account. When I titled that story "The Oranging of America," it never occurred to me that it would come to readers as *The Oranging of America* by Max Apple. The punning and color stuff were absolutely lost on me until it was pointed out. It's just unconscious. I have no answer for that.

AV: There is also the extended metaphor of pomegranates in *The Propheteers,* supposedly painted by Dalí for C. W. Post, being depicted on canvas as if they were people: round, hard, mysterious, pitted, tender, thick-skinned—above all, useless. Essentially, isn't C. W. Post more like a pomegranate than a cornflake, just as Birdseye was more kale than orange juice?

MA: Yes, you're right. Nicely said. The honest answer that comes to mind is because I am acquainted with the Bible. I spent a lot of years at Hebrew school.

AV: Other than the fact the French word *pomme* means apple, why pomegranate?

MA: I *wondered* about pomegranates. When you're a kid, it's hard enough reading Hebrew and then you think "Why are pomegranates all over? Why a land of milk and honey?" Milk and honey were things that weren't particularly interesting to me, either. I probably would have preferred Rice Krispies and milk. I never thought about this before, but I always wanted to eat cereal in the morning. For some reason my grandmother insisted that I drink coffee. My deepest longing, if you wonder why I write about cereal or why I have Dalí talking about cornflakes moving, was to eat cereal. Also, I think I recaptured my childhood longing. I didn't want to sit in the house and have hard toast and coffee with my grandmother and watch my grandfather drink tea with a piece of sugar in his mouth. I was sitting with my immigrant grandparents having breakfast and imagining that they were in Odessa, and I wanted to be in Grand Rapids and Battle Creek. I think that explains some of it, too, but when you see them in the supermarket, it seems like more work than they are worth. I guess I could have picked artichokes, but the Bible is not littered with artichokes. You are right, I did describe it as people.

AV: It is interesting to go back to Shakespeare's sonnets, which state there are two types of immortality: procreation and creation. *The Propheteers* seems to suggest the artist has a certain type of immortality with his creative work. On the other hand, so-called famous people, like C. W. Post at the end of the novel, are forgotten. They become a generic company like General Foods with their real names lost in time.

MA: Even Shakespeare will disappear. I would also say that people who do create don't understand what life is all about. Believe me, I don't pose to know what life is all about. Writing for me is *a continuing act of wonder.* I make small discoveries along the way. I get the felicity of a line now and then, such as at the end of this novel, or the passage about Disney, or the chapter about the tongue. When I get something—I don't always get it the way I want it, believe me—that's what I'm struggling for. When I get parts of the story or novel, that's pure bliss, pure felicity, and that's as close to understanding the world as I can get. Maybe a craftsman gets it in another way, such as when the feel of the wood is just right. I'm sure it's available to other people, when you feel things are just right and great. Every once in a while, the world seems luminous: being in love or with your children.

The other thing we carry with us is our death. Maybe I'm obsessed with those things, and it's possible I am. I've told you about the relations with my grandparents and how I grew up living close to old people. One of my earliest jobs—I recently wrote a short essay about this—was taking care of my grandpa, not that he needed any care. He was a vivid and active man who lived to be one hundred and seven years old, but he was an old man when I was born. He was over sixty-five. So, in that sense, I lived close to death. One of my big fears was that my grandpa would die, even though he was more vivid and alive than people much younger, because he was working eighteen hours a day. That's why I think death is with me, because I've lived so close to it.

AV: Disney makes the analogy on pages 166-67 that the artist is like God drawing lines (life) and then erasing them (death). This recalls Ebeneezer Cooke's existentialist notions of killing the ant in Barth's *The Sot-Weed Factor.*

MA: I wonder about the erased lines. What happens to a line that is erased? What happens when there is a page that's covered with things that disappear? What happens to people when they die? These are things that people have always wondered about. They go one way into religion, which becomes solidified. I'm not a theologian, and I don't pretend to be, but all people wonder about what life is and what death is.

I don't remember if there is any connection with *The Sot-Weed Factor*. It might have stayed in my own unconscious, because *The Sot-Weed Factor* is one of the greatest novels I've ever read. So I wouldn't be surprised. I would like to say any borrowings I got from *The Sot-Weed Factor* or Barth can only enrich one's work.

AV: In chapter nineteen, Nurse Bloom is unable to get any blood from Disney. Essentially, he is like an animated character, isn't he?

MA: Exactly. I wanted him to be as depressed, as lifeless, as full of death, as I possibly could. It's the blank page idea again. The novel in part is about how the imagination creates words or people out of nothing, as God did the world. I've made an anatomy of melancholy with Disney's character, but I've also made the kind of affirmative statement, I hope, that I described earlier. It's a comic novel. Like the Disney children, we're all attracted to humor and humorous people because we sense the sorrow and pain behind the humor, and that's real life.

AV: With the deaths of Camus and Sartre it seems existentialism has died. I can't think of one major writer who has said, "God is dead." What was once a major movement now seems dormant. Why?

MA: I have no way to answer that except that it isn't. Writers don't have to make such statements because it is so obvious. I hardly even know in any academic sense what existentialism is, except in my own life. I think it is so much the mood and the understanding of the world, since there are people who read and think that it doesn't have to be stated anymore.

That's why everybody is so busy being something else, Born Again or whatever, because you've gotten beat over the head about something that isn't there. The reality is existentialism. How you live with it is another matter.

AV: What are your feelings about contemporary fiction? Do you feel comfortable with labels like metafiction of experimental fiction, which are sometimes applied to your work?

MA: The truth is I don't like to categorize. I'm as likely to enjoy fiction that is old-fashioned as something avant-garde. My current colleague Lynne Sharon Schwartz's novel *Disturbances in the Field* is a perfectly realistic, conventional narrative and could have been written, stylistically speaking, in the nineteenth century. It's wonderful. It is one of the great novels in the way that George Eliot's and Joseph Conrad's are great—intricate plot, richly realized characters, acute social commentary. So I can appreciate that. I can also appreciate Frederick Barthelme or Raymond Carver and other writers who shade away from the mainstream. I consider what I do as sometimes experimental, sometimes very conventional.

AV: Or postmodernist?

MA: I was invited to write "Post-Modernism" (reprinted in *Free Agents*) for a panel discussion at a museum. First, I went to a library to find out what postmodernism was. I ended up reading a book of literary criticism that used my work as an example. So I thought, if I'm part of it I ought to be able to describe it. But, of course, it's critics who make the categories. That's what I was playing with in the "Post-Modernism" piece: writers don't say, "Today I'm a realist," or "Now I'm going to write a minimalist story." We write what we can, including the bad writers. I think Louis L'Amour might have his existentialist days and Judith Krantz now and then feels minimalist. You hope that the critics won't stick you with a label—Georgian poet, Decadent novelist—that will diminish you. You hope that, like Dickens or Joyce, your work will defy any one label and accommodate all of them.

The real question is, when will I have time to read all the contemporary fiction I want? I think there is an enormous number of good writers in the country today. I think this is a golden age in fiction writing. I know the critics, those people who are taking the measure and who have their hand on the pulse of the times, are never going to get it. You have to wait another generation or two for it. People are upset there is no Faulkner they can pick out. Of course, in Faulkner's lifetime, until almost the end, no one picked him out either.

AV: Would you be willing to name writers you admire? Or those who have influenced you?

MA: There are so many that I would just as soon not answer. As soon as you mention Barth, certainly. He has brought so much joy to my life, especially when I was young. Now I read my contemporaries with admiration and respect. I know a lot of them now, too. That's why I'd feel bad if I'd start giving a list and I'd leave some out.

I can tell you that when I was young, and by that I mean eighteen or so, it was a great discovery for me to find the Jewish writers. Not only Bellow and Malamud, but Herbert Gold. A whole group of writers who seemed so different from me, though their idioms and characters were intimately familiar.

I knew as a teenager that I was going to be a writer, whatever that meant. I was living close to stories. My grandmother was a great storyteller. And I knew that being a writer meant being a reader too. Reading was the most important thing in the world to me. When I was sixteen or seventeen, I read everything I could get my hands on. I didn't know when I read Dostoyevsky that I was reading a translation. I just read any book I could find, and given my later practice, I was strangely attracted to immense and realistic novels like *Les Misérables*. I made the jump, literally, from juvenile fiction to that book; I couldn't stop reading it. It turned out that I was reading great fiction, though I didn't know it at the time.

I thought that real writers were not people like me. I thought they were Englishmen or Frenchmen or Russians. I thought you had to be full of high seriousness like T. S. Eliot. Then when I got to college and got a closer look at all that high seriousness and great tradition, I knew I didn't belong to any of that. When you realize that you're not going to be writing about the Russian aristocracy or the French bourgeoisie, you look around for models closer to home, and this is where Malamud and Gold, especially, were so helpful.

I feel enormously close to E. L. Doctorow's writing too—both to the life he recounts, the autobiographical stuff, and to his style as a fiction writer. I also love Grace Paley's stories. Some of these stories just sing to me. Once I was teaching a short summer session at Berkeley with Grace Paley and E. L. Doctorow. Students would go from one class to another. One of the stories reminded me of a certain Chekhov story which I made an allusion to. A student stood up and said, "This has got to be a fix! I was in Doctorow's class and Grace Paley's class and they were both talking about the same Chekhov story!" Of course, we had not mentioned it between us, but it shows our affinity as readers and writers.

AV: Your review titled "Merdistes in Fiction's Garden" lambasted John Gardner's *On Moral Fiction.* It seems Gardner accomplished three things: (1) he made a lot of writers and critics mad; (2) he escalated critical attention on John Fowles by making him out to be the greatest writer of the century; and (3) Gardner may be remembered more for *On Moral Fiction* than *October Light* or *Sunlight Dialogues.* Do you have any comments ten years after your review of his book?

MA: I would stay with what I said, except that I later met Gardner and I found him to be charming. A very nice man. I liked him a lot. He had no animosity about the review. I took him seriously, by the way, because I spent a lot of time on that review. He was just wrong, and you know what, he knew it. I think he wanted to make large statements. When you try to do something on a large scale, you're going to fail most of the time. I gave him credit for what he tried to do. Of course, in a way, he was right; but in all the specifics he was wrong. I found it very objectionable to bring in Homer to pommel Ron Sukenick. It was disproportionate. So I brought out Homer to pommel him.

AV: Your stories are often set in Michigan, where you were raised and educated, or in Texas, where you teach at Rice University. Do you choose these settings because they have had an impact upon you, or is it just their familiarity?

MA: Not consciously. Things happen to you in a place in the world.

I know names of streets in Grand Rapids and Houston. I don't know them in Paris. Some of the *The Propheteers* takes place in Italy when Margery goes to look at *The Last Supper.* A friend gave me a guidebook to Italy so I could look up some street names. What I do know are the places where I've lived, but places are not important to me. I used to talk to Bill Goyen, who is a friend and a great writer from Texas. He didn't live in Houston, because that was his place and he had to go away from it. He is so much rooted in place. His fiction is the place. To me, it's the opposite. My characters, I think, could just about live anywhere, but I don't know the street names.

AV: *The Oranging of America* was one of the most distinctive collections of short stories to appear in recent decades. How did these stories develop?

MA: I knew when I was ready. I sent "The Oranging of America" to Ted Solotaroff at *American Review,* and after he published it, other stories came rapidly. When I started to be published, I realized I had some readers. I wasn't alone, as I had been all those years in graduate school, writing my secret stuff in the back of my Shakespeare and Milton notebooks, almost as if it were Hebrew starting from the other side of the page. None of these was published—typical juvenilia set down in my mid-twenties without any real hope.

I felt I was going to be a writer someday, and I thought I was going to be a teacher, but I knew I was never going to be a literary critic. Writing a dissertation was a pose for me, but I wrote it on a text that was intriguing: *The Anatomy of Melancholy,* a seventeenth-century book that addresses subjects I take up in *The Propheteers.* The career I have now is the one I still want. I still teach. I spend some hours almost every day being a writer, but I spend more hours being a reader. If you ask me what I am, I'm a reader.

AV: Regarding your narrative style, you have said in an interview with the *Mississippi Review* (Fall, 1984) that "Gas Stations" was a crucial story for you "because it was the first time I consciously trusted my fantastic impulses completely." Can you elaborate on this statement?

Does this following of fantastic impulses apply only to the short story?

MA: I hope so. I don't want to follow too many fantastic impulses in the world, though I have them. About "Gas Stations," Nora Ephron had called me from *Esquire* and said she liked my work and wanted to know if I'd write something for their bicentennial issue. She started running through a list of possible topics, which always strikes dread in my heart. I had never had anything published in any large-circulation magazines. I said I would write on gas stations, my suggestion. And yet I began to follow her advice in writing the essay; it was more than advice, it was directions. There was a lot of money at stake, and I nervously produced a rather dull essay on gas stations, which I threw away. Then I wrote what I wanted. I remember this so distinctly because I sent it to her with trepidation—with real fear that I'd blown my big chance for money and fame.

I was on vacation when Nora tracked me down and told me how much she loved the piece. I said, "But it's not an essay." She said, "Who cares! When it's that good, who cares!" I needed to trust my own instincts and personal style. Maybe that dull essay would have been published anyway, but I wouldn't have *emerged* as a writer, following my own directions.

AV: The last line of "Gas Stations" reads: "Careful on the curves, amid kisses and hopes I gave her the gas." This autoerotic metaphor recalls e.e. cummings's poem "she being brand new." Was this a conscious attempt to imitate cummings?

MA: Not conscious, but you picked up something good. No, I didn't know it. I just do it. I remember working those lines carefully. I do it all by rhythms to get it just right.

AV: What was the inspiration for "Vegetable Love"? Also discuss Annette's concept of Ferguson's fidelity depending more upon abstaining from meat than from other women.

MA: I haven't read it in so many years that I really couldn't answer that. But my wife and I had a small health food store, right down the street here on Morningside, and on the porch we used to be referred to as the Gypsy Market.

AV: What was the store called?

MA: Apples, Arts, & Herbs. It was a really tiny place. We sold toys on consignment. It was closed down by the health department because Jessica, our daughter, was playing with lima beans on the floor. No one ever bought any dried lima beans. We had about forty pounds of them, but the health inspector said you couldn't have children playing with food and then sell it. I suppose the eating I've talked about was on my mind when I wrote "Vegetable Love."

AV: What prompted an ivory tower PhD to write his first novel, *Zip,* about a poor Jewish manager of a Puerto Rican middleweight fighter? Also, what problems did this present as far as your authorial voice, in connection with the novel being related in an unusual semi-foreshadowing style?

MA: I just don't remember. A writer has to forget, like anyone else; otherwise, I would still be writing *Zip.* I'm busy forgetting *The Propheteers.*

AV: At the end of *Zip,* J. Edgar Hoover sits in a balloon above the ring. Any connection to similar scenes in Waugh's *Vile Bodies* or Barth's *Giles Goat-Boy*?

MA: I haven't read Waugh's *Vile Bodies,* but I did read *Giles Goat-Boy.* I tell you what it is. Writers that live at the same time, given all our differences, we're like radios since we're playing back certain images. The language is finite.

AV: "Bridging" (from *Free Agents*) is an incredibly poignant story made even more so because it is difficult to separate the fiction from the reality of your own life: a widowed father raising two children. You also stated in your interview with the *Mississippi Review* that your father's death affected you "in all sorts of ways that must filter into my fiction," but that you also lost "that intense ambition to be a writer." How has the death of two people so very close to you affected your writing and your view of life?

MA: I can't answer that in any other way except that it shows up in the work. I just can't answer any more than that. Except that it is there.

AV: The two-pronged sword of writing and teaching beleaguers most writers with not enough time for both. What are your thoughts on this, since you have vacillated between writing short stories and novels as well as screenplays?

MA: I don't get ideas. The screenplays or the things that are commissioned I only do if it is offered. I don't sit around and dream up screenplays. I've learned something about writing screenplays. It's not a form that's a happy one for a writer, because in the final version the words aren't everything. I like to be close to words.

With the fiction sometimes I'm interested in all the forms. When I start, I'm with a blank page. I don't know that a story is ever going to be a story. I can feel it about halfway through. I start to know. I feel it is going to be a story and not a novel, but some things are just going to be novels. It's happened a couple of times. Talking about an existential situation, I don't know what I'm writing. The majority turns out to be nothing—neither novels nor stories—just an interesting passage here and there. They turn out to be fragments. I just have to trust my judgment.

AV: Finally, in what direction do you see your fiction going?

MA: In an article published this year in the *New York Times Book Review* I talked about finding my place on the dying body of fiction. This goes back to Henry James's phrase, about the novel being the body of American fiction. I said: "Finally, I found a place. It was under the left-middle fingernail, an aging subdivision called 'Jewish, Jewish-American, not so Jewish and not so American either.' It was one of the noisiest sectors on the body, but I slipped in and found a place that had been vacated when the inhabitant moved to Hollywood. As crowded and argumentative as the subdivision was, I was relieved to have finally found my own place."

In the act of writing a novel or story, I'm dreaming. I'm daydreaming. It's the most real, the most profound *me* there can be, which doesn't mean it's very real or very profound. I was learning, even before I went to the University of Michigan, how to tell a story and also what to leave out. I don't consider myself a master of this. I give myself assignments. They come from my unconscious, and when the raw materials are there, I work with it as well as I can. I'm still learning. I hope to learn to do this better and better. That's the work of my life. My writings are my motels. My hope is to have a chain.

Paolo Bacigalupi. Courtesy of JT Thomas Photography.

The Author with the Unpronounceable Name: An Interview with Paolo Bacigalupi

Paolo Bacigalupi was born in western Colorado and raised by hippie parents on a fifteen-acre farm. He later attended Oberlin College, where he decided to major in Chinese. This strange choice of a "horribly hard" language enabled Bacigalupi to teach in China and visit such countries as China, India, Laos, Thailand, Malaysia, Singapore, Hong Kong, and Japan. After writing four novels which were not accepted for publication, he drew upon his experiences in the Far East and writing environmental columns for *High Country News* to write short stories that were eventually published and collected in the book titled *Pump*

Six. Bacigalupi eventually followed this up with his novel *The Windup Girl,* which, after several publishing house rejections, was published by Night Shade Books. *Windup* is a science fiction novel set in a dystopian future of Thailand where foods are genetically made to feed a world starving from bioengineered plagues; yet the main focus are the numerous multidimensional characters. The primary character is a nonhuman named Emiko—a genetically designed geisha girl designed to obey, but primarily used as a sex toy—who might be the most human character in the novel. *The Windup Girl* swept the awards for Nebula, Locus, Campbell, and Hugo. Subsequent publications include *The Water Knife, The Tangled Lands* (with Tobias Buckell), *The Drowned Cities, Tool of War,* and *The Doubt Factory.* Bacigalupi's other awards include the Locus Award for Best Novelette for his short story collection *Pump Six* and the Michael L. Printz Award for Best Young Adult Novel for *Ship Breaker.*

Allan Vorda: Terry Bisson gave you a backhanded compliment for your writing when he said, "Luckily, he has an unpronounceable name." Can you tell us a little about yourself?

Paolo Bacigalupi: Well, I'm not Italian. Let's start with that. Or at least I'm so watered down that I've got no legitimate claim to the culture, despite the name. This seems to cause great disappointment for anyone who comes across my name before meeting me—I'm more exotic in print, apparently. As far as my background: I was born and raised in rural Colorado. My parents were hippies who wanted to get back to the land, and I grew up on fifteen acres of apple orchards and hay fields and a lot of sagebrush and juniper trees. I attended Oberlin College, where I studied Chinese. I picked the language for no good reason, but I thought that an educated person should speak more than one language and I was sick of studying Spanish, so I went rooting through the course catalog and came across Chinese. I thought, *Hmm,*

I've heard Chinese is hard. So I picked it. And it really was hard, horribly hard. But I stuck with it, and because of that one casual choice, I ended up spending a fair amount of time on the other side of the Pacific, and some of my most formative years in China. I'm traveling less now, but my wife has family in India, so we at least get a chance every few years to go over for weddings and such.

AV: Christy Tidwell wrote an article called "The Problem of Materiality in Paolo Bacigalupi's 'The People of Sand and Slag,'" which focuses on the meaning of posthumanism. She concludes by saying: "A truly ethical posthuman future would, as Sherryl Vint has argued, be an embodied posthumanism and it would also be a posthumanism that is post-Humanist and post-Cartesian, a posthumanism that neither defines humanity in opposition to nonhuman nature and the environment nor defines nonhuman nature and the environment in terms of the human. Bacigalupi presents a strong argument for precisely this by revealing what happens in the absence of such an ethical and embodied posthumanism." Do you agree with this assessment? Does your story have a moral premise in light of an amoral future with a lack of ethics?

PB: This is one of those moments when I realize that my education is lacking—I had to read your question a couple times to get all my humanisms and posthumanisms straight. At root, my assumption is that humanity is intertwined with nature. We are part of it, and the more we pretend otherwise, the less human we become. In "The People of Sand and Slag," humanity has transcended all the things that require us to partake of what we might call ecosystem services. They live off sand and mine waste and don't notice the loss. They don't need nature, and that has implications for how they interact with their world. I'm not sure that the characters in the story are less ethical than present-day humans, they're just more sharply defined.

AV: Ursula K. Heise states in "From Extinction to Electronics: Dead Frogs, Live Dinosaurs, and Electric Sheep," that there is "the possibility of a different relationship between species: one that no longer privileges the right of humans—feminine or masculine—over those of all other forms of life, but that recognizes the value and rights of non-human species along with those of humans." This takes into consideration such characters in your fiction as human and posthuman—centaurs, bio-jobs, animals, and windups. Based on the relationship of the characters in "The People of Sand and Slag," the future for humanity does not look promising. What is your vision of the future for mankind in the twenty-first century and beyond?

PB: I think—if we're honest with ourselves—that we all know that we will be making do with less, even as we try to convince ourselves that we've actually got more. We'll enjoy less open space, fewer species and less diverse ecosystems, less clean water, less clean air, less ecosystem resilience, less cheap energy. Life today is probably as good as it gets. Of course, we could actually start planning and preserving and living as if we've got a long-term interest in the planet—as if we're embedded and part of a much larger web, which I think is what Ms. Heise is referring to—but we haven't showed any signs of change so far. I'm betting we're going to stay selfish, and hand our kids a shitstorm.

AV: I am curious if any of the following writers had any influence on the writing of "The People of Sand and Slag": Ursula K. Le Guin (*The Left Hand of Darkness*), Dan Simmons (the *Hyperion* quartet), and Harlan Ellison ("A Boy and His Dog").

PB: I've read *The Left Hand of Darkness* and "A Boy and His Dog." I got about fifty pages into *Hyperion*. I can't say exactly how those things might have tied into the final story; everything is mulch. What I can say specifically is that I was inspired by a news story of a dog living in a superfund site in Butte, Montana, and by an argument that I had with one of my bosses about human ingenuity and his confidence that we humans are so clever that we'll always keep thinking our way out of every problem. Those were definite seeds. The rest of it is all probably fertilizer of some sort or another, but I can't really say how all that works.

AV: There's been increasing demand for grains as our planet's population has doubled since the 1960s. What do you see as the dangers of genetically produced grains, which is a theme in "The Calorie Man" as well as *The Windup Girl*?

PB: I see genetically modified food as being worrisome in any number of ways: (1) we don't really understand the technology very well. GM research seems to be running forward willy-nilly, and we risk letting genies out of bottles that we don't understand; (2) companies want to replace existing seeds with their own profit-generating seeds, often in conjunction with their herbicide products, which have their own cascade effects; (3) it seems to encourage monoculture planting, which strikes me as shortsighted; (4) I don't like it when my food is owned by corporations who, let's face it, aren't in the business of feeding people, but are in the business of generating quarterly profit. They may talk about feeding people, but that's PR—they're about profit and they're about control. You don't patent genetic material to feed people, you patent it so no one else can have it and you can make money off of people's needs.

As far as the question of addressing the ever-increasing demand for food, it strikes me that GM tech is the shortsighted solution to the larger problem of how we deal with the fact that we as a species are overtaxing our planet's ecosystems. GMOs seem like a successful bid to squeeze a bit of blood from the stone, but at some point, we still face the fundamental question of how we deal with runaway population growth.

AV: Short stories from *Pump Six* such as "The Calorie Man" and "Yellow Card Man" are precursors for characters and themes in *The Windup Girl*. When did these the ideas coalesce into the larger work?

PB: Actually, the novel's seed came first. I created a short story that just refused to work. When I showed it to a friend of mine, she commented that it felt like a dwarf star, with too many characters and too many plotlines all jammed against one another. It was more like a novel, compressed, and needed to be a novel, uncompressed.

At the time, I was burned-out on writing novels, having written four, which didn't sell, so I was horrified at the suggestion. Instead, I went back to the short story and started harvesting interesting bits. "The Calorie Man" was an attempt to explore part of the world—the GMOs and peak-oil world—without anything else getting in the way. "Yellow Card Man" was a chance to do a character study, and fill in the backstory of one of the characters.

At one point, I thought I could probably harvest stories out of that one packed short story for years. It looked like there were at least a dozen other possible stories just waiting to be mined. Instead, I finally got up the guts and wrote *The Windup Girl*. All told, from the initial story idea to the final version of the book, I think it was something like five or six years. Three years of serious work on the novel, and then all that other time while I hid my head under the bed and avoided it.

AV: Since *The Windup Girl* is set in Thailand, tell us how your time in Asia affected you and your writing. I have to say the country is absolutely beautiful, and I have never seen people as *jaidee* (good-hearted) as those in Thailand.

PB: The Thai people really are wonderful, and the people I met were very warm both to me and to one another. If there's one thing I really regret about *The Windup Girl*, it's that the book doesn't sufficiently illuminate that facet of Thai culture. My stories are almost always about the worst of humanity, extrapolated. Broken worlds, and broken people. There were things about Thailand that I loved, but I wasn't sufficiently clever to find a way to illuminate those positive layers in my larger narrative. It makes you aware of how storytelling can illuminate, but it can also distort.

AV: What writers have influenced you and your writing?

PB: When I was first learning to write, writers like J. G. Ballard and Cormac McCarthy and Le Guin and Hemingway and Gibson inspired me and drove me to try to excel. For *The Windup Girl*, it was sort of a crash course in Thai literature, mostly in translation: Botan and

S. P. Somtow and Kukrit Pramoj and Chart Korbjitti, among others. It was exhilarating to be taking in so much writing that I'd never encountered before, but sometimes it was frustrating as well. I found myself wishing more than once that Chart Korbjitti had a more nuanced translator—I couldn't help feeling that the transition to English did some damage to his voice. And it frustrated and frightened me that I couldn't learn enough Thai fast enough to read it myself. It emphasized how much on the outside I was going to be as I tried to write *The Windup Girl.*

AV: One of the themes throughout the novel has to do with the worldwide susceptibility of grains to blister rust and ivory beetles. Was this concept partly developed due to the spread of beetles in your state of Colorado, a spread that was triggered by global warming?

PB: It was one of the inspirations, yes. I used to work as the online editor for an environmental journal, and it is terrifying to be immersed in the details of our changing world. As far as rusts go, look no further than Ug99, a wheat rust that is destroying crops in Africa and the Middle East, and looks likely to attack wheat crops worldwide unless we engineer a solution. One of the things that interests me about our food supply is that it is a monoculture. Billions and billions of people all depending on monoculture to survive. And monocultures are vulnerable. So I use news stories and then extrapolate to what the world would look like if those stories proved out. Unfortunately, many of my worst imaginings don't seem nearly as far-fetched as I used to think.

AV: It seems there is an anti-*farang* (Westerner) message throughout your novel, as when Hock Seng states: "We're working for ourselves, now. No more foreign influence, yes?" Is this sentiment something you developed for your story, or is this something you detected when you were in Thailand?

PB: I developed it for the story, based on the way I've seen people behave when they're put under pressure by outside forces. The Thailand of the future is very much beset by *farang* agricultural companies. My assumption is that we all get a little more nationalistic when we're fighting for survival.

AV: Your characters are not the stereotypical ones we meet in most novels. Anderson Lake seems like he might possibly be a hero early in the novel, but he is a hard one to read. Jaidee seems to harbor conflicting feelings toward his wife and Kanya. Characters like Carlyle, Raleigh, Akkarat, and General Pracha are hardly respectable or honorable, but the only truly evil person, or so it seems, is Gibbons. Perhaps the most moral or ethical character with feelings is the windup girl Emiko. How did you come up with these multidimensional characters?

PB: I don't think anyone wakes up in the morning and decides, "Today, I'm going to be the bad guy." We just end up there, and we've all got a good excuse for why we failed to live up to our higher ideals. I actually think most of the characters in the book are heroes. They're all trying, and they're hanging onto their ideals as best they can, whether it's Tan Hock Seng and his dream of rebuilding his wealth and a family, or Jaidee and Kanya trying to protect their country. Anderson Lake came from a place where people starved and where rock candy was such a childhood treat that it still remains in his mind to adulthood. If you remember starvation, staying out of starvation by any means necessary doesn't seem so crazy. I don't judge any of the characters too harshly. I doubt I'd do half as well as any of them in the circumstances that I throw them into.

AV: *The Windup Girl* has genetically made cheshires, described as "a high-tech homage to Lewis Carroll," and megodonts, which seem to be a DNA reproduction of the extinct mastodons. What was your inspiration for these creatures?

PB: I wanted to use megodonts because I wanted to illustrate the connection between calories and joules—the connecting tissue between food and energy—in this world. And, let's face it, a giant elephant-like creature is pretty fun when it goes crazy in a factory. Cheshires were a way to illustrate the unforeseen consequences of an invasive species. Something that initially seems harmless and entertaining turns out to have ecosystem consequences as it tears through the songbird population. And, of course, invisible cats are cool, too. I try not to deny myself the fun of creation as a writer.

AV: You portray the religious sect called Grahamites in a fairly bad light, as most are fat while the rest of the world is starving. Did you choose the name from Billy Graham and his followers? What do you see for the role of religion in the future?

PB: Grahamites, at root, are believers. All that's good in that—in that they want to protect the natural world—and all that's bad in that, because they do tend to get carried away and burn things down. I don't really view them as a commentary on religion per se, except that I think religion will continue to adapt to the needs of its parishioners. Religion drives people to fanaticism, but so does politics. So does economics. The people who celebrate the genius and wisdom of free markets are just as crazy as the ones who tell you Jesus is the only way to salvation. Let's face it, we've never been a very logical species.

AV: There is a scene in which Kanya takes the elevator down into the bowels of the Quarantine Department, perhaps suggesting Dante's *Inferno.* Why is the Quarantine Department looked upon negatively, since it helped Thailand survive while the Empire of America no longer exists and the Asian nations are broke and starving?

PB: The Quarantine Department is a frightening place. I don't think it's looked down on so much as feared, because of the kinds of genetic material it works with. I actually based some of the Quarantine Department's underground labs on descriptions of the CDC's own biological containment facilities.

AV: How did you come up with the concept of the windup girl? It's interesting that Emiko, a genetically produced creature, is perhaps the most human of all the characters in your novel.

PB: I've always been interested in people who are required to serve someone else. It shows up in my short story "The Fluted Girl," and it shows up again with the bioengineered soldier named Tool in my new young adult novel, *Ship Breaker.* I only recently noticed that I keep returning to this theme. I think, at root, I'm interested in what makes us loyal—what binds us to other people. As far as Emiko's original inspiration, she came to me during an international flight. A Japanese stewardess caught my eye, because she was moving with a strange sort of herky-jerky motion. I almost thought she was acting a role because the movements were so robotically stylized. I couldn't get the image out of my head.

AV: Gibbons is the mad geneticist who pictures himself as some sort of god, a Conradian Kurtz with little empathy or feeling for mankind. He says: "If we wish to remain at the top of our food chain, we will evolve. Or we will refuse, and go the way of the dinosaurs and *Felis domesticus*. Evolve or die." How do you see this character?

PB: Gibbons is the ultimate pragmatist. He looks around at the world, sees what's wrong, and then adapts to it. He's not sentimental about loss or change. He just does what he has to do in order to survive and to please himself. And he is powerful. When he claims a sort of godhood for the changes he can inflict on the world, and in fact has already inflicted, he's not mad, he's stating a fact. The thing that's scariest about him, to me, is that he might be right. We may already be past the point of sentimentality for nature or what we used to have. From now on, it's adapt or die.

AV: Your use of the Thai superstition of ghosts and Kanya's ongoing discussion with Jaidee's ghost recalls John Burdett's use of ghosts in his novel *Bangkok Haunts*.

PB: I haven't read *Bangkok Haunts*; I was actually more inspired by some of S. P. Somtow's short stories. But I liked the presence of ghosts in Thai folklore and I wanted them there, as another part of Jaidee's and Kanya's world. I've always sort of felt that the soil of different countries emanates its own rules of reality and you need to respect that when you journey to those shores, so having active *phi* (ghosts) in the story seemed like a good way of acknowledging a different country.

AV: Kanya speculates that Jaidee might be reincarnated as a windup, a fascinating concept.

PB: I'm really interested in how religion adapts to the changes that science and technology introduce. At least since Copernicus, science has challenged religious cosmology, and forced adaptation. Windups challenge almost all of our religious conceptions of soul—given their hybrid, manufactured nature.

AV: The rape of Emiko by Somdet's men is a powerful scene. How did you develop this degrading and violent moment in the book?

PB: I still feel a little uncomfortable about that scene and the first one where Emiko is introduced, but it seemed like the reader needed to be in the room during her abuse, so that her later actions would seem acceptable. I have no idea how I wrote it. My wife sort of looks askance at me as well.

AV: Violence also ensues when the ghost of Jaidee tells Kanya, "What good is a city if the people are enslaved?"—and of course when Emiko goes against her training and kills Somdet and his men.

PB: We all hit breaking points, moments when we decide to stop going along, and change paths. So much of the world wants us to obey and not make waves, to be good workers and consumers and soldiers and parents and children and what have you—even when it goes against our own best interest, and even the best interest of others. I like it when characters make cathartic changes, and act according to their truest selves. And I like pushing them to that breaking point.

AV: Let's talk about your newest book. What was the inspiration for *Ship Breaker*? Did you consciously write it as a young adult novel?

PB: There were a couple things going on. One was that I write a lot of science fiction for adults that focuses on questions of the environment and sustainability, and pretty soon I realized that while adults will often nod their heads in agreement at what I write, they aren't going to make a change in their lives—we're simply too fixed in our positions to accept the sort of change that's necessary. Kids, on the other hand, haven't made all of our dumb decisions about cars and mortgages and jobs yet, so it seems possible to influence them more readily. So, yes, *Ship Breaker* was always going to be aimed at teens. The actual inspiration for the novel came from watching a documentary about Edward Burtynsky called *Manufactured Landscapes* that featured shipbreaking operations in Bangladesh. I was so struck by the imagery that I couldn't get it out of my head.

AV: A key element in the book is Nailer's and the crew's belief in Fates, luck, and superstition.

PB: One of the things you figure out eventually is that there's no rhyme or reason to why one person ends up living a life of privilege and another person doesn't. We get born to whomever we get born to, and then deal with the consequences. Short of a sort of karmic worldview, whatever we're born into is random, and in many cases the opportunities that come before us are random as well. But the other side of that equation is what we do with whatever opportunities we have, and what opportunities we're willing to create through work and force of will. It's always a combination. For Nailer, he's feeling his way into the question of how much he can change the cards he's been dealt.

AV: As in *The Windup Girl*, there is the theme of slavery in *Ship Breaker* with the half-man Tool. When asked why he doesn't obey as trained he responds, "They made a mistake with me... I was smarter than they prefer." What is the impetus for using this as a social metaphor in your fiction?

PB: I'm interested in characters who don't do what they're told. Most of society asks all of us to do as we're told. To be good workers, to be good consumers, to be good, to stay in our place, and not to break out or think too many dangerous thoughts about why our world is the way it is, and why we're participating in many of its horrors. I keep wondering why we're all so obedient, and maybe that's making its way into my fiction.

AV: The issue of slavery is also present with Nita "Lucky Girl" Patel, who has a true owner-slave mentality based on her family's treatment of half-men—she believes that "genes are destiny" and opines, "we treat [them] well." Is there an analogy to be made between the half-men characters and the issue of slavery as it occurred in the United States?

PB: I wasn't consciously aiming for that, but I think that wealth provides a certain sense of privilege and ownership and entitlement, whether or not there's actual slavery involved.

AV: The half-men such as Tool are described as a "genetic cocktail of humanity, tigers, and dogs." How did you develop this creature and the role they play in *Ship Breaker*?

PB: Tool's archetype has been with me for a long time. I recently reread "The Fluted Girl," and it turns out that he's there in a different form, as Burson, the head of Madame Belari's security. For me, the half-men provide a lens to examine questions of loyalty, because they are engineered genetically from dog DNA to obey, but also to play with questions of nature versus nurture, which are very much on Nailer's mind as he tries to figure out who he is in relation to his father.

AV: Indeed, the idea that "genes are destiny" worries Nailer a great deal.

PB: We all get certain things from our parents—some are taught, some are genetic—and yet, we are not clones. And yet the ghosts of our parents haunt us. If our parents were abusive, we fear becoming so ourselves, because sometimes we do repeat the failures of our parents. If they were addicts, or couldn't relate with others, or failed to succeed in life, or if they succeeded too well, our parents loom large. For Nailer, whose father is so powerful and awful, and who is growing up under the exact same pressures that his father grew up in, there is a strong chance that he will become precisely the monster that his father represents.

AV: Both here and in *The Windup Girl* you often reverse male-female stereotypes. Overall, your female characters are usually stronger, whether mentally or physically, than most of the male characters. Why do you use this theme so consistently in your fiction?

PB: I don't really see it as a reversal, I guess. Strong female characters don't mean male characters are weak. What I think I'm trying to do is show characters of both sexes who are strong in a variety of ways. The thing that makes Blue Eyes dangerous to Nailer is that she's a fighter and an adult who is bigger than he is, but the thing that makes the girl Sloth dangerous is actually that she's smaller than Nailer and she's smart—someone who could take his job away from him. Pima and Sadna are both strong physically, but so is Tool, the ultimate masculine figure. Nailer isn't as strong as a lot of people, but he's quick and he's a thinker. I just like to see lots of people showing their strongest aspects, and sex isn't necessarily the determinant for any of those things.

AV: Nailer's father, fueled by amphetamines and alcohol, is the embodiment of evil: he breaks Pima's fingers and scavenges a ship before getting medicine to save his son's life. What made you choose this unorthodox father and son relationship to drive the underlying themes of your story?

PB: I've always hated the idea that children owe their families, and particularly their parents, anything. Our children didn't ask to be born. We decided to create them for our own selfish reasons. So I don't think our children owe us for their care, for their feeding, or their education. That's their right, and we owe it to them for dragging them into our world.

Even more, I hate the idea that because someone is family, they deserve greater respect or obedience or care than a friend, regardless of their actual behaviors. Too often, it seems like family relationships and obligations and the clichés that we use to describe them are used to justify abuse. Family doesn't matter. Marriage doesn't matter. Day-to-day good behavior does. I wanted to make the family relationship conditional on good behavior, and when that good behavior doesn't exist, I'm happy to see family broken in favor of something better.

AV: It's ironic that the uneducated Nailer is able to defeat his father due to a half-man who teaches Nailer how to read.

PB: The written word is powerful. I come back to that, again and again. It gives us access to so much information, assuming that we have the keys to that initial code. Without it, we're dependent on slower oral traditions, and have no indexes for information. The area where I live in rural Colorado has a fair number of kids who were never taught to read and are ignorant because of it, and it ticks me off, so I was happy to slide that bit of my own values into the action of the book.

AV: Can we anticipate a sequel for *Ship Breaker*?

PB: Yeah. There's definitely going to be a sequel. Some characters will return, and new ones will show up. Tool is definitely coming back, though.

AV: What can your readers look forward to with your next work of fiction?

PB: After the *Ship Breaker* sequel, it's a little up in the air. I'm contracted to write another couple science fiction novels for adults, and I've got some more young adult ideas as well, but if I talk about them, they'll sound stupid, and then I won't have the guts to actually write them.

Greg Bear. Courtesy of Astrid Anderson Bear.

The Forging of Science Fiction: An Interview with Greg Bear

Greg Bear was born on August 20, 1951, in San Diego, California. His father was in the navy, and he spent much of his childhood traveling throughout the Pacific. He wrote his first short story at the age of nine and sold his first story at fifteen to *Famous Science Fiction*. He graduated from San Diego State University and worked at various jobs until he was able to support himself full time as a writer.

Some of the numerous books he has published include *Beyond Heaven's River, Strength of Stones, Blood Music, Eon, Eternity, Legacy, The Way of All Ghosts, The Forge of God, Queen of Angels, Anvil of Stars, Moving Mars, Dinosaur Summer, Vitals, City at the End of Time,* and *Hull Zero Three.*

Besides numerous award nominations, Bear has won five Nebula Awards (which include awards for *Moving Mars* and *Darwin's Radio*) and two Hugo Awards (which include the novelette for *Blood Music*).

Bear cites Ray Bradbury, with whom he carried on a lifelong correspondence, as the most influential writer in his life. In 1983 Bear married Astrid Anderson, daughter of science fiction icon Poul Anderson. He lives outside Seattle in a home that has a library with over twelve thousand books.

The following interview was conducted March 17, 1989, when Bear came to Houston to sign copies of his novel *Eternity* at Future Visions bookstore. The interview was conducted between book signings at a Motel 6 on the outskirts of Houston.

Allan Vorda: Since you are a graduate of San Diego State University, how did you develop an interest in science fiction when most college classes are geared toward conventional literature?

Greg Bear: I was a big science fiction fan long before I went to college. I was interested in science fiction by the time I was eight or nine years old. I sold my first story in high school.

AV: What was your attitude toward the standard English classes?

GB: They were fine. If the teachers were good. I enjoyed them. I'm a very diverse reader. I don't have any particular prejudices.

AV: Your books contain references and allusions to various writers. For example, *The Infinity Concerto* acknowledgement mentions Jorge Luis Borges, while *Eon* and *Eternity* character Konrad Korzenowski is the actual Polish name of Joseph Conrad. Just as Borges has stated that "writers create their own precursors," can you mention some of the writers that influenced you?

GB: I'll start with the science fiction writers first. The usual gang of suspects: Robert Heinlein, Arthur C. Clarke, Isaac Asimov, and Ray Bradbury, of whom the latter probably influenced me the most. Bradbury, in particular, because I know him personally. He was a direct model of what a writer did and could be. I started corresponding with Ray when I was about sixteen and continue to this day. He has been a very big influence. Arthur C. Clarke, of all the living science fiction writers, is probably the most influential on the kind of stories I write and what I think science fiction should be. Clarke concerns himself with both science and philosophy at the same time. He is a true visionary.

AV: What about Kurt Vonnegut?

GB: Vonnegut is a fine writer, but he came to my attention after my formative period. *Slaughterhouse-Five,* I think, is a masterpiece. Outside of American pulp Science Fiction, Olaf Stapledon has had the most influence on me. His works inspired Arthur C. Clarke. After seeing *2001,* I traced Clarke's roots back to Stapledon. *Last and First Men* and *Star Maker* were very formative. Then, of course, the old-timers like H. G. Wells had an enormous impact on me as a child and teenager. Wells and Verne, Asimov and Clarke, and Bradbury and Heinlein all built the bedrock; Stapledon and other writers laid on the superstructure.

Outside of science fiction completely, I enjoy reading James Joyce, Joseph Conrad, and in my college years, Nikos Kazantzakis. I found a resonance between the philosophies of Kazantzakis and Stapledon. Later, I found a similar vein in Bradbury's work. Bradbury was very fond of Kazantzakis. *Other Inquisitions* was the collection of Borges's essays that I read first. I enjoyed it immensely. Borges was a literary writer not in the least afraid of ideas. He reveled in them. What he was afraid of was long narrative—he thought it was unnecessary. Yet he adored Cervantes.

AV: Borges also has an element of science fiction in his works.

GB: Borges read a lot of science fiction. I met him when he was lecturing at San Diego State around 1970. I came up after his talk and managed to get one of his books autographed. He was nearly blind, and the autograph is a seismograph scrawl. "You mentioned H. P. Lovecraft," I said. "How much of Lovecraft have you actually read?" Borges replied, "I've read a little bit of him. But Lovecraft—that's a wonderful name for a writer, don't you think?" And he laughed. Of course, Borges had read Bradbury and A. E. Van Vogt—he talks about them in his essays on American literature. An absolutely unprejudiced man. Maybe he was prejudiced against Argentine literature, but he looked at English and American literature as a vast foreign thing which he had to absorb, and he valued English and American fantasy and science fiction for the wealth of ideas.

AV: I recall in some of his interviews that Borges said American writers had the greatest impact on him. This was probably because his father had a sizable library that contained a lot of American literature.

GB: I think we all love most what we start reading in our teenage years.

AV: You also mention Anthony Burgess in "The Wind from a Burning Woman," where one of the characters in the story was reading Burgess.

GB: Yes, and I've neglected to mention James Blish, who wrote several novels which were very influential on me. Chiefly, *Black Easter* and *A Case of Conscience,* but also books like *Jack of Eagles.* He had wonderful science fiction ideas. He also came up with some philosophical ideas that were really quite startling, even if he didn't develop them fully. In *Black Easter,* he talked briefly about radiation destroying the physical soul. That really stuck with me, and it turned into *Psychlone,* which is in part dedicated to him. In *A Case of Conscience,* Blish referred to *Finnegans Wake* by James Joyce. So I immediately hustled off and bought a copy and became a real Joyce fanatic. I still appreciate *Finnegans Wake* more than *Ulysses.* I started with the most difficult book of all.

AV: Borges has also referred to the library as a universe. I understand you are a voracious reader in a variety of fields, which has resulted in the collection of over twelve thousand books in your own library at your house in Washington. What is your daily reading and writing schedule like?

GB: If you count books by weight, my library came to seventeen thousand pounds when we moved about two years ago. As far as my reading habits, I read in the bathtub, I read before going to bed at night, and if I'm doing research on something, I'll be reading in the daytime.

My writing schedule is not really fixed. I write each day until I've amassed five pages, but I don't stop myself if I'm really rolling. I seldom reach ten pages a day because I start getting ahead of myself if I do. The plotting has to go on in the background.

AV: How did you make that transition after you graduated from college to be a self-supporting writer? I think at one time you worked in a bookstore.

GB: That's almost all I did. Actually, my first wife, Tina, helped a lot because she was gainfully employed. I was able to repay her in part by giving her a year off later on. Astrid was also gainfully employed. She only got off work three years ago, which was just before our son was born. She hasn't worked since because we are doing quite well. Mostly it's been a matter of working very, very hard and having the support of a spouse.

AV: How did you work in those days? Did you work full time in the bookstore for forty hours a week and write at night?

GB: It was sporadic because I was going to school. By 1975, I was freelancing full time. Before that I was going to school and working part time or full time in the space theatre in San Diego. I had different odd jobs, but no sense of a career other than being a writer.

AV: Do you feel there is less pressure to write such as when you had a job, or is there more pressure to write when writing is a full-time profession?

GB: You can call it pressure, but I think it's more *internal* pressure since you don't have someone leaning over you. I found very early that I could work with people who I knew were as smart or smarter than I am, but I had a really difficult time working with people who were dumber, and that's what you have to do in the workaday world as a general rule. You quite often have to get along with people who are less intelligent.

AV: Something like the Peter Principle. You run into those people on the way up.

GB: I'm fortunate since publishers are never dumb, at least my publishers aren't! I really don't have to worry about them. I really don't have any bosses. I just have people who are happy if I'm getting the work done on time.

AV: To quote from the preface of *The Wind from a Burning Woman*: "The future will come, and it will be different, unimaginably so." And to quote a line by Kawashita from *Beyond Heaven's River*: "the future is not appetizing." Would you concur that this is an ongoing theme in your books—that the future for mankind is ever-changing and not necessarily pleasant and predictable? Or, to be more precise, that Heisenberg's uncertainty principle is a scientific metaphor in your books?

GB: As far as the future being unimaginable, yes. Human beings are a chaotic system. Certainly, history reflects a chaotic system, which means you cannot predict how humans are going to behave over the long term. You might be able to do gross analogies by characterizing our role in a biological system. You might say that at this point, if human beings belong to a giant biological system on the Earth, they are equivalent to the Earth's gonads. Perhaps cultures will grow old and stagnant and will be replaced by new cultures. There is no way beyond that generalization to pin down what might happen.

AV: And that's probably good, in one sense.

GB: It's wonderful in one sense, and it's horrible in another sense. If you think history should be a lot of people having a very good time and not being in any great pain, history is not like that. History is in a very, very nasty, prolonged, painful adolescence right now. The twentieth century is the bloodiest century we have ever been through—and it continues to be. We have seen so-called developed people who, at the same time as seeming to be fairly reasonable and rational people, are capable of doing the most nasty, mean, rotten things. And yet if you met them on the street, they would be fairly good party guests.

AV: Are you referring to people like Hitler or Stalin?

GB: Hitler or Stalin probably would not have been very good at a party. Hitler got into power because Germany was twisted by WWI and its aftermath. Germany was just basically ground under and stomped on by all the European nations, whereupon it went crazy. Germany expressed its craziness in an urge to suicide, which is particularly Germanic. They picked Hitler to lead them to the funeral parlor.

AV: What about the Japanese?

GB: The Japanese are a different problem. The Japanese came out of the feudal period into the twentieth century in a period of about forty years. By 1900 they had battleships and they had all the modern war machines that all the other nations had. They had already whipped the Chinese and the Russians by the time the nation had been out of the feudal period only forty-five years. You might think of Japan as coming out of childhood and going immediately into late adolescence and having to catch up with everybody else, yet still living by a philosophy and creed of a society that was back in the feudal period. They had to shake that loose, and unfortunately, they had to shake it loose in the middle of all this other stuff. They got very badly burned. Interestingly enough, they recovered from World War II with the help of the United States. The Marshall Plan was unheard of in the history of warfare. Nearly every nation that we defeated came out stronger than they were before the war. Japan certainly did so, although the US can't take all the credit for that. There is an innate genius in Japan. It perhaps even transcends the innate genius that you still find in Germany. A lot of their problems had to do with major cultural difficulties. For example, Germany did not become a unified country until the nineteenth century. It never had a sense of unified culture. The US had to acquire that in the Civil War. Before that time, each part of the US thought of itself as a separate nation. We still have those tendencies. You know, the Pacific Northwest thinks it's far better than California. California is despised by New York. And New York is loathed by everybody else. All these schisms exist.

AV: In your novel *Eternity,* the Recovery reminded me of the Marshall Plan. The Hexamon group tried to help the native Earthlings recover economically and psychologically to the level where they were before the battle with the Jarts.

GB: It's a good comparison, although we were not at war with the Hexamon. They had a chance to redeem their past. For example, try to imagine someone going back after WWI and teaching Europe how to organize to avoid the next forty years of misery and to avoid a Europe and a Russia driven crazy by deprivation and war.

Almost every problem we have now in the Western world comes out of that period. It comes out of the decision after WWI to start grinding nations down. The Depression perhaps came out of that. Winston Churchill thought so. It seems a good theory to me because there was so much bad money being pumped out of Germany to pay off war debts that they couldn't possibly repay. Russia got caught up in a revolution that was misdirected because of WWI. You wonder what would have happened if some decent, reasonable men had been in place instead of some massive incompetents that were in charge of Europe at that time. After WWI, there were decent men with ideas of how history operated. Men like George C. Marshall, and MacArthur in Japan. For a conquering war hero, MacArthur was an amazingly sophisticated social worker.

AV: He was more of a diplomat than a soldier after the war.

GB: He was far more important to the world as a diplomat than as a soldier, and these things are to America's credit. I hope the future looks back on us for that reason and not for the things we screwed up. In other areas, we screwed up horribly—for example, in the occupations of Central America and Haiti. Even today we continue to screw up in these countries. We just don't know what to be: a strong-arm world police force or a benevolent world helper.

AV: A number of your characters and ideas seem to grow into a more full-bodied development. I'm referring to such short stories as "The Wind from a Burning Woman" (*Eon* and *Eternity*), "Mandala" (*Strength of Stones*), and "Blood Music" (*Blood Music*). Can you explain how this happens?

GB: Some ideas develop a life of their own. There's a tradition in science fiction that if your book takes off like a rocket, then you write a sequel to it. In most of these cases, the stories didn't take off like rockets, although "Blood Music" did very well. I was actually planning the novel before "Blood Music" won any awards. The idea contained in the story was not fully developed in the short version. It was there, it was nicely handled, it came to a striking conclusion, it got its point across, but there were a lot of other implications that had to be developed, so I wrote a book.

AV: What about "The Wind from a Burning Woman," written around 1976, which was a prelude to *Eon* that came out in 1984?

GB: I started writing *Eon* about 1979. I think "The Wind from a Burning Woman" was fairly well developed as a story, but it had an interesting culture in it that posed some curious problems. I think it was Orson Scott Card who reviewed the story and said it was an interesting story but that he couldn't believe that the society could have ever existed. Of course, there was no history in the novelette. I went back and filled in the history and stuck it into *Eon* as a support for this big idea of this infinite, artificial universe.

AV: *Blood Music* was one of the most distinctive science fiction novels in recent years. How did this novel develop, particularly your knowledge of genetics?

GB: To write the short story, I had to do just a little bit of research. It was short enough that I could get by with just a few references. To do the novel, I had to go out and really add to what I knew about genetics—which was very little. I have a pretty good background in astronomy and physics, less in biology and genetics. I've been around enough scientists to pick up their jargon and know their personalities. What I really had to do was go out and visit biology laboratories where people were working that were like my people in the story. I did that by making appointments with several professors at the University of California at San Diego and the Scripps Institute of Oceanography. I found several young people, who are mentioned in the back of the book, who were very sympathetic to my work. They were all professors or researchers at the university or at the institute. They went to work in the labs while I sat watching them and their techniques, noting the types of equipment they worked with, and using the Stephen King technique of putting in brand names if you can because it makes the story more authentic.

AV: What about Vergil I. Ulam's name? I assume it's an anagram or that "I.V." could stand for intravenous.

GB: Oh, it's much simpler than that. It's a real name, but it's also an anagram. You will have to work out the anagram. Switch around the letters, and it spells out the name of a well-known literary character who was also involved with the very small.

AV: Please discuss the idea of the Thought Universe and its ongoing dialogue with Dr. Bernard, which is an interesting concept in *Blood Music*.

GB: I'm not sure who first came up with the notion behind Thought Universe. If we go back far enough, we get some hints of it in Alfred Bester's *The Stars My Destination*. I think the first author to really write about it in detail was John Varley, but I could be wrong. Someone like Fred Pohl or Jack Williamson is sure to have done it at some point in time. William Hjortsberg used it to some extent in a book called *Gray Matters*. John Varley wrote stories like "Overdrawn at the Memory Bank," where he talks about the computer being a receptacle for the human spirit. We must not leave out *Neuromancer* by William Gibson, who invented the term "cyberspace." Cyberspace may be a better name for what we're talking about than Thought Universe—it's certainly caught the public imagination and will likely end up in the dictionary—but I think Thought Universe is more descriptive.

The possibility occurred to me when I was doing research on an article on computer graphics that if you could simply move computer graphics into the human brain or the brain into the computer, as in *Tron,* then you've got a simulation of existence for the actual soul or spirit or programming, that is the equivalent of reality. And that's a huge metaphor for life itself. You can think of the entire universe as nothing but information running back and forth. A Thought Universe then becomes a less rigorously controlled metaphor for the universe.

AV: Many readers might see the end of *Blood Music* and the end of humanity, as we know it, as disquieting. Yet I think you were trying to convey that this change to a different life form is just another example of evolution. Is this a correct analysis? You made a point earlier about the whole earth having a consciousness as a collective biological system. Does this analogy apply here?

GB: I'm not a complete believer in James Lovelock's theory of Gaia—the Living Earth. I don't think the Living Earth is a conscious entity, and I don't think you can say it's a biological organism like a human being. To compare them would be like comparing a human being to a cell. A human being is an entirely different structure from a cell. Gaia would be a completely different structure from a human being. For example, it might not have parents. A planet is very likely to be self-generating.

There is natural evolution, and there is man's evolution. Most evolution is blind. It doesn't have soft sensibilities about cuddly, furry animals. Many millions of deaths or trillions of deaths have to occur for an evolutionary process to take place.

AV: At least until this century. We may have a say in what may or may not be here.

GB: Right now, natural evolution is not the only path to large-scale change. We are now in the process of controlling evolution as a means to our own ends. I suspect we will be surprised. I wrote a metaphor about how we might be surprised. Turning into lime Jell-O is a pretty surprising way to evolve! Especially when you find out it's wonderful.

AV: You think that would be wonderful? What do you think would be the pros and cons of this type of evolution?

GB: Well, very few people actually died in *Blood Music*. The whole world is gone as far as we know it, and the whole structure is different, but if you look at the last chapter, one of the characters (Bernard) goes back and is able to correct the mistakes of his youth in a simulation.

AV: Yes, but it's only thought. It's like a dream with no physical contact.

GB: But you wouldn't know the difference. Remember—they're fully sensory. They're disembodied spirits provided with a completely simulated environment. For example, right now you could be in Thought Universe, but you wouldn't know it. Maybe it's already happened, and we're just sitting here discussing it, and this is an artistic jape on behalf of the noocytes. You wouldn't know the difference so long as you were in that simulated environment. It's a bit of a conundrum, of course.

AV: So you are saying that if Bernard and the girl, whom he missed having as the love of his life, had been reunited at an earlier age, and that if they had had intercourse, then it would have been the same as having real physical intercourse?

GB: Yes, they could simulate the entire existence of that other life and then they could go off and try marriage. In other words, they experience a kind of heavenly immortality, unbounded in space and time unless they choose it.

AV: Wouldn't this be restricted to the past and not to the future?

GB: In Thought Universe you can simulate anything. You can change the rules of the game, including metaphysical rules. You can tweak Euclid's fifth postulate and end up with unimaginable varieties of experiences you simply cannot do within the limited context of our physical universe.

AV: What about exploring outer space from the Thought Universe?

GB: Outer space is *within* you. Look what happened at the end. Everything, including the planets, is sucked in. The universe has been attacked from the bottom level, from the level of all smallness in creation and reconstructed as thought and information. Space exploration is unnecessary if all of space and time are contained within your universe. You have basically digested the entire world all at once.

AV: *The Forge of God* is an apocalyptic novel that delves into such topics as politics and religion. Please discuss the exchange in which Crockerman asks, "Do you believe in God?" and the Guest replies, "We believe in punishment."

GB: The Guest was playing with the President's head. But the Guest itself is just a tool of the machine intelligence that is already dissolving the planet. The Guest is just sitting there going boogey-boogey—saying I know you are a lowly human being; we know how to mess with your mind, and we're curious what happens when we do.

AV: I thought the Guest was just a parasite.

GB: That's only what it claimed to be! It was lying. And so were the robots who were saying "Welcome to the galactic culture." It becomes pretty obvious to the characters later on in the book that they're being tested like ants in a nest, having a stick poked at them by "intellects vast and cool and unsympathetic." The intellects already know basically what the human reactions are going to be. They know how to prod this low-level culture. You hit these particular buttons. Most humans are in a particular religious phase, and the president is the leader of a fairly religious society. The machine invaders know religion as we could not possibly know it—complete from the outside, seeing it as a morphological phenomenon. It's like observing hormone flows inside the human body. They know how religion works. They take a look at us and say, "We can poke them here and see what happens, and we'll run our experiment before we destroy the Earth."

The robot probes have three functions. One is to reproduce themselves. Two is to destroy species that could compete with their original masters. Three is to study everything they get their hands on. Everything the killer probes do in *The Forge of God* is explained by these three provisions. There are also machine intelligences opposed to the planet-killing probes. They arrive when the humans are completely confused. (It's possible the reader will be confused for a while as well.) They have different motives. They consider it a gross breach of galactic law to create self-replicating machines that go off and do your dirty work for you.

AV: I read a review of *The Forge of God* by a critic who said that by having the bogus spaceships, you had cheated the reader by "injecting false suspense into the narrative."

GB: My reply to the critic is, "Do your homework! Slow down. Read the book carefully." There are whole chapters in the novel that answer his criticism in plain text and not hidden away in some obscure metaphor.

AV: What about *The Forge of God* being an apocalyptic novel? Many people have the idea that if there are beings out there of higher intelligence, they must therefore be good, but you seem to be saying that isn't necessarily the case.

GB: A long time ago, David Brin and I were talking about a galactic ecology. He was trying to find an explanation why von Neumann probes hadn't filled the entire galaxy. If you had one civilization develop efficient von Neumann probes, then in one hundred thousand years they would suck up virtually the entire galaxy.

It occurred to me that you don't have straightforward developments in any natural system. For example, on Earth we have many biological systems or species competing with other species. One system develops here, another system develops there, and if they're going to fight for the same territory, then they start fighting each other. That spurs evolution. It spurs change. It also creates a dynamic stasis and dynamic interaction where one gives and the other takes.

Occasionally one will dominate completely, and then it will weaken or fall prey and another will take its niche. It's an evolutionary process. So why not extend that to the entire galaxy? This critic, as so often happens with critics, is just not thinking broadly enough. He hasn't broken out of the old mindset. He thinks, "Oh gee, he's talking about God here." No, I'm not talking about God. The machines are using God to torment the poor president of the United States. They don't give a damn about God! In this novel, God has nothing to say about what the killer probes are doing. God is far removed from the discussion of this novel—if he exists at all. In *Eternity,* I talked about God. I mean there is a version of God, if you want one, coming to save us. God is ourselves, but infinitely older.

AV: Are you referring to "The Final Mind," or the "Descendent Command," as the Jarts called them?

GB: Yes, I have religious elements in many of my books, but they can't be understood in the standard fashion.

AV: What about your fellow writers? Do they understand and respond to your writing better than the critics?

GB: I haven't received too many bad comments from fellow writers. Books are funny that way. You'll find some writers are really opposed to some books. One writer didn't like *Eon* very much at all. He thought it was too metaphysical and too undisciplined, but he absolutely loved *The Forge of God*. He just keyed in on everything that happened in it. In some respects, he's right. *The Forge of God* is a better formal novel than *Eon*. It was written a few years later. Hopefully, I'm getting better. I'm taking themes that involve strong human emotions and expanding them to a larger scale. *The Forge of God* is a book about the death of friends—up to and including the death of the Earth.

One of the characters (Harry Feinman) has cancer. His cancer serves as a microcosm of the Earth, which also has a cancer. The kid, Rueben Bordes, has just lost his mother, and it has not only torn up his family, but it's going to happen to Rueben again when the Earth is destroyed. It's not apparent to most readers what's going on here, but it should echo subconsciously in their heads. When you emphasize the story from several different angles, then the story becomes triply strong. That's what I love doing. I've just finished a book called *Queen of Angels*, which spins a story through several viewpoints, reflecting at least five strongly echoing themes.

AV: It seems there has always been an unholy war between art and religion as well as between science and religion; yet, *The Forge of God* seems to walk the middle ground. What are your thoughts about religion in contemporary society?

GB: I think it is more science than religion. Religion has always managed to subvert art to its own purpose, and then art sneaks around and subverts religion. But science is a more direct, cantankerous individual, and consequently science and religion have usually squared off pretty drastically.

AV: It's going on right now, with the Creationists trying to influence the content of the textbooks used in high schools.

GB: The Creationists want to go back three thousand or four thousand years and have a static society that has never existed on this Earth. They want to force it on everybody. I've got one thing to say to them: "You can go live in Iran and have a good time. It's not going to happen here."

AV: When asked if he was an atheist, Woody Allen's character in *Annie Hall* responded that he considered himself "part of God's loyal opposition." What is your notion about God?

GB: If God were any sort of decent God at all he would certainly have a loyal opposition. I spend most of my life not telling God what to be. I certainly haven't the slightest clue as to what a God should be. I keep playing at describing what a God could be, but I'm not going to be dogmatic about it. It's ridiculous. I'm not equipped. None of us is intellectually equipped to handle the concept of a God. It's a toy for our own development.

AV: What about the role of Crockerman and his use of religion as a crutch?

GB: Crockerman is not a political statement about any particular party. Crockerman is a very good politician. He's the kind of politician we find commonly in the United States today. He's just not an intellectual politician. He can't handle big, philosophical problems. Yet suddenly, he's got one laid in his lap. He strives for a solution that allows him to continue to be a good leader. Obviously, his religious background is such that he believes in some deep sense that the Apocalypse is at hand. And he asks us to prepare for it.

AV: Both *Eon* and *Eternity*, your latest novel, offer some fascinating ideas about the future of mankind. How did you develop the concept for these books, especially about the Stone and the Way?

GB: The seven chambers of the hollowed-out asteroid come from the story "The Wind from a Burning Woman." After the asteroid has been flying around for five hundred years or so, the people inside get very tired of waiting to arrive at their star system. You have the equivalent of millions and millions of people inside this thing. They create this artificial universe using the physics that had been pioneered even before the end of the twentieth century by people like Patricia Vasquez. They look back upon her as a pioneer. It's more than a literary twist of fate that she shows up on board the Stone and gets to meet Korzenowski. This is stretching the filaments of history considerably, but it's fun. She gets to meet all the people for whom she was the godmother. The last chapter of *Eon* is given considerably more detail in *Eternity.* We explore the alternate universe that she fell into rather than getting back home where she wanted to be.

AV: Can you briefly discuss the role of the Jarts (originally described in *Eon* as monstrously aggressive fleas), which seem to be somewhat analogous to Milton's satanic angel in *Paradise Lost*?

GB: I suppose that's not a bad comparison. The Jarts are alien and domineering and as advanced physically and technologically as the Hexamon. You're never quite sure what they were originally, because they have shape-changed so much. They can be whatever they want to be. The original Jart figure that we see locked in stasis was identified by a reader who wrote a letter to me and asked, "Is this based on the Cambrian creature found in the Burgess Shales (*Hallucigenia sparsa*)?" Wee, damn right it is! That's one of my favorite creatures—this little spiked thing running around in the Cambrian period. The kid read it and recognized it. That's great. Kids are my best critics sometimes.

AV: Your next novel is *Queen of Angels*. What can we look forward to in this book?

GB: I just finished it recently. I'm probably too close to it right now to say, but it's probably the best thing I have ever written. It's a near-future novel—comparable to *Stand on Zanzibar* or *Brave New World.* It has to do with self-awareness and punishment as well as our society's preoccupation with both of those things and the really weird mix of the two. As far as I can tell right now, it works better than any novel I've written. Virtually everything ties together and echoes the central themes.

AV: When will it be out?

GB: Probably early next year, around January of 1990.

AV: What do you mean when you say our society is preoccupied with punishment?

GB: If someone came along and murdered your daughter, would you sit down and recommend psychological therapy for him, or would you want to put him in an endless hell?

AV: Endless hell, of course!

GB: You see, you're preoccupied with punishment. We don't care so much about other people so much as we want them to either leave us alone or face eternal damnation. We see it throughout human cultures. Poor Salman Rushdie. What are they going to do with him? They're going to send him straight to hell because he offended their sensibilities. Well, it's pretty obvious that Salman Rushdie didn't offend Allah one bit—I don't see Allah pinning him down with a thunderbolt! Allah sends his little children out to do the dirty work, I guess.

AV: It helps to get the dirty work done when there's a five-million-dollar fee on Rushdie's head.

GB: This kind of nonsense extends into our culture. I'm not immune to this. I'm just as glad that Ted Bundy is no longer with us. On the other hand, would I have put Ted Bundy in eternal hell? Would I put Hitler in eternal hell? Of all people, you wonder about Hitler or some of the tyrants of the twentieth century, like Stalin or Mao, who put so many countless millions of people through unbelievable misery—what should their fate be? Very likely, in nature they're just dead. That's going to happen to me, too, and I haven't done anything nearly as evil, which isn't fair. Society's answer is to punish the bastards! In the society of *Queen of Angels* it is possible to do so.

Thus, in *Queen of Angels,* not only is the potential for really nasty punishment there, but the potential as well for therapy, in the sense of taking a person who has done a horrible thing and finding out what's wrong with him. And then correcting him without removing his personality or substantially affecting him as a self-aware individual.

AV: From where does the title derive?

GB: You'll have to read the book to find that out. It's pretty deeply embedded and has at least three meanings.

AV: If therapy ever reaches the stage of curing the evil that men do, then aren't you putting us in the position of a god?

GB: We are beginning to understand more and more about human personality and how the brain works. It's almost inevitable there will come a time when effective psychological therapy will exist. Right now it's all magic and smoke and occasional miracle cures. We are like children in dealing with our own brains because we don't know what's going on in them, but there will come a time when we will. This book has to address all those questions.

We are a lot more civilized than we used to be. I think we are in a transition state. We are growing toward a time when we don't want revenge so much as we want to cure people who behave in evil and destructive ways. We see their behavior as a disease.

AV: If we can correct these people, then are we turning mankind into a kind of robot?

GB: Good question, isn't it? What's the difference between Ted Bundy and you and me? He's the robot. He's the one who is stuck on one particular, very nasty habit. Here's Ted Bundy telling us all about pornography. How pornography sent him off in this direction. There are millions upon millions of young American males out there who read the same things Bundy did, and they didn't turn into mass murderers. What is Bundy? He is a monster. An aberration. He's like a giant cancer. If you can cure his robotic behavior, give him back self-control, does that turn you into a robot maker?

AV: Hopefully, more of a doctor?

GB: Exactly. You are curing this illness, this aberration that he has. There is a question that occurs in *Queen of Angels*: What if you find out that the root of evil is the root of a personality? Then, as a social worker, do we have the right to expunge the personality and put in a new one?

AV: There is a project going on at Jet Propulsion Laboratory (JPL) whereby a spacecraft would measure the distances between stars, thereby revealing if the universe is expanding or contracting. What are your thoughts on these two polar (universal life versus entropic death) possibilities?

GB: It's expanding. It's pretty obvious. We just don't know how it's expanding or how fast or how long it will go.

AV: Do you think it will ever collapse?

GB: It's possible. We just don't know. We don't have solid answers yet. I tend to like the notion of a cyclical universe. On the other hand, the options may be unknown.

AV: With science fiction writers such as Benford, Brin, Card, Gibson, Le Guin, yourself, and others, science fiction seems to be coming closer to literature. Do you like the thought that science fiction is being considered as "serious literature," or would you prefer it to maintain its own separate genre?

GB: It's there. We're not coming close. We're better than most of the writers writing today because we handle important questions like "Whither mankind?"

I think someone quoted John Barth as saying, "Science fiction writers are not like you and me. They have more fun!" That's a wonderful quote. And it's true! You get a bunch of serious literary writers together, and they're good company because they're intelligent. But then you put them in a room with a couple of freaks like me or Brin or Benford, and we're going to be running all up and down the spectrum. We're going to switch from hard physics or xenobiology to the course of Muslim history in the twentieth century. What are they stuck with? They're stuck with the past or the twentieth century. Most know nothing about science or physics or astronomy.

Now with some of them, this is not true. Pynchon is apparently able to swim in these waters pretty well. John Updike is an extremely bright man who has written science fiction-like stories and fantasy stories. *Witches of Eastwick* is an out-and-out horror-fantasy story with sexual overtones. The really good writers aren't prejudiced in what they address. Unfortunately, there are too many writers who are wallflowers at the orgy. Science fiction writers are definitely not wallflowers at the orgy. They *are* the orgy! They're the vast wellspring of ideas and to see them at work is amazing.

Other writers can go off and pontificate, and we'll see whose name is remembered four hundred years from now. That's the challenge. It's probably not going to be mine, and we will all be equal under the grave—but at least I will have laid down that challenge.

AV: Finally, is the name Vergil I. Ulam an anagram for Gulliver?

GB: Close. It translates to "I am Gulliver."

Madison Smartt Bell. Courtesy of Jerome DePerling.

The Productive Procrastination of Robert Stone: An Interview with Madison Smartt Bell

Madison Smartt Bell was born and raised in Nashville, Tennessee, and graduated from Princeton University. He has published a total of twenty-two books, more than half of them novels. He is perhaps best known for his trilogy of historical fiction works focusing on Toussaint Louverture and the Haitian Revolution; *All Souls' Rising*, the first of the trilogy, was a finalist for the National Book Award and the PEN/Faulkner Award, and it ultimately won the Anisfield-Wolf Award for the best book of the year dealing with matters of race. He and his wife, the poet Elizabeth Spires, teach at Goucher College.

Bell's latest work, *Child of Light: A Biography of Robert Stone* (Doubleday, $35), reflects his lifelong love of the work of that novelist, and inspiration Bell has drawn from Stone and his contemporaries. We discuss the biography in the following conversation, held over email in early 2021.

Allan Vorda: You have produced the definitive biography of a great American author. Walk us through the origins of how you got started on this project. Did you have full access to Robert Stone's manuscripts and letters? Did his widow give you permission to discuss Stone's alcohol and drug issues, as well as their open marriage?

Madison Smartt Bell: Yes, I had extraordinary support from Janice Stone, and couldn't have written the book without that. I was good friends with her before Bob's death, but working on the project together deepened that friendship a good deal. At the time of his death, there were twelve crates of papers in the Stones' New York apartment scheduled to go to a Stone archive at the New York Public Library. Janice delayed sending them so that I could have the convenience of working on the material at her place. (Later I also worked with the Stone archive already housed at NYPL, whose staff was wonderfully helpful.)

Early in the discussions of the biography I called on Janice at the Stones' house in Key West, and said I needed to know two things: how frank she wanted to be about drugs and about other women. She thought for a bit (Janice has no fear of silence) and said that she wanted the whole truth told and believed that Bob would want the same. Early on I interviewed her a couple times about the early period of Bob's life and sent her questions by email. Janice eventually responded by writing her own memoir, sending it to me serially; that was an amazing asset to have, as any reader can see from the amount that I quote from it. Gerry Howard, the editor at Doubleday, worried about that; he said reviewers are going to quip about your having a coauthor. I said I don't mind if they do. It really was a partnership.

I don't know that I'd choose the term "open marriage," since it was not really in use before the early '70s. By then, the Stones had been married more than ten years and had passed through the Kesey orbit. I believe Jane Burton said, "Everybody was in love with everybody," and they all expressed that fully. What Janice told me, while Bob was still living, is that they'd agreed to cut each other some slack in that area since they had married so young and then entered the gigantic cultural upheaval of the 1960s; she felt that this leeway made it possible for them to stay together, which is what they both wanted. You might say that their arrangement prefigured the open marriage trend, but I wouldn't say it was part of it.

AV: Can you briefly describe Stone's upbringing regarding his mother, his Catholic education, and his joining the navy?

MSB: Gladys Grant was a single mother, so single that Bob never knew his father; nothing is known of Homer Stone beyond the name on Bob's birth certificate. In Bob's early childhood Gladys maintained them fairly comfortably on what she earned as a schoolteacher. But she lost that job, probably thanks to mental illness, and that early stability went with it. Still a small boy, Bob spent a few good years as a boarder at St. Anne's School on Lexington Avenue in Manhattan, a school run by Marists which took in supernumerary children from large Catholic families. Bob was a student there through high school, and was in and out as a boarder for several years, but more in than out during his young boyhood. Gladys next tried to move them to Chicago, where they stayed less than a year. On their return to New York, they were briefly homeless, then shared a single room in various SRO hotels, with Gladys earning money as a maid or by stuffing envelopes.

In his teens Bob had some involvement with a street gang (and also an incipient drinking problem), but he was a good enough student to get a top score on the Regents exam as a senior at Saint Anne's, and to win a scholarship to NYU. Around the same time, however, Saint Anne's expelled him for coming to school drunk and (worse) talking a classmate into renouncing Catholicism. Street life in New York was becoming more dangerous; Bob was involved in one fracas where someone was fatally wounded with a knife, and heroin use was becoming more common in this milieu. No doubt he was also ready to get out of his mother's single room, so he took advantage of a navy program that allowed a seventeen-year-old to make a three-year enlistment.

AV: Stone met Janice, his future wife, while both were students at NYU. They later dropped out of school, got married, and then moved to New Orleans in January 1960. How did this move affect Stone's writing and lay the groundwork for Stone's first novel, *A Hall of Mirrors*?

MSB: Well, first she got pregnant and then they got married. Bob had taken up his NYU scholarship at the end of his navy enlistment, but he had to be a full-time student to keep it, and he couldn't sustain that while also working at the *Daily News* full-time. He'd promised Janice a European tour (having seen a good deal of Europe while in the navy), and New Orleans was as close to that as they could manage at the time. They got decent jobs as census canvassers at first; Janice having to conceal and work around her pregnancy until she gave birth to the Stones' eldest. When the census finished, Bob tried factory work, briefly, and sold Bibles in the boonies, briefly and unsuccessfully. Finally, they returned to New York, where Janice could at least get some support from her family.

New Orleans furnished the setting for *A Hall of Mirrors*—Rheinhardt and Geraldine live in the Stones' French Quarter apartment (later to be reconstructed as a set for the movie starring Paul Newman). And the Stones got around all over town, what with Bob's various short-term employments, and most importantly the census work—that took Bob into the Black community, an important factor in the novel.

AV: Would you agree the most momentous event in Stone's life was being granted a Stegner Fellowship at Stanford? Pretty amazing, since he only had a GED certificate and less than three full semesters of college; yet this seemed to help propel him on the road to a writing career.

MSB: It was certainly a life-changing event, especially since Bob had never assumed he would go to college—his childhood produced the expectation that he'd enter the workforce after high school, like most of his peers, although his restlessness opposed that prospect. He would not have applied for the Stegner if not pushed to do it by Mack Rosenthal, an NYU professor who'd seen Stone's promise from some early stories written for Rosenthal's class. On the other hand, Stegner had invented the program to serve students who fit Bob's profile: young men leaving the military after World War II, with incomplete educations and uncertainty about what they could or should do.

A byproduct of Stone's zigzag path through conventional higher education is that though in maturity he was encyclopedically knowledgeable and immensely well-read, he was also very much an autodidact and so had little traffic with received ideas.

AV: While at Stanford, Stone was working on his manuscript for *A Hall of Mirrors,* but this is also where he met Ken Kesey. Tell us about his relationship with Kesey—which included taking LSD, being part of the Merry Pranksters, the parties at Perry Lane, and going to Mexico.

MSB: *One Flew Over the Cuckoo's Nest* had recently come out when the Stones arrived in California, making Kesey the biggest star to have come out of the Stegner. The Perry Lane scene was a Petri dish for the enormous cultural changes on the way, with free love aplenty and many doors of perception being kicked open by mescaline, psilocybin, and LSD. At the same time, most of the people living there were much like the Stones: young couples trying to take care of babies while also finishing novels or dissertations. Kesey had some gravitational force in the community, but was not yet the quasi-cult leader he would become once he moved up to La Honda.

Bob was extremely enthusiastic about any and all hallucinogens on offer. He and Kesey were good, close lifelong friends, but Bob was always resistant to the cult-building aspect of Kesey's charisma (and Janice even more so). The sense grew that Bob's novel would never be finished if the Stones stayed in Kesey's orbit. The Stones were back in New York by the time the Merry Pranksters moniker was coined.

Bob was still working on the novel, in a more disciplined manner than before, when the Prankster bus rolled in for the 1964 World's Fair. The Stones rode the bus around town with their friends, but they were not really "on the bus" in the cult sense of the phrase.

Kesey fled to Mexico in 1966 to avoid drug charges, taking a handful from his inner circle with him, including Neal Cassady. Bob had finished *A Hall of Mirrors*, and didn't yet have a good start on a second novel. He got an assignment from *Esquire* to write a piece on Kesey's Mexican camp—unlike most other reporters, Bob knew how to get there. He eventually wrote nearly a hundred pages of a piece which addressed the whole Kesey phenomenon very astutely, but *Esquire* passed on it. Bob shared the material with Tom Wolfe, and eventually published a much shorter version in *The Free You* as "The Man Who Turned on the Here."

AV: Right—Stone wasn't actually on the Further bus except briefly, when it arrived in New York City, but he had been exposed to Neal Cassady while in Mexico. When I interviewed Stone in 1990, I asked him about Cassady, and he said: "He was a walking cautionary tale about speed. If you wanted to think of one hundred reasons not to take speed, then Cassady could provide you with at least eighty of them." Can you add any other insights about Cassady?

MSB: That's a great line about Cassady. I don't think I can top it. I never knew the guy, and he has been well mythologized by other writers. Bob did once tell me that Cassady had achieved a sort of immortality in the form of his parrot, who could say a lot of Cassady dialogue in a perfect impression of Cassady's voice, and who may still be doing it somewhere, given the longevity of parrots.

AV: If getting the Stegner Fellowship was not the most important, life-altering event in Stone's life, then working as a journalist in Vietnam had to be right up there. Stone stated: "I realized if I wanted to be a 'definer' of the American condition, I would have to go to Vietnam. In many ways it changed my life."

MSB: Bob went to Vietnam from London, where the Stones had been living for quite a while, increasingly cut off from the American scene. Bob was struggling with a second novel set in the US. He agonized terribly about making the trip, but he was so stuck in the novel that in the end he felt he had to go. Getting killed in Vietnam would be no worse than atrophying in London. He spent most of his time with the fringier Anglophone journalists in Saigon, but he did manage to come under fire once and that was certainly a key experience—one that he gives to John Converse, a protagonist of *Dog Soldiers*.

I think that before the trip he had a suspicion that Vietnam was such a key factor in the American experience at the time that you couldn't write anything that didn't somehow include it—*Dog Soldiers* is the expression of that idea. Vietnam is omnipresent in the novel, though mostly offstage.

AV: Stone was given a teaching position at Princeton (despite having no college degree), where he slowly churned out the manuscript for his second novel. It is amazing to think he didn't know what he was doing when he began writing *Dog Soldiers*, since it is one of the great American novels of the twentieth century, but this is what Stone said about writing the book that would win him the National Book Award: "I didn't really research it. I didn't know what I was doing when I began it."

MSB: Princeton had one of the first undergraduate creative writing programs in the country (one reason I went there a few years later). Bob got on board at a moment where the main qualification to teach in that field was achievement in the craft as proven by publication and recognition; degrees didn't matter so much.

My sense is that he was unable to get any real start on *Dog Soldiers* before going to Vietnam; he was, among many other things, a great procrastinator, but I also think that he began with a very inchoate sense of what he wanted to do, and that his Vietnam experience somehow unlocked the problem for him.

AV: Do you think Ray Hicks in *Dog Soldiers* was based on Neal Cassady—and, if so, in what ways?

MSB: Not much, although Hicks's Zen death march scene is probably inspired by Cassady's having died while walking a Mexican railroad track in 1968. Hicks isn't a speed freak (speed was one of the few drugs that didn't much appeal to Bob recreationally, although he did sometimes take Ritalin to write), and he doesn't have Cassady's manic, nonstop-jabbering personality.

I think, rather, that Bob did here what he often did: split aspects of his own personality to create two separate characters for a story, which in some ways opposes them to each other. Hicks is what Bob might have become if he hadn't married, had gone from the navy into the merchant marine (he had a brief encounter with the latter at the end of the New Orleans stay), and drifted into a life a few steps outside the law. Hicks is a man of action, not entirely unreflective but far less reflective than Converse, who's a writer with problems completing his work, who shares much of Bob's ironical insight, and whose ability to imagine the worst that can happen makes him far more timorous than Hicks.

AV: Fans of Robert Stone probably wish he had written more novels. It seems Stone would always procrastinate while writing, and he even referred to himself as a "slothful perfectionist." What are your thoughts on Stone's productivity?

MSB: It's a very solid body of work, and I think one of Bob's novels is worth three or four of most of his contemporaries. We occasionally talked about a difference between him and me: I write with facility and have a good time doing it. For me, it's almost never not fun. For Bob the writing was often a painful experience, especially in later stages when he would push himself further than most of us do, to make every scene and every sentence diamond-hard. Completing each of his best novels was a more taxing experience for him than it is for most of us, so he might not have been quite as eager to turn around and do it again as the average novelist. It's also true that he was very amenable to distraction and inclined to be a rolling stone in the gathers-no-moss sense.

AV: In *Child of Light* you write, "In the summer of 1983, my mother handed me a paperback copy of *A Flag for Sunrise*. We were on our way to spend a few weeks with friends in the Roman Campagna and a couple of other places. It was my first trip to Europe; my first novel had been published a few months earlier. Before I got on the plane, I had never heard of Robert Stone. By the time the wheels touched down in Rome, he was the writer I wished I could become." What other recollections can you share about being captivated with Stone's work and how it affected your own writing career, which has now spawned twenty-two books?

MSB: Stone is one of the few contemporary writers (along with Cormac McCarthy, Mary Gaitskill, William Vollmann, and Eudora Welty) that I can read many times over and still get more out of it. And I've read the great Stone novels so many times I'm sure I just internalized them, and at that point one stops being aware of the influence. I think there's some bleed of Stone's style into mine, although not so much that many people have noticed.

During the years of our friendship, Bob was very admiring of my work, particularly the Haitian novels, which was nice but also felt a little weird; I'd be thinking, "You're 2.5 times the writer I'll ever be—what are you talking about?" I mean, I don't take a back seat to practically anybody, but to Stone I do. I think maybe the fact that I did it easily impressed him, perhaps excessively, and surely more than it does me—it's lucky in a way, but I don't consider it a virtue.

AV: There is an interesting and sublime metaphor in *A Flag for Sunrise* when Holliwell is scuba diving; fear overtakes him as he imagines he is being watched by something unseen, probably a shark. The symbol of fear is also evident when Heath declares, "I'm the shark on the bottom of the lagoon. You have to sink a long way before you get to me. When you do, I'm waiting." It seems that fear was ingrained in Stone's consciousness on the day he went out on patrol in Vietnam. How do you think fear drove Stone in both his life and his writing?

MSB: Proverbially, it's easier to be brave if you're stupid—or maybe unimaginative would be a better word. Active imaginations project bad outcomes, which are hard for courage to overcome, and sometimes those outcomes materialize. I think Stone's experience under fire was not symbolic at all, but a primal, visceral experience, a self-annihilating nadir he was always aware of afterward.

AV: Pablo Tabor from *A Flag for Sunrise* is a scary character for me as a reader. Every time a passage occurred with his name, my antenna came up, anticipating some horrific act of violence. Pablo has been referred to as an "institutional personality" and as an "affectless sociopath"; he's certainly one of Stone's most fascinating characters. I wonder if you see any similarities between him and Ray Hicks.

MSB: I think both are in some ways there-but-for-the-grace-of-whatever self-portraits. Bob had a very evolved idea of the institutional person as someone whose character, in the absence of much in the way of parenting, is shaped by orphanages, juvey, prison, and the military. His childhood and youth gave him the opportunity to become that person, but he didn't. Pablo did.

AV: Stone had a lifelong battle with religion and the existence of God, nurtured early on due to harsh Catholic school discipline, against which he rebelled, eventually being expelled due to being "militantly atheistic." As you note, Stone seems to espouse various philosophical concepts, including atheism, Heidegger, and even psychedelic mystical beliefs. This struggle seemed to weigh heavily on him as he was older and nearing death. How do you view Stone's concept of religion?

MSB: He told some interviewer somewhere that you can't stop being Catholic any more than you can stop being Black. He also wasn't always fighting Catholicism; he had a period of intense devotion in his early teens before adopting the posture of apostasy that got him kicked out of Saint Anne's.

Catholics who renounce the faith and become atheistic live in opposition to what they've renounced, which defines them as much as if they hadn't renounced it. Bob understood that and avoided it. He had instead a much more open-minded kind of skepticism, which you might call agnostic, though I don't think that's exactly right. He had a religious sensibility which is always felt in his work, one way or another. For *Damascus Gate* he got very involved in Kabbalah and was attracted to the idea that Creation was a sort of Big Bang event that scattered tiny sparks of God all over the universe, leaving humanity the task of reassembling them. At the end of his life I think his attitude toward divinity was a sort of hopeful "maybe."

AV: There is sometimes a question of whether a writer is more productive with a wife and children as opposed to not having them, but Stone's productivity does not seem fathomable without Janice. You state: "There's a Janice avatar somewhere in almost every Robert Stone novel." How important was Janice to Stone, not only as a wife, but one who gave balance to his life and even helped with his editing?

MSB: Hugely. Michael Herr called her "the patron saint of writers' wives." It's not an exaggeration. Janice was muse, assistant, secretary, logistician, travel agent, manager, editor, and continuity person for the later novels. Bob knew how important all those roles were, having asked her to quit her job in social work to assist him full-time. (I got the benefit of many of her skills myself, while working on the biography.) Their marriage was founded on love, with the troubles love is heir to, but also on tremendous respect. The Janice avatar in the fiction is there to straighten the protagonist out, and if the protagonist ignores that, it can be fatal. From a childhood where his only family was his mother, Bob derived the idea of "two against the world." In adult life the two were he and Janice. The sexual straying is trivial compared to that; their first and strongest loyalty was always to each other.

AV: Do you think *Children of Light* was a drop in terms of quality from Stone's first three novels, and if so, can this be attributed to the great amount of alcohol and drugs under whose influence Stone wrote it? Your biography gives incredible insight for the decades-long battle Stone had with drugs and alcohol. By chance, I was looking at my interview with Stone in 1990 (after *Children of Light* had been published and right after Stone had completed the manuscript for *Outerbridge Reach*), and I asked him about taking drugs and his response was: "I never became addicted to drugs. I don't think drugs particularly interfered with my life. Obviously, around the electric scene described in *The Electric Kool-Aid Acid Test* drugs were taken. I don't know how different my writing would be without drugs. I certainly don't write in a state of intoxication of any kind. I do not take drugs or drink in order to write. I don't write stoned in any way." This seems to contradict what your biography reveals, and I can only assume Stone was lying to cover up his addiction.

MSB: Doubtless there was an element of classic addict's denial (and wishful thinking) in what Stone told you. I'm sure he imagined a self that could take it or leave it alone. But also, I heard him say the same sort of thing in other contexts and for a different, more practical reason. He depended on teaching for a stable income, and for most of his teaching career drug use was classed as "moral turpitude," for which tenure can be revoked, etc. I saw him get baited about drug use in public; he'd have to deny it, for the reason given.

Meanwhile I think *Children of Light* stands with the best of his books, although, like many, I was disappointed when I first read it. Aficionados of *A Flag for Sunrise* wanted another big, world-historical novel about grand sociopolitical struggle, and *Children of Light* didn't look like that . . . at first. I was reading it for the sixth time when I thought, hey, there must be something about this book that I like. In the end, it's very seriously about good and bad faith in the making of art—a topic as important as any Stone tackled. And the protagonist is the most complete self-portrait Stone ever put into fiction: abjectly addicted, yes, but also possessed of a lethal wit and a kind of real brilliance (at least sometimes), whose self-destructive impulse is matched by a capacity for redemption.

AV: There is a quote from Gordon Walker in *Children of Light*, essentially echoing Stone's own inner voice, about squandering his vocation: "If I was that good, I would never waste a moment. I'd be at it night and day. I'd never drink or drug myself or be with a woman I didn't love." What a great statement, and yet how ironic.

MSB: Heartbreaking too, because if Walker's never really that good, Stone most definitely was. Maybe he just didn't believe it, or not strongly enough.

AV: What do you make of the critics who compared Stone to Hemingway, Graham Greene ("whom he consistently loathed"), and especially Conrad, whom he often mentions as an influence?

MSB: Conrad is, as you say, an influence that Stone avowed; he frequently quoted Conrad to students. Certain statements Conrad made about the practice of writing were crucially central to Bob, particularly this one:

> *To snatch in a moment of courage, from the remorseless rush of time, a passing phase of life, is only the beginning of the task. The task approached in tenderness and faith is to hold up unquestioningly and without fear the rescued fragment before all eyes in the light of a sincere mood. It is to show its vibration, its color, its form, and through its movement, its form, and its color, reveal the substance of its truth—disclose its inspiring secret: the stress and passion within the core of each convincing moment. In a single-minded attempt of that kind, if one be deserving and fortunate, one may perchance attain to such clearness of sincerity that at last the presented vision of regret or pity, of terror or mirth, shall awaken in the hearts of the beholders that feeling of unavoidable solidarity; of the solidarity in mysterious origin, in toil, in joy, in hope, in uncertain fate, which binds men to each other and all mankind to the visible world.*

Being grouped with Greene under the rubric of "Catholic novelist" irritated the hell out of him, for fairly good reason. Even as Catholics they are dissimilar: Bob a lapsed cradle Catholic, Greene a vigorous convert—a difference strongly expressed in their work. The far-flung settings of their novels are another superficial commonality. Bob detested Greene's personality, as he understood it; that's expressed in his preface to a late edition of *The Quiet American*—though alongside some serious respect for the work.

Comparisons to Hemingway are also superficial—two bearded adventurers with abodes in Key West and a taste for world travel and international narratives. I do think they share a strong interest in the meaning of human suffering. Bob probably thought more deeply about Hemingway than about Greene, given this interesting line in a letter to Sven Birkerts: "I think a lot about Hemingway. His work is the best argument I know for the principle that style represents moral perspective."

AV: Conrad can be categorized as a writer who writes fiction with a moral purpose, which writers such as Stone and John Gardner subscribed to as well. You mention John Barth in *Child of Light* on several occasions, whom Gardner castigated in his nonfiction book *On Moral Fiction*. It appears Stone was not on intimate terms with Barth when they were both teaching at Johns Hopkins. What are your thoughts about their relationship? What is your opinion of Barth, whose early fiction was exceptional, but who is now in his nineties and sadly almost forgotten by the literary community?

MSB: First wave metafictionists (Barth, Pynchon, Donald Barthelme, et. al.) generally went past me. Reading Barth's early work felt to me like watching a magic trick without the magic. Not that there's anything wrong with it. *C'est pas mon truc, c'est tout.* I never read his long novels either, it would be fair to say, and perhaps unfair to say that the reason was that they bored me. He published a couple of collections of stories while I was teaching at Hopkins, and those I thought were wonderful, so go figure.

I didn't know Barth well when I was teaching at Hopkins, but he was always cordial. He gave good weight (precisely measured) as a teacher. A nice precision was built into him, perhaps. If someone had set out to design two personalities to abrade each other at every point of contact, Stone's and Barth's would have filled the bill to perfection. In theory, Stone was hired to replace Barth; they should have overlapped by only one year, but Barth changed his mind, resulting in a new situation in which Stone and Barth would share not only the theoretical throne but also the physical office. Barth had a very ambivalent attitude toward retiring from Hopkins and did it in very slow motion. Stone was caught in the consequences of Barth's last second thought. Coexisting with Barth ad infinitum was not something he could tolerate. That Stone's work and Barth's were completely opposite in motive and intention was also a factor, I'm sure.

John Gardner was a really good novelist who might have been a great one had he lived, but *On Moral Fiction* is a self-serving work, not to be taken seriously except for the good bits, all cribbed from Tolstoy. In that vein, Stone's "Reasons for Stories," published in *Harper's* in 1986 as part of a public argument with William Gass (representing the first generation metafictionists), is a lot better, and doesn't suffer from being a lot shorter.

AV: Will anything ever appear from Stone's manuscripts of *Opus 5/Opus 6/Charlie Manson's Gold* and *Arcturus*, the latter of which seemed to have great potential?

MSB: Who knows, but I doubt it. Very little was actually written of *Arcturus*, though somebody might play off Stone's truly amazing plan for the work (that would be on the order of my long-ago fantasy of writing Dostoevsky's unwritten novels). Janice and I actually joked about the notion of my finishing *Charlie Manson's Gold*, which, at two hundred-plus strong pages, should have been over the hump. Those pages show an aspect of Bob's personality that he never really put into any other fiction, and there's a much larger role for the Janice avatar than usual; those are two reasons I wish he had finished it, and also why I don't think anyone else could.

AV: *Bay of Souls* is likely Stone's least effective novel, but *Death of the Black-Haired Girl* was a good read. One wonders what he could have written without having so many physical issues. You saw him in the later stages of his life, and this must have been difficult for you to see. I can only imagine how Janice coped with everything.

MSB: I'll still say that Bob Stone's worst novel is better than most people's best. *Bay of Souls* has got problems—he almost died during the writing of it, and in some places that shows—but still eminently worth reading. The last scene, in particular, is remarkably strong.

But more importantly, he was determined to come back from that low. There were a handful of books he wanted to write, and he was determined to live long enough to write them (he told me that in person, one day we ran into each other in Paris). And he fought to live, not only via the trips to rehab, which improved things for a spell even if they didn't stick long-term, but also in doing everything possible to fight off his COPD, which is what actually killed him in the end. He didn't live to finish all the work he wanted to, but *Death of the Black-Haired Girl* and *Fun with Problems* do show that the effort was worth it.

AV: Finally, I was wondering who your favorite character is from Stone's novels, your favorite novel, and how should Stone be remembered?

MSB: I don't want to play favorites with either characters or novels. But I can say that even minor Stone characters, as Ford Madox Ford recommended, are so real you can smell their breath. If you put yourself in the mind of God, how can you love one more than another?

I think Robert Stone is the writer of his generation who, like the great nineteenth-century novelists and those of the early twentieth, pushed the possibilities of realistic fiction—the representation of who we are in the time we live in—as far as they can go.

Paula Byrne. Courtesy of Guillem Lopez.

Evelyn Waugh and the Secrets of Brideshead: An Interview with Paula Byrne

Paula Byrne was born in Birkenhead in 1967, the third daughter in a large working-class Catholic family. She studied English and theology at the college that is now Chichester University and then taught English and drama at Wirral Grammar School for Boys and Wirral Metropolitan College. She then completed her MA and PhD in English literature at the University of Liverpool. She is now a full-time writer, living with her husband, the Shakespeare scholar Jonathan Bate, and their children in an old farmhouse in a South Warwickshire village near Stratford-upon-Avon. Her nonfiction books include *Perdita: The Life of Mary Robinson, Mad World: Evelyn Waugh and the Secrets of*

Brideshead, Jane Austen and the Theater, Belle: The True Story of Dido Belle, The Real Jane Austen: A Life in Small Things, The Genius of Jane Austen, and *The Adventures of Miss Barbara Pym.* Byrne also has written two novels titled *Look to Your Wife* and *Mirror Mirror.*

For any reader who is a fan of Evelyn Waugh and especially *Brideshead Revisited,* then reading Byrne's *Mad World: Evelyn Waugh and the Secrets of Brideshead* should be a must read. The history and insights that Byrne provides are remarkable.

The following interview was conducted July 2010.

Allan Vorda: What was your inspiration to write a biography of Evelyn Waugh primarily focusing on his involvement with the Lygon family at Madresfield?

Paula Byrne: I started this book with one question in mind—why do people fall in love with other people's families? That led to other questions about Evelyn Waugh and the family which inspired his masterpiece, *Brideshead Revisited,* such as: Where and when was he happiest and unhappiest? What were the relationships that mattered to him most? What was he looking for in life, and how did his quest shape his best novel? I kept coming back to his relationship with the Lygons of Madresfield. I came to the conclusion that his feelings about them provided a key that could unlock the door to his inner world.

AV: Please stress the importance of Brian Howard and Harold Acton (both of whom were flagrant homosexuals and had American mothers) upon Evelyn Waugh and the other students at Oxford.

PB: Brian Howard and Harold Acton had a huge influence on the young Evelyn Waugh. They were undoubtedly the most notorious figures of the Brideshead generation; they were Old Etonians, charming, intellectual, artistic, stylish, and hilariously funny. They were unlike anyone Evelyn Waugh had ever met, and they were a huge inspiration. Brian Howard was also the model for Ambrose Silk, a flamboyant homosexual, who regularly appears in his novels. Evelyn had mixed feelings about Howard, but he adored Acton and dedicated his first novel to him.

AV: Waugh said to a friend shortly after arriving at Oxford University: "All I can say, is that it is immensely beautiful and different from anything I have ever written about except perhaps, 'Know you her secret none can utter?'" This is a reference to Arthur Quiller-Couch's poem "Alma Mater" that alludes to homosexuality. Aside from the lack of female students, why was homosexuality so prevalent at Oxford? Your book seems to make it seem this was just a phase for many of students including Waugh, but I think a lot of readers would be inclined to think this was their actual preference. Please comment on the sexual atmosphere in the 1920s at Oxford among the students.

PB: Homosexual relations were more acceptable than heterosexual relations at Oxford in the twenties. There were very few women at Oxford and the Dons, many of whom were homosexual themselves, frowned upon male/female liaisons. The majority of young men came from single-sex boarding schools, had little experience of female relationships, and shared intense romances with other young men fueled by alcoholic excess. Some of the young men were in rebellion with their fathers, some were homosexual and remained that way all their lives (such as Acton and Howard); others, like Evelyn, went through a homosexual phase that they outgrew. The twenties was a time of unprecedented freedom and experimentation.

AV: Evelyn began to write after leaving Oxford. His first novel, *The Temple of Thatch*, was rejected (by Harold Acton), and later the manuscript was burned by Waugh. Do you think the rejection helped Waugh write a better first novel with *Decline and Fall*?

PB: Yes, the rejection of his first novel was probably a good thing. *Decline and Fall* is one of the funniest novels in the English language.

It is hard to imagine a more perfect debut novel. Thank God he burned his first novel about black magic.

AV: After Waugh divorced his first wife, he basically had no permanent home from 1930-37. It seems his relationship with the Lygon family, especially the sisters, seems intrinsically tied to his development as a writer.

PB: Yes, after his divorce, Evelyn had no permanent home. He did not find his own family home a congenial place, and Madresfield became the closest place to a home. He was able to write in peace, drink to excess, chat with his friends, and enjoy their lavish hospitality. Most importantly, it was a home without parents, an arcadia, where the rules were made up by the young people.

AV: The relationship of Waugh with the homosexual Hugh Lygon and his sister Maimie ("she was a female version of a beautiful Hugh") might seem strange to an outsider. The relationship was subtly played upon in both the novel as well as the movie *Brideshead Revisited* that was directed by Julian Jarrod. As close as Waugh was with all of the Lygon sisters, it seems strange there was no romantic involvement. Why?

PB: There was no romantic involvement with the Lygon sisters because first and foremost they were friends. Evelyn was a little in love with beautiful Maimie, but he would not have dared to spoil the friendship. He knew that he was not her type and valued the friendship above all.

AV: Lord Beauchamp's ouster from politics and England, due to his flagrant homosexuality, inspired Waugh's writing of *Brideshead Revisited.* This is an historical incident little known to Americans, but certainly famous in British history. He was a fascinating and very cultured man who was loved by his children, as evidenced that the Lygon sisters took to his defense. The relationship was so strained that, many years later, Coote and Maimie did not attend their mother's funeral. What did you find in your research about Lord Beauchamp that made him such an interesting figure?

PB: Lord Beauchamp started off as a rather marginal figure in my book, but by the end of my research I was enthralled and fascinated by him. He was cultured, adored by his children, a patron of the Arts and Craft Movement, a talented artist. The treatment of him was outrageous. He was hounded out of the country for being homosexual, and yet he refused to let society break him. The love and adoration of his children toward him speaks volumes.

AV: It is interesting that Waugh dedicated *Brideshead Revisited* to his wife, Laura, yet she never read the novel. Any reason why she didn't, and what kind of marriage did they have?

PB: Laura Waugh was not a great reader. I think that Evelyn would have felt deeply sad that she never wanted to read *Brideshead*. He dedicated the novel to Laura and, as it was about Catholicism, I believe he thought she would love it. Nevertheless, they had a strong and happy marriage and he had plenty of female friends to discuss literature with—I'm thinking here of Nancy Mitford!

AV: How do you look upon Waugh's conversion to Catholicism? Do you think it inspired him as a writer? On the other hand, do you think the conversion scene in *Brideshead Revisited* is a weakness in the novel, as some critics have suggested?

PB: Evelyn's Catholicism was deeply central to his life. Though critics disliked the conversion scene in *Brideshead*, Evelyn said that it was "all true" and a piece of reportage of a deathbed conversion that he witnessed.

AV: Waugh's life was drastically affected in 1961 when Ann Fleming (wife of Ian Fleming) told Waugh that Lord Hailes and his wife found Waugh to be a great bore. This was something Evelyn could not accept and made him reclusive. How could such a seemingly bland comment affect Waugh as greatly as it did?

PB: Ann Fleming's unkind remark hurt him deeply. It was one thing to be a bore, but as he tried to explain to Nancy Mitford, what was far worse was not to realize that one is a bore.

AV: You state that Evelyn Waugh "was the funniest man of his generation." How do you think his reputation as a writer has evolved over the years? Do you think it has been enhanced or has it dwindled, both in England and America, by readers of British literature?

PB: Evelyn Waugh's reputation in England continues to grow and grow. His reputation has not diminished since his early success. He is valued very highly as a satirist, and a great stylist. In my view, he is unable to write a bad sentence.

Elizabeth Crook. Courtesy of Kenny Braun.

The Which Way Tree: An Interview with Elizabeth Crook

Elizabeth Crook has lived most of her life in Texas and is deeply rooted in the Austin scene. She has written five historical novels: *The Raven's Bride, Promised Lands, The Night Journal, Monday, Monday,* and *The Which Way Tree.* These novels, which differ in aspects of style, subject matter, and time, share a theme of characters who face grave, often violent situations, and their attempts to overcome difficult odds. Her most recent novel, *The Which Way Tree,* is the only one told in the first person, yet shares a certain lyricism with the narrative voice in her other novels, with sentences occasionally tied together by a quiet interior rhyme.

Because her novels tend to take place in the Old West, they sometimes get consigned as "Western" genre, as has been the case with *The Which Way Tree*. This is both misleading and miscasting since the novel, which is set in the Hill Country of Texas during the Civil War, is basically a quest novel, where a young man and his half-sister have to overcome numerous obstacles. Samantha Shreve—a young mixed-race girl who is disfigured by a large panther—wants to seek revenge, and is just like Captain Ahab in her relentless pursuit. Benjamin is Samantha's half-brother, who tells the story in letters to a judge. These two siblings are joined by a diverse cast of characters whereby unexpected bonds are formed in the face of danger. This epistolary novel was going into film production, with Robert Duvall to play a minor role, but was temporarily stopped due to COVID-19.

This interview was conducted during August 2019. Even though we lived less than two hundred miles apart, we ended up conducting the interview via email; this included exchanging numerous emails before and after the interview to make sure everything was done correctly. My one regret, based on her mellifluous responses, was that we couldn't meet in person.

Allan Vorda: You have a fascinating background. Your father, William H. Crook, was the director of VISTA for Lyndon Baines Johnson and later the US ambassador to Australia. What was it like growing up in Texas and Australia, and how did this help shape your life?

Elizabeth Crook: I grew up mostly in San Marcos, Texas—which was a small town back then—but my father became tangentially involved in Kennedy's administration and then more integrally in President Johnson's as part of the War on Poverty program. I was seven years old when Johnson appointed him as national director of VISTA (Volunteers in Service to America) and we moved to DC.

From there we moved to Canberra, and were in the embassy for only a year before Nixon was elected and sent Johnson appointees packing. We came home to San Marcos and I've lived in Texas ever since.

I remember those months in Australia as a magical time, in a beautiful country, where I was surrounded by a large and very kind household staff and by more press than was comfortable for a chubby little nine-year-old. I had attended only public schools in the US and found myself at Canberra Church of England Girls' Grammar School, where we wore uniforms and were expected to pledge allegiance to the Queen every morning, and uphold a certain level of decorum that was foreign to me. It was advanced from the US public schools I was used to: I went into fourth grade and was totally out of my depth. I remember we were given a timed test on the multiplication tables 1-12, and counting on my fingers only got me through the sevens. We were told to pass the tests to the front, and I carried mine up instead, and asked the teacher if she would please take me to the third grade. She did, and I was taken in by a lovely teacher, Mrs. Atchison, who got me through.

AV: You dedicated *The Which Way Tree* to your grandparents, Howard E. Butt and Mary Elizabeth Holdsworth Butt. Not everyone may know about your grandfather's grocery store chain known as H-E-B, but it is quite a phenomenon. Are there any tales that you can tell us about this extraordinary man who built his mother's grocery business from the ground up?

EC: I can tell you I'm very proud of who he was and what he accomplished. There's plenty of history about him, and about the company online, but I remember him more personally as "Big Dad." He wasn't a large man, but my cousins and I all saw him that way. He loved stories of honor and adventure, especially Westerns, and one of my favorite tales of him is how he hitchhiked to San Francisco and worked the grape harvests the summer after graduating valedictorian of his high school class in Kerrville. While he was there, he took a train to Jack London's house near Santa Rosa to knock on the door and shake the author's hand. He apparently was a little disappointed when Jack London thought he had come for a handout, but he didn't regret the journey. Nearly eighty years later I stood at the same door and tried to imagine the meeting.

In business, he was known to be spotlessly honest and always generous. He drove himself hard, loved the outdoors, and had a great laugh. When I was growing up, he used to challenge us to swimming races and leave us all in his wake. My grandmother sometimes asked him if he could let us win now and then, but he didn't see the point in it. Frankly, neither did we. We adored him.

My family knows I didn't inherit a shred of his business sense, so they got a big kick out of the fact that my "skill set"—whatever that might be—landed me on a *Forbes* list recently. This happened when the Spanish translation of my novel, *The Which Way Tree,* made it onto a recommended reading list in the Mexican edition of *Forbes*. He would have chuckled at that.

AV: You attended Baylor University for two years and then transferred to Rice University, where you graduated with an English degree in 1982. Was this transition difficult? What was your time like at Rice? Perhaps you can also comment on Max Apple, the author of the wonderful short story collection, *The Oranging of America,* who was one of your professors.

EC: It was certainly a switch going from Baylor to Rice, but my boyfriend at that time was living in Houston, so I took the leap. I took Max Apple's writing class there twice. He was extraordinary. I adored him as a person and admired him as a teacher. Frankly, I was a late bloomer as a writer, and my stories were probably pretty bad, but he was always remarkably kind when it came to critiquing his students.

AV: Jacqueline Kennedy Onassis edited two of your books, *Promised Lands* and *The Raven's Bride,* for Doubleday. Did you have any contact with her before she died?

EC: I met with her several times while she was editing my books, but I was living in Austin and she was in New York, so we did most of the editing by fax machine and mail. She made numerous, sometimes very funny notes on my drafts. Our relationship was professional, not personal, but she was warm and generous and wrote lovely notes to me, signed "Love, Jackie." I never knew how to sign my name to her, because I felt anything reciprocal might seem presumptuous. She was a real champion for my books; I believe she was a champion for all her authors. She passed away on the publication date of my second novel, *Promised Lands,* and although I had known how sick she was, her death still somehow took me by surprise. Having worked closely with her on two books, real labors of love, I felt a little disoriented watching her formal and beautiful funeral procession from afar, on television, and being reminded of her extraordinary place in history.

AV: You were seven years old when the shooting at the University of Texas Main Building tower occurred. Did you have any memories of this tragedy where Charles Whitman killed sixteen people? How did this become the impetus for writing the novel *Monday, Monday,* which won the Texas Institute of Letters' Jesse H. Jones Award for the Best Work of Fiction?

EC: I was attending my grandmother's funeral in Ingleside, Texas, that day, so I wasn't one of the people watching events unfold on television. I don't remember when I learned of it. It became integral to *Monday, Monday* when I read Pamela Colloff's piece in *Texas Monthly,* in which she related the events of that day through first person accounts of eyewitnesses. At the time, I was planning to write a light, contemporary story, but had found myself unable to get emotionally involved with it, or to care deeply about the characters. When *Texas Monthly* landed in my mailbox, my would-be light, funny story turned into something entirely different. It was after I wrote that book, and then wrote *The Which Way Tree,* that I realized four of my five books are spun from violent massacres. I suppose in order to care deeply about my characters, and preside over their lives with a degree of emotional intensity, I need to place them at risk. And what greater risk than to be in the sights of an unhinged killer?

AV: *The Which Way Tree* is a masterful novel that centers around a brother and sister whose lives are forever transformed by a panther. This story actually germinated from your own real-life experience. Can you briefly recount what happened?

EC: When my son was fourteen years old, he and a friend went for an overnight camp-out near Camp Verde in the central Texas Hill Country. They overshot the cabin where they had planned to spend the night, and got lost in the ravines. We went to check on them before dark and realized they had never reached the cabin. The nine-hour hunt that followed was the most frightening night of my life, spent making my way with other searchers by flashlight along waterways, shouting my son's name through dark canyons and a web of narrow ravines, and praying for him to answer. We feared there had been a water accident at the dams. Halfway through the night, the Bandera deputy sheriff and two other searchers spotted an enormous mountain lion weirdly trekking alongside them in the canyon they were searching, and our concern, after that, intensified. The boys were finally spotted by helicopter shortly before dawn, having made a small campfire in a deep arroyo, and were brought home safely. But I wasn't able to stop thinking about mountain lions after that.

AV: One of the compelling things about *The Which Way Tree* is your use of language that totally captures the essence of south-central Texas in the year 1863. The story is told in an epistolary form, letters between the boy Benjamin Shreve and Judge Carlton. Benjamin's letters, with their poor grammar and vibrant colloquialisms, ring so true they make the readers feel as if they are living in that time. How were you able to write in this manner?

EC: I've read so many journals and letters and documents from that time period that the language has lodged in my brain. It was pretty easy to fall into it while I was writing. I can't exactly describe the rules of how the speech rolls out, except there's a formality along with the faulty grammar and punctuation, and a certain rhythm. The sentences often go on a beat longer than you would expect them to. It's a little strange, but I have to whisper things aloud while I'm writing if I want to be sure the sound hits right. My dog, eternally by my side, often catches a strand of a whisper and goes tearing through the house in search of intruders.

AV: How did you decide on the title of the novel?

EC: My friend Stephen Harrigan first suggested it, but I wasn't sure I loved it. There's an actual Which Way Tree that figures in Texas history—and mine isn't that one. So the title was up in the air, but then Robert Duvall, who first optioned the book for film even before I sold it for publication, loved the title. Duvall said if the movie were to be made he planned to call it *The Which Way Tree* no matter what I titled the book. That clinched it for me.

AV: If the visitor named Luke hadn't visited the Shreve home, or had been kicked out of the house by Juda due to her hatred of lice, this story about the panther probably would not have happened. All of the events that unfold are due to Juda wanting to put kerosene on the heads of Benjamin and Samantha. It's amazing how one thing leads to another.

EC: I guess that's pretty much how life works. I like for my stories to play out as they would in real life, for things to happen for a reason, and for my characters to behave as they would if they were actual people. If a story fails in any of those respects, then I stop believing it. And if I stop believing, then I stop caring. And why keep going, after that?

AV: Six years go by before the panther returns. Since Benjamin is afraid of both the Comanche Indians and predatory animals like panthers, wolves, and coyotes, why doesn't he get a better gun, or at least some good gunpowder instead of "bat shat" to protect himself and Sam?

EC: There were shortages during the war. The Union army blockaded the coast and prevented shipment, even of staples like salt. Texans got by with cheap gunpowder made from bat guano—which Benjamin calls "bat shat"—collected out of the caves in central Texas. I've been in these caves, and believe me, there's a lot of guano!

AV: Benjamin reads *The Whale* twice from a copy given to him by captured Union soldiers. It made him "see how Ahab acted the way he did about the whale, as I seen how Samantha acted about the panther." This is an astute observation by Benjamin. It is hard to fathom who is more vengeful—Ahab or Sam.

EC: Samantha (Sam) seeks revenge on the panther for scarring her face and killing her mother—so yes, she's out to settle a score. But there's the added fact she has nothing else to do with her time, or with her life, given her circumstances. She's a young girl, of mixed race, disfigured, and at risk of being mistaken for a runaway slave if she ventures out. Revenge on the panther becomes her sole purpose, partly because she's denied any other.

AV: Sam says, "You seen my face. You seen my mama's dress there without my mama in it. I don't care about songs. That panther was on top of me. I want its hide laying right here on my floor to tromp on day and night. I will be on top of it! I will make that happen myself, not you!" Even though Benjamin is the narrator of the story, it is Sam who drives the novel with her Ahab-like lust for revenge. How did your creation of this twelve-year-old girl come about?

EC: I actually don't remember. She sprang up out of nowhere. Some readers might find her need for vengeance unlikeable, but I love the passion. In spite of the fact that her sex, age, and appearance would normally have made her the least powerful person in the story, time and again she rises up and turns things her way. Her brother Benjamin, Lorenzo Pacheco, Preacher Dob, and even the dog Zechariah all find themselves at the mercy of her will.

AV: Preacher Dob recounts the story when he was a young man and joined a group of ruffians who are captured by Mexicans. The Mexicans tell the prisoners to reach into a pot that has black and white beans. If the person picks a white bean then he lives; if he picks a black bean he will be executed. As Preacher Dob "watched the other men draw their beans, one after another, he noted the fact the black beans was a touch smaller. And when the blindfold was put on, and he reached his hand in, there was but two beans left, one for him and one for the man behind him, who was hardly more than a boy. He got hold of the small one first, and felt of it, and feared it, and let go of it, and felt of the bigger one, and took it." Was this account based on a true story or something you created?

EC: It's based on the fate of men who were taken prisoner during the 1842 Mier Expedition, and what is known as the Black Bean Episode. One out of ten of the 176 men was to be killed, and they were selected by drawing beans from a pot that held 159 white beans and 17 black ones.

AV: There is a scene where Sam says if they kill the panther then the hide has to stay with her and not be taken to Mexico for the $2,000 bounty: "Look at me! All of you look at me! You want songs, you want money, but I want payback. And I own the say-so! I own the right! I own all the right! Preacher Dob said, Vengeance belongs to the Lord, Samantha. She said, Only if he can beat me to it." This is one of several scenes where Sam and Preacher Dob disagree; a lot of readers might side with the preacher in these battles of wit, but I love Sam's tenacity and obstinacy. Is there a winner in your mind between two people who have totally different personalities and different thought processes?

EC: Stories are driven by conflict, and the fact that the characters tracking the infamous panther are four individuals of different backgrounds, different ages, various races, each involved for a different reason, and with completely separate goals in mind, lends itself to conflict at every turn. For the scenes to be real, and the arguments to come off as genuine, I had to see things only through the eyes of whichever character was speaking at that moment. Whoever had the floor, that's the one I agreed with.

AV: While Sam is the person who drives the novel, the other person who creates multiple confrontational scenes is Clarence Hanlin, probably the only evil character in the novel. Your portrayal of Hanlin is pitch perfect. How did you conceive of him?

EC: I love Clarence Hanlin as a villain because he's both sinister and inept. He wants to terrify, but Preacher Dob and Lorenzo Pacheco constantly put him in his place. His attempts to lie his way out of trouble are transparent to the preacher and consistently backfire. Preacher Dob tells him, "You're a liar, Clarence. Before you could talk you laid in your cradle and thought lies." Benjamin writes, "The preacher then hollered at him about being immoral and good for nothing. He said, Your mother has wept buckets over you and cursed herself for bringing you into the world. Your father would likely shoot you if he was to run across you. You are the worst seed I ever saw. We known it when you drowned them cats for the fun. You are not right."

AV: Alfred Pittman's letter to Jackson Beck in 1925 states: "Concurrent with sending the original pages to you, I have placed photostats in the Bandera County Courthouse and the archive held by the Texas State Historical Association at the University of Texas." Do these letters or similar letters actually exist?

EC: No, the letters are entirely fictional. It was a lot of fun to tell the story in Benjamin's voice, through the letters, and then have Alfred Pittman and Jackson Beck, both seemingly insignificant players in the tale, step forward from the shadows at the end, and provide the closure. In real life it's so often those backstage figures who, when they're allowed to talk, can give us the broadest perspective.

AV: Benjamin's last letter to the Judge states: "I will do what you think I aught to and write other accounts of events that befall me in my life as you suggested." This being said, do you have any thoughts about writing a sequel to *The Which Way Tree*?

EC: Not a sequel—no. But maybe Benjamin will have another adventure someday. He follows that statement with this: "I have been reading *The Whale* again, and I seen where Ishmael says that a most perilous and long voyage ended only begins a second, and a second only begins a third, and so on, for ever and for aye."

AV: I came across *The Which Way Tree* by chance, but along with Ron Hansen's *The Assassination of Jesse James by the Coward Robert Ford* and *Butcher's Crossing* by John Williams, I consider it one of the best Western novels I have read. Thank you for a marvelous reading experience and for doing this interview.

EC: What a nice compliment, Allan—thank you. I've enjoyed your thoughtful questions. This has been completely my pleasure.

Kim Echlin. Courtesy of Michelle Quance.

Arranging Memory: An Interview with Kim Echlin

Kim Echlin was born in Burlington, Ontario, where her high school teachers noticed her writing talent early on. She has received degrees from McGill University and Paris-Sorbonne University, as well as her PhD in English literature from York University; her thesis was on the translation of Ojibwe Nanabush myths. Echlin has been a documentary filmmaker, editor, and teacher, and has travelled around the world, often infusing this experience into her novels, which include *Under the Visible Life* and *The Disappeared,* a critically acclaimed book heralded by Khaled Hosseini as "nothing short of a masterpiece." She currently teaches at the University of Toronto's School of Continuing Studies and for the Vermont College of Fine Arts.

Echlin's most recent novel, *Speak, Silence,* is a fictionalized account of the Bosnian women who testified at The Hague about their experiences of crimes against humanity, focusing on the estimated sixty thousand women and children who were raped during the genocidal Bosnian War. This novel celebrates the courageous women who spoke out against this brutal and widespread tool of war and, in doing so, changed both international law and the world's consciousness.

In this interview, Echlin references Homer's *Iliad,* where Agamemnon tells his troops to rape faithful Trojan wives. Echlin's response is: "Where is the heroic literature about this? Where is the story of a woman's survival of war that is as beautiful as the *Iliad*?" Where is the heroic literature? Here it is.

This interview was conducted May 2021.

Allan Vorda: *The Disappeared,* your novel about the relationship of a young Canadian girl with a Cambodian man, seems to have some similarities to your most recent novel, *Speak, Silence*.

Kim Echlin: Yes. In both novels, characters live with grave historical events—in *The Disappeared,* a genocide, and in *Speak, Silence,* an international war crimes trial. The characters in these novels live in a world that is connected by international travel and communications. They have romantic relationships and friendships and work affiliations across cultures and languages and international borders. This is my world, and it is the world I want to reflect in my storytelling. In *The Disappeared* and in *Speak, Silence,* Canadian characters have relationships with men who are not Canadian. One begins in Montreal, the other in Paris, and characters explore other parts of the world as a result of these relationships—Phnom Penh, Sarajevo, Toronto, The Hague. Their powerful and complicated love affairs are lived against a backdrop of international turmoil. If we can bear to look, we know what is happening. We are electronically and visually connected as never before. My characters want to look. They want to act. They leave home to explore the world and they find love. They also find genocide and international trials and they do not turn away. Their consciousness compels them to look, and to act. The question I ask myself, in my writing and in my life, is, "What do we do once we know?"

AV: I want to mention also your previous novel, *Under the Visible Life,* which deals with the relationship of two multiethnic young women (Katherine Goodnow is Chinese and Canadian, while Mahsa Weaver is American and Afghani). Why did you choose to write about multiethnic characters?

KE: There are many reasons for this. From the point of view of the story, Katherine's mother is prosecuted under the "Female Refuges Act" in Ontario (Canada) for having a relationship with a Chinese national working in Canada. Under this act, women could be charged with being "incorrigible." This word was widely interpreted and applied to control women's behaviors, everything from playing cards and prostitution to interracial relationships. This act was not removed from our legal system until 1969. Mahsa's parents were persecuted by both state and religious law, and in the end were murdered for their relationship. Their marriage was transgressive because of their differences of religion and nationality. I wanted to explore law and custom in different parts of the world—in Canada, in Afghanistan, and Pakistan—and to look at how law and institutionalized religion can limit love and human connection.

My city, Toronto, is diverse. Half of our citizens speak a language other than French or English at home. Our school system is set up to support students who are acquiring English and French at different ages. Important city information from our 311 telephone number is available in 180 languages. Naturally, in such a place, culture and ethnic origins mix. In my novels, characters of different origins and religions marry, have love affairs, create families, and work together. Why? Because that is the world we live in.

Multicultural or pluralistic societies are not new. They have been with us since the beginning of recorded history. In ancient Mesopotamia,

Akkadians and Sumerians mixed, and their stories and documents were written on bilingual tablets, even though the two languages share no common roots. People have travelled, intermarried, traded, and lived together since 5000 BCE. I think it is time to see that such interconnectedness is, in fact, the norm. Human cultures have never not mixed! I want to tell that story. Cultural connection is as ancient as the written word. Our consciousness can no longer deny this. Storytellers have always traded stories. Musicians, sculptors, painters have always shared their forms of expression.

AV: My kids, one of whom lives outside Ottawa and is married to a Canadian woman, are Asian American, so these are issues that are near and dear to me. It is very disturbing to see anti-Asian violence here in the US, partly in response to COVID-19. What do you make of this, and is there similar anti-Asian violence in Canada?

KE: This is a question that is both literary and social, and it demonstrates our experience of imagination in the world. We, as a world community, have a very long way to go as we search—eternally and without hope that the work is ever finished—for equity across race, gender, sexual expression, and social class. I am sure you experience this in your own family as I do in mine. The violence we are witnessing around race in this moment is not only disturbing, it is criminal. We need to continue to use the principles of our democracies and our laws to defend everyone's pursuit of self-definition. The Canadian Charter of Rights and Freedoms is an elegantly written document that not only articulates ideals of citizenship but is the basis of our laws meant to defend and explore the responsibilities and rights of *all* citizens.

In your question, I feel you reaching into that almost ineffable place where lived experience and lived imagination become one. This is the greatest moment in art. It is the moment in which consciousness shifts and we see the world fresh.

The first time I saw Georgia O'Keeffe's series called "Sky Above Clouds" I suddenly perceived the world in space differently. O'Keeffe captures flying and looking down on clouds. In my writing, I want to capture the complicated relationships people have with each other and create a moment of seeing afresh. Language has the power to understand more expansively, from above the clouds. Beautiful language can take us into pain that we perhaps cannot otherwise tolerate, and also into fresh consciousness.

AV: What research did you do for *Speak, Silence*? Did you travel to Sarajevo and The Hague? If so, in what ways did this help with writing your novel?

KE: I worked on *Speak, Silence* for ten years. I watched this war on television. I was fascinated when the international court was established. I travelled to The Hague, saw the courts, interviewed prosecutors and case managers, visited the evidence vaults and library and courtrooms, saw the mechanisms behind the courts, the translation booths and visitor galleries and witness waiting rooms. I really loved meeting the people who were working in the courts. Several have become dear friends, which does not always happen when one is researching. I admire their international optic, their dedication to this difficult work and the shared ideal of international justice. Without a doubt, this group of people are the best listeners I have ever met, and novelists are accustomed to listening deeply.

My visit to Bosnia-Herzegovina was transformative. I travelled with a former soldier and UN driver to parts of the region that are normally difficult to access. A friend from The Hague who is a case manager travelled with us and brought detailed files. Throughout our days I heard personal experiences of the war from someone who fought in it and statistics and evidence about the war from someone who has spent years in the courts studying it.

On my own, I visited the office for Women Victims of War, and met the NGO's founder, Bakira Hasečić, who is a survivor. With her I could feel the tragedy and violence of what happened to the women. I remember a moment with her in which I looked at a wall of files and suddenly grasped that the files were the testimonies of thousands of courageous women finding a voice to tell about their experience of war rape. In this moment the walls seemed to tremble, as if the voices were speaking aloud.

AV: Did you give Edina's husband the name Ivo in reference to Ivo Andrić, who wrote *The Bridge on the Drina* and who won the Nobel Prize in 1961? In what ways was Andrić's novel an influence in writing *Speak, Silence*?

KE: Ivan is a common name in the region and means "God is gracious or merciful." Edina calls him both Ivan and the diminutive, Ivo. Theirs is a great love affair. They grew up together and their families loved each other, and they shared Muslim and Christian traditions with ease and hospitality and caring. I wanted the love between Edina and Ivan to be one in which readers experience the grace of the spirit, unimpeded by politics, religion, or war.

Ivo Andrić is an important writer. I read a lot of his work and learned many traditional stories that most people who grow up in the region would know. On the night they meet, Kosmos tells Gota about the long history of conflicts in his home and some of Andrić's stories. She responds by telling him about her own culture's history of violent colonialism and the principle of Terra Nullius. But neither of them has any idea of what the other is talking about. They just want to make love!

AV: The main character, Gota Dobson, goes to cover a film festival in Sarajevo during the Bosnian war. Is this scene referencing Susan Sontag, who made a famous trip to produce a play during the war?

KE: I'll just sort out a few historical dates for clarity, because these events happened in an intense three-year period. Susan Sontag worked on a production of "Waiting for Godot" in 1993. She is much beloved in the community, and a square in Sarajevo in front of the National Theatre is named for her. The ICTY (International Criminal Tribunal for the former Yugoslavia) was established in 1993, and the indictment for the trial that I fictionalize in the book was in 1996. The first film festival in Sarajevo began in 1995.

Artists played a prominent role in this war, especially in Sarajevo. They kept radio broadcasts going during the siege, and there was underground theatre and music. They impatiently started the film festival which continues to this day. Artists and their work became the embodiment of memory, activism, and future. In my book, Kosmos, the father of Gota's child whom she travels to Sarajevo to find, is the eternal artist trying to capture in his work the psyche of the place where he was born.

AV: In your novel, Zarko Dragic is the defendant who is indicted and stands trial at The Hague for crimes against humanity. Your portrayal of Zarko depicts him as a person with no feelings of guilt or remorse. What can you tell us about these men and what they were really like?

KE: This is perhaps the most complicated question in this interview. In earlier drafts of my novel, I tried to work from Dragic's point of view and I wrote his backstory based on research. I read first-person perpetrator accounts and the testimonies of the defense carefully; but I have never felt able to inhabit this psychology.

The three common features that I understand about the individual rationale for war crimes are: the pressure to act as others do or be killed oneself; the conception of the enemy as "other" and therefore not-quite-human; and the idea that there are no rules of war, and therefore anything is permitted. But there is more to war crimes than this—power, individual conscience—and I cannot get to the bottom of all of it.

In my novel, I decided not to try to enter into Dragic's inner perspective because I felt my attempts were inauthentic. Was my imaginative empathy too limited? I don't know, but I never felt that I was being true to Dragic. His inner voice escaped me. I decided to use language from the trial transcripts, physical descriptions from watching the video footage of the trial, and the women's responses to him in court. This was as accurate as I could get.

AV: Centrally in your novel there is the silence of the Bosnian women, but there is also the silence between Gota and her daughter Biddy. Can you extrapolate on this allegory of silence and the need for communication?

KE: People live with all kinds of silences. In my novel, the women defendants must find the courage to testify in court, *to break the silence* in order to have their stories on the record.

The silences between mothers and daughters are periodic and change throughout our lives. In my story, Gota and her daughter are living their unique relationship through both silence and deep connectedness. Edina and her daughter Merima have also had to learn to deal with secrets they kept, out of both shame and the desire to protect each other. Merima did not want her mother to know what she went through and yet, her mother urged her to testify in court, to tell her story, which meant that she would have to know. This was excruciating.

Ultimately, grandmothers, mothers, and daughters had to accept knowing each other's dread stories in order to change the law. I do not know how people live with these truths. But I do know, even in my own more ordinary life, that secrets destroy families. It is better to tell and work to bear the pain.

AV: On the first page Gota is watching TV about the Bosnian war and ruminates: "To watch people falling like clay pigeons in skeet practice. To change the channel. To live in the unattended moment. To be where I was not." Later on, after the war, Mak takes Gota to Srebrenica to see the memorial and graves at Potocari. This is quite a journey that Gota makes, from distant to first-hand observer. Is this something that you can relate to in your own experience visiting places like Srebrenica and Foca?

KE: Yes. I have been able to travel and to see. In part this may be why I am drawn to certain themes. My parents created our family after World War II. They both came from insecurity and poverty and they were both curious about the world and they liked to read. My father had a chance for education on a veterans' plan and he became a dentist. Even though my mother did war work calibrating airplane engines, there were no education plans for women, and she continued her own work independently. Later, when my parents had a chance to travel, they took us with them. We watched them work together on outreach dental programs in remote areas, the Northwest Territories and northern Labrador. We were always expected to help when we could and to give back. This was woven into who we were as naturally as breath. I think this has had a great impact on how and why I travel. I want to see. I want to know.

AV: Grief is a vast wasteland. An example of this is where you state: "People were still collecting and identifying, bone by bone, arranging memory." I cannot conceive how the Bosnian people afflicted by the war can live with the horrors every day.

KE: Yes, I think you're right. We are becoming aware, since World War II, that war experience is held by generations. The children of survivors carry the pain and grief. If, as a world community, we were able to conceive of ourselves as interconnected, we would all share the pain and grief. We would be less likely to turn away from each other. This is why I believe that the international courts are very important. People from all over the world find new ways to work together in these courts, to create new laws and to attempt a shared culture of ideas around justice.

AV: After the war in which these women were raped, "Some men supported their wives and some refused to live with them after the war." Have there been any post-war studies about these families regarding the various traumas that occurred?

KE: Yes, a great deal of work has been done in this area. There is more to do. The trial I describe in *Speak, Silence* is one in which rape was found to be a "crime against humanity," which is important because this means that the crime is not an individual crime against an individual woman but a crime against all of us, and, in certain cases, a constitutive part of genocide. These are legal definitions and they are important to all of us because with them comes a shift of our consciousness about rape in war. Women's bodies are no longer spoils of war. But the crime goes on, most recently in Myanmar with the Rohingya, in northwest China with the Uyghurs, in the Democratic Republic of Congo. We have so much more to do.

AV: At many points in the novel, you seem to imply there was a directive by the Serbian leaders to commit genocide. Is there proof there was such a directive, and what are your thoughts about this?

KE: The Foca (Kunarac, et al.) case from which my story is drawn was the first international case to exclusively prosecute sexual violence. The legal intricacies are critically important and there is a high legal bar to prove its part in genocide.

I think of the evolution of our thought since Homer's *Iliad* in which Agamemnon rallies his troops by saying, "Now, let no man hurry to sail for home, not yet / Not till he beds down with a faithful Trojan wife." Now, several thousand years later, our collective imagination is shifting with the recently developed legal jurisprudence that sexual violence can form part of convictions of genocide, crimes against humanity, and war crimes.

Where is the heroic literature about this? Where is the story of a woman's survival of war that is as beautiful as the *Iliad*? The work of representing a woman's experience of war in fiction requires deep listening.

AV: When you discuss the cross-examination by the defense attorney Mutaruga of Edina, you state: "Both acted within the law. Like a king sliding in and out of check with no clear resolution." This is analogous to the chess matches that Edina and Gota play. What brought up this effective metaphor of comparing the trial to a chess game?

KE: Chess is very popular in Bosnia-Herzegovina. In Sarajevo, I watched a wonderful game of street chess using pieces that were four feet tall. The two players walked through their game, moving the pieces with two hands. It was really fun to watch. Spectators called out advice and insults and it was entertaining for everyone on the square.

In schools, it was an activity that boys and girls did together and Edina had real mastery. I wanted to show her as she was before the war, fun, competent, competitive. Gota isn't a good player but they can play together, even over the telephone, and chat. Edina is more relaxed playing chess than in any other activity and she is able to tell Gota difficult things while they play.

I had a beautiful moment of synchronicity when I was researching chess for this novel. This often happens to me when my research goes well. I was looking for someone to help me design the games in the book. I wanted them to show Edina's spirit and competitiveness and humor. I checked online for a chess master near me and the first person's name that came up was a name that looked Bosnian. I told him that I was writing a novel and needed instruction and when we met he agreed to teach me and a few lessons later he told me that he himself had escaped from Sarajevo during the war. Suddenly the pieces I was studying on the board seemed alive in a fresh way.

AV: There is a brief scene where you mention the seventeenth-century Dutch painter Judith Leyster and her painting *The Proposition,* where a man is offering money to a seamstress, ostensibly for sex. Leyster's painting originally included her initials with a star, but a person named Franz Hals put his name over hers and it was not discovered and restored for three hundred years. This could be analogous to the Serbian military trying to cover up or deny their responsibility. What else can you tell us about seeing this painting and incorporating it into your novel?

KE: I like how closely you read. The fabric of images is part of the story and all art is interconnected, if we can bear to see. We know that in the Western tradition, women have been "silenced," not only in war, but domestically. One of the many forms of silencing is appropriation of voice and creativity, which is what happens to Leyster when Hals steals her painting. Gota sees this painting during the time that she is watching the court case and she wonders if the legal process is not in some way appropriating the women's experiences. Gota becomes acutely aware of the age-old harassment of a woman in her own home and also that Leyster's work itself was disappeared under a male artist's name. It is unbearable—in that moment—and she leaves the gallery. Then it makes her more determined to tell the story she is witnessing.

AV: Even though the trial at The Hague occurred ten years ago, *Speak, Silence* is an important book telling the reader we cannot, just like the

Serbians and Bosnians, forget what happened. Perhaps you can comment on this.

KE: I hope that *Speak, Silence* transcends the particular trial which took place in 2000. The International Criminal Court work is ongoing. Women's domestic lives, sexuality, and political freedoms have been silenced for millennia. I have experienced this in my own work and mothering and domesticity. I hope that this novel helps communicate the emotion of emerging from silence, the feeling of finding one's voice. I write from emotion and feeling. Reading fiction allows us to enter into a shared imaginative experience in which we can feel what the characters feel. I have always, since childhood, read for the expansiveness that using the imagination gives me. I hope readers will experience this in my books.

Jennifer Egan. Courtesy of Pieter M. Van Hattem.

Habit of Mind: An Interview with Jennifer Egan

Jennifer Egan was born in Chicago but raised in San Francisco. Her education includes an undergraduate degree in English literature from the University of Pennsylvania and a graduate degree from Cambridge University. While on a hiking trip throughout Europe she decided to become a writer. Her first book publication was a collection of striking short stories titled *Emerald City* (1993), which was subsequently followed by the novels *The Invisible Circus* (1995), *Look at Me* (2001), *The Keep* (2006), *A Visit from the Goon Squad* (2010), *Manhattan Beach* (2017), and *The Candy House* (2022).

Egan was a recipient of a National Endowment for the Arts Fellowship and a Guggenheim Fellowship. *Look at Me* and *Manhattan Beach* were nominated for the National Book Award, while *A Visit from the Goon Squad* won the Pulitzer Prize and the National Book Critics Circle Award.

The following interview took place on November 6, 2017, at the Four Seasons Hotel in Houston before her book reading of *Manhattan Beach* at Rice University for the Inprint Reading Series. When I turned on my digital recorder and asked her my first question, Egan caught me off guard and said she didn't want prepared questions, instead wanting something off-the-cuff. Since all my questions were prepared, I was temporarily stumped, but once we got going everything was fine. Once the interview was over and I left the hotel, my thought was that *Manhattan Beach* was a good novel, but not up to the level of *Look at Me* and *A Visit from the Goon Squad,* which I think are extraordinary. My overall impression of Egan was that she takes her writing very, very seriously and her next novel will be something special.

Allan Vorda: Before getting into your latest novel, *Manhattan Beach,* I would like to briefly discuss some of your earlier writing. *Emerald City,* a collection of short stories, often depicts characters who initially might be described as not worldly or perhaps naïve, yet who experience some epiphany or awakening. I am thinking of Sam in "Why China?," Sarah in "Sacred Heart," and Rory in "Emerald City." Was there a particular enlightening experience that you can share that contributed to your own self-awareness?

Jennifer Egan: Yes. I took a year off between high school and college, and I went to Europe and traveled with a backpack. I flew to London, got a Eurail pass, and traveled around Europe, which a lot of European kids did and probably still do. I didn't see too many Americans. It was very alienating in certain ways because my family was in San Francisco and, of course, those were the days without cell phones or the internet. It's hard even now for me to imagine this. I felt very cut off and I think in that cut-off state, I discovered that writing was an essential part of my connection to the world. It was an epiphany, although I don't remember a specific moment when it happened. I remember by the time I came back I knew I wanted to be a writer. I guess you can't really ask for more from a year off, right? I knew what I wanted to do with my life, but like so many discoveries I've made, it really came through adversity.

In other words, it was not a fun trip in many ways. It was very hard. I felt very isolated. I wonder sometimes whether anyone experiences that isolation anymore. I wonder whether without that isolation I would have discovered I wanted to be a writer. I don't know nowadays if I would have. I don't know if I would have been just chatting on Instagram the whole time and never reaching that discovery.

AV: How have your other traveling experiences affected you as a writer?

JE: I think a great deal, because I'm very influenced and informed by place. That's my entry point into fiction. I think it starts with the fact that I'm originally from Chicago, but my parents divorced when I was two. I moved at seven to San Francisco with my mother and stepfather, and the textures and feeling of that place were very different from Chicago. Right from the start I was attuned to the fact that in some ways geography and biography intersected. I used the places that I had been and experienced as both a traveler and a citizen very heavily. In fact, it's the only part of my own life that I knowingly use in my fiction. So, in some ways, the places I've been offer me stories to tell. They're my access points.

AV: Several of the husbands in *Emerald City* are unfaithful, leading to divorce. Charlotte Swenson, the protagonist in *Look at Me,* observes of her one-night stand with a married man: "It was obvious he was a regular cheater. So many were." You are a happily married woman with children, but should readers read into your characters that you do not have a high opinion of men in general?

JE: I think that would be presumptuous on the part of the reader because I think there are also a great many happy marriages in my work.

However, it is fair to say that I have witnessed a lot of broken marriages. My parents divorced when I was very young, so I didn't grow up with an example of a very happy marriage in front of me.

AV: Taking a line from *Look at Me,* Charlotte ponders: "Seeing her mother beside her annihilated that hope, leaving Charlotte to wonder whether someone so unbeautiful as herself would be allowed to go on, to have anything. Wouldn't someone more beautiful get it, whatever it was?" You seem to have a lot of references to women's beauty or even their unattractiveness. I'm curious what your concept of beauty is and its importance to women in general.

JE: I think we live in an image-saturated world, a culture in which physical appearance ends up having excess importance, in which people of all sorts are focused, have to be focused, especially younger people, on this self-marketing. That's really what social media is on some level. I think physical appearance has outsized importance in our culture, and no one has much of a choice but to care about it. I think that's unfortunate in certain ways. It impacts people in ways that are different for every person, and I think it often has very little relationship to their inner lives. I guess I feel that physical appearance is a bit of a distraction, but it ends up mattering more than it should in a culture permeated by mass media.

AV: Throughout several of your stories you mention Rockford, Illinois. I believe your mother grew up there, but did you spend any time there, and what is it about Rockford you like to use as a reference?

JE: I did spend a lot of time there because my grandparents lived there. Until they both passed away, I would go there in the summer and other times. I think what interested me in Rockford is it is a quintessentially industrial, mid-sized midwestern city, but whose industrial peak gradually subsided over the last century. When its industry gradually began to die out, and to some degree its economy, its identity also changed. When other changes happened, like the highway systems in the 1950s, which left downtown Rockford sort of like a shell of itself.

There were a lot of trends one sees all over America that were manifested in Rockford. I guess what I found interesting is it seemed like a way to look at a larger phenomenon in the progress and decline of American cities; yet it was also a place that I knew well and for which I had an affection because of my childhood.

AV: When writing fiction and doing your research, do you have time to read for your own pleasure? If so, do you feel this distracts or energizes your writing?

JE: I am definitely always reading for pleasure. For *Manhattan Beach,* I was reading mostly about the first half of the twentieth century for several years. There's always the danger that what I'm reading starts to make a stamp on what I'm writing. What I find is if that happens, the influence tends to fall away in later drafts. I don't really worry too much about it. I love reading and I'm very inspired by it. I'm always looking for ideas and approaches. It's true I might grab onto an idea or approach that doesn't really fit in the context that I'm working in, but I can usually spot that at a later point and let it go.

AV: You state in the book *Why We Write***:** "Read at the level at which you want to write. Reading is the nourishment that feeds the kind of writing you want to do." What kind of writing provides nourishment for you?

JE: First of all, I like to read fiction and nonfiction, but ideally writing that has a strong intellectual bedrock and a deep structure of ideas. Writing that is ambitious and pays attention to the music and rhythm of language.

AV: *Manhattan Beach* is your first novel since *A Visit from the Goon Squad.* What was the genesis of the story? Tell us about Lucille Kolkin—did you base any of Anna's character on Lucy?

JE: Lucille Kolkin was a woman who corresponded with her husband during World War II in a series of letters that are now at the Brooklyn

Historical Society, and they're wonderful letters. I discovered them in 2005, and it took me a few months to read them all since I had limited access to the library. The reason I was reading these letters was to try to learn about the Brooklyn Navy Yard, where Lucy was working after her husband, Al, had joined the navy. I did not base Anna on Lucy, but I felt like Lucy was kind of an inspiring spirit in all of it, because she was sassy and strong. Lucy was crazy about Al—head-over-heels in love—so it was very sweet to read the way she wrote to him. Certain little anecdotes from her experiences did find their way into the book, but it's hard to remember, because I read interviews and interviewed so many women who worked at the Brooklyn Navy Yard. So I can't quite say to what degree I've used details from Lucy's experience, but certainly she was one of many voices in my head that provided a kind of texture of women's experience at the yard, apart from all the stuff I made up.

AV: Since we are talking about the letters that Lucy was writing, hasn't this become a lost art? Nowadays people just correspond by email and writing by script is gradually disappearing.

JE: They don't know script, even my kids don't know script. It's very unsettling. First of all, who prints their email to save it? What are we going to do? We'll have no correspondence of which to have a record. Not only is the handwriting in Lucy's letters wonderful, but she and Al also made diagrams of things for each other. For example, at one point she kissed the letter paper, which was so eerie because you could see the little creases of her lips. It was like she did it yesterday! There was a human element that is simply not present if you read email. You're interfacing with a machine, not a person. One time Lucy was on a streetcar and her handwriting would be messy and she'd say, "Oh, my stop is almost here!" and it's just so much more intimate than reading email. There were a few letters that were typed, but I think that was because someone had typed them later to make them easier to read. Even a typewriter was an unwelcome intrusion into this prose. I wrote letters for a lot of my life. I have lots of letters that people wrote to me. I still save cards and notes, but no one writes letters. Yes, you might get a thank-you note, but who writes a handwritten letter? I don't even do that, and I handwrite my first drafts. Future generations are going to have nothing. We're going to have screenshots of people's Instagram accounts to see what they were doing and thinking.

AV: The story of *Manhattan Beach* is set primarily in the 1930s and '40s in which ethnicity plays a key role. "Dexter liked the Irish, was drawn to them, although time and again they had proved untrustworthy. It wasn't duplicity so much as a constitutional weakness that might have been the booze or might have been what drove them to it. You wanted a mick to help you dream up schemes, but in the end you needed a wop or Jew or a Pollack to execute them." Can you explain to readers who were not part of that generation what it was like to be Irish, and the ethnic differences that existed that you bring out in your book?

JE: First of all, it was very strange to use terms like that. My husband is Jewish, and when he was reading the book the first time, he was really shocked to find that I was using the term shylock or shyster in the first chapter. He was brought up short by that because it's an ethnic slur, and the book is full of ethnic slurs. There was no way to be true to the period without making those characterizations. I spent a lot of time talking to the painter Alfred Leslie, who was very much a part of the abstract expressionist movement and had a wonderful career and is still very active in his eighties. Leslie said people identified each other ethnically, but there was actually less ethnic prejudice than today. That was the first thing you wanted to know about someone, right up front—you're a mick, I'm a wop, he's a Jew, and this person is a Negro. Once our ethnicity was established, now let's move on. According to Alfred, we now have this fallacy that everyone is the same, which is not true, and ethnic tensions are actually made worse by the fact that we don't acknowledge our differences right up front. If you read someone like John O'Hara, it's striking how insecure Irish Americans were. The Irish came to America in large part because of the famine, which was a catastrophe arising from the really cruel and negligent treatment they received from the English. The Irish already had a chip on their shoulders. Then they came here and they were treated pretty badly. It's amazing to think of how that prejudice has disappeared. I mean, who isn't Irish? We're everywhere! But there really was a strong sense of ethnic identity and also of insecurity and inferiority.

AV: This was a long time ago, but I remember my grandfather in Evanston who would look out his window and refer to a neighbor walking down the sidewalk and say, "There goes the Swede." I was just a kid, but to call your neighbor by his ethnicity and not even his name was very telling of those times.

JE: I never even thought of my name as an Irish name until much later. Chicago is one place where Irish Americans have an ethnic identity, and definitely Boston, but not so much in New York.

I remember when I first moved to New York and got my phone number, I was working at a temp job calling the phone company. The woman gave me this great number that was really easy to remember, and I said, "Wow, thank you, that's such a nice number!" And she said, "One Irish girl to another," and it was so surprising. She had recognized my name as Irish and she was looking out for me. I don't think I'd ever had that experience before.

It's interesting to think about it in light of Ta-Nehisi Coates and the idea of whiteness as a construct. I really understand why he says that, because you rarely hear the word "white" in the first half of the twentieth century. White—what did that mean? You were a wop, you were a mick, you were a Pollack, you were a Jew. The idea of all those people being combined into a category called white is something people from those ethnic groups would have had trouble comprehending. The Irish, for example, tended to hate the Italians. They certainly didn't see themselves as bound to Italians by any shared "whiteness."

AV: I once read the Irish were paid less than Black people in the late-nineteenth century because they were considered the lowest class of people. And yet due to Irish fortitude and pride, they built themselves up and made great lives for their children.

JE: The Irish had a lot of problems—alcoholism was extreme, physical abuse was rampant, and consequently, so was a lot of abandonment. There are a lot of similarities with the urban poor that we now think of as being more often African American: a lot of children raised without fathers, which often leads to further fatherlessness. A lot of strong mothers holding families together. My character, Eddie Kerrigan, grows up in the Catholic protectory in the Bronx, and I think some of those buildings—or at least the grounds—still exist. A lot of the guys on the Irish waterfront did come from that protectory, but growing up in an orphanage did not necessarily mean you were an orphan. A lot of these "orphans" were kids whose families just abandoned them or couldn't raise them because they had so many children. Actually, it was Alfred Leslie who first told me about this. He didn't know about the Catholic protectory because he was Jewish, but there was another orphanage where members of his family were placed even though they weren't orphans. This kind of fatherlessness and rootlessness and trauma really existed in these Irish American families, and it perpetuated a lot of pain that took quite a while to work through. And the alcoholism persists: my father and my uncle were alcoholics for decades before they became sober.

AV: Anna Kerrigan has a special relationship with her handicapped sister. Why did you create Lydia? What secrets does she know about Anna?

JE: I don't really create characters. I start writing and I see who enters the story. Lydia was there right from the beginning. I questioned that. I was unsure that I wanted to write about someone who was handicapped. But she felt inextricable. She's in some ways the fulcrum around which a lot of the story turns. So I rolled with that. I often don't feel I'm in control of who populates the stories. As long as I feel they organically need to be there, I just try to the best job I can to tell their story.

I think the main thing she knows about Anna is that she has a sexual history, which was not an acceptable fact for an unmarried girl at that time—certainly not a young teen. Although there was plenty of sexual activity going on, which is another thing Alfred Leslie talked about. He said in these tenement neighborhoods there was a lot of promiscuity among young kids. This placed girls in a strange position, because the mores governing their behavior were very different from what they are now. This often had very little to do with the reality of the situation, yet it led to a lot of guilt and bad feeling. Anna's parents are somewhat estranged, partly because of Lydia. Her father finds it impossible to feel good about his handicapped daughter, and his difficulty in being affectionate toward her has created a huge divide in his marriage. Anna alternates time with her mother and her father; yet she says very little about either world to the other parent. Lydia, in a way, is the only person that synthesizes Anna's family life. She's the connection. It's through Lydia that Anna experiences her whole self, her whole life, and that continues when she develops another secret life that neither of her parents know about.

AV: *Manhattan Beach* is partly about the evolution of women's rights brought about by the Great Depression and World War II, when women got involved in the workforce. Can you talk a bit about the role of women during this transitional period in our history?

JE: It was an incredible period for women. I always knew this in a vague way. Women were called upon to do work that they'd been told all their lives they could not do. The fact is they did it very well, and then they were told they could not do it anymore. Rosie the Riveter was a propaganda campaign designed to get women to do industrial work because they were needed so badly. One of the women I interviewed for the oral history project, who was an amazing welder, talked about how she had become so proficient and so excellent at welding during her time at the Brooklyn Navy Yard that she wanted to use those skills later, but she was laughed at when she applied for welding jobs. All of this came home to roost in the women's movement and the '60s counterculture. There was no way to make this discovery go away, and I think it was a really head-spinning moment for women. Interestingly, I think a lot of them really did just go back to much more domestic women's work and lives. They were back to the telephone company or to be secretaries. It's not true that they stopped working, although that's what some people say about the '50s. But that wasn't possible for working-class families. The women still had to work. A lot of the women that worked at the Brooklyn Navy Yard had already been working; they were just doing more of these "women's jobs"—lots of telephone operating, secretarial work, and childcare. So they went back to that kind of work. If they could afford not to, then they didn't work. It was really their daughters that had to lead the charge and say we need to rethink all of this. The war in general was such a time of tumult. Women's lives were one of many different kinds of accepted patterns that were disrupted. I think that a lot of what happened in the '60s, in terms of the civil rights movements and all kinds of other things, were the result of that disruption. They sort of skipped a generation, and then they really came to the fore.

AV: Anna wants to be a diver to repair naval ships, which was considered a man's job. Why did you choose this role for her, and what kind of research did you do?

JE: I don't know why I chose it. I was interested when I learned that deep-sea diving was a part of ship repairing and I saw a picture of an old diving suit, with the spherical helmet. I was very moved by that. The sea is a deep inspiration for this book. In a way I followed the sea into the various different elements of the story. One thing about using the ocean in fiction is that it's both real and metaphorical. I guess it was exciting to follow the sea into its physical manifestations and also reap its metaphorical rewards. Anna is trying to understand things that she can't see. The thought of her physically walking around the bottom of the sea just seemed incredibly thrilling to me. I couldn't resist.

AV: It is not just Anna but many of the female characters in your novels and short stories who exhibit mental toughness and the ability to eventually make sound decisions. Is this a theme you consciously try to address in your fiction?

JE: I'm always interested in strength and weakness in both genders.

Stories of surmounting odds are not that interesting. We've all read those stories. I'm just as interested in marginal people who cannot master mainstream culture, both male and female. In the end, I'm more interested in those people than the ones who manage to triumph.

AV: Dexter Styles has a high opinion of himself. How should we judge Dexter?

JE: I guess the only way I can answer that is that in art and in life, I'm not very interested in judgments. I think that people are contradictory and imperfect, and my job as a fiction writer is to try to capture those imperfections and to try to condense some form of the complicated mess which is human life. Judgments don't interest me; they're always reductive.

AV: Literary critic Matthew Carl Strecher wrote that Haruki Murakami has the unique ability to "include movement in and out of the protagonist's mind." I think the same is true of your work. How do you make each of your character's thoughts ring so true?

JE: That's one of the key things I think about with a character: their unique habits of mind. I think we all organize reality in our own way, and a lot of that has to do with our individual past and our experience, which is unique to us. Finding the way a person interprets reality and makes it legible for him or herself is the number-one thing I try to find about every person. I *have* to find it. If I can't find it, maybe that means I shouldn't be in that person's point of view.

In other words, if I'm going to go into a point of view, I am making a promise to the reader that I can deliver the habits and mind of that person; if I can't, I haven't earned the right to represent that person's point of view. This actually happened a little bit in *Manhattan Beach*. I go in and out of various points of view, mostly with my three major protagonists, but a little bit here and there with other people like Lydia and her mother Agnes. At one point I was in Agnes's point of view a lot more, but what I found was that I couldn't give the reader much more than the reader already knew about her. So I pulled back on her point of view because I was not delivering on my promise to the reader to justify my presence inside her mind.

AV: All of your books are excellent, but is there one you personally like the best?

JE: *Look at Me* is my favorite. It's flawed, but it's the most ambitious, in my opinion. I have not topped it. I'm still trying. It is all about understanding the deep mental landscape of individual characters. This is the number-one goal I have as a fiction writer. This is one thing fiction can do that other types of media—film, YouTube, video games—cannot achieve, which is to deliver a deep knowledge about how someone else's mind works.

My fear was that lovers of *Goon Squad*—and that's where I found a lot of my audience—might not like *Manhattan Beach*. I've had that happen before. For example my novel *The Keep,* which was a gothic thriller, is where I found a whole world that loved the gothic. Yet the gothic readers weren't so thrilled with *Goon Squad,* since there's nothing gothic in the book. I feel I ask a lot from my readers to make these transitions with me, but I'm finding that I'm getting a better reaction than I thought I might from people who loved *Goon Squad.* A number of people have said, "Look, I don't like it as much." They're honest with me about that. That's okay, they've given it a try and in some cases really enjoyed it. I'm hoping my next book will be a companion to *Goon Squad.* I'm happy to keep those readers with me and move back into that territory. If I can do it well is the big question mark.

AV: To quote from *Goon Squad*: "Time's a goon right? You're gonna let that goon push you around?" Your readers waited seven years before *Manhattan Beach* was published. How long before Jennifer Egan knocks out that goon so we can read your next book?

JE: [*Laughter.*] Very fair question. I'm *hoping,* and hoping should be italicized, to be publishing every three years from now on through the rest of my career. I can't have those long gaps any more, or I won't get done what I want to get done. There are a number of reasons that this book took so long. One reason was that *Goon Squad* had such good luck, and I spent a lot of time trying to capitalize on that luck by speaking and traveling. Also, my kids were still young, so I was with them the rest of the time. Now that they're teenagers—they've got their own lives to some degree—they don't want my help and involvement to the degree they once did. In fact, they're probably a little relieved that I'm not at home constantly right now. Frankly, it's just time for me to pick up the pace. I hope it will be every three years, max four, and never again seven. Of course, you say never, and you find out you're not in total control, but I feel adamant that I don't want to have those gaps anymore. One concrete way I try to prevent it is while I was writing the first draft of *Manhattan Beach,* I also worked on the first draft of another novel for the first eight months. I actually have a lot of material which I need to type and get into, but that's very different than having nothing. That is where I found myself in 2012, two years after my last book had come out, and starting on page one. I don't want to let that happen again.

AV: Winning the Pulitzer Prize must be a blessing and a curse. You get all this popularity and sales, but when you're sitting at your desk writing you must feel this enormous pressure that you need to duplicate that success. Can you share what this has been like?

JE: I thought that I wouldn't feel pressure, but I totally felt pressure as it turned out. I think because of the delay, and I was very rusty when I finally started writing again, and the fact that I was taking on writing a book outside of my lifetime, was especially hard for me. I had always used times and places from my life. I did feel a worry about doing a horrible job and really being pounded for it. It was hard. I'm relieved that *Goon Squad* is not my last book anymore. The goal is always to keep getting better. The danger with having a book be so rewarded is that it starts to take on this iconic quality, and it can be hard to move past it. The big danger is not that you feel bad or that you feel worried, but that you actually cannot continue to improve. That's the biggest concern. I really hope that I've moved out of that weird loop of worry.

Aminatta Forna. Courtesy of Nina Subin.

The Paradox of Happiness: An Interview with Aminatta Forna

A writer with both a Scottish and Sierra Leonean background, Aminatta Forna was born in 1964 in Scotland near Glasgow, where her father, Mohamed Forna, was working on a medical internship. After her parents' divorce, Aminatta moved with her father back to Sierra Leone, where he remarried and became involved with politics: Mohamed was the Minister of Finance before being imprisoned by his own government (he was named an Amnesty Prisoner of Conscience) and subsequently executed. Aminatta returned to England, where she received a law degree before writing a memoir of her father's life, *The Devil That Danced on the Water.* She then turned to fiction and has published four acclaimed novels: *Ancestor Stones, The Memory of Love, The Hired Man,* and her latest, *Happiness.*

Happiness revolves around Dr. Attila Asare, a Ghanan psychiatrist, and Jean Turane, an American social biologist who is studying the habits of foxes in London. It is an unlikely relationship that develops slowly but inevitably; the novel tells the tale of two middle-aged professionals who are trying to solve problems in their respective fields while dealing with their own problems. Jean is going through a divorce and combatting the forces trying to exterminate London's foxes. Attila is trying to help his niece avoid deportation and find her missing son; he is also attending an ex-lover who is battling early onset Alzheimer's. The unspoken theme is that Attila and Jean are searching for happiness in a world where struggles and conflicts abound, and it is this elusive emotion Forna so deftly reveals through the two characters; although they come from such disparate backgrounds, they might actually find happiness in each other.

The interview was conducted during March 2018 with the able assistance of my friends, Nina Shanu and Jennifer Otalor, who provided questions based on their African backgrounds. Forna, along with Samanta Schweblin, later gave a reading for the Inprint Reading Series held at Rice University. The one thing about Forna, besides being beautiful, is she has this wonderful lilting voice that is subtly British, which made the reading so enjoyable.

Allan Vorda: By the time you published your first book, the memoir *The Devil That Danced on the Water,* you had already received a law degree from University College London. What made you decide to write a memoir?

Aminatta Forna: In the later 1990s, when the war in Sierra Leone was ongoing, I felt there was an urgent necessity to address what was happening in our country in a way that went beyond news reporting. By then I had been a BBC journalist for ten years and knew well both the limitations of the form and the way the Western media served and continues to serve the African continent poorly. The question I wanted to answer was how had Sierra Leone lost its way? My father's and my family's story held part of the answer. In a final letter to the nation shortly before his death in 1975, my father had foretold the country's future if people allowed our then nascent democracy to be subverted. He warned about the end of the rule of law and of coming war. The causes of the war were political; there was a chain of cause and effect. I wanted to write about that, to trace the place where the country left the path. To me it is the task of the writer, of the artist, to address these moments in a country's story.

AV: What writers have influenced you, and can you name a few of your favorite books?

AF: I grew up reading the South African writers: Nadine Gordimer, Alan Paton, Andre Brink. These writers revealed to the world what the apartheid regime denied, stripped away the lies to reveal the brutishness beneath. I recently met Isabel Allende for the first time; as a young woman I had been utterly absorbed by *The House of the Spirits*. Her life could have been my life. I looked to South American writers in my twenties, for the ways in which they addressed political upheaval and social injustice. I teach my students *Death and the Maiden* by Ariel Dorfman. Can you imagine the impact of going to the theatre to see that play in Santiago in the 1990s, when Pinochet was still alive? Dorfman has said he thought of writing it as a novel, but decided the story needed to be made into a play so that the experience of seeing it would be a collective one. He was forcing a nation to address its conscience. Nearly three decades later the play still resonates, and it could be set anywhere: Indonesia, Syria, Egypt, El Salvador. I adore *Anil's Ghost* by Michael Ondaatje. Those are some of the books that shaped my writing mind. I don't have favorite books, but I am drawn to works which ask questions about the human condition. People write and read for many reasons, but for me what fiction does best is to offer the opportunity to interrogate the way we live through the self.

Nina Shanu: *The Devil That Danced on the Water* is a wonderful, heartbreaking memoir. However, it seems your father, Mohamed Sorie Forna, underestimated the maliciousness of President Siaka Stevens. Do you think your father, who was a physician, was naïve not to think Stevens would try to malign him, especially considering the public response to your father's resignation as Minister of Finance? Why didn't he get himself and his family out of the country?

AF: My father was thirty-nine when he was killed—he was young, not naïve. Stevens's regime was gathering pace and power, but he had not yet begun to murder his opponents. I'm often asked why my father didn't leave. I have to say I struggle with this question, as I understand perfectly why he stayed. For a political activist, danger goes with the job description. My father was a political activist who chose to stay and fight. He loved his country, and he wished to remain there. After his death my stepmother stayed, and I continued to go home to Sierra Leone from my boarding school in Britain during the holidays. We never left. I asked my stepmother about that once, given how very tough it was for her as my father's widow. She said my father very much wished her to stay, and she wanted to as well. She told me: "I would not give them (Stevens and his acolytes) that satisfaction."

NS: After uncovering the events that led to your father's death and writing your memoir, how has this changed you?

AF: It gave me a hard-earned wisdom. When I told my sister what I was planning, she said, "Be careful, what you discover may be worse than what we think." I didn't know how much worse it could be, but it was. I thought I was going to uncover a sophisticated plot that would take me months to unravel. What I discovered instead was that Stevens, when he wanted my father dead, merely let his wishes be known, and those around him were all too willing to play their part. The level of complicity was astonishing, and the discovery of how it penetrated almost the whole society led me to write *The Memory of Love*. This, of course, is not unique about Sierra Leone.

I also discovered the face of courage via the elderly couple who hid me as a child. I asked them why they did it, and they replied that they couldn't have lived with themselves if they had done anything else. I've heard this predicament called the "Anne Frank test"—it poses the question of whether someone you know is a good enough person that they would hide you if the worst happened. I find myself thinking about people this way now. Which one would they be, the complicit or the quietly courageous? This question has informed a great deal of my writing ever since. It is one we should all be asking ourselves.

AV: Was it a difficult transition to move from nonfiction to your first novel, *Ancestor Stones*?

AF: The writer of creative nonfiction and the writer of fiction have much in common. Both employ the techniques of narrative, plot, pace, mood, and tone, considerations of tense and person, the depiction of character, the nuance of dialogue. Where the difference lies is that the primary source of the fiction writer is first and foremost their imagination, followed by their powers of observation and maybe a certain amount of research. The primary resource of the writer of creative nonfiction is lived experience which is, above and beyond all, memory. Then you can add observation and research to that. The big difference is that the writer of nonfiction works within the limitations of the story as given, remembered, or told. Nonfiction can be also untidy—there are usually too many characters—whereas in fiction, you would use one character for multiple purposes. These are some of the challenges of nonfiction. The challenge of fiction is that there are no "givens" to rely on. It's easy to lose track of what story you are telling, to lose direction or even inspiration.

Jennifer Otalor: It seems *Ancestor Stones* used the stories and lives of the women to portray the evolution of the West African nations and their communities. Were these women symbols of this evolution?

AF: Each woman in *Ancestor Stones* is born into a different period of her country's history. Asana is born into a pre-colonial world; Hawa is a child of the colonial era; Mariama comes into contact with the missionaries and their ambitions; Serah comes of age at the same time as her country. The women are not so much symbols of this evolution—or transition might be a more accurate word—as they are impacted by political events of which they were often not even aware and in ways they do not realize.

JO: Reading *Ancestor Stones* reminded me of what I experienced in Nigeria as a child. Were most of the experiences you wrote about in your novel based on true events?

AF: The stories in *Ancestor Stones* are fiction. Like many writers, if not most, I find inspiration in something seen or heard. Some of the stories grew out of such a kernel. During my research I spoke to many older women about their lives from the 1930s to the present day, for this was not the kind of information you could read about in a library or on the internet. They were the kinds of lives that had gone more or less unrecorded. Once or twice a woman said something that prompted an idea. For example, I first heard about the stones from a woman whose father had thrown her mother's stones away. Her mother pined and died thereafter. This woman did not know what the stones represented; she only saw that they meant a great deal to her mother. Later I discovered the significance of the stones, that they represented a woman's line of descent, her mother and her mother's mother and so forth. Each woman added a stone to the collection before she passed it onto her daughter. I found that woman's single memory so moving and so compelling that I built a narrative around it.

AV: Your second novel, *The Memory of Love,* won the Commonwealth Writer's Prize Best Book Award in 2011. What was the genesis for writing this multilayered story that revolves around Elias Cole, his love for the beautiful but married Saffia Kamara, and his betrayal of her husband?

AF: The genesis was talking to people about the 1960s and 1970s in Sierra Leone, people who had been witnesses and sometimes party to events. I was interested to know how those who had been silent or complicit could live with their choices. What was the story they told themselves that made this possible?

AV: Attila runs a mental hospital in *The Memory of Love.* What made you choose this name and why did you decide to make him one of the main characters in *Happiness*?

AF: Attila stayed with me, as simple as that. I kept thinking about him. I wrote a couple of short stories in which he is featured. I became very curious to know what he thought of the West and its values. Attila is not such an unusual name in West Africa since there was a fashion for the names of historic characters at one time.

AV: You have described how Sierra Leoneans, in living with the memory of the civil war, existed with a "disassociative condition in which the mind creates an alternative state. This state may be considered a place of safety, a refuge." You also touch upon this with Duro in *The Hired Man* (his memory of Anka is based on smell), and you discuss PTSD with Adama and Rosie's battle with Alzheimer's in *Happiness*. How important is memory, both the good and the bad, to you as a writer?

AF: Memories are what shape us. Memories are based on experience, but how we remember the experience is more important than the experience itself. Consciously or unconsciously each one of us creates the narrative of our lives, and that is both informed by and informs the way we see the world.

AV: The first thing that struck me about *The Hired Man* is how physical your prose is—at times I felt like I was reading Hemingway. How do you feel about writing from a man's perspective?

AF: When I create a character I create a voice for them. I listen closely to people from their world. Croatians in general are economical with words, to the point of dispensing entirely with definite articles. Duro is an excellent hunter, an occupation which demands patience and silence; he prefers his own company to that of other people. So it is his voice that speaks in *The Hired Man.*

AV: One of the ironies of *The Hired Man* is that Kos, the blind hunting dog, can easily find his way, yet Laura and Duro are blind to what is around them. It seems inconceivable that Duro can remain in the company of Fabjan and Kresimir after what they have done to those he loved. The same can be said for Agnes in *The Memory of Love,* who witnesses her husband's beheading by rebel soldiers and later discovers her sole surviving daughter is married to one of these soldiers. How can these people live amongst people who have been so cruel?

AF: We all live among people who are that cruel, or at least potentially cruel. In peacetime most people don't get the opportunity to live up to their full potential. They need something like a civil war, some breakdown in law and order, which removes the restraints of ordinary society. Duro knows this because he is close to nature and its ways; he has no illusions about human nature. Agnes has no illusions either. Agnes would have grown up knowing poverty and hardship, and she would have had few romantic illusions about the world. However, she must endure the consequences of people's cruelty at even closer quarters than Duro. Both must stay silent, yet Duro has found a way to turn that silence into a weapon against his enemies by threatening to break it. Agnes has no such resource; her silence is turned inward, and her mind has found the only way it can to cope with the horror of her predicament.

AV: Your latest novel, *Happiness,* revolves primarily around Dr. Attila Asare, a Ghanan psychiatrist, and Jean Turane, an American social biologist who is studying the habits of urban foxes in London. One of the reader's first glimpses of Attila is where you state: "He liked to watch the English perform, enacting a conception of Englishness still held sacred in some quarters, amongst expatriates who went about their parties, bashes, and games of golf with a kind of strained urgency, but also here on home turf, in this room, were gathered the guardians of the flame." Why is it that writers, such as you and Kazuo Ishiguro, can describe the English so well? Also, since you are Sierra Leonean and Scottish, do you feel English?

AF: There's a Chinese saying: "A cow can tell you what it feels like to stand in a field and eat grass, but it cannot tell you what that cow looks like standing in a field eating grass." Possessing more than one cultural influence has gifted me a double consciousness—the ability to view one through the lens of the other. So in a way Ishiguro and I are both the cow and the viewer of the cow.

Do I think of myself as English? Identity is multilayered and overlapping, far more untidy than I have just suggested. I went to boarding school in England for twelve years, and then university. I have lived in London for thirty years, and for the last three years in Washington, DC. I am married to an Englishman. I am probably far more culturally English than I am Scottish, having spent much more time in England than Scotland.

AV: Is it fair to assume from your novel that foxes are fairly common in London? Also, based on your research of wolves, coyotes, and foxes, what did you find most surprising?

AF: Foxes are everywhere in London. I've seen a fox wander past Buckingham Palace. I've seen a fox cross the road in Piccadilly. I have foxes in my garden, where a vixen raises her cubs every year. Like all Londoners I am very used to the proximity of foxes. I never realized coyotes were equally prevalent in American towns and cities; I had assumed them to be mostly rural. A wildlife biologist told me that in Boston you are probably never more than two hundred meters from a coyote. The speed at which coyotes evolved from a desert to an urban environment has been astonishing. Their adaptability is what has allowed them to survive strenuous efforts to kill them. You have to admire them for it.

AV: "She stroked the fur of his underbelly. Finally she laid her cheek against his chest and felt the beating of his heart, turned to bury her face in his fur . . . The coyote had been Jean's first. She had never forgotten." This scene describes when Jean tags her first coyote; a few years later she remembers "the smell of this animal's coat the day she felled him and collared him, the warmth of his body, the blood beat of his life." These scenes seem to have sexual connotations. Is Jean, who is divorced from her husband Ray, in some kind of sexual limbo before she falls in love with Attila?

AF: I would not have said this was intended to be sexual. The moment for Jean is in the transition between studying the animal in the abstract and feeling it as a living, breathing creature. If I were to use an analogy I would say, like a parent having a child placed in her or his arms for the first time, the emotions produced in that moment are far deeper and more complex once the idea of a child becomes a reality. Also, Jean isn't in a state of sexual limbo in London; she has had a couple of lovers, of which the Romanian truck driver was the most recent before Attila.

AV: Jean has a very contentious radio interview. Was this scene based on something you experienced?

AF: The style of British radio broadcasters is very different from NPR. They are far more direct, even hectoring, especially on more populist shows—although still not in the league of American talk radio. I know how the inside of a radio studio operates because I have been in them many times, both as guest and presenter.

AV: At one point, Attila says "I'm not being cynical, just realistic. War is in the blood of humans." Do you believe this statement is true?

AF: Look around you. I recently spoke to a conflict negotiator who was very much like Attila himself, a trained psychologist. He had spent many years working in Northern Ireland, which is where he was from. He told me that human beings reflexively want what somebody else wants and will try to take it by one means or another. A friend of mine, a war correspondent with thirty years of experience, put it even more succinctly. He said, "War is armed robbery." Somebody wants what someone else has got and sets out to take it. The ancient Greeks stole women. Most modern wars have been fought over land, and increasingly, wars are fought over resources such as oil—and soon enough, water. People think wars are fought over religion, race, or ethnicity, but those things merely act as a justification. Look beyond and you'll see what is really being fought over is material wealth.

AV: Attila thinks to himself that "he knew, every morning when he woke up, what he had been put on this earth to do. Or he had anyway, the knowledge had nourished him for decades. He could not imagine what it was like not to wake up with that sense of purpose." Do you feel similar to Attila in this regard?

AF: When I became a writer, I felt this overwhelming sense of relief that I had found the thing I wanted to do for the rest of my life. My restlessness was over. I feel profoundly lucky.

AV: In the novel you mention a statue in Greenhampton, Massachusetts, called *The Wolfer*—does this statue actually exists?

AF: No, I made it up. I made up Greenhampton too. My inspiration for the statue came from those statues to settlers who murdered Native Americans, a few of which still exist in American towns. The statues exist to commemorate not those killed but the killer, to venerate slaughter.

AV: Attila notes just before his conference speech "what [people] desired so badly wasn't happiness but a state of prelapsarian innocence, the things that babies possessed." Is happiness a paradox?

AF: The paradox is that happiness is not contingent on the absence of suffering, but the reverse—that surviving difficulty can lead to happiness. In this culture we are conditioned to believe that anything other than pleasure is a threat to happiness, that happiness is an all-or-nothing condition. The central question in *Happiness* is this: Can you know happiness if you have never known unhappiness?

AV: Do you think being in love is a contingency of happiness? What can we do to make ourselves happy, since it seems happiness is a fleeting thing for so many?

AF: Are you asking whether you have to be happy to be in love? I'm sure it helps. I think happiness remains elusive when it becomes a goal in itself. The more you chase it, the more elusive it is likely to become. The happiest people I have ever met are those who have committed themselves to an endeavor that goes beyond the self. Happiness is a byproduct of that activity, whether it is building hospitals or playing the piano. We tend to assume that all people are capable of achieving happiness, but I think a good many people simply don't have the temperament for it.

AV: The novel ends with Attila writing a letter to Jean that he decides not to send, but to deliver in person in two days. This recalls the letter Attila did not send to his late wife, Maryse, although this time there appears to be some hope for happiness for the older, more mature couple. Nevertheless, doesn't it seem the older we get the less we laugh and the less happy we are?

AF: Gosh no, I wouldn't go back to being in my twenties for all the tea in China. I may have had more fun then, but that's entirely different from happiness.

Cristina García. Courtesy of Ann Trinca.

A Fish Swims in My Lung: Two Interviews with Cristina García

Cristina García was born on July 4, 1958, in Havana, Cuba, to a Guatemalan father and a Cuban mother. She was only two years old when her family decided to leave Cuba for the United States, after Castro came to power, and grew up in New York City. She earned a bachelor's degree in political science from Barnard College and a master's degree in international relations from Johns Hopkins University. After school she worked as a correspondent for *TIME* magazine in Miami, San Francisco, and Los Angeles before quitting to write full time.

Her first novel, *Dreaming in Cuban,* was nominated for the National Book Award in 1992. Her second novel, *The Aguero Sisters,* won the

Janet Heidiger Kafka Prize. Subsequent novels include *Monkey Hunting, A Handbook to Luck, The Lady Matador's Hotel, King of Cuba,* and *Here in Berlin.*

The first interview was conducted by phone on January 23, 1993. Ms. García spoke from her home in Princeton, the only break occurring when she had to pause to feed her daughter Pilar. The second interview was conducted May 18, 2018, to discuss *Here in Berlin.*

Dreaming in Cuban

Allan Vorda: You were born in Havana, Cuba, in 1958, and moved to the United States when you were only two years old. What effect did this have on you and your family?

Cristina García: We moved to New York and had a different experience growing up than the larger exile community, which moved to Miami. I think we were just like any other immigrant family that comes to New York or any other big city. We grew up bilingual, and my parents worked very hard. I was so young when I left that I had no memories of Cuba, and my parents were so busy working they weren't necessarily nostalgic the way many other Cuban families are. It had no direct effect on me because I was simply in the wake of this dislocation of my parents. I grew up very Americanized and was much too young to remember the trauma of moving. For me, a larger effect was that my family was split up. All of my mother's side of the family stayed in Cuba—by choice—and all my father's family came here. I grew up with that political schism as the backdrop of my family life.

AV: What was it like growing up in New York during the 1970s, and what was your educational background like?

CG: I was educated in Catholic schools through high school. I received a degree in political science from Barnard College, and then I went to Johns Hopkins University, where I received a master's degree in international relations. Growing up in New York was great. I grew up partly in Queens, the other part in Brooklyn Heights, and then I went to high school and college in Manhattan. I've always felt like a New Yorker through and through.

AV: Where you lived in New York, was that part of a Cuban neighborhood?

CG: No, not at all. I lived in Brooklyn Heights, which is right across the river from Wall Street. It's just a corner of Brooklyn, and it's quite an upscale neighborhood.

AV: Which writers influenced you? Your style seems to have elements of García Márquez and Borges. I was also wondering if John Barth influenced you, since you attended Johns Hopkins.

CG: I did attend Johns Hopkins, but since I went to their advanced international studies program, I had nothing to do with their English department or their graduate writing program. I've read Barth, but I couldn't consider him influential in my writing. I have read and loved all the great Latin American authors, including García Márquez and Borges whom you mentioned, but also Jorge Amado from Brazil and Julio Cortázar from Argentina. I also loved great poets such as Octavio Paz, Pablo Neruda, and Federico García Lorca. Strangely enough, I came to them rather late, as I was in my twenties. When I was growing up, I read most of the great Russian, French, and American writers before encountering any Spanish or Latin writers.

Among contemporary writers, I love Toni Morrison and Louise Erdrich, who writes about Native American life in the Dakotas. I'll tell you who I had on my desk when I was writing *Dreaming in Cuban.* I had a copy of poems by Wallace Stevens, García Márquez's *One Hundred Years of Solitude,* and Morrison's *Song of Solomon.*

AV: Did your background as a *TIME* correspondent assist you in becoming a writer?

CG: It's totally different. In fact, fiction for me is a kind of anti-journalism, since it uses a different portion of my brain. The only way journalism was helpful to me was the sheer physical comfort I had when sitting in front of a computer for hours at a time. It was more of a physiognomic advantage.

AV: You left Cuba in 1961 and returned to visit your family in 1984. You said your trip to Cuba "was like finding the missing link in my own identity." For five years you couldn't get the trip out of your mind, whereupon you wrote *Dreaming in Cuban*, which reveals how strong memory can be. To what extent was the writing of *Dreaming in Cuban* a cathartic experience?

CG: I have no memories of Cuba prior to going back in 1984. The only memories I have of Cuba are the two weeks I spent there in 1984, whereupon I learned a lot of my family history. It definitely enlarged my perspective on the choices family members made, particularly those who chose to remain in Cuba. Furthermore, it enlarged my sense of self and my own identity and how Cuban I was—which I never realized until then.

AV: Was it hard to get into Cuba?

CG: In those days, before Radio Marti started up in south Florida, it was not that difficult. They had charter flights leaving Miami on a fairly regular basis. It was quite expensive, and that was prohibitive. And there were waiting lists, but it was not impossible to go at that point. Since then, it has been very difficult.

AV: Do you see writers such as Sandra Cisneros, Oscar Hijuelos, Julia Alvarez, Victor Villaseñor, and yourself as being hybrids of such Latin American writers as Borges, García Márquez, and Vargas Llosa? Or, are the American-born and/or raised Hispanic writers offering a different perspective of their ethnicity from their South American counterparts?

CG: I think probably the latter. I think the experiences are so different, and yet I'm sure we all draw on our reading and from such writers as Borges and García Márquez. It's part of our literary heritage, and I think for those of us who grew up in the US, we are talking about a different experience entirely. I also think we're not so much on the periphery. I think what's happening in what was once considered "mainstream America" is changing, and I think American literature is reflecting that.

AV: In Earl Shorris's book *Latinos: A Biography of the People,* which chronicles the past and present influences of Latinos in the United States, he writes, "There are no Latinos, only diverse peoples struggling to remain who they are while becoming someone else." Do you agree with this statement regarding Cuban Americans? And doesn't this statement also work conversely as sundry new ethnic groups exert their influence upon Americans who lose a little of their own heritage as part of the proverbial melting pot?

CG: I think so. I think the idea of a melting pot is an arcane one. I think what happens is that by the third generation most immigrants would not be speaking their parents' native tongue or their grandparents' native tongue. I think there's an emphasis now and a value placed on the diversity of speaking more than one language in a way that didn't exist before. For example, I hope my daughter, Pilarita, will grow up and speak Spanish because I'm going to speak Spanish to her. My husband is half Japanese, and I will encourage his mother to speak Japanese to my daughter in order to continue the heritage. There is an emphasis and a value placed on the continuation of heritage whereas before, assimilation was the key to success. Now the broader your background and the more languages you speak, the more advantageous it is in society.

AV: When Felicia is six years old she brings home a mother-of-pearl shell that Celia says will "bring bad luck." Shortly thereafter a tidal wave hits. It seems bad luck, especially concerning her romantic relationships, follows Felicia everywhere. Even her use of Santeria with its black magic doesn't help. Why is Felicia cursed? Is it because she is the only offspring of Celia to remain in Cuba?

CG: I don't think it's any one reason why Felicia is cursed. It's a panoply of factors that have worked against her in her life. Felicia was a daughter born into an unhappy marriage, a daughter who never got the approval of her father the same way her elder sister did, a daughter who didn't have the same kind of resolve or talent that her older sister did, and a daughter who was always searching for something, After the revolution she didn't find it in politics or in volunteerism. So in a quest to find some satisfaction in her life, I think she was drawn to Santeria through her friends and into love affairs. I think that was her way of giving meaning to her life. I don't think there was just one thing. I can't really agree that she is cursed. I think that is the way her life turned out, but I certainly didn't plan it that way.

AV: Did you have to do any research, and did your family provide any information when you were working on the Santeria scenes?

CG: My family provided no information on the Santeria. It was not something I grew up with. It was something the character Felicia led me to, and then I had to scramble and research to keep up with the forays into Santeria.

AV: Why did you switch from a third-person to a first-person narrative with the appearance of Pilar Puente? Don't you think some readers will assume Pilar is a persona for the author?

CG: I think a lot of people have erroneously assumed that. I tried to write her in the third person, but her first-person voice kept punching through the third person. I guess it was appropriate for her in the way she spoke and her vernacular that she would have her own voice in a way the others didn't. I would also like to point out that Celia has a first-person voice through her letters. Even though it is a more formal outlet, we do get a sense of her and how she thinks through the first-person narrative in her letters.

AV: There is an interesting thought that Pilar has: "My father knew I understood more than I could say." Can you comment on Pilar's thoughts, since this expresses a basic challenge for writers—to articulate their innermost thoughts?

CG: I think Pilar was kind of blessed with special powers as a baby, which may be viewed as a type of magical realism. Pilar could make the nanny's hair fall out, she could will things to happen, and she could talk to her grandmother late at night in the dark. She was someone who had some connection with the supernatural, which she could control as a child. I think she lost this special power to some degree when she was in the US, but it came back to some degree when she discovered Santeria quite by accident. I think her father had a sense he had a very special baby, in that there was something luminous and intelligent about this child. When he spoke to her, she knew more than what she could say at that point.

AV: What was the inspiration behind the beautiful sentence that Celia writes to Gustav: "A fish swims in my lung?"

CG: That just came to me. When you have a heartbreak, it describes what your chest feels like. It does feel like a fish swimming in your lung: that intense and fluttering and pressured uncertainty that one gets when one is heartbroken.

AV: There is the scene where Lourdes is raped by the Cuban soldier and she smells all the major events of his life. How did you create this scene? Also, why is Lourdes's vision of the rapist based on smelling, while Felicia's gift of perception is based on the sense of hearing?

CG: That scene was a total surprise to me. I can remember very distinctly when I was writing it that it was summer in Los Angeles. I didn't plan for Lourdes to be raped or visualize it moving to that inevitability. It was just one of those moments, if you are lucky, that happens occasionally in fiction. It feels as if it's being not dictated to you but that a little part of the sky opens up to you and it flows down upon you. It wasn't planned. It was a gift.

AV: The rapist carves something illegible into Lourdes's stomach. What is this supposed to mean? Also, are the rape and carving scenes, which foreshadow her bloody miscarriage, symbolically connected to the sacrificial blood rites of the Santeria?

CG: No, I don't think they are connected to the Santeria. The way I wrote it was simply a vicious act by a deranged soldier. I think what happens is it leaves a scar she carries with her the rest of her life. It reminds her of that dreadful day and about her hatred of the Cuban system after the revolution.

AV: The color blue is used frequently throughout the novel, often in the form of magical realism. Since García Márquez is considered one of the innovators of magical realism and has used the color blue as a device in his fiction, have you experienced any criticism for covering the same territory?

CG: Nobody has ever mentioned that, and I didn't have García Márquez in mind. What I had in mind with the color blue is the mental image one has of an island. Cuba is surrounded by water, and that is why there is so much blue in the book. Celia has a house on the beach, and so her entire horizon is blue. It colors her entire life and perspective.

AV: It's ironic that Lourdes rejects Cuba for the cold of New York City while her daughter wants to return to the warmth of Cuba. Does Lourdes unconsciously think the weather will freeze her bad memories (e.g., her rape by the Cuban soldier) of Cuba?

CG: I think there was an element of that, because when she and her family arrived in Miami, she insisted they drive north. I think she just wanted to get so cold, almost a numbing cold, that it would free her of her memories.

AV: Felicia thinks her mother has an unnatural attraction to El Lider—an attraction that is almost sexual—and then later on, Felicia fantasizes about having sex with El Lider. Does Castro represent the missing man in each of their lives?

CG: I think Castro for many years was a powerful sex symbol in Cuba. He did sleep with many women in Cuba and has many children scattered around the island. I think he represented a kind of sexual fantasy for many women.

AV: Javier del Pino, Celia's son, is a professor of biochemistry in Czechoslovakia who lectures in Russian, German, and Czech. Does the distancing between Javier and his daughter—who cannot speak fluent Spanish—show they are losing their Cuban heritage since they no longer speak the same language as their ancestors?

CG: I think so, in the fact that Javier loses his entire family and later his wife runs off with someone else. Javier returns to his homeland and becomes a broken man who has no family and no country of his own.

AV: What is your attitude toward Communism, since certain elements in your novel seem to express a negative viewpoint?

CG: I grew up in a very black-and-white situation. My parents were virulently anti-Communist, and yet my relatives in Cuba were tremendous supporters of Communism, including members of my family who belong to the Communist Party. The trip in 1984 and the book, to some extent, were an act of reconciliation for the choices everybody made. I'm very much in favor of democratic systems, but I also strongly believe a country should determine its own fate. I realize I couldn't write and be a journalist and do everything I've done in Cuba; yet I respect the right of people to live as they choose.

AV: What is the significance of Hugo making love to the prostitute with the black mask?

CG: There is no particular reason the prostitute wears the black mask. There is an earlier scene of Hugo with his wife having sex in the hotel, which shows he was interested in rougher or sadomasochistic rituals. I think that was his personal preference, but I don't think it has any larger significance. I think the significant thing wasn't the woman wearing the mask, but that his son Ivanito, whom he had never met, unfortunately saw Hugo for the first time under these conditions. It was a big disappointment and a shock to the boy.

AV: Lourdes decides "she has no patience for dreamers, for people who live between black and white." Do you consider Lourdes a tragic figure because she is more of a realist than a visionary like her mother and daughters?

CG: I wouldn't call Lourdes tragic, but I think she's a character with enormous blind spots. I think she is someone who lives and accomplishes things her way, and in that sense considers herself a mover and a shaker and a success. I think this is how she measures other people. Perhaps Lourdes is tragic in the larger sense, but Lourdes would not consider herself a tragic figure.

AV: Felicia's unjustified attack on Graciela Moreira is sadistically bizarre, as she applies a mixture of lye and menstrual blood when she gives Graciela a permanent scar. Why did you choose this action? Was it based on any particular incident?

CG: It wasn't based on any particular incident. I think Felicia was just mad. It made no sense, but she was deranged and upset after her second husband was killed. She became very paranoid—such as being distrustful of people with glasses. Graciela was just a victim of Felicia's deteriorating mental condition.

AV: After her attack on Graciela, Felicia is unaware of the passage of time. Can the same thing be said metaphorically about Cuba, which has been isolated from most of the world?

CG: I think Felicia has a bout of amnesia and drops out for a while, but I don't think a comparison should be made to Cuba. I think, for its size, Cuba has had an incredible influence and presence in the world. I don't think anybody has ever forgotten about Cuba. Even though it has been isolated, Cuba is constantly in the news. I believe it gets a disproportionate share of the world's interest.

AV: The role of the artist is a minor theme in the novel. Could you expand upon the differences between Pilar, who is an abstract painter in America, and Simon Cordoba, a fifteen-year-old Cuban boy, who is told by Celia to reorient his short stories toward the revolution? Have you ever wondered whether you might have been like Simon Cordoba and not had any creative freedom if your family had stayed in Cuba?

CG: I used that scene with Simon Cordoba only to illustrate the militancy and single-mindedness of Celia, especially when it came to her system and her way of life. It was written to illustrate one of Celia's blind spots and to see how people, if you keep them in dreams, are sacrificed by politics.

AV: It is ironic that Celia and Lourdes, who are estranged from each other by philosophy and distance, are alike in the sense that both are involved in the application of justice—Celia as a local judge and Lourdes as an auxiliary policeman. Why did you present the contrast where Celia presided as judge over a love affair contested by the postmaster's wife and Lourdes, who indirectly caused the Navarro boy to jump into the river and drown?

CG: To answer the question of why there is such a contrast, it's because I was intrigued by the possibilities of interpretation when it came to patriotism. For Celia, patriotism in Cuba meant judging a variety of pieces from the sublime to the ridiculous. For Lourdes, patriotism in the United States was achieved through patrolling in order to maintain law and order. I would also like to say that I don't think Lourdes caused the Navarro boy, not even indirectly, to jump into the river and drown. I think he was planning to jump, and she was trying to save him.

AV: Are there any similarities between the author and Pilar? For example, liking the music of Lou Reed, modeling nude at art school, being an atheist, or the belief that one has to live in the world to say anything meaningful about it.

CG: I have never modeled nude. My husband loves Lou Reed, which is how I started to love his music, but I didn't know anything about Lou Reed as a teenager. The whole punk element is not from personal experience, but this was also borrowed from my husband and I picked his brain a lot for that aspect of Pilar. I would say I identify with being an atheist and the belief that one has to live in the world to say anything meaningful about it.

AV: Jorge del Pino committed Celia to an asylum and then to a home by the sea to make her forget her Spanish lover, but Celia's unmailed letters prove she hasn't forgotten. Aren't these unmailed letters similar to Celia's children and grandchildren who can't forget their memories and love of Cuba?

CG: I think for her it's simply a kind of diary. I think it's a private act of rebellion and optimism, in a strange way. That's what those letters are for Celia.

AV: Why didn't Celia mail the letters or try to go to Spain if she was so desperately in love with Gustavo?

CG: Celia did send him that first letter and never got a response. When she decided to marry Jorge del Pino, I think Celia gave the public side of herself over to Jorge del Pino, but I think there was a private corner of herself that would always be for her lover. I think the cache of unmailed letters is illustrative of her private love for Gustavo.

AV: "Cuba is a peculiar exile, I think, an island colony. We can reach it by a thirty-minute charter flight from Miami, yet never reach it at all." The act of dreaming is a major motif that permits characters to take off on a mentally chartered flight whenever they have the notion.

While Pilar's dreaming can be viewed as nostalgic, Celia's dreaming seems to have more in common with the madness of Felicia, since she never mails her love letters to Gustavo. How do you view the different types of dreaming by Pilar and Celia?

CG: I think it's just extensions of their individual obsessions and concerns. When I was writing the book, I did not have any larger agenda, nor was I parceling out information to the characters. What I was doing was trying to stay as close as possible to their idiosyncrasies, obsessions, compulsions, and joys. The dreams they have stem simply from their individual traits.

AV: Pilar starts "dreaming in Spanish" after arriving in Cuba and wakes up "feeling different, like something inside me is changing, something chemical and irreversible." This scene shows Pilar regaining her Cuban heritage, but if this change is irreversible, why does she have to return to New York?

CG: I don't think it's irreversible in the literal sense, but I think it's irreversible in terms of her own identity since her "Cubanness" is now taking place.

AV: *Dreaming in Cuban* ends with Celia's death and her last letter to Gustavo. It doesn't matter whether one lives in America or Cuba, since virtually the entire book seems to be full of lost loves, family estrangement, painful experiences, and various types of insanity, is there any hope for your characters to be happy, to live with their loved ones, and to have their dreams fulfilled?

CG: Probably not.

AV: What future do you see for Cuba, including her relationship with the United States?

CG: It looks pretty dismal right now. I think they have retrenched themselves into a terrible hole both financially and politically. There doesn't seem to be any flexibility in Cuba's policy. Similarly, I think the persistent isolationism and ostracism of the United States is unconscionable and should stop.

AV: Do you think this might change with the election of Bill Clinton, or perhaps with the death of Castro?

CG: I think it will be more likely with the death of Castro. I think Clinton has already indicated the US policy will change very little toward Cuba.

AV: What were your thoughts when you heard you were nominated for the National Book Award?

CG: I don't know if it was coincidental, but I went into labor and had the baby the next day. After I gave birth, the next six weeks were like a baby blizzard until the National Book Awards. I was barely conscious at the ceremony, but I think it will sink in, in retrospect.

AV: Will your next book deal with your Cuban heritage, and what direction do you see yourself going as a writer?

CG: I do have a second novel in the works. The characters are Cuban, but aside from that, there is no direct link with the first novel. I prefer not to discuss it at this point since it's in an early stage, and things often change. For example, the original title of my first novel was *Tropic of Resemblances.*

AV: Since you have a political background, I wonder if your writing will function as political commentary.

CG: I think the nature of the exile is inherently political. I think there will always be politics, just because that's a part of the fabric in the characters' lives, but it won't be political in the sense of agendas or axes to grind. It will be political to the extent that my characters are vastly interested in politics because I am an exile.

Here in Berlin

García's seventh novel, *Here in Berlin,* was released in 2017. The story revolves around an unnamed Cuban narrator known simply as "the Visitor" who travels to the German capital in 2013; she then recounts thirty-five varying tales of Berliners she meets, many of whom recall personal episodes of World War II and its aftermath. It is a fascinating addition to García's body of work, one that expands upon her recurring themes of politics, cultural memory, and how identity can be constructed from multiple viewpoints.

Allan Vorda: *Here in Berlin* is narrated by the Visitor, a Cuban American middle-aged woman who has been divorced and has a daughter living in Barcelona. What was the inspiration for the Visitor (who is perhaps not unlike yourself), as well as the concept of relating thirty-five vignettes in which Berliners discuss their past?

Cristina García: The Visitor was the hardest character for me to write. At first, I used her as a kind of scaffolding to elicit stories from the characters and fully expected to cut her out once the stories were harvested. Eventually, I realized that her presence was essential. Listeners are as crucial to storytelling as storytelling itself.

AV: "On her twelfth day in Berlin, a young father asked the Visitor for directions in German, to which she correctly replied . . . Thus, her mission began." Are the stories you tell based on people you met or read about, or are they purely fictional characters? If they are based on actual people, then how did this come about?

CG: The characters are fictional but emerged out of a great deal of historical research, eavesdropping, casual conversations with Berliners, and, of course, my hyperactive imagination—such as the story about the Cuban boy who was kidnapped by the crew of a German submarine during World War II. But I wanted the format to blur the distinction between fiction and fact.

AV: In one of the early "the Visitor" chapters you state: "Berlin was altering the Visitor, carving out space for silence, hallucinations, distortions." Then in a later chapter you write: "People asked her: 'Why are you here? What do you want?' Her reasons had changed. Now it was war that kept her here; also Eros and pathos, the impossibility of looking away. A different mission." Did your perspective change in any way, the longer you stayed in Berlin? Also, did you feel that because you are an outsider, your writing might be criticized for bringing up a past that Germans want to but cannot forget?

CG: Yes, I went to Berlin, much like the Visitor, in search of stories about Cuba's relationship with the old Soviet bloc. But the city itself seduced me, provoked me, coaxed me into telling stories other than what I had planned. The city whispered in my ear continually for the three months I was lucky enough to live there. Also, I felt that my outsider status gave me the freedom to probe where others might not.

AV: You have so many memorable characters in this book, such as Ernesto Cuadra (a Cuban who is kidnapped onto a German U-boat), Sophie Echt (a German Jew whose husband helps her hide in a sarcophagus), and Christine Meckel (a nurse who kills her patients). Out of the thirty-five stories, is there a particular character you like the most?

CG: I think I'm most fond of the characters in the opening and closing stories of the book: Helmut Bauer, who was a young boy during World War II and gives us the wonder and horror of that perspective; and Lukas Böhm, who grows up to be a classical clarinetist. Both boys lost their fathers—a zookeeper and a musician, respectively—during the war and carried those scars, with a poignant dignity, their entire lives.

AV: You use a quotation by Klaus Filbinger, a former Nazi judge, to open the chapter titled "Hunters": "What was right yesterday, can't be wrong today." This is a fascinating sentence, since several of your characters try to justify their actions for Nazi Germany during World War II. How did you deal with coming up against such examples of what Hannah Arendt called "the banality of evil"?

CG: History of all kinds—official, revisionist, national, familial, personal—endlessly fascinates me. To create narrative, to choose one version of events over another, tells us everything about the storytellers themselves. Every narrative has an emotional urgency that conforms to what the storytellers *need* to convey for their own reasons, conscious or not.

AV: There are numerous references to the atrocities committed by the Russians when they entered Berlin at the end of World War II. Were these stories ones that still linger in the minds of the Germans who still remember those days? What are your thoughts about the Russians and international diplomacy today?

CG: There were no shortages of atrocities on both the Russian and German sides of the war. Yes, I believe the horrors that were perpetrated live on not only in the survivors themselves but in those who come after them. There is a whole new branch of brain research focused on the intergenerational inheritance of trauma. In my opinion, the best chronicler of Russia today is the fearless journalist Masha Gessen. *The Road to Unfreedom*, the most recent book by Yale historian Timothy Snyder, is a brilliant, penetrating look at contemporary Russia. I defer to them.

AV: While you do not mention Günter Grass's allegorical novel about Nazi Germany, *The Tin Drum*, you do allude to its two main characters, Oskar and Roswitha. What made you bring up Grass's novel in this subtle fashion?

CG: I remember reading *The Tin Drum* in college and the huge impact it had on me as both a work of extraordinary literary merit as well as historical testimony. The novel took me deeper and further into the damaged psyches of war than any history book ever could. I couldn't have known it then, but Grass ultimately opened up this possibility as an ideal for my own work.

AV: Rudolf Hess was convicted of Nazi war crimes and was incarcerated at Spandau Prison from 1947 to 1987. He lived out his life as the sole prisoner in the entire prison until he committed suicide at age ninety-three. The utter loneliness he had to have experienced is incomprehensible. Was there any consideration about using Hess in your novel?

CG: His story is an astonishing one, and I was riveted by it. But Hess's story is also one of World War II's most well-known ones. I was more interested in exploring the hidden interstices of the war—particularly in Berlin, the epicenter of the Third Reich. The stories that rarely, if ever, get told.

AV: Several of your characters have problems with their vision, such as needing cataract surgery. Lukas Böhm is one such figure, who states at the end of the novel: "My eyes are clouded, my hands no longer steady. And I wait for death, without Father's courage, to end it on my own terms. Dear Visitor, upward of two hundred sparrows a year die against my windows, blinded by what they can't see." Essentially, many of the old Berliners have a distorted vision of their past. Did you find this to be true even in the twenty-first century, during your time in Germany?

CG: I'm married to an ophthalmologist, so I have more than a passing acquaintance with eye disease. More importantly, I thought it an apt metaphor for examining the distortions of memory. What, how, and why we remember what we do is inextricably connected to what we allow ourselves to see.

AV: In 2015, Angela Merkel stated that Germany would accept hundreds of thousands of Syrian refugees. Do you think Merkel's decision is based on a sense of guilt about Germany's haunted Nazi past, which is also a theme in your book?

CG: As unpopular as her resolve was with her own citizens, I believe Merkel's decision was an ethical, humane, and generous one, no doubt informed by Germany's Nazi past.

AV: Do you foresee a backlash by conservative German groups against the Syrian immigrants, especially in light of such books as Douglas Murray's *The Strange Death of Europe?*

CG: I'm not an expert on the refugee crisis in Germany. However, history tells us that the newest immigrants anywhere—especially in times of political and economic upheaval—often become scapegoats. We need look no further than our own shores for evidence of this.

AV: I've heard that a play based on your 2013 novel *King of Cuba* is coming out this summer. Can you discuss how this came about?

CG: Yes, I adapted *King of Cuba* as a two-act dark comedy, and it premieres this summer at Central Works Theater in Berkeley on July 21. I'm thrilled! After twenty-five years of writing novels, I wanted to try my hand at another genre—and this is the result. I'm loving the collaborative nature of it, too.

AV: The epilogue you use to close the novel is wonderful: "And now? What did she want? Quiet, resplendent days in the light. Her daughter a breath away. And a butterfly net with which to swipe the air, trapping bits of flying color here and there. Yes, she might spend the rest of her life doing nothing more than that." I hope you are not implying that your writing days are over.

CG: Not at all! I don't think writers ever retire, do they?!

Mark Haber. Courtesy of Nina Subin.

The Quixotic Search for Melancholy: Two Interviews with Mark Haber

Mark Haber was born in Washington, DC, grew up in Florida, and moved to Houston with his wife in 2012. He has taught middle school as well as high school, and currently is a bookseller and operations manager at Brazos Bookstore. He previously published a collection of short stories titled *Deathbed Conversions* (2008), yet his star seems to be on the rise with the publication of his first novel, *Reinhardt's Garden* (Coffee House Press), which was nominated for the 2020 PEN/Hemingway Award. Written in the form of a single, blistering paragraph covering 150 pages, the novel details the travails of a Croatian named Jacov Reinhardt, who is in the midst of writing a treatise about melancholy. *Reinhardt's Garden* offers a unique and playful take into the heart of darkness. His second novel, *Saint Sebastian's Abyss*, is scheduled to be published in 2022 by Coffee House Press.

This interview developed in an unusual way. I had contacted Coffee House Press, who generously sent me a copy of Valeria Luiselli's *Tell Me How It Ends*, so I could do some research on her to prepare for an interview. While speaking with Daley Farr, I asked her if Coffee House Press had any other writers they might recommend. I was told there was a writer named Mark Haber who she said worked at Brazos Bookstore in Houston. I asked her to send me a copy of Haber's *Reinhardt's Garden*, which I thoroughly enjoyed. Then I went to the Brazos Bookstore and met Haber, who agreed to do an interview, all the while he was pontificating and showing me books I should read. Thus, by chance and luckily for me, I was introduced to Mark Haber.

This interview was conducted on July 26, 2019, in Houston.

Reinhardt's Gardern

Allan Vorda: Melancholy has a long cultural history dating back to medieval medicine; it is also linked to creativity and writers such as Robert Burton, Milton, Keats, Goethe, and Tolstoy who have written about it. Was Burton's *The Anatomy of Melancholy* a major source? What motivated you to write about melancholy in the first place?

Mark Haber: I didn't set out to write about melancholy. Writing fiction is a sort of nebulous act, even magical, and I've always wanted to keep it that way. I think setting out with an agenda, or a subject or a "big idea" if you will, is the territory of nonfiction. If you want to tackle your life, write a memoir. If you want to write about the Cuban Missile Crisis, do research and write about the Cuban Missile Crisis. If I went into a story or a novel knowing *exactly* what I was aiming for, I think I'd be in trouble. Fiction writers don't write what they know, but what they *want* to know. Fiction is storytelling, but it's also asking questions and looking into yourself. I believe in improvisation; I need to sit down each morning unsure of where the story is going to take me. No storyboard. No organizing chapters. In a word, intuition. I knew certain things I wanted to do, of course, but only aesthetically: I wanted the book to take place in a jungle; I wanted the text to be dense yet accessible; I wanted it to be digressive. I let my imagination take over from there.

The Anatomy of Melancholy wasn't so much a source of inspirations, but I'm certainly a fan and love to dip into it once or twice a year. It's endlessly digressive and very, very funny.

AV: *Reinhardt's Garden* consists of 150 pages of a single paragraph provided by an omniscient narrator who is the factotum for Reinhardt. How did you decide to write your novel in this style?

MH: I wish I could take credit, but the book is heavily influenced by Thomas Bernhard, an Austrian writer and, in my opinion as well as many others, a master. The relentless cadence, the musicality, the repetition—that's all influenced by Bernhard. He would riff for four or five pages on a single, obsessive thing and then move on to something else, only to return to it five pages later after riffing or complaining about something else. Bernhard's novels are basically literary rants, angry and poetic monologues. To me there's such joy and pleasure in the darkness, but his novels never struck me as particularly depressing, which is a common complaint. There's also a command of language that's incredible.

So the idea of a single paragraph novel is nothing new. I did, however, want my book to be filled with incident and action. Whereas Bernhard's books are almost solely "interior" so to speak, *Reinhardt's Garden* vacillates between the internal and the external world. Another influence was Bolaño's *By Night in Chile,* a slender novel but also an unbroken paragraph, and it's a magic trick to me. I've read that book probably three times cover to cover, and it's only 130 pages, but it goes *everywhere*. I should also mention László Krasznahorkai's *The Last Wolf,* a small novella that's actually a single sentence; *Zama* by Antonio Di Benedetto, a Latin American classic; and Conrad's *Heart of*

Darkness—all were influential.

The single paragraph is an aesthetic choice. I think a page of unbroken narrative, if it's really good, is beautiful to just look at. It wasn't to make the book difficult or literary, but to capture the stream-of-consciousness of the narrator, and, of course, to have pages and pages of beautiful unbroken text. I can read a page by Mathias Enard or Bolaño or Clarice Lispector, who are incredibly dense writers, but for me their unbroken text is simply beautiful.

AV: Early on you describe Jacov's adoration of dust: "dust, in a window, for example, creates a film that distorts the natural world. Just as melancholy darkens one's worldview, he continued, not to alter reality but to transpose reality, to elevate reality, to *improve* reality, dust does the same." What inspired this unusual analogy?

MH: I'm not sure. Probably the idea that we spend our lives trying to get rid of this thing that never really goes away. The battle against things like dust or old age or decrepitude are futile, no? There was no deeper meaning. I just attempt to get inside my character's heads, and this is what Jacov would've likely thought of dust. Plus, he's certainly a person who seeks to be contradictory, so setting himself apart is important: "People hate dust? Fine! I worship dust!"

AV: The narrator tells Jacov that "the absence of melancholy was a thing to aspire to . . . a life in search of happiness seemed the acme of a life well lived." Jacov laughs at this comment and responds that melancholy "is transcendental, divine, and nothing a wise person should run from, but instead something to meet head on." Can you briefly explain what is behind Jacov's obsessive search to describe melancholy?

MH: I'm not wholly convinced Jacov cares about melancholy—I think he wants to be thought of, looked upon, and regarded as a celebrated intellectual. That's why he resents Klein and his followers so much, because Klein is respected and talked about. Despite his so-called abhorrence to fame, I think Jacov is frightened of obscurity.

AV: The narration of *Reinhardt's Garden* meanders across time and geography, with no paragraphs to indicate shifts. Was it difficult to write these non-chronological scenes?

MH: It was hard and it wasn't hard, if that makes sense. I did it, but if I had to go back and tell you *how* I did it, I would be at a bit of a loss. I wrote the book chronologically, the way the reader reads it. I would go back, of course, and edit or change things as I went along, but I wrote the book in order. So the challenge was in knowing when it was time to leave the jungle or return to the jungle; in other words, when to have a flashback or when to be in real-time. If I found myself floundering, I'd tell myself, "Okay, let's go back to Germany or Croatia." It was very organic. I was concerned with making sure the narrative was easy to follow. Sometimes it was a challenge and I would get lost in my own text; sometimes it felt like I was in the jungle myself. But it was also a very easy book to write, in that I saw what I wanted and just sprinted after it. I was extremely focused and just chased the story so it wouldn't get away. That's part of the reason the book feels like a sprint—because I was chasing the story.

AV: Reinhardt in old German means "brave counsel." Why did you choose this name—and any correlation to Robert Stone's character of the same name in *A Hall of Mirrors*?

MH: I did a little research and saw that Jacov was a common name in Croatia. It's really that simple. He had a different name for about the first third of my writing the book; it didn't feel right, so I changed it to Jacov, which seemed to fit. I've never read *A Hall of Mirrors*, although I've heard of it. I don't try and put too much emphasis on character's names; there's no symbolism or deeper meaning, I just want the name to feel natural and not draw attention to itself. I don't want the names of characters to be distractions.

AV: When Jacov moves to Stuttgart, he decides to build a second castle. Its hallways "gradually narrowed into dead ends, stairways assembled to climb straight into walls . . . giving even the most well-balanced visitor an impending sense of vertigo; every ceiling vaulted to convey emptiness and desolation." If Jacov's building of a castle is his attempt to recreate his garden memory of his sister Vita, who died when he was nine, then why does Jacov build a second castle that is like a labyrinth?

MH: I'm not sure. I mean, the entire book is really about *not* communicating—the inability or refusal to communicate and understand. We have a man who created a language around his dead sister Vita. Reinhardt then spends his adult life switching the meaning of his so-called favorite philosopher/writer to fit his understanding. They're in a jungle with an interpreter who can't speak or understand any of the languages. The entire novel is filled with people not being able to communicate, or hearing only what they want to hear. The castle is really for comic effect, and to illustrate the absurdity of Jacov's vision or obsession.

AV: "As Jacov spoke, a ringlet of light would descend above his head, and though I never mentioned it, I saw it countless times, no matter if the day was bleak and beclouded, those obstinate days of gray so copious in Stuttgart, and though there appeared no scientific reason for the halo to exist, throbbing and trembling like a star, it was perhaps a reminder of why I fell in love with the immensity of this great man. . . ." Is this a narrator the reader can trust?

MH: The narrator is genuine; *he* believes what he says. But can the reader? I don't know. That's for you to decide.

AV: "Success and praise in one's lifetime, Jacov said, is repulsive; it's merely strutting in front of the mirror like a rooster—fun perhaps, but an utter waste of time." What are your thoughts about success and praise for a writer?

MH: I think success is fine. Of course, everyone's definition of success is different. The fact that Coffee House is publishing my book, a press I greatly admire, is success for me. It's a dream. Being able to continue writing and (hopefully) getting published—that's success for me. Anything more would be great, but I don't expect it. There are so many writers who struggle to get their work recognized. It's nice to see my book as a finished "thing" that can be discussed, and to show people something they haven't seen before. The fact is, I sat in my apartment in Houston and created this weird story. Now it will be read by others who are willing to escape and go to that place I created—so in my mind I've already succeeded.

Spending my twenties and thirties writing and mostly failing was a great lesson. It's very humbling. I take nothing for granted. I wrote two so-so books in my twenties and, thank God, they were never published; yet it taught me to just do the work. You have to love the work and feel compelled to do it. I stopped writing almost completely when I was teaching high school, and the part of me I love the best went to sleep. I was literally hibernating.

AV: Ulrich is hired by Tolstoy's wife to get rid of the mongrel dogs that ravage Tolstoy's estate. Should the reader look upon these wild dogs as a foreshadowing of the Bolshevik revolution, or perhaps read these "hellhounds" as akin to those from Milton's *Paradise Lost*?

MH: I have no idea. I wanted Tolstoy's estate overtaken by dogs because it's funny! Does that mean there's a deeper meaning? I don't know. It's up to the reader to take what they want from a novel. It makes perfect sense to me now that you say it, but it never occurred to me.

AV: Jacov was extremely close to his younger sister, Vita, who dies at a young age. Vita is not wholly visible in the novel, but she permeates the book through Jacov's thoughts and is the catalyst in his search to understand melancholy. What prompted you to create the character of Vita, who is almost like a ghost in the novel?

MH: Jacov needed a catalyst to support his extreme view and obsession, and the death of his sister is that catalyst. The strange tongue they spoke in, the memories he has of their brief time together—these are all infused with an importance that only has meaning for Jacov. It's like our youth: what matters to most of us is of very little or no importance to a stranger. Vita hovers over the story but, in most ways, the novel is really Jacov's story.

AV: A major influence on Jacov was reading Tolstoy's *The Death of Ivan Iylich*. What made you choose this as a lodestar for Jacov?

MH: I'm a huge fan of nineteenth-century Russian literature—all the big names, and the more obscure names, too. I wanted to use *The Death of Ivan Iylich* because it's so small that Jacov, who detests literature, would probably give it a go. It's one of my favorite stories, since it deals with many of the same themes as *Reinhardt's Garden*, as far as mortality and the meaning of life. You know, the big stuff. It was also sort of a tip of the hat to small books. I love *War and Peace* and *Anna Karenina*, but they get all the press.

AV: *Reinhardt's Garden* takes place in various locations, such as Stuttgart, Prague, Budapest, Berlin, San Rafael, and Montevideo. Have you been to any of these places? If so, how helpful was it for your writing to be there?

MH: The biggest influence has been literature and books. I've been to Europe only once, which was to Sweden, and as far as Latin America, only to Mexico. It's a mixture of research, invention, and the mystery of a place. Sometimes it's better not to go because you can invent it for yourself and, hopefully, for the reader. You end up inventing not a real place or the memory of a place, but a third place that only exists in the mind.

AV: You work as a manager at Brazos Bookstore, so you must come across a lot of hidden gems. Can you name a few you admire?

MH: My choices for reading are definitely not methodical. I tend to choose books based on publisher. If you find books by a good publisher then you can trust they always have something interesting. Some of those publishers would be: Two Lines Press, New Directions, Transit Books, Coffee House, Dorothy, Open Letter, Seagull Books, Coach House, Graywolf, and New York Review Books, to name a few. I'm also passionate about books in translation, which most of these publishers specialize in. You can look at my influences and see almost all of them are translated from another language.

AV: I was alerted to your novel by chance, but I want to state *Reinhardt's Garden* is a fascinating, even tremendous, work of literature. Thank you for doing this interview.

MH: This was a pleasure, Allan. Thank you.

Saint Sebastian's Abyss

Allan Vorda: What was the inspiration for writing *Saint Sebastian's Abyss*, and how long did it take to write it?

Mark Haber: The book came extremely fast; it took about three months. I was working on another, bigger novel, and this idea about a piece of art came to me, and when something is tugging at my imagination, I've learned to put other things on the backburner. My best work usually comes quickly. And I always want to write the book that I feel compelled to write, not simply write because I'm supposed to. It's a cliche, but I want to feel inspired and excited by what I'm doing. If you aren't inspired (not every single day perhaps, but by the *thought* of the work) then what's the point? There wasn't a specific inspiration, although I love art, and the idea of writing a book about art or painting was very appealing. Quite a few books have been published recently about art or a specific work of art, and I was excited about writing something, but in my particular voice.

I should add that I obviously went back and edited and worked on the novel. It wasn't simply three months of writing and boom, the book was complete.

AV: The reference to Northern Renaissance art made me think of Richard Powers's *The Gold Bug Variations* and his reference to the Flemish painter Herri met des Bles. Which Northern Renaissance painters were of particular interest to you in your research?

MH: There was no specific painter or artist. My mind doesn't work like that. I'm drawn more by words and expressions or historical/academic terms. I love "Flemish School" and "Dutch Mannerism," for example, because they sound so academic and specific. I hear these terms and my mind sees possibility, possibility for a story, as well as digression, the gateway to a particular world, so the order or the initial spark is almost always dictated by words. Then I might do a little research and say: "Okay, this is something I can write about, this triggers something." That being said, I do love Renaissance art, especially Jan Van Eyck. Especially the colors. But I'm a real novice as far as art is concerned. The trick was making my characters sound knowledgeable.

AV: "Art, he believed, and I along with him, should be the centerpiece of one's entire world." Do you subscribe to this in any way?

MH: I subscribe to it utterly and completely! And this has often made my life difficult, my own fault, I should say. Art is the *only* thing that makes sense to me! The only language I understand. A poem I *don't* understand makes more sense to me than most things I do understand. It's what I love most. But when you love art (music, film, literature) it can make life hard. The world isn't designed for artists. It simply isn't. In America especially. I spent years of my life writing ideas in a notepad while waiting tables or ducking away at a job to write down an idea. There are guerilla filmmakers and I'm sort of a guerilla writer. As an adult I've never had the luxury of ten or twelve unbroken days to write.

The other stuff, the *practical* stuff, seems just insane to me. Practical things have always been hard for me, and I just don't care about them. In short, I've never cared a lot for the things the world tells you you should care about.

AV: The nameless narrator speaks of his fascinating relationship with Schmidt. Do you see any similarities with the narrators of your first two novels as well as with Reinhardt and Schmidt?

MH: Yes. It wasn't intentional, but there's definitely a mentor-mentee relationship in both books. The narrator in *Saint Sebastian's Abyss* has a little more agency than in *Reinhardt's Garden*, who was more starstruck by Jacov, but there are definitely similarities. Both narrators sort of follow in the footsteps of their mentors. One important distinction is in *SSA* both are contemporaries of one another, both have success with their various books, whereas in *RG* it was more of a leader-and-follower chemistry.

AV: You italicized a lot of words, seemingly for emphasis, and often repeatedly, on almost every page. I don't remember any writer doing this as extensively as you have done. Why?

MH: Like a lot of writers, I often write according to the sound. To me sound is as important as anything else. I want a certain rhythm and stressing certain words, repeating certain words, is one way to do that. My characters are also obsessives, and this is a reflection of that obsessiveness. A certain emphasis on words, to dramatize the intensity (and ridiculousness) of their feelings, and the italics helps. And, if I'm doing it right, there should be a musicality and cadence to the writing.

AV: The unnamed narrator has two unnamed wives that he divorces. Both wives, however, have a considerable dislike of Schmidt. Was this basically to show Schmidt was a truly despicable person because he never seemed to get along with anyone, including his later falling out with the narrator?

MH: Yes, I think that's part of it. Schmidt isn't a sympathetic character. I think I was poking fun at the type of people who don't like anything, enjoy not liking things, and consider themselves to be the smartest people in the room. I think that's a very lonely existence. Also, if you express your love for something, if you're an enthusiast, you're exposing yourself in a sense, right? You're saying: this is something I like, something I care about, and this can be revealing. It's much easier to simply dislike things and criticize. Disliking things is a sort of defense mechanism—although I don't mean not thinking critically.

Personally, I love getting excited by things. And I don't mind not-knowing things either, because then I'm able to learn something new. So it's a bit of a satire on elitists and critics who dissect something so much they take the life out of them. There's a line in an LCD Soundsystem song that goes: *killing it with close inspection.* And there's a bit of that too. Analyzing the life out of something, instead of letting it be. Of course, it's human nature to want to investigate something that evokes feeling, art especially. Sometimes, though, it's better to be led by the mystery. There's a beauty to not fully understanding something and letting it simply be what it is.

AV: Schmidt's books of critical commentary of *SSA* borders on the absurd. *August in Rhapsody* is twelve hundred pages long detailing why *SSA* is the "greatest painting in human history." Schmidt's third book, *The Descent,* "spent several chapters illustrating why the tumbrel, or wheelbarrow, contained sacks of seed and not corn." Even the narrator admits to being "more interested in the hems of the apostles" and his "affection for the holy donkey . . . was unrivaled." It is hard to imagine how Schmidt could write so much about one painting and contemplate what is in the sack of the wheelbarrow or for the narrator to contemplate about the hems of the apostles and the holy donkey. Why did you make these statements so outlandish?

MH: That's just my sense of humor, my aesthetic. If going a bit far seems too much, then I want to go even a little bit further than that. I love the contradiction of Renaissance art, its utter seriousness placed beside two men holding their hands to the sides of their faces, talking about the end of the world as well as which one of them saw the painting first. Highbrow and lowbrow.

That being said, it isn't hard to imagine someone writing so much about a single painting. Careers have been made on less. There are Kafka scholars who have written more pages *about* Kafka than Kafka ever wrote in his life. So it's outlandish, and yet, it's not.

AV: Since there is no picture of *SSA* for the reader to view, did you sketch out a picture with the apostles, the cliff, and the holy donkey? Why did you choose these images, which imply the end of the world?

MH: I didn't sketch anything out, but I wanted certain symbols in the painting. I wanted it to be strange and ecstatic, bizarre yet realistic. I made sure images didn't contradict one another. At the end I realized the reflections in the eyes of the donkey are described, and knew I had to have the donkey facing the viewer, or how would they know about the reflections in his eyes?

But I didn't sketch out *Saint Sebastian's Abyss*. I like that gray area where it's described but never fully; that way it will look different to every reader. I wanted to leave some blank space for the reader's imagination.

AV: Talk about when you are writing. Do you get into a rhythm when your sentences, very often long-run sentences, just keep evolving as you write? When the writing is just flowing, do you just keep going for as long as you can?

MH: I usually get into a good rhythm and just go. Often it's simply a word or a phrase that hits me. A single word can be the impetus. Often I'm reading a book and I notice a word and I decide I want to use that specific word, and before I know it I have a page or a couple pages, simply because I saw this word I liked. I'm largely driven by words and rhythms. The long, sinuous sentences are me simply getting into the mind of the narrator (my books are first-person), so I'm simply writing, or speaking (and thinking) the way the character would, and before you know it the sentence is very long! There are bad days too. On the slow days, or the days when I'm not inspired, I just try and go back and edit what I've already done.

Nothing is plotted out. Obviously with *SSA* I knew there would be the two characters meeting in Berlin at some point, so right at the start I was building toward a confrontation. But I didn't know how it would play out until I arrived there. I don't like planning things too much; I like the excitement of not knowing exactly where you're going; I like building the bridge as you cross it. I also think thoughtful readers can tell when you're simply painting-by-numbers, and if you're not excited, why should the reader be?

AV: You manage the Brazos Bookstore, which is considered Houston's best independent bookstore. What are the advantages and disadvantages of working in a bookstore?

MH: The advantages are huge, and the disadvantages are there too. I've gotten the chance to know some of my favorite writers and publishers, which has been fantastic. At the same time, it's a public-facing job, so I have to talk to people. I *have* to. I don't work in an office or a cubicle where I say "hi" to my coworkers and then get to work. I can't hide. If someone wants to talk about a book, it's my job, too. And as much as I love talking about books, I also love solitude too. That can't happen working at a bookstore. So sometimes I get tired of hearing myself talk about books. I get tired of myself!

As a side note, people in general have been very contentious amidst the pandemic, so that's been hard. It's hard for everyone. Customer service can be rough. Getting yelled at, people not realizing books don't just show up when you snap your fingers. Amazon has done a number on people's expectations. It's ridiculous.

On the other hand, I've been able to champion books that I love, usually small press and translated books. That's been a dream for me. Getting to share great things is what it's all about. And Brazos *is* Houston for me. It's what made the city special when I first moved here. And keeping it going, being a part of a city's literary culture, a small blip in the store's legacy, is not something I take for granted. It's a very special place, and it's important. We're the fourth largest city and often the only place a person can go to get a new book from an amazing publisher. Millions of people live here, but if you want to get a new book by César Aira or Maggie Nelson, you're coming here.

AV: There are two deathbed conversions: Father Vogel trying, unsuccessfully, to convert Beckenbauer, and Schmidt asking the narrator to admit he was wrong for saying *that horrible thing.* Please comment on this interesting parallel, where one deathbed conversion is about religion and the other is about art.

MH: That's interesting. I knew there were two deathbed conversions in the novel (with varying degrees of success), but I didn't think about the idea of one being about art and the other religion. But there's no deeper meaning than what the reader gets from it. Although my first collection of stories is titled *Deathbed Conversions*, so there must be some underlying thing going on. Time for therapy.

Ron Hansen. Courtesy of Chuck Barry.

A Hard Kind of Play: Two Interviews with Ron Hansen

Ron Hansen was born in in Omaha, Nebraska, and received a BA in English literature from Creighton University in 1970. Following military service, he enrolled at the University of Iowa, where he received an MFA from the Iowa Writers' Workshop. He studied under John Irving and also one semester with John Cheever. Hansen received the Wallace Stegner Creative Writing Fellowship at Stanford, where he studied with John L'Heureux, and later received an MA in spirituality from Santa Clara University. Hansen's first novel, a historical novel about the Dalton gang titled *Desperadoes,* received critical acclaim, whereupon the *New York Times Book Review* listed Hansen as one of the five best new writers in 1979. His next novel was *The Assassination of Jesse James by the Coward Robert Ford,* which finished as runner-up for the William Faulkner Award. The novel was later made into a movie starring Brad Pitt and Casey Affleck, which is one of the most realistic Westerns ever made.

In 1987 Hansen published two books: *The Shadowmaker*, a highly praised children's book, and *You Don't Know What Love Is*, an anthology of contemporary American fiction. His own short stories were collected and published in a volume titled *Nebraska* in 1989, the same year that the American Academy and Institute of Arts and Letters presented him with an award in literature.

Mariette in Ecstasy, the story of a seventeen-year-old postulant nun who experiences the stigmata of Christ, was chosen by the *Nation* as one of the best books in 1992. *Atticus*, his next novel, follows the life of a sixty-seven-year-old Colorado rancher who goes to Mexico to retrieve the body of his son, who supposedly committed suicide. *Atticus* was made into a Hallmark TV movie which starred James Coburn in his last film.

Subsequent novels were *Hitler's Niece, Isn't It Romantic?, Exiles, A Wild Surge of Guilty Pleasure,* and *The Kid,* which tells the tale of Billy the Kid.

Hansen teaches at Santa Clara University, where he holds the Gerald Manley Hopkins Professorship. He is married to the novelist Bo Caldwell.

Ron Hansen was the first writer I ever interviewed, primarily because we both attended Creighton Prep High School and later Creighton University. Even so, I don't know if we ever spoke, because we weren't in the same classes. Nevertheless, I reached out to him when he was teaching at the University of Arizona, and he was gracious enough to do an interview. Probably the only interview I have ever done with a writer where we exchanged questions and answers by mail. I had just returned with my wife from our honeymoon on the Virgin Islands when Hansen's responses arrived in my mailbox. The interview was subsequently published by the *Sonora Review*. Ron and I finally met at our twenty-fifth high school reunion at Creighton Prep in Omaha in 1991 and again later when he gave a reading at St. Thomas University. The original interview was amended with a few questions about *Mariette in Ecstasy* in order to update the interview that was published in my book *Face to Face: Interviews with Contemporary Novelists* (Rice University Press, 1993).

The second interview, conducted in May 2008, primarily discusses his novel *Exiles* as it relates to the death of five nuns who drowned in a shipwreck, and who were later immortalized in Gerald Manley Hopkins's brilliant poem "The Wreck of the Deutschland." Additional questions were provided by Wipanan Chaichanta.

Desperadoes, The Assassination of Jesse James by the Coward Robert Ford, and *Mariette in Ecstasy*

Allan Vorda: I recall that you were listed in 1979 by the *New York Times Book Review* as one of the five best new writers of the year when *Desperadoes* was published. Yet the road to critical success had its bumps. Can you trace your educational background as well as some of the jobs you had before the publication of *Desperadoes*?

Ron Hansen: I've been tinkering with fiction ever since grad school, so I feel I've had a long apprenticeship in the writer's craft even though I'm just getting used to my thirties. My high school years at Creighton Preparatory School were those of many an Omaha boy, as were my years at Creighton University, except that I edited and contributed to the literary magazine and was the newspaper's political cartoonist. I sought escape from the Great Plains by accepting a commission as a second lieutenant in the army. I thought I could write about the Vietnam conflict as Crane, Hemingway, and Mailer had written about other wars—the notion seemed neither callow nor preposterous then—but instead I served two years in southern Arizona, where I was the senior officer in the casualty branch. I notified next-of-kin about their missing or dead in Asia, I escorted returning corpses to funeral homes, I oversaw burials, and in order to remove myself from that saddening work, I wrote short stories in my room—one was a prizewinner in the

Armed Forces Short Story Writing Contest—or I took flying lessons, played tennis, read deeply in American history.

It was the stories that sent me to the Iowa Writers' Workshop, where I studied under John Irving and for one semester, John Cheever. I earned a fellowship and a teaching assistantship in literature and completed a master of fine arts thesis entitled "No Cares Have I to Grieve Me," a fictional memoir that was so apparently influenced by Frank Conroy's masterpiece *Stop-Time* and so unprotected in its revelations that I have since locked the book away until the time comes when I can read it without pain.

Following graduation in 1974, I attended the Cummington Community of the Arts on a summer scholarship, and thereafter worked at a number of jobs, among them housepainter, leasing agent, jack-of-all trades, while toiling at night on the weekend at fiction. I sold stories to *The Little Magazine, Carolina Quarterly,* and *The Iowa Review*—none of the stories much like the one that preceded it—but my real concentration was a novel about my army service, a novel called *The Escort.* It was not an entertainment. It was as serious and surly as any book ever submitted, and I recalled it from the marketplace when I saw each editor's rejection contained a synonym for "grim."

I got a job selling college textbooks in Illinois, Indiana, and St. Louis, and in the late afternoons I would return to my motel room and scratch away at a novel that was not about me or even about the puzzling twentieth century, but about an outlaw gang in 1890s Oklahoma. I wrote as always in pencil and in a large black book of blank pages, carrying it with me like letters from home. And I can still recall writing *Desperadoes* with all the zest of a man who feels good fortune is just around the corner. And I reached that corner in April 1977. I sold another story to *The Iowa Review,* I learned I was a winner in the *Penthouse Magazine* New Writers Short Story Contest, and I was given a Wallace Stegner Creative Writing Fellowship at Stanford University. I moved to California and wrote a story about a salesman that the *Atlantic Monthly* published, and I revised my novel about the Dalton brothers with the canny advice of John L'Heureux, director of the creative writing program at Stanford. I sent *Desperadoes* to Robert Gottlieb at Alfred A. Knopf, who read it over the weekend and bought it on Monday. And it was a nice coincidence that on that same night I was hired to teach basic and advanced fiction writing at Stanford as a Jones lecturer. And it has been writing or teaching that has occupied my time since.

AV: Most contemporary writers choose to experiment with their particular narrative style in contemporary setting, yet you decided upon historical fiction for your first two novels.

RH: Many contemporary writers use contemporary settings because they want to explain their own lives or speak about what is important to them, a subject or problem that usually came up just recently. I'm really too private for that sort of exploration—I suppose the closest I'll ever get to my own life is my master's thesis at Iowa, a series of linked stories about a character who was very much like myself. Even there, however, the relationship between "Jack Baker" and myself is many degrees away from the parallel. Historical fiction gave me the opportunity to say all I knew about the West and about philosophical questions I thought were important, and it kept me away from the contemporary world that I find comparatively boring. And I liked the idea of using a popular genre, such as the Western or the historical novel, as a way of expanding the appeal of my work to people who wouldn't normally pick it up.

AV: In *Desperadoes*, Emmett Dalton's elderly reminiscence of the Dalton gang reminded me of the structure of Thomas Berger's *Little Big Man*, a recollection by Jack Crabb. Did Berger's book influence you?

RH: Yep. I came across *Little Big Man* in a paperback edition in 1970, and it was love at first sight, a superb book, and though I purposely didn't reread it prior to writing *Desperadoes*, Thomas Berger's great novel was very much on my mind during the composition.

AV: Throughout *Desperadoes* and *The Assassination of Jesse James by the Coward Robert Ford* the reader cannot help but notice the language, which is historically accurate, and your choice of words, which is remarkably descriptive. For example, on the first page of *Jesse James* you write this beautiful sentence with a wonderful simile: "a rope swing looped down from a dying elm tree and the ground below it was scuffed soft as flour." To what do you attribute your writing style?

RH: You develop a writing style—at least when you're young—by imitating the styles of those published writers you most appreciate. I began with the greatest affinity for the work of John Updike and have learned from writers as unalike as Ernest Hemingway and Elizabeth Bishop, as E. L. Doctorow and Normal Mailer, as William H. Gass and Thomas McGuane. I was a painter as a boy, and I liken my style to a painterly one, with emphasis on color, comparison, and metaphor. I'm uncomfortable with abstractions and generalities and vagueness, and what I'm conscious of, as I'm writing, is of putting words down that will somehow convince me of the reality of the scene I'm trying to render. William Gass once said he couldn't read contemporary poetry because the words slide right off the page—a comment I interpret to mean too little attention is paid to imagery and heightened language, and the plainness of much of contemporary writing in America threatens to make our literature imprecise, inarticulate, and as easy to forget as yesterday's noodle soup. Historical accuracy is important to me because I want my characters to be at ease inside my paragraphs, but descriptive writing is important to me because it pleases me to reread it.

AV: Although your first two novels share a common theme of Old West outlaws who meet a tragic fate, there is a distinct difference between the lighter side of *Desperadoes* and the darker side of *Jesse James*. Why?

RH: I would have been repeating myself if I told the James gang story as I did with the Dalton gang, and I wanted to correct the impression that approved of the empty-headed notion that these criminals were expressing something important about America. *Desperadoes* was a joy to write, *Jesse James* was a job. I didn't want to produce a popular entertainment, but the deepest book I had in me at the time. There are sentences, and even pages in *Jesse James* that I'm very proud of, but it's a hard book even for me to love; the penance is there in every word.

AV: Bob Ford and Jesse James seem to evoke the Doppelgänger motif as Nabokov used it in his novels *Lolita, Pale Fire,* and *Despair*. Is this a fair assessment?

RH: I agree that the Doppelgänger principle is at work in the novel, but Nabokov is simply too foreign for me to think of in the context of Jesse James. Joseph Conrad, perhaps. There's a great deal of *The Secret Sharer* in the relationship between Jesse and Bob. I was blithely writing one scene in which Jesse and Bob were at a dining room table, and for some reason having to do with this idea of the Doppelgänger, one of my characters urged Bob to list all of the things that he and Jesse had in common. Bob and I started listing those things together, and I was frankly surprised by how long the paragraph was getting. From this I got a new appreciation of why Jesse James—who was otherwise so protective—would allow this disciple into his home. He says to Bob at one point, "I figure if I can get you right, I'll be just that much closer to me." My best explanation for Jesse permitting Bob Ford to come to St. Joseph, and for Bob Ford's courting of Jesse James, is that they both saw in each other a counterpart, a spirit in harmony with his own.

AV: Of course, such a realization reflects the process of character invention, which raises the issue of how to reconcile the historical aspects of the work with the fictive aspects. When you research a historical novel, what are your basic sources, and what steps do you take? Any interesting stories you could share about visiting these small midwestern towns where the Dalton and James gangs rode nearly a hundred years ago?

RH: The steps I take for writing historical fiction are pretty much the steps I take for writing contemporary fiction. I read virtually everything that has any relationship to the subject at hand, read more deeply as the writing progresses, go to movies that handle the same themes, and compare my work with other novels of the period. Interviews with relatives are usually disappointing—for example, how much do you really know about your grandmother? And visits to Coffeyville, Kansas, and St. Joseph, Missouri, were helpful only inasmuch as they gave me a chance to see a good many photographs of the Daltons and the Jameses. I use photography to a great extent, and also maps, dictionaries of idiom and American slang, and graphs that remind me of birthdays, eye color, handicaps, and characteristic phrases. Somewhere between all this factual and semi-factual information—and my imagination of the way these people were, based on the knowledge I have of them—the story emerges as a kind of balance between my individual assessment of the characters and their actions as recorded by those alive at the time.

AV: Historical fiction seems to take advantage of the old adage "truth is stranger than fiction." Perhaps we sometimes find historical fiction more engrossing than so-called "pure" fiction because we know the events depicted have in some sense happened. In that regard, it's ironic that the Daltons were once lawmen and that, with the exception of Grat, the Dalton brothers did not seem evil. Rather, they were simply poor, lazy cowboys who preferred theft to ranch work. They were prisoners of the events that happened to them. Is this the way it really was?

RH: A good many apologists for Old West outlaws try to extenuate crimes with claims of poverty, but of course many people were poor back then, but only a few became thieves. I composed *Desperadoes* and *The Assassination of Jesse James by the Coward Robert Ford* with the benefit of some fine scholarship on crime that has been published lately, and I used some conclusions about contemporary outlawry in writing about the past. In the same way that rapists are not really after sexual gratification but use rape as an expression of power, many thieves do not really need the money, many killers feel no hate for their particular victims, and many people who are in jail deny they've done anything wrong. Emmett Dalton certainly did, and it's because Emmett narrates *Desperadoes* that it works as an entertainment. You like the gang more than you ought to. When I decided to do a companion book about Jesse James and Robert Ford, I decided to write it in an omniscient voice so readers could see the criminals as history does. I adopted a documentary style and the unsurprised-by-anything tone of a nineteenth-century god in order to convince my readers that this was exactly what was going on back then, and not the gentlemanly things they'd imagined from movies.

AV: Speaking of movies, I understand that work is under way on screenplays for both *Desperadoes* and *Jesse James.* Aren't you concerned that the printed word will lose that built-in tension and effectiveness, that implicit reality, when transcribed to celluloid?

RH: You can't be certain about a film's effectiveness in the way you can be certain about a book's, mostly because so many people have a hand in the final product. As for what happens to a book once it's made into a film, I like James M. Cain's reply. A reporter once asked Cain if Cain approved of what Hollywood had done to *The Postman Always Rings Twice* and *Double Indemnity* and *Mildred Pierce.* Cain pointed a finger toward his bookshelves and said, "Hollywood hasn't done anything to them; they're all sitting right there." You can't expect a movie to repeat every aspect of a book. You can only hope the movie suggests some of the overriding ideas and that people are moved enough to go back to the prose.

AV: To return to the development of the prose, in the dedication to *Jesse James* you list three people named John: Irving, L'Heureux, and Gardner. What influence have these three writers had on you?

RH: I give a lot of thought to dedications—I guess most writers do—and sentimentality is my last consideration. I look for some connection with the novel's material, with what I was trying to get across. My father died during the writing of *Jesse James,* and for some time the book was dedicated to him, but I couldn't remember him ever mentioning the James boys, and I hope someday to get a project that will tell the story of my mother's and father's relationship, so that dedication for him is still forthcoming.

John Gardner worked with the *James* manuscript over three Bread Loaf Writers' conferences, giving the book a great amount of attention, giving me great advice. I'd made preparations to go to his wedding to Susan Thornton when he had his motorcycle accident. I planned to dedicate the book to his memory in appreciation for his help, and then I considered the subject matter of the novel and what was, in Jesse James and Bob Ford, a perverse master-and-pupil relationship. My own experiences with writing teachers were exceptionally positive, and if John Gardner expressed all that was good in a teaching relationship, so did John Irving, with whom I studied at Iowa, and John L'Heureux, with whom I studied and worked at Stanford. I thought of that dedication as a way of thanking three good men for their help and support, and also as a way of honoring the teaching profession.

AV: Since you have taught and are teaching creative writing on the university level, perhaps you could discuss some of the advantages and disadvantages of being a teacher/writer—or is it a writer/teacher?

RH: I miss teaching when I'm away from it, and when I'm at it I find I'm always looking for ways to get away from it again. I find it appealing, compelling, frequently overwhelming, inspiring, disappointing, depressing, and generally invigorating. The problem is that a good writing teacher is doing pretty much what a good writer does, but he's doing it for other people who may or may not accept his ideas. You're called upon to rewrite sentences, reimagine scenes, suggest other plot developments, pinpoint weaknesses, punch up dialogue, and much of the time while you're doing that you've got a manuscript of your own that needs to have its sentences rewritten, its scenes reimagined, its dialogue punched up. I once taught a course at Michigan that met only once a week, on a Wednesday night, so that I could spend the other six and half days per week on my own work. And yet, on Wednesday, at two or three in the afternoon when I really had to begin preparing for class, I'd be filled with anger over giving up those hours when I could be going ahead with my novel. On the other hand, there was a period when my novel was as plain and simple as cheese, and nothing I did made it jump, and I was called up and offered a course that I loved every minute of. My students were princes and princesses. Their stories would have made Chekhov weep, golden sunlight filled the room, and if I went to my manuscript it simply stayed in its place like old pudding. Well, I was teaching now and could put the writing off. And in fact, I went back to the novel with fresh insights about what was right with it and what was wrong. The teaching of writing forces you to say things about grammar, style, characterization, and design that you may forget as you're pushing words around. Going back to a novel after a class often has the effect, for me, of giving instructions to myself, or rehearsing what I said to some poor soul yesterday and realizing that it was my subconscious speaking and that the words were meant only for me. I'm making myself sound like a slipshod teacher, but I think I'm a pretty good one if only because I'm as deeply involved in the subject at hand as my students are. Our energies generate us, and we go out of the classroom with a feeling of excitement about what we're going to say next. When I'm in my house and the page won't get better, the only thing I can do is keep at it. I sometimes wind up looking at the phone and hoping it will ring—anything that will pull me away from my own misbegotten prose. Right now, I can't imagine not teaching. It's good for my writing, my peace of mind, and I hope it's helpful for my students.

AV: In this regard, most of your students start out writing and submitting short stories, as did you. You recently had a short story published in *Esquire* titled "True Romance." How did this story evolve, and have you published any other short pieces?

RH: I've been writing short stories for a long time but only get to publishing one out of every four or five that I complete. I write some very quickly and in a spirit of whimsy. Good judgment prevents me from mailing them out. Others have been published over such a space of time, and in such little-read publications that very few people, perhaps only myself, could have seen all of them—ten at present. The stories have been collected together and will be published under the title *Nebraska*.

"True Romance," the short story, had its origins in 1975 when I was living on a lake that was close to Columbus, Nebraska. A stockyard and auction barn were close by, and I'd see young farmers who didn't fit all the world's image of good men of the soil. I thought at times about writing an article about them, but journalism is something I can easily pass up. About this time there were some cattle mutilations and a good number of theories explaining them, including devil worshippers and close encounters of the second kind. And there was a week in life when I was at a fishing resort and it was raining perpetually. I kept to myself on a screened porch of the main lodge and read anything I picked up. As it happened, all I picked up were confession magazines. I kept waiting for their article's narrators to break up into laughter, but they remained fascinatingly sober about their petty and crazily complicated lives. So, in desperation, one rainy day in a fishing lodge in 1975, I began a short story about young farmers whose cattle are being mutilated and they don't know why or by whom. And there I stopped. I didn't know what would happen next, but there was a paragraph or two that I liked, so I kept the pages. About once a year I'd go back to that story, and eventually I came up with a long, very zany piece about a monster who spoke in gobbledygook. I rewrote that story completely, making it a simple horror story that could have been a teleplay for *The Twilight Zone*. I went back to my original conception and made the style closer to that of the poker-faced comedy, working in more about soap operas, confession magazines, all those distancing mechanisms that keep people from seeing the real horror in their lives. And I came up with a peculiar story called "True Romance" that I really don't expect people to understand completely since I'm a little up in the air about it myself.

My methods are pretty much the same for every story—it's always happenstance, putting together, delaying, rewriting, putting away, picking it up again until the story is nearly presentable and I can slap a postage stamp on it.

AV: Could you elaborate further on your writing habits or disciplines?

RH: I get up at six-thirty or seven, read the morning newspaper with a pot of coffee, read or reread some poetry, and by eight-thirty usually get around to opening up my blank book and picking up my pencil. I don't know why I have to trick myself in this way, because usually, once I get the pencil in my hand, the words start spilling out and my main job is to cross out one or give some thought to another or to check the dictionary to see if this word's proper meaning is the one I want. Often I'm looking for both practical sense and euphony, and there are some quirks I have that hamper my writing process—my own kind of discipline—but I won't go into them for fear of appearing crazy. I may quit at noon for lunch and come back for another two hours in the afternoon, or I may go on until four o'clock and then run in a nearby park. I'm surprised, when I count up the hours, that I have so few pages at the end of the day.

AV: But the number of pages is only one byproduct of your method; meaningful prose seems to take on a higher order of importance because you work slowly. Since you were a student and clearly an admirer of John Gardner, do you agree with his contention that fiction should have a moral point of view?

RH: *On Moral Fiction* has engendered a good many arguments, particularly because of the arrogance of a chapter in which Gardner points out those writers of whom he approves and those he does not. You'd have to know John Gardner to know he was playing the rogue in parts of that book, that there was an impishness, a wink of the eye, in many of his most upsetting statements. He was a man who, in the most good-hearted way, would call a person stupid, an idea goofy, and in class get away with it because his caring and sympathy were always so apparent. In print, his words seemed vituperative and preachy, and for that reason the book was probably a mistake.

I buy the premise of it, however. And that premise appears to me to be that all great fiction is moral; that is, all great fiction pretends that human beings have the willpower to do good or evil, that ideas have consequences, and that existence matters. I've read some people's complaints that Gardner's thesis would pitch out as junk most of Shakespeare's plays; those people either didn't read the book or they weren't paying attention, for Gardner specifically mentions Shakespeare as a moral writer, a playwright who, when dealing with villains like Richard III, or culpable kings like Macbeth, permitted his characters to be complicated and not pushed around by happenstance—not victims—but actors in the world. Gardner's premise was that the rules that applied for Sophocles ought still to be applied today.

AV: It seems that critics today are more interested in trying to lump writers into certain camps than they are in paying attention to the rules that applied for Sophocles—however central a concern those rules may be for fiction writers. What is your opinion about artificial groupings such as postmodernism, black humor, historical fiction?

RH: My agent was afraid I would be pigeonholed by doing two novels set in the Old West. That's an occupational hazard, but I didn't let it perturb me. I knew, after all, that I'd written an unpublished contemporary novel and plenty of stories and that my plans were not to stay in the Old West. Any categorization would simply be premature and wrong. Groupings exist for the purpose of newspapers and PhD theses. I know John Barth is supposed to be a postmodernist and John Hawkes a fabulator, but I don't know if these labels can be switched, or where Robert Coover fits into the picture. John Irving, for example, published a novel that was indebted to Günter Grass and another that brings to mind J. P. Donleavy; a third that continues the stories of Ford Madox Ford and John Hawkes, and so on. The only constant element is John Irving's perspective on these stories—would Grass and Donleavy even speak to one another? And what would Dickens—the writer Irving is most like now—make of the writing of John Hawkes? I'm a great fan of every writer I've mentioned in this interview, and yet I can't think of anything I could say, in general, about all them except they're very good writers. Groupings and stereotyping would pit them against each other, and that sort of competition accomplishes nothing at all.

AV: Even so, it seems that all writers are in danger of falling prey to that qualification of their accomplishments. So twenty or even thirty years from now, when you look back at the substantial body of work you've produced, how do you imagine you will have reconciled the tension created by writing what might be termed commercial or "genre" fiction and writing what you yourself have so elegantly referred to as the deepest books in you at the time?

RH: Way too many people approach the writing profession with the same frightened and queasy attitudes fostered by grade-school report cards. They're afraid their teachers or peers or reviews will issue them reprimands for bad deportment. When I published *Desperadoes,* one guy in a creative writing program said he'd been eager to write a Western but didn't think it was okay to do that sort of thing. One of the more peculiar aspects of our creative writing programs is the tendency to "permit" a certain kind of fiction writing while disapproving of many others. It's as if the job of the serious writer were akin to the priesthood of tenth-century monks who could pray in Latin six times a day, but who could neither gossip nor joke.

Entertainment and popular storytelling have become such secondary considerations in creative writing classes that when I mention a story's commercial potential it's frequently seen as a *sub-rosa* rebuke. And yet we writers keep on reading books by Isaac Asimov and Elmore Leonard and P. D. James and Stephen King. In my own case, I know that Jules Verne, Edgar Allan Poe, and Robert Louis Stevenson had a great deal to do with my desire to try writing my own stories as a boy, and I would like to make that same impression on someone young or incompletely educated with my own, more accessible books. We unnaturally cripple our intelligence and imagination if, for reasons of pride and narcissism, we deny ourselves the possibility of creating any sort of thing that appeals to us. And any fiction writer who depends on critics or academics for sanction or ratification will end up being insipid, unimportant, and hopelessly mediocre. Writers ought to be instinctive, experimental, perverse, risky, apprehensible. Writing ought to be a natural act, like singing, or a hard kind of play, not a prison of wardens and screws and the jail of "one's career."

AV: *Mariette in Ecstasy* is your third novel. What is it about?

RH: *Mariette in Ecstasy* concerns a seventeen-year-old woman,

Mariette Baptiste, who joins the Convent of Our Lady of Sorrows as a postulant in upstate New York in 1906. Her older sister, Annie, or Mother Celine, dies of cancer and is buried. On the next day, Christmas, Mariette is given the stigmata—those wounds in the hands, feet, and side resembling those that Christ suffered on the cross. Whether Mariette is a sexual hysteric full of religious wishful thinking or whether her physical wounds are indeed supernaturally caused is the subject of the novel.

With *Mariette in Ecstasy,* I was not attached to a particular geography or historical period as I was with my previous novels on the Dalton gang and Jesse James. Given that liberty, I roamed freely from France to Nebraska and finally put the convent in upstate New York because I'd taught at Cornell University at Ithaca and was presently teaching at SUNY-Binghamton. I floated through history too, from the 1700s to 1940, until I finally settled on 1906-1907 because I wanted a historical period far enough in the past that psychoanalysis would just be getting started, and medicine would be fairly primitive. I looked for what was necessary for the story, and I did not make historical or technical research harder than it needed to be.

Some parts of the letters Mariette writes in the book, for example, are paraphrased from confessions written by Gemma Galgani in 1900 and included in a hard-to-find book called *Letters and Ecstasies.* Quotidian life in my fictional religious order, the Sisters of the Crucifixion, is based on the Thomas Merton's account of the Cistercian life in *The Waters of Siloe.* The mass hysteria hinted at in my book was a product of my looking into Aldous Huxley's wonderful history, *The Devils of Loudun.* Simple scenes of the sisters at work and recreation were inspired by a book of photographs taken at the Carmelite convent in Lisieux by Therese's sister Celine. The first investigation of Mariette's stigmata is taken from the medical diagnosis of Padre Pio's stigmata in the 1920s.

I cribbed and stole and adapted from hundreds of sources, but always allowed the factual information to be distorted and transmuted, whether by language or by my own purposeful forgetfulness.

Exiles

Allan Vorda: Your Catholic upbringing has greatly influenced your writing, particularly *Mariette in Ecstasy* and now *Exiles*—which is dedicated to "all my friends in the Society of Jesus." Can you tell us a bit about your Jesuit foundation?

Ron Hansen: I greatly admired the Jesuits who taught me in high school and college, not just because of their idealistic commitment to difficult vows that identified them more closely with Jesus, but also because of their ease with the world, their refusal to see it contaminated as so many with serious religious impulses do. Without sacrificing their faith in the transcendent or their intention to live up to high moral standards, they found a way to feel at home with cultures and arts that others might have labeled profane. It's an extension of the genius of Ignatius: In the world, but not of it. Over the years, many, many Jesuits have become great and influential mentors and friends, so it seemed easier to make an all-encompassing dedication than to name them each individually.

Wipanan Chaichanta: Since you hold a chair named for Hopkins where you teach, writing a novel about him must have been a joy for you. When were you first exposed to Hopkins's poetry, and when did the idea germinate to write a fictionalized account of his life?

RH: It was because I was already involved in Hopkins research and the president of the university was also a fan of his poetry that the chair was named after him. I had actually prayed to Hopkins about the job offer before I heard the position was to be named after him. That naming seemed to be Gerard's reply that I ought to accept the offer. And he was right: I've been very happy at Santa Clara. I don't remember reading Hopkins in high school, but I was a Dylan Thomas enthusiast by then and I gradually learned how indebted he was to Hopkins. Little by little I became better acquainted with Hopkins's poetry, and like so many others who have dabbled with him, I got hooked. Eventually it was not enough for me to teach a sonnet or two. I wanted to reflect on his life and the source of his poems in the way that only fiction can do. But *Exiles* had a long gestation. Perhaps fifteen years.

AV: You seem to have perfectly captured the British Jesuit community of the nineteenth century—in the very first chapter you refer to newspaper advertisements for "Bailey's elastic stockings, ladies' abdominal belts, Pulvermacher's Galvanic Chain Bands, Antakos corn plasters, Iceland Liniment for chilblains," and other period goods, as well as to William Gladstone's anti-Catholic commentary that Jesuits were "the deadliest foes that mental and moral liberty have ever known." Describe your research and the particular joy of finding such arcane items.

RH: My method with *Exiles* was similar to my method with *The Assassination of Jesse James by the Coward Robert Ford*: I read every book available on the subject, and then I read the newspapers that the protagonists would have been reading. There's nothing like a daily newspaper for plunging you into the world you're writing about, and in some ways it's a wake-up call to realize that an advertisement for types of coal would be as prominent as an ad today for Diet Pepsi or Yoplait. At once you're reminded: no electricity, no natural gas, no propane. And on the same front page of the *Times* of London, there were appeals for work from nursemaids and cooks and other servants, and it became apparent to me how labor-intensive households were then. Three or four "domestics" seemed necessary to help even middle-class families function. We're not talking Jeeves or other impeccable butlers, just water haulers and fire tenders. An intricate symbiotic arrangement was required for the homes of the English gentry to work. Encountering such things or random entries like that obnoxious bigotry of William Gladstone's carried for me the same fascination as of visiting a foreign country.

AV: In a previous interview we did (published in *Face to Face: Interviews with Contemporary Novelists*, Rice University Press, 1993), you made the following comment about *Mariette in Ecstasy*: "I cribbed and stole and adapted from hundreds of sources, finally, but always allowed the factual information to be distorted and transmuted, whether by language or by my own purposeful forgetfulness." Did you use the same methodology for *Exiles*?

RH: Exactly the same methodology. Basically, if you're stuck with the nonfiction data, there's not much of a story to tell unless you're dealing with very famous people. Consequently, we rely on historical novelists to fill in the gaps in probable ways. I never violate known information, but I'm forced to imagine a good deal in order to connect the dots in a life.

AV: How has your approach to writing changed over the years? For example, when I first interviewed you in 1987, you commented: "I get up at six-thirty or seven, read the morning newspaper with a pot of coffee, read or reread some poetry, and by eight-thirty usually get around to opening up my blank book and picking up my pencil."

RH: The pattern is almost precisely the same except that I don't drink much coffee and I type on a computer now. One thing I've noticed is that my responsibilities have increased and I don't have as much free time for writing now, but the compensation is I'm faster when I'm at it—not as many false starts and more ease at finding conclusions. I could be wrong, however. Maybe I've just lowered my standards.

AV: Your similes and metaphors are often brilliant. For example, in *The Assassination of Jesse James by the Coward Robert Ford* you set the scene with "a rope swing looped down from a dying elm tree and the ground below it was scuffed soft as flour." *Exiles* also begins with a noteworthy image: "Wednesday, December 8th, 1875. A soft confetti of snowflakes was fluttering down upon Wales." Do you stockpile similes and metaphors or is the process more often spontaneous creation?

RH: Thanks for noticing, and no, I don't stockpile anything. I just try to make an image as tangible as possible. Sometimes the simile or metaphor is instantaneous; sometimes I brood over it for a while. Anyway, I'm glad you like them. I'm rather ashamed of the unseemly pleasure they give me.

WC: I assume you traveled to Wales, Germany, and Ireland to do your research on *Exiles*. How did being there help with your writing about Hopkins and the five nuns who died on the *Deutschland*?

RH: Wales was especially important. Seeing what Hopkins saw, walking the hallways of the Theologate at Saint Beuno's where he wrote the poem, was absolutely essential. I wanted to make a sea voyage from Bremen to London in December to get a better feel for what the nuns went through on the *Deutschland,* but probably it's just as good to have imagined it. But we're talking about a subject that's 143 years old as I write this; so much has changed or is irrecoverable. I depend on libraries for much of my information. Always have.

AV: I know you have traveled extensively throughout Europe and Mexico. I was wondering, not just about the experiences you gained by physically being there, but how your exposure to different languages has affected the way you write.

RH: I love languages, but am fluent only in English. Still, I'm aware of cognates and origins, so it pleases me to be exact (or sometimes punning) in my word choices. I consult etymologies all the time.

AV: I notice you include Hopkins's "The Wreck of the Deutschland" in an appendix. What are your thoughts about its arresting first stanza and especially the last line: "Over again I feel thy finger and find thee"?

RH: The first stanza reflects on the hugeness of God as a "mastering" entity, likening Him to the "world's strand" and "sway of the sea," and marvels that God has not only stooped to create something so unimportant as Gerard, but has taken great interest in him, touching him afresh with poetic inspiration. Responding to that impulse, Hopkins finds the God who can seem absent otherwise.

AV: In *Exiles* you tell us "the scruples to which he was prey caused Hopkins to consider the worldly pursuit of poetry writing in conflict with his vocation to the priesthood. Just before entering the Society of Jesus in 1868, Hopkins resolved to pen no more verse unless his religious superiors requested it, and in a theatrical act of renunciation he incinerated some copies of his Oxford poems in a secret ceremony." One wonders at the magnitude of brilliant verse never realized by this decision.

RH: But what you notice is how much his poetry improved. What we have from his Oxford years are some nice but hardly memorable things and a great many fragments. Seven years later and Hopkins is doing something entirely grand and original, works of genius that will be anthologized for centuries to come. Lying fallow seems to have been good for him. And very little is fragmentary after that.

WC: The day before the five nuns leave Bremerhaven, Germany, they eat at a restaurant under the spiteful gaze of other patrons. This appears to be a microcosm of anti-Catholic sentiment prevalent throughout Europe during this time. Were you surprised by its pervasiveness as you researched the period?

RH: I had read a good deal about anti-Catholicism in Europe before starting the book, so I wasn't surprised. The Reformation was joined by the tyranny of King Henry VIII and Elizabeth Tudor, the so-called Enlightenment, the rise of Puritanism, and the age of revolution to create menacing conditions for anyone who adhered to the Church of Rome. I highly recommend Alice Hogge's *God's Secret Agents: Queen Elizabeth's Forbidden Priests and the Hatching of the Gunpowder Plot* for a chilling look at the murder and torture of Jesuits in England in the sixteenth century.

AV: In *Exiles*, Hopkins responds to a question about his meter by saying, "I call it 'sprung rhythm.' You scan it by accents or stresses alone, without counting the number of syllables." What are your thoughts about Hopkins's poetic style—one that seems, at times, brilliantly disjointed and non-rhythmic?

RH: Counting metrical feet and scansion had developed to a point of weird obsession in the century, producing the artificiality of rotten greeting card verse. Hopkins wanted to return to the qualities of colloquial speech that you find in nursery rhymes such as: "High diddle diddle, the cat and the fiddle, the cow jumped over the moon." To Victorian ears, that does not scan and the syllabic count isn't correct. But Hopkins heard only the stresses, just as we do, which is why the verse works. The difficulty with Hopkins is not that he's disjointed or non-rhythmic, but that he deliberately slows the reader down, often by employing a word whose antique meaning is precisely right, but which is strange for us now. Entire papers have been devoted to his choice of the word "Buckle!" in "The Windhover." There's an orneriness about him that I can identify with.

AV: Hopkins's letter to Robert Bridges about "The Wreck of the Deutschland" asserts: "I cannot think of altering anything. Why shd. I? I do not write for the public. You are my public and I hope to convert you." It appears he doesn't care for public praise, but years later he writes to Bridges in all capitals, "AND WHAT DOES ANYTHING AT ALL MATTER?" This makes it appear that Hopkins, near the end of his life, did care.

RH: Hopkins was extremely confident, intelligent, and prescient. In one letter to Bridges he hypothesized that he was too far ahead of his time in his poetic inventions, but that perhaps in a hundred years readers would be ready for him. And he was right. Like any good scientist, he felt a duty to his theories, but it must have been galling to see so many minor talents extolled when he knew he was onto something. His friend Bridges became poet laureate of England (selected over Rudyard Kipling), but hardly anyone reads Bridges now. Tastes change. We can forgive Hopkins for capitalizing the vexation that most writers have felt at one time or another.

AV: In an email you sent to me in March of 2006, you stated: "I'm calling the novel *Exiles*, and its last chapter, which I'm working on now, will conclude with Hopkins's death in Ireland, linking his feelings of having foundered there with the poem's subject of the ship *Deutschland* stuck on its shoal of sand. He wrote a poem in Dublin titled

'To Seem a Stranger,' recording his feeling of having been cut off from his family, his beloved England, even Christ 'my sword, my strife,' and now considers himself at 'a third remove.' Hence my title of exile." Perhaps you can comment on the multiple implications of exiles, not only for Hopkins and the five nuns, but especially for the extreme estrangement he endured from his Anglican parents, who didn't even bother attending his ordination.

RH: It was shocking to discover how shunned Hopkins was by his parents, who were dutiful, perhaps model, Anglicans, but no more. Religion was not something they were deeply invested in. Yet Hopkins lived as a Jesuit on the west side of London off and on for four years, and near Hyde Park for another year, while they lived in the northeast suburbs—short railway rides away—and still they never visited him; they did not attend his vow days or his ordination to the priesthood in Wales; the only time they ever saw him in his surroundings was on his sickbed in Dublin the day he died. Even a child who marries badly or is convicted of a serious crime is treated more cordially. Also, because of his Catholicism, he seemed to be for Bridges a cause for despair or a figure of fun. Only his brilliance as a critic kept their friendship alive. So Hopkins had every right to feel as persecuted as those religious orders that were ostracized from Germany simply because Bismarck could not command the fidelity of Catholic voters and wanted to subtract from their power base.

WC: When the *Deutschland* is sinking, Sister Barbara remarks: "We sometimes seem God's playthings. The dice he rolls. But even though he can seem the source of our miseries, our faith tells us that God is good. Always." What were you hoping to convey through this statement and its allusion to Einstein?

RH: Encountering peril, especially when we have the time to consider our probable finality, often occasions speculation about either the goodness or omnipotence of God. Philosopher Gottfried Leibniz created the neologism "theodicy" as a term to deal with the vindication, or not, of the Holy Being for the presence of evil in His creation. With the five nuns, I sought to address different ways of looking at the terror of death—fear, resignation, anger, etc. Hopkins's way struck me as perfect, the way of a saint, as with his father and mother near him he saw death approach and said, "I am so happy," recognizing that life is changed, not ended.

WC: Hopkins's *Poems* was published in 1918, almost thirty years after his death; his reputation, like Melville's, has risen astronomically since. Why did it take so long to recognize his genius?

RH: The Great War, as it's called, changed the rules of warfare, the rules of etiquette, the rules of living in the world. Remember that Gertrude Stein called Hemingway and his fellow soldier survivors "a lost generation"—meaning cynicism, contradiction, and rebellion against society would do them in. But there was also a liberation from the old norms that allowed Hopkins's poetry to be printed and then to flourish, as he predicted. We care a good deal more about language now, and far less about scansion or meter, as I've said, but also we note an intimacy with the Holy that was far from orthodox in the platitudinous nineteenth century.

AV: There have been a plethora of books lately that proclaim not only the logic of atheism, but that many of the world's problems are due to religion. Have you read any of these books, and what do you make of the attention they have garnered? What do you think about atheism since it is diametrically opposed to your belief in God?

RH: I have read reviews of their books, but not the books themselves. I find their reasoning lame and some, if not most, of them seem unfamiliar with the greatest theological thinkers. One approving review tossed out supposedly knotty problems that I could remember discussing and having shot down in my high school religion classes. Atheism is based on a philosophical or scientific premise that simply runs counter to many people's actual, lived experience of a God who loves them deeply, loyally, and intimately. That such books are momentarily popular has been typical throughout history. But on a far greater scale is the faith of billions who feel connected with a loving, supernatural creator. For them, and for me, the arguments of atheism seem as empty as the arguments against the existence of one's sister Alice.

AV: What are your thoughts about your novels being made into movies (such as *The Assassination of Jesse James by the Coward Robert Ford*), and what book are you working on now?

RH: I have always had a great fondness for film, have enjoyed working at movie-making even when the final product didn't turn out especially well, and rejoice in any film sale, not just because of the potential extra income, but because I can reach so many more people with that "text" than with my stories in print. I loved what Andrew Dominik and Brad Pitt and Casey Affleck and so many others did with my interpretation of Jesse James and Robert Ford. I felt honored by their dedication. And I guess I'm a cinematic writer, not in the sense that I'm hankering for a film sale, but in that I have already seen the movie in my mind as I produced each scene.

Right now I'm collecting the short stories I've written since *Nebraska* was published in 1989. I ought to have a book of them in a couple of months; then I'll submit it to my publisher and hope for the best, just like I've always done. One of the things I like most about fiction writing is the adventure of it, the risk. Some people may think of me as an established writer, but I submit my manuscripts with all the anxieties of a rookie. And when any fiction of mine is actually published, I always feel I've gotten away with something.

Kazuo Ishiguro. Courtesy of Jeff Cottenden.

Stuck on the Margins: An Interview with Kazuo Ishiguro

Sir Kazuo Ishiguro was born in Nagasaki, Japan, in 1954 and left Japan when his parents emigrated to Britain in 1960. He received his undergraduate degree from the University of Kent at Canterbury and received his MA in creative writing from the University of East Anglia. In 1982, he was included in the original "Best of Young British Novelists" after having become a British citizen earlier that year. He is a deliberate writer, as can be seen from his having published only eight novels in forty years. His novels include *A Pale View of Hills* (awarded the Winifred Holtby Prize), *An Artist of the Floating World* (awarded the 1986 Whitbread Prize), *The Remains of the Day* (winner of the Booker Prize), *The Unconsoled, When We Were Orphans, Never Let Me Go, The Buried Giant*, and *Klara and the Sun.* His other awards include the Nobel Prize in Literature in 2017, Order of the Rising Sun in 2018, and Knight Bachelor in 2019.

Writers who have influenced him include Junichiro Tanizaki, Dostoyevsky, Chekhov, and Proust. He has been married since 1986 to Laura MacDougall, and they have a daughter.

The interview with Kazuo Ishiguro occurred on April 2, 1990, in Sugar Land, where the author was a guest of the Houston International Festival. (Since I was doing the interview for a special edition of the *Mississippi Review,* additional questions were provided by Kim Herzinger of the *Mississippi Review* which greatly enhanced the interview.) Originally, Ishiguro and I were to conduct the interview at his hotel, but when I called his hotel Ishiguro said he had been cooped up for three days in downtown Houston and wanted to get out. Since he had just won the Booker Prize for *The Remains of the Day,* I asked him how his book reading had gone at the Houston Downtown Central Library. He said one person showed up! He then asked if the interview could be conducted somewhere else so we drove to my house in Sugar Land, a sprawling suburb southwest of Houston; the interview was conducted in my kitchen with Ishiguro talking and sipping ice water with lemon. As we talked, I studied his face with its broad Oriental planes and features and listened to his very British accent which, at first, was a startling juxtaposition. During the course of the interview, I came to realize that this was an extraordinary young writer with a tremendous understanding of his craft. At the end of the interview, Ishiguro asked if we could have a late lunch of Tex-Mex food, since he could never find it in England.

Kim Herzinger: Last year, just before you went back to Japan for the first time since you left at the age of six, you were somewhat worried that the Japanese would expect you to know a great deal more about the culture and country than you actually did. Were your fears realized?

Kazuo Ishiguro: Not really. It's partly because they knew I was coming. I had a very kind of closeted journey to Japan. I was invited by the Japan Foundation, which is part of the government, so there was always an escort hanging around. In fact, there was far more media interest in me than I had anticipated. I caused a great stir in the press—not because they were particularly interested in me as a literary figure—but because I touched a strange nerve from the social aspect. Japan is, at the moment and perhaps for the first time, facing the idea that they cannot remain a homogeneous society.

This question about immigrants from Southeast Asia as well as a greater number of Western people living in Japan has started up a process. They now have to start thinking about what it means to be Japanese and what sort of country Japan might be. This has suddenly become a live-wire issue. This idea that somebody who is racially Japanese and looks very Japanese could go to England and have lost his Japanese-ness in some ways is at the same time fascinating and I think rather threatening. There was all this interest in what kind of person I was and what messages I could bring and what the West thought about Japan. They somehow thought I was somebody they could actually ask. So I found myself put in that sort of false territory there.

I was on TV and I did a lot of interviews—but very rarely talked about literature. There were always these questions about what people think of Japan and what did I think of Japan.

Allan Vorda: Did you respond in Japanese?

KI: No, I spoke English all the time and I was advised to do so. Really just to avoid this confusion—that was my way of saying I'm not a regular Japanese guy. My Japanese isn't good enough anyway to speak correctly. I could make myself understood, but in Japan that is not enough. There are about seven or eight different ways to say the same thing, depending on how you perceive the status of the person you are speaking to, vis-à-vis yourself. To get this kind of thing even slightly wrong produces tremendous offense. It's a terribly hierarchy-conscious society. It means people aren't worrying about whether they are upper class or middle class or working class. They are worrying about what number they are on the ladder.

AV: Did the people there like the answers you gave them, or did your answers increase their xenophobia?

KI: I avoided giving any clear-cut answers, but I think just my very being is a kind of embodiment of the whole issue.

A lot of Japanese are starting to properly travel for the first time, and I don't mean just as tourists. Business and international trade means they are spending more time abroad. Of course, there are Japanese children who are growing up abroad. This is something that some people say is good and others say is horrifying because their Japanese-ness is going to become dissipated. The fear is that these people and their children will come back to Japan having lost something, such as eating with chopsticks, which is part of the cultural tradition.

A lot of the younger Japanese, particularly in Tokyo, know very little about things people in the West consider to be traditionally Japanese. They don't even know how to put on the kimono. (I suppose I would be a good example, since I don't know.) If you do it the wrong way around—the left on the inside or the right on the outside or whichever way it is—it's a terrible blunder because one way you only do to a corpse; living people have it the other way, and I never can remember which way it is. But what was interesting is a lot of the young Japanese don't know because they don't wear kimonos and they don't know a lot of the basic things. The younger kids, particularly in Tokyo, are kind of like Western kids in that sense. It is a kind of baffling, weird thing from a bygone era.

They also eat meat all the time. I was shocked at how tall they were as well. Anyone under thirty is six or seven inches taller on average than anyone over thirty. This is partly due to eating American junk food, so of course they may not live as long. The older Japanese are small, but they live a long time. I think they still have the longest life expectancy in the industrialized world, although sometimes the Scandinavian countries compete in this area.

Thus, the whole trip was interesting, and I think it's the way the world is going now since we're becoming much more international. America has always had this melting pot reputation, and now Britain has to face up to the question of multiculturalism. The Japanese are beginning to realize it's going to be their turn since Japan is the last large industrialized country that hasn't yet faced the problem.

AV: You stated in the *New York Times Book Review* that "Publicity for me has to a large extent been fighting the urge to be stereotyped by people." Do you think the stereotyping is due to your ethnicity and to the fact that your first two novels were set in Japan?

KI: There is a kind of paradox about my books being set in Japan and whether this stereotypes me or not. In Britain, around the time when I published my first novel, the climate had actually turned toward a great deal of interest in writers who wrote books set in that particular setting. I think there was a very peculiar thing going on in Great Britain at that time. I tend to think if I didn't have a Japanese name and if I hadn't written books at that stage set in Japan, it would have taken me years longer to get the kind of attention and sales that I got in England with my first two books. What happened in Britain, certainly during the time when I was at university, contemporary fiction was, I won't say dead, but it seemed to be the preserve of a very small strata of a very small British society. We all had this image of contemporary British novels being written by middle-aged women for middle-aged, middle-class women.

Some of them are good and some of them are appalling, but that wasn't one of the exciting things that was happening when I was growing up. Anyone interested in the creative arts was interested in theater. There was a whole explosion with a kind of radical theater. Rock music, cinema, and even television—because we have quite serious arts television in Great Britain—were the kind of things everyone was talking about, while the novel had a kind of sleepy, provincial, cozy, inward-looking kind of image, and no one was interested in it.

Around 1979 and 1980 things changed very rapidly. There was a whole new generation of publishers and a whole new generation of journalists who came of age at that time, and they desperately wanted to find a new generation of writers to rediscover the British novel. I think there was something wider going on in English society at that time too. There was an awareness that Britain was a more international place, a more cosmopolitan place, but it wasn't the center of the world. It was a kind of slightly peripheral, albeit quite wealthy country. It started to be aware of its place within the context of the whole international scene. In the early 1980s there was an explosion of tremendous interest in literature that suddenly appeared almost overnight. This occurred in foreign-language literature with people like García Márquez, Milan Kundera, and Mario Vargas Llosa, who became very trendy people. At the same time, there was a whole generation of younger British writers who often had racial backgrounds that were not the typical white Anglo-Saxon. Even some of the "straight" English writers were also using settings or themes that tend to be international or historical. There definitely was this atmosphere where people were looking for this young, exotic—although exotic may be somewhat of an unkind word—writer with international flavor. I was truly fortunate to have come along at exactly the right time. It was one of the few times in the recent history of British arts in which it was an actual plus to have a funny foreign name and to be writing about funny foreign places. The British were suddenly congratulating themselves for having lost their provincialism at last.

The big milestone was the Booker Prize going to Salman Rushdie in 1981 for *Midnight's Children*. He previously had been a completely unknown writer. That was a real symbolic moment, and then everyone was suddenly looking for other Rushdies. It so happened that around this time I brought out *A Pale View of Hills*. Usually first novels disappear without a trace. Yet I received a lot of attention, got lots of coverage, and did a lot of interviews. I know why this was. It was because I had this Japanese face and this Japanese name and it was what was being covered at the time.

I tend to think I got a very easy ride from the critics. I subsequently have won literary prizes with each book, which is very important in Britain, career-wise. It's one of the things that help you climb the ladder. All these things sort of happened to me, and I think it greatly helped that I was identified as this kind of person.

Yet after a while, this became very restricting, and the very things that helped me in the first place started to frustrate me as an artist and as a serious writer. I don't want to be confined by these things, even though they were quite helpful publicity-wise.

KH: In Britain there is a rather large community of extremely important and active writers who come from, or often write about, cultures quite different from the English, Irish, Scottish, and Welsh. I'm thinking of V. S. Naipaul, Salman Rushdie, William Boyd, Lisa St. Aubin de Terán, Doris Lessing, Ruth Prawer Jhabvala, and even Americans like Paul Theroux, David Plante, and Russell Hoban. Do you find yourself grouped with them often? Do you mind it? Do you resist it? Do you think such a grouping is of any use in coming to grips with your work?

KI: Like any writer, I resist being put in a group. The group you mentioned is quite an eclectic one. I'm usually put in a much narrower group—usually with Rushdie and a writer called Timothy Mo, who probably isn't that well known in America. Mo is a Chinese-British writer who is quite prominent in Britain and has been nominated for the Booker Prize twice. He hasn't won it yet.

I write so differently than someone like Rushdie. My style is almost the antithesis of Rushdie's or Mo's. Their writing tends to have these quirks where it explodes in all kinds of directions. Rushdie's language always seems to be reaching out—to express meaning that can't usually be expressed through normal language. Just structurally his books have this terrific energy. They grow in every direction at once, and he doesn't particularly care if the branches lead nowhere. He will let it grow anyway and leave it there, and that's the way he writes. I think he is a powerful and considerable writer.

I respect Rushdie's writing enormously, but as a writer I think I'm almost the antithesis. The language I use tends to be the sort that supresses meaning and tries to hide away meaning rather than chase after something just beyond the reach of words. I'm interested in the way words hide meaning. I suppose I like to have a sparse, tight structure, because I don't like to have this improvised feeling remain in my work. From a literary point of view, I can't see anything that links me with someone like Salman Rushdie or Timothy Mo.

I think there is something that unites most of the writers that you have mentioned, especially the younger writers of Britain at the moment. There is something different about them, if you compare that group with the older generation of writers of Britain. The one possible valid thing that unites the younger group is the consciousness that Britain is not the center of the universe. There was a time when Britain thought it had this dominant role in the world, that Britain was the head of this huge empire. I think for a long time it was thought you could just write about British issues and about British life and it would automatically be of global significance, since people all around the world would be interested. British writers didn't have to consciously start thinking about the interest of people outside Britain, because whatever concerned them was, by definition, of international interest.

I think there was this gray period—because literary habits take a long time to die—before the British finally, both intellectually and consciously, accepted that the empire had gone. No longer did they have this dominant, central place in the world to go to anymore. I think perhaps the styles of writing and the assumptions of writing took a while to catch up with that, and I think this was a rather dull period in English writing. The writers were writing things in which nobody was interested, since it meant nothing to anyone outside of Britain. Yet, they carried on with the assumption that Britain was the center of the world. In fact, it was this that turned it into this provincial little country.

I think the younger generation of writers not only realized that but are now suffering from a kind of inferiority complex. There's a great sense that the front lines where the great clashes of ideologies were happening elsewhere. Whether you are looking at communism and capitalism clashing, or the Third World and the industrialized world clashing, or whatever it is—people have this idea if you're actually based in Britain and British life is what you know—then you have to make some sort of leap. Either you go out there physically and start searching around as V. S. Naipaul and Paul Theroux did, or you have to use your imagination. It's much more normal for the younger generation of British writers, and apart from the people you mentioned

I would also include Julian Barnes and Ian McEwan, that they will very often not write books in the contemporary British setting they live in. They will search far and wide in the imaginations for mythical settings or historical settings. For example, McEwans's novel *The Innocent* is set in the Cold War period in Berlin. This is not atypical of the differences that separate the younger generation from the older generation of writers.

KH: Americans like to believe that English language literature somehow became theirs after World War II. We pay some lip service to Greene, Golding, Lessing, Amis, Fowles, Larkin, Heaney, Hughes, Powell, Murdoch, and the rest, but not much. In fact, I would say that Americans half feel that English literature never quite recovered from the deaths of Joyce and Woolf and the war itself. How do you see yourself, and other young contemporary British writers, in terms of the twentieth-century tradition of British writing?

KI: What I just said previously raises questions about style and technique as well as setting and theme. If you happen to actually live in a country that you think won't actually provide a broad enough setting to address what you see as the really crucial issues of the age, that inevitably means you start moving away from straight realism.

If you happen to be, let's say, living in East Germany at the moment, perhaps there is no overwhelming reason to not write realism. I think there is a natural instinct to write realism. It takes much more to start thinking of other ways to write. It's when you are actually *stuck on the margins*. Then you start to become conscious that you are stuck on the margins and the things that you know intimately on that concrete, documentary level just won't do. Yet on the other hand, you realize you won't have the same authority as someone who lives in Eastern Europe, or someone who lives in Africa, or the Soviet Union, or America to write about the places that you think are rather central to the things you would like to talk about. What can you do? You know about English life and the texture of English society, but it's something you feel you can't use that well. So you start to actually move away from realism. You have to start looking for other ways in which to work. I think here you start to move, not so much into out-and-out fantasy, but you start to create a slightly more fabulous world. You start to use the landscape that you do know in a metaphorical way. Or you start to create out-and-out fantastic landscapes. Perhaps Doris Lessing got caught up in that when she went off on her science fiction venture.

It may well be that Americans are going through some of the stages that British writers once went through because American society is today so central to the world community. What are the international themes that are of interest to everybody? In America there is no need to ask this question consciously. Americans are almost exempt from having to ask that question. Perhaps they shouldn't be. In any case, at this moment I think people can write about American society and American life and it will be of interest to people in Kuala Lumpur or the Philippines because American culture has a broad appeal. It has reached the point that some people say American culture is invading or taking over everywhere you go in the world. Thus, a lot of people are trying to stop it, but a lot of people are bringing it in. It's very difficult to think of any point on the globe—or any society in the world today—where people shouldn't have a valued interest in American culture.

For the time being, just because of the way things are, I think American writers find themselves in this position—that they can write in a way that at other times might seem very inward-looking and parochial. Just by virtue of America's cultural position in the context of international culture. American writers are going to be relevant. Writers who haven't tried to be of great interest to people all over the world end up being so; sometimes, precisely because they're so inward-looking and unconscious of the world beyond, that they reveal where a lot of these influences are coming from. I think there was a time when British writers were in this position. Perhaps American writers need to be aware of a time when it will no longer be the case for them.

AV: Do you see your prose as participating in the more traditional, twentieth-century style of such writers as W. Somerset Maugham, E. M. Forster, Evelyn Waugh, and Joyce Cary?

KI: Not really. Most of them I haven't even read. With *The Remains* *of the Day* it's like a pastiche where I've tried to create a mythical England. Sometimes it looks like or has the tone of a very English book, but actually I'm using that as a kind of shock tactic: this relatively young person with a Japanese name and a Japanese face who produces this extra-English novel, or perhaps should I say, a super-English novel. *It's more English than English.* Yet I think there is a big difference from the tones of the world in *The Remains of the Day* and the worlds created by those writers you mentioned because in my case there is an ironic distance.

AV: Maybe I misread you somewhat. Are you saying that readers have to get past the realism in order to reach—as Barth or Borges or García Márquez have termed it—the irrealistic or fabulist world? This is more your intent with *The Remains of the Day* than just writing a traditional British novel?

KI: Absolutely. I think it's almost impossible now to write a kind of traditional British novel without being aware of the various ironies. The kind of England I create in *The Remains of the Day* is not an England that I believe ever existed. I've not attempted to reproduce, in a historically accurate way, some past period. What I'm trying to do there, and I think this is perhaps much easier for British people to understand than perhaps people abroad, is to actually rework a particular myth about a certain kind of England. I think there is this very strong idea, which exists in England at the moment, about an England where people lived in the not-so-distant past that conformed to various stereotypical images. That is to say, an England with sleepy, beautiful villages with very polite people and butlers and people taking tea on the lawn.

At the moment, particularly in Britain, there is an enormous nostalgia industry going on with coffee table books, television programs, and even some tour agencies who are trying to recapture this kind of old England. The mythical landscape of this sort of England, to a large degree, is harmless nostalgia for a time that didn't exist. The other side of this, however, is that it is used as a political tool—much as the American Western myth is used here. It is used as a way of bashing anybody who tries to spoil this Garden of Eden. This can be brought out by the left or the right, but usually it is the political right who say England was this beautiful place before the trade unions tried to make it more egalitarian or before immigrants started to come or before the promiscuous age of the '60s came and ruined everything. I think it is one of the most important jobs of the novelist to actually tackle and rework myths. I think it's a very valid ground on which a novelist should do his work. I've deliberately created a world which at first resembles that of those writers such as P. G. Wodehouse. I then start to undermine this myth and use it in a slightly twisted and different way.

I was asking you earlier on, and this is a question I ask a lot of American people who know American literature, about the genre of the Western myth. It's always puzzled me that serious writers have not tried to rework that myth to a greater extent, because it seems to me a nation's myth is the way a country dreams. It is part of the country's fabulized memory, and it seems to me to be a very valid task for the artist to try to figure out what that myth is and if they should actually rework or undermine that myth. It has happened in the cinema as far as the Western is concerned, but when I ask this question people don't seem to be able to offer many serious literary works that go into that area.

To a certain extent, I suppose I was trying to do a similar thing with the English myth. I'd have to say that my overall aim wasn't confined to British lessons for British people because it's a mythical landscape which is supposed to work at a metaphorical level. *The Remains of the Day* is a kind of parable. Yet this is a problem I've always had as a writer throughout my three books. I think if there is something I really struggle with as a writer, whenever I try to think of a new book, it is this whole question about how to make a particular setting actually take off into the realm of metaphor so that people don't think it is just about Japan or Britain. Because ultimately, I'm not that interested in saying things about specific societies; and if I were, I think I'd prefer to do it through nonfiction and follow all the proper disciplines to actually produce evidence and argument. I wouldn't do it by emotional manipulation.

AV: Perhaps it is less interesting to do it through nonfiction because it is less imaginative. I guess that is one of the joys of writing fiction.

KI: I think one of the joys of fiction is that you are saying things that are universal and not just about Great Britain or America or whatever. It can be about America or Britain, but I think when fiction really takes off it is because you can start to see how it is relevant to all other kinds of context and how there is a universal streak to these things. I always have this real problem because on the one hand you have to create the setting in your novel that feels firm enough for people to be able to find their way around it. On the other hand, if you make it too concrete and too tied down to something that might exist in reality, that fictional world doesn't take off at that metaphorical level and people start saying, "Oh, that's what it was like in Japan at a certain time," or "He's saying something about Britain in the 1930s." For me, it is something I feel I haven't quite come to terms with yet, but I'm trying to find some territory, somewhere between straight realism and that kind of out-and-out fabulism, where I can create a world that isn't going to alienate or baffle readers in a way that a completely fantastic world would. Essentially, a world which at the same time can actually prompt readers to say this isn't documentary or this isn't history or this isn't journalism. I'm asking you to look at this world I've created as a reflection of a world that all kinds of people live in. It's the movement away from straight realism that is actually the real challenge. You get that wrong and you could lose everything, whereby no one identifies with your characters or they don't care what happens in this funny, weird, bizarre world. I just wanted to somehow move it away so it's just a couple of stages from straight realism and let it take off with that metaphorical level. I think I've come closer to doing that in *The Remains of the Day* than I did with the two Japanese novels, but I still feel this is a challenge I have to meet.

AV: Your prose is a joy to read. For example, on page twenty-seven of *The Remains of the Day* you write: "I was then brought up to this room, in which, at that point of the day, the sun was lighting up the floral pattern of the wallpaper quite agreeably." And shortly thereafter, the butler

Stevens thinks that the "greatness" of Britain paradoxically comes from "the lack of obvious drama or spectacle that sets the beauty of our land apart." Can the same analogy be made to your writing style?

KI: When Stevens says that about the British landscape, he is also saying something about himself. He thinks beauty and greatness lie in being able to be this kind of cold, frozen butler who isn't demonstrative and who hides emotions in much the way he's saying that the British landscape does with its surface calm: the ability to keep down turmoil and emotion. He thinks this is what gives both butlers and the British landscape beauty and dignity. And that viewpoint crumbles during the course of Stevens's journey.

To a large extent, when I wrote *The Remains of the Day*, that was the first time I started to become very conscious of my own style. And of course, quite rightly, these references that Stevens makes are also a reference to my own style. I think what happened was this: in my first two novels I just wrote these sentences without really thinking about style. I was just writing in what I thought was the clearest way possible. Then I started to read review after review which talked about my understated or clipped style. It was the reviewers and the critics who pointed this out to me—where my style seemed to be unusually calm with all this kind of strange turmoil expressed underneath the calm. I started to ask myself, "Where does this style come from then?" It's not something I consciously manufactured. I had to face the possibility this was indeed something to do with me. It's my natural voice. In *The Remains of the Day*, for the first time, I started to question to what extent it was a good or bad thing from the human point of view regarding this whole business about the suppression of emotion.

Perhaps this was revealed by this style, by this inner voice, that I produced in my first two books. To a certain extent, *The Remains of the Day* tackles on a thematic level the implications of that kind of style. Stevens's first-person narrative is written in that style, but of course his whole life is led in that style. In the book I try to explore to what extent it is indeed dignified and to what extent it is a form of cowardice—a way of actually hiding from what is perhaps the scariest arena in life, which is the emotional arena. It is the first book I've written in which I was actually conscious of my own style and to a certain extent tried to figure out what it is, why it's like that, and where it's coming from.

KH: Despite a comparatively paltry audience in the United States, there is a feeling that you, along with Ian McEwan, William Boyd, Martin Amis, Salman Rushdie, Julian Barnes, Graham Swift, and a few others—plus the international success of *Granta*—are leading an energetic new wave in English fiction. How does it seem to you?

KI: It is very hard for me to assess what is going on in America because I have just visited, but it does surprise me the extent to which the Atlantic does seem to create this huge gap between the two literary cultures. There are household names here that aren't even available on the bookshelves in Britain and vice versa.

When I came over here to do my tour with Knopf in November, I discovered that there were these people who are literary giants here. For instance, Ann Beattie, who I don't think is readily available on the bookshelves in England. You might be able to track down a copy of an Ann Beattie book, but you could talk to a lot of literary journalists in London and they will not know her. Quite likely they would not have heard of Russell Banks. On the other hand, Raymond Carver has become very well respected in England, as has Richard Ford. I would say these two writers have broken through to significant respect and readership in Britain.

All the time I'm coming across books that I realize are very well known over here, but quite often these names mean very little to me. I've been given a book by Pete Dexter called *Paris Trout*, which I think is quite a well-known book here and I've noticed he's won the National Book Award. Personally, I had a hell of a time breaking through here. I don't know why there should be this huge gap, but I think it just points to the fact that even though we share the same language, the literary cultures are so different.

The other factor has to do with the actual publishing industries, because so much of publishing has to do with contacts and literary politics. I think one of the real weaknesses of the system as it operates at the moment is that there is a tendency toward insularity. If you start operating any contact games, then the mediocre domestic talent is always going to get promoted over more interesting stuff from abroad.

KH: Since you studied American literature at university, were there any American writers who influenced your work? I hear that you think Hemingway wrote great titles, but that perhaps the books that followed were a bit of a letdown.

KI: I think Hemingway did write marvelous titles. I like Hemingway's early work, but I find some of his later stuff pretty mediocre, almost embarrassingly so. His standard of title writing remained high right to the end. I think *Across the River and into the Trees* is a marvelous title, but the discrepancy between the quality of the title and the book is one of the greatest discrepancies I've come across in world literature. It is staggering someone could write a title like that could write such an appalling book, but he did write some fine stuff early on.

With American writers I tend to like the older guys from the nineteenth century, such as Mark Twain. I think *Huckleberry Finn* is a very beautiful book with a real liveliness to the language and the vernacular is very exciting. *Moby-Dick* is a crazy book, yet very interesting. I like Edgar Allan Poe, who raises some very interesting questions about literature as a whole.

AV: What about contemporary American writers such as Pynchon, Gass, and Barth?

KI: These are all people that I should say that we don't really read in England. Pynchon is read . . . well, I don't know . . . he is bought. Usually the only book of his that anyone has read is *The Crying of Lot 49*, because it is short. A lot of people possess *Gravity's Rainbow* and *V.*, but I know very few people who have gotten over one-third of the way through. It remains to be seen if people will finish *Vineland* in England, but people are buying him. Pynchon may very well be a very important writer, but I've only read *The Crying of Lot 49*, so I'm not in a position to say. From what I've read, it is a little too overintellectualized for me. I suppose one of these days I should tackle one of his big novels.

AV: I can't think of one writer in America who gets more critical attention than Pynchon.

KI: Perhaps he is a great writer, or it could be because there will always be a certain kind of writer who is good for academics.

AV: Can you name one thing that separates American literature from British literature?

KI: One feature in your literary scene that we don't have in Britain, and generally in Europe, is the creative writing industry. I think that is one of the enormous differences in the two literary cultures. It's probably true to say, and I've heard it often said, that you can't find a single American writer today of any significance who hasn't, in some way, been directly touched by the creative writing world, either as a teacher or student. Even someone who kept away from it is going to be affected by it indirectly, because so much of the criticism and so much of the opinions of his fellow writers are going to be touched by it. I think this is something that would certainly make me nervous if I were living in a literary culture where the role of the universities and faculties who teach creative writing began to have that sort of dominant influence.

I'm not actually suggesting that the Thomas Pynchon phenomenon is something closely related to this, because I'm not in a position to comment on him. All I would say is that I would want to assess quite carefully what the role of the creative writing faculties actually is. Thus, within the whole literary culture, whether you like it or not, American literature is going a certain direction and I would want to determine if the influence were benign or whether it was actually leading us up a garden path.

KH: Lately in this country there has been some debate over the virtues of fictional "minimalism" (*Granta* called it "dirty realism")—Raymond Carver, Ann Beattie, Frederick Barthelme, Max Apple, Mary Robison, Richard Ford, Tobias Wolff, and a number of others have been called "minimalists." Readers seem to like the work, but it has sent critics into spasms of concern over the death of the novel, the end of American fiction, and so on. Do you have any thoughts on the subject? Is there anything like minimalism and the subsequent outcry from the critics in contemporary British writing?

KI: No, there isn't a comparable movement or phenomenon in British writing at all. Minimalism isn't a word that you hear very often in British literary debate. I should say in relation to the previous question that Richard Ford and Raymond Carver are two American writers that I admire enormously. Raymond Carver is a profoundly moving writer, while Richard Ford has written two or three short stories that are amongst the finest short stories I've ever read. Perhaps it is the influence of the creative writing industry that somehow led to that sort of style. If that's the case, then that is an aspect I'll be quite well disposed toward because I think these two writers write with great emotional honesty about things that strike me as being genuinely deep at the human level.

The thing I fear from the creative writing industry and universities in general is that people elevate priorities I would not consider to be terrifically important. They'll elevate to some special status issues like the nature of fiction or some rather cerebral intellectual ideas. Such issues become esteemed in that kind of environment because, after all, that is what that kind of environment celebrates. For me, however, while the nature of fiction or fictionality are things writers might need to be concerned with to get on with their work, I don't believe the nature of fiction is one of the burning issues of the late-twentieth century. It's not one of the things I want to turn to novels and art to find out about. I think reading Ford and Carver for me is a kind of antidote to those over-intellectualized or self-conscious literary creations that almost seem to be created for the professor down the corridor to decipher. Carver and Ford seem to write about life in a way that is profound. Also, at the technical level I think they are in a different league from a lot of these people who are just trying to show off or make comments about their literary techniques. The technique applied by Ford or Carver is one at the highest level and, to the point, perhaps it's not that obvious. I think they say great things about the emotional experience of life.

Minimalism is not something that is discussed very much in Britain. Short stories haven't really caught on in Britain recently. You can bring out a volume of short stories and you know that only about one-third of the people read it, as opposed to the number of people who read a novel that you have written. For some reason the British don't get into short stories.

KH: To what extent has Japanese fiction influenced your work? If we look around for writers who sound a bit like Ishiguro, it would seem that Tanizaki—especially his cool precision and delicate touch—is closer to you than anybody else.

KI: Tanizaki wrote in various styles, and a lot of his books I wouldn't describe as cool or delicate. I think the book that is best known in the West in one called *The Makioka Sisters*. It is really like a Western family saga. It is one of those stately, long books like Henry James, Edith Wharton, Theodore Dreiser, or George Eliot would have written. It's about this rich merchant family where nothing terribly dramatic ever happens, but it follows the different family members through a period of social change. I think a lot of people think that Tanizaki always writes like that, but he also writes kind of weird, kinky, perverted stuff.

AV: What book would you be referring to?

KI: *The Secret History of the Lord of Musashi*, which is about a medieval lord who, the first time he gets sexually turned on, is wandering around a battlefield shortly after a battle and he sees these severed heads. I think that night he peeks through a hole and sees some women dressing the severed heads of fallen clan members and he starts to get sexually turned on.

AV: I'm sure Freud would have a good time with this.

KI: It gets even weirder because the thing that really turns him on is a particular head that has a nose missing. Later on, he becomes a powerful lord and has a real sexual craving for severed heads with missing noses. It gets really funny because there is a particular guy that he takes a liking to and he really wants to see this guy without a nose and so he keeps trying to arrange it so that his nose will get cut off, but it never quite works. This poor guy doesn't know what the hell is going on. Every few weeks he loses an ear, or something happens to him, or somebody is after him, but he doesn't know why. There is this weird scene where the lord gets his servant to impersonate a severed head without a nose while he is making love to one of his concubines.

I mean, this is real Tanizaki territory, and this is where Tanizaki is really interesting. And there are a few other books like that. This is by way of saying, that there is this tendency, just because I have a Japanese name, to pull out one or two other Japanese writers somebody else has heard of and say there is a similarity to my writing. Yet the critic perhaps is basing this comparison to a Japanese writer whose book is not typical of others he has written. For example, Tanizaki wrote in a lot of different styles, and he wrote for a long, long time. Tanizaki actually went into his eighties, and he produced an enormous number of books as he went through lots of different stages. I can't really see that anybody would particularly compare me to any Japanese writer if it weren't for the fact that I have this Japanese name. Now if I wrote under a pseudonym and got somebody else to pose for jacket photographs, I'm sure nobody would think of saying, "This guy reminds me of that Japanese writer." I often have to battle against this kind of stereotyping. I wouldn't say it's wildly unfair, but then I can think of a dozen other writers with whom I could just as easily be compared. I would say I am not wildly dissimilar to the Tanizaki of *The Makioka Sisters*, but then someone could equally say that for anybody almost—whether it was George Eliot or Henry James or the Brontë sisters.

KH: How about Chekhov? He would seem to be the one overwhelming influence on American writing over the past ten to fifteen years.

KI: Chekhov is a writer I always acknowledge as one of my influences. When people ask me about writers I really like, I always say Chekhov and Dostoyevsky.

To backtrack just slightly on my refuting any affiliation with Japanese literature, there are some things I have learned from Japanese movies. I think it is the same thing that perhaps I've taken from Chekhov, and that's from reading these people and seeing movies by the filmmakers like Ozu and watching the plays of Chekhov and reading Chekhov's short stories. I think it's given me the courage and conviction to have a very slow pace and not worry if there isn't a strong plot. I think there is an overwhelming strong tradition in Western literature—at least I should say in British literature and American literature, since I think the French have a slightly different thing going—in which plot is pretty important. By fiction I also mean movies and the way television stories are told and so on. It is almost assumed that plot has to be the central spine around which the story is fleshed, and that is almost the definition these days. When you actually think about Chekhov, it is really rather hard to actually see his pieces as plots-with-flesh on it. What is interesting is in Japan, until very recently, this kind of plot-with-flesh model just didn't exist in Japanese fiction.

There are writers like Kawabata, whom I find quite baffling and alienating, because he's from such a different tradition, but at the same time fascinating because he writes kind of long short stories. I believe he is the only Japanese Nobel Prize winner for literature. Kawabata's stories are often completely plotless. They are not only plotless, but the pace goes so slowly sometimes it almost stops. These things seem to break all the rules people teach about how to write screenplays for Hollywood.

This business about pace, you read these books on how to write a screenplay or books on how to keep the narrative drive going; yet reading Chekhov or some of these Japanese writers has indicated that you don't have to worry about that very much. I've really started to get into this idea of slowness, with things almost stopping.

AV: This seems evident in *The Remains of the Day,* where the plot is loosely based, yet you are able to piece things together. For example, Miss Kenton disappears for much of the novel, but she is always there when you need her to pull things together. The use of Miss Kenton's character seems to allow you to intermingle different elements.

KI: I don't structure my books around plots, and I find it a great liberation. If you have to worry about making a plot work, you often have to sacrifice other priorities to mechanical workings of the plot, and you start to distort characters and all kinds of psychological insights. I find a great deal of freedom in not having a plot, but that does actually mean you have to face lots of new challenges about not boring the reader and how to structure your work. These are some of the things in Chekhov which I find a continuing revelation. How does he keep you absorbed when all these people are doing is just sitting around a field and asking whether or not they are going back to Moscow? He should be crushingly boring. In fact, one or two of those great plays are boring, but some of his short stories are masterpieces.

AV: Which ones in particular?

KI: It's probably not that well known, but I like "Ionych." Other stories that come to mind are "A Boring Story," "Lady with Lapdog," and "The Kiss."

AV: You stated after you wrote *A Pale View of Hills* that, "If you really want to write something, you shouldn't bring things into your book lightly. It's a bit like taking in lodgers. They're going to be with you a long time. I think the most thing I learned between writing the first and second novels is the element of thematic discipline." Do you now feel you have control of your thematic discipline after having written *The Remains of the Day?*

KI: I'll never say I've got control, but I think I've gotten more and more control with each book. When I read reviews, I've always read the opening and closing paragraphs to see if they're saying this is good or not so good, but then after that the next thing that concerns me is the summary. Have they actually summarized the book in a way that I wanted the book to come over? For a long time, at the beginning of my career, I would actually get favorable reviews that praised me for a book that I didn't wish to write. They were emphasizing all the wrong things and praising me for things I didn't intend to do. So I would keep quiet about it and accept unwarranted praise. Of course, this isn't very satisfying, and the question of thematic discipline comes in here. There is a real satisfaction from being praised for exactly the right things you wanted to be praised for and not for some accidental effect you created. Because that is what you're trying to do. You're not just trying to get people to like your book—you're trying to communicate a vision. This is why thematic discipline is so important to me. I used to read all these reviews recommending people to read my first book for the weirdest reasons, but it had nothing to do with what I was wanting to do. I was pleased because they were favorable reviews, but that was a very frustrating experience for me.

The one point I still feel an element of frustration about, and I mentioned this before, is that people have a tendency to say *The Remains of the Day* is a book about a certain historical period in England or that it is about the fall of the British empire or something like that. They don't quite read it as a parable or see it take off into a metaphorical role. Now, a lot of reviewers have understood my intent and said this is not just a book about a butler living in the 1930s. It is interesting that reviews vary from country to country. It tells you something about that country, but it also reminds you that as a writer you're going to be read by lots of different people in lots of different social contexts coming at the book from lots of different directions. I think it's always a healthy thing to remind oneself that you shouldn't assume every reader's assumption is going to be the same as a British reader's assumption. There are going to very obvious reasons why some people see it in a completely different way. And usually the further I get from Britain, the happier I am with the readings, because the people are less obsessed with the idea of it just being about Britain. In Britain, I suppose I'm still slightly locked into this realist reader and I recognize that a part of that is my own responsibility. I hate to use the word "fantastic," but the book is still too realistic for the metaphorical intentions to be obvious if people actually come from the society which the book superficially resembles.

I've been very happy about the way the American reviewers on the whole have read *The Remains of the Day.* One or two have thought it was specifically about British history, but by and large, most people read it the way I intended them to. As I say, I think I had more trouble in Britain, where some people thought it was about the Suez Crisis or it was about British appeasement of Nazi Germany.

KH: *The Remains of the Day* and *An Artist of the Floating World* both seem to be about men who have an extraordinary capacity to lie to themselves while presenting themselves as very precise and cautious truth tellers. Should we imagine that this is going to be the central obsession in your work? So far, the central notions in your work would seem to demand first-person narration. Are you planning to work in any other forms?

KI: I think this is always a difficult question about how you're going to develop as a writer. I find it rather difficult to plan more than one book at a time, and I can't really say now which other themes I'm going to be obsessed about two or three books from now. I think certainly with my first three books I was actually trying to refine what I did over and over again, and with *The Remains of the Day,* I feel that I came to the end of that process. That is why the three books seem to have a kind of similarity. It's not a similarity for which I can apologize; I have no other way of working.

I don't actually think of my writing as being an attempt to cover this territory and finish it, and then move over to a different territory altogether and have a go at that. I don't see it like that. I feel like I'm *closing in on some strange, weird territory* that for some reason obsesses me, and I'm not sure what the nature of that territory is, but with every book I'm kind of closing in on this strange territory. And that's the way I see my development as a writer. Quite often I will have an idea for a story which is intrinsically quite interesting, but I know immediately that I can't use it because I know it's not going to help me close in on this territory. It has gotten to the point now that I recognize this. I know the things that apply to this territory which will be relevant or might be relevant from the ones that are quite diverting and therefore irrelevant. If I'm reading a newspaper and I come across an item occasionally something will hit me, something that is perhaps quite banal, but it rings some kind of strange bell. The item doesn't necessarily have to be some kind of weird human-interest story, because quite often some ordinary situation will just spring out from the page at me and I'll think that's something I could use.

I don't intend to write about old men looking back over their lives all the time because I think I've come to the end of that, but I think the real challenge that always faces writers is what to keep and what to cast off from their previous concerns and previous books. I think it is important to try to identify those things that still mean something to you, that still feel unfathomed in some way, and that is the way you close in further and further on this territory. I think most writers do write out of some part of themselves—that is, I wouldn't say "unbalanced," but where there is a kind of lack of equilibrium. I'm not suggesting that writers are usually unbalanced people, but I think a lot of them do write out of something that is unresolved somewhere deep down, and in fact it's probably too late to ever resolve it. Writing is kind of a consolation or a therapy. Quite often, bad writing comes out of this kind of therapy. The best writing comes out of a situation where I think the artist or writer has to some extent come to terms with the fact that it is too late. The wound has come, and it hasn't healed, but it's not going to get any worse; yet the wound is there. It's a kind of consolation the world isn't quite the way you wanted it, but you can somehow reorder it or try and come to terms with it by actually creating your own world and own version of it. Otherwise, I can't see any other explanation for why people should actually do this time-consuming, antisocial activity of locking themselves away and obsessively writing. I think serious writers must try, in some way or the other, to keep moving in a direction that moves them toward this area of irresolution and lack of balance. I think that's where the really interesting, deep writing comes from. This is partly why I'm very wary of the creative writing industry. I think it could actually deflect potentially very profound individual voices away from what their muses are trying to tell them.

AV: Please comment on such characters as Etsuko, Ono, Miss Kenton, and Stevens, who have misused their talents or have not led lives of fulfillment because of a lack of insight. And conversely, would their lives be better off if they had insight and no talent?

KI: I wrote about these people not actually to pass judgment on them, because I am interested in people who do have a certain amount of talent—not just talent—but who have a certain passion, a certain real urge, to do a little bit more than the average person. They've got this urge to contribute to something larger.

AV: I can see where this applies to Ono in *An Artist of the Floating World,* but do you think it applies to Stevens?

KI: Yes, definitely. Stevens is somebody who desperately wants to contribute to something larger, but he thinks he is just a butler and the only way he can do this is to work for a great man. He gets a lot of his sense of self-respect from an idea that he is serving a great man. If he were someone who didn't care at all about how his contribution was being used, then he wouldn't end up a broken man at the end. He is driven by this urge to do things perfectly, and not only do things perfectly, but that perfect contribution should be, no matter however small a contribution it is, to improving humanity. That is Stevens's position. He's not content to say, "I'll just get by and earn money so that I can feed myself."

AV: But then again, it doesn't seem that Stevens has any great insight as to why he does things. Nor does he seem to have a great understanding of the world.

KI: That's true; Stevens doesn't have a great understanding. I think this is where my characters go wrong. Their lives are spoiled because they don't have any extraordinary insight into life. They're not necessarily stupid; they're just ordinary. (I write out of this fear that I will waste my talent—not only waste my talents, but indeed end up backing some cause that I actually disapprove of or one that could be disastrous.) Yet these ordinary characters often are going to get involved in a kind of political arena even if it's in a very small way. The reason I chose a butler as a starting point was that I wanted a metaphor for this vehicle. Most of us are like butlers because we have these small, little tasks that we learn to do, but most of us don't attempt to run the world.

We just learn a job and try to do it to the best of our ability. We get our pride from that, and then we offer up a little contribution to somebody up there, to an organization, or a cause, or a country. We would like to tell ourselves this large thing that we're contributing toward is something good and not something bad, and that's how we draw a lot of our dignity. Often, we just don't know enough about what's going on out there, and I felt that's what we're like. We're like butlers.

AV: You also briefly present the lives of Lisa and the footman with whom she elopes. This seems to be a microcosm of what could have been a more fulfilling or happier life if Stevens had allowed himself to fall in love with Miss Kenton instead of denying his feelings.

KI: I had this story of Lisa and the footman because I just wanted a scene where they were confronted with just such a situation and how they (Stevens and Miss Kenton) would actually talk about it and discuss it. It refers to something they're both painfully concerned with, and yet they have to discuss it as a kind of professional incident or setback. When Stevens is thinking back over his life, this is one of the things that comes back to him, which is the closest they ever got to discussing their romantic possibilities. So even when Stevens and Miss Kenton are discussing their unfulfilled romance, they do it indirectly by discussing Lisa and the footman.

AV: Stevens's vision is very myopic in that he never seems to give a thought to anything, nor is sex an issue. Do you agree that he is a pathetically tragic figure that is almost nonhuman in his thoughts and feelings?

KI: I wouldn't want to say nonhuman.

AV: Maybe if I could digress just one second. You had that interesting metaphor in *The Remains of the Day* where Mr. Cardinal suggests to Stevens it might be better if people were created as plants "firmly embedded in the soil," then there wouldn't be any disagreements about "wars and boundaries." Then Mr. Cardinal adds, "But we could still have chaps like you taking messages back and forth, bringing tea, that sort of thing. Otherwise, how would we ever get anything done?"

KI: I think he's in danger of turning himself into something less than human partly because he's got this sense of perfectionism. It's this kind of terribly misguided sense of perfectionism, which if he actually achieves it, would actually mean turning himself into something less than human. But it's not just perfectionism. It's a kind of a cowardice. That is what I'm trying to suggest, and hence the juxtaposition of his ambition to be a great butler with his avoidance of romantic life with Miss Kenton. I suppose I'm suggesting that often that kind of drive to that kind of professional perfectionism is rooted in some kind of cowardice about the emotional arena. It's not just a determination to be the best. Once again, I was drawn to use a butler in this kind of metaphorical way because that seemed to be a profession in which at least a stereotypical view of the professional butler is that you have to kind of erase the obviously human from yourself. This was probably a social requirement, because people wanted privacy at the same time as wanting to be served. Thus, the butler was obliged to be a kind of robot-like figure.

AV: Nevertheless, it seems as if Stevens is devoid of any feelings. For example, his proudest moment as a butler is during Lord Darlington's political conference when his father is dying upstairs. He ignores being with his father since his duty lies elsewhere—primarily trying to get bandages for the sore feet of the snotty Dupont. Even after his father dies, Stevens does not go to attend to the corpse, whereupon Miss Kenton sarcastically says, "In that case, Mr. Stevens, will you permit me to close his eyes?" It's as though Stevens is made of cardboard, without any identity or feelings.

KI: The role of the butler is to move inconspicuously while creating the illusion of absences and at the same time being physically on hand to do these things. It seemed to me appropriate to have somebody who wants to be this perfect butler because that seems to be a powerful metaphor for someone who is trying to actually erase the emotional part of him that may be dangerous and that could really hurt him. Yet, he doesn't succeed because these kinds of human needs, the longings for warmth and love and friendship, are things that just don't go away. This is what Stevens probably realizes at the end of the novel when he starts to get the inkling about this question of bantering. He starts to read more and more into why he can't banter, and this is an indication of the fact that he's somehow cut off from other people. He can't even make the first steps in forming relationships with other people.

AV: In the *New York Times Book Review*, you say your next book will not be repetitive stylistically and that you might "like to write a messy, jagged, loud kind of book." What kind of book can your readers expect next?

KI: It is very difficult to say. I write very slowly, and most of my writing time I'm not actually writing prose. *The Remains of the Day* took me three years, and during that time I did nothing else. I don't have any other job, and I turn down any offers to do journalism. I was full-time working on that book, but I realized afterwards looking through my diary, that I actually spent only twelve months writing the words that ended up in the book. It horrifies me to think that I spent two years just working up to it, but I find that I have to have a very close map of where I'm going to go before I actually start to write the words. I have to have it almost all in place in my head first. This is once again quite unusual, because I know plenty of writers who write brilliantly, although they know very little of where they're going when they start the first draft. I must have all these things worked out and researched. Now things may change obviously, in the execution, when I'm actually writing the words, but I usually have to know fairly precisely what I'm trying to achieve with every paragraph. It takes me a long time to get to that situation. I fill folders and folders up with notes and ideas which look like excerpts from a longer work. I may experiment with a particular tone or a character during the very early stages when it's very difficult to say even where the book is going to be set. All I know are the themes.

Jamaica Kincaid.

I Come from a Place That's Very Unreal: An Interview with Jamaica Kincaid

Jamaica Kincaid was born into tropical poverty as Elaine Potter Richardson in 1949 on the island of Antigua. An only child, she lived with her father, a carpenter, and her mother in a house that had no electricity, water, or bathroom facilities. In her story "In the Night," the narrator refers to a time in her youth when she would prepare the family outhouse every Wednesday for the night-soil men to pick up their tub and replace it with a clean one.

Since Antigua was a British colony, she was educated in the British system, but grew to detest everything about England except the literature. (Antigua became self-governing in 1967 and an independent nation with the Commonwealth in 1981.) After completing her secondary education at seventeen, she was sent to Westchester, New York, to work as an au pair. Later, she studied photography at the New School and attended Franconia College in New Hampshire.

In 1973 she changed her name to Jamaica Kincaid, and her writing caught the attention of William Shawn, editor of the *New Yorker*. Kincaid later married the editor's son, Allen Shawn (brother of the actor Wallace Shawn), and they had two children. They divorced in 2002.

Kincaid has published numerous books, including *At the Bottom of the River, Annie John, A Small Place, Lucy, The Autobiography of My Mother, Mr. Potter,* and *See Now Then.* Various awards include the Anisfield-Wolf Book Award, Lannan Literary Award for Fiction, Prix Femina étranger, American Academy of Arts and Letters, and the Dan David Prize in Literature.

It was very difficult to set up an interview with Jamaica Kincaid. She was scheduled to speak at the Museum of Fine Arts in Houston as part of a reading series, but weeks of effort trying to arrange the interview through her publisher had been to no avail. Finally, Frederick Barthelme, the editor of *Mississippi Review,* said he could put in a good word for me to an editor at the *New Yorker,* and the day before Kincaid arrived her publicist said that she would indeed do the interview the day after her reading. We met February 13, 1991, in a large conference room off the main lobby of the very grand Wyndham Warwick Hotel (now the ZaZa Hotel). When Kincaid stepped off the elevator, I was struck by her appearance. A tall woman, she was dressed in what looked like a Catholic schoolgirl's uniform: a plaid skirt, white blouse, white socks, and black shoes. Her hair was in pigtails, and she appeared to be a teenager even though she was over forty. I found her to be highly opinionated and steadfast in her beliefs, fiercely determined as to what she deemed morally correct and what she believed were social injustices. When the interview concluded, we went to eat Mexican food. She was very pleasant and interesting to talk with during our time together.

Allan Vorda: Caribbean writer Derek Walcott, while writing about your work, stated that "Genius has many surprises, and one of them is geography." In what ways has geography both helped and hindered you as a writer?

Jamaica Kincaid: I can't say it has hindered me at all and, if it has, I don't know of it. It seems to me it has been more of a help since I can find nothing negative to say about the fact I come from the place I'm from. I very much like coming from there. It would be false for me to take pride in it because it's an accident, really. It just seems to be sort of happenstance that I was born in this place and happenstance that I was born with black skin and all the other things I was born with. All that aside, the fact that I was born in this place, my geography has been, I think, a positive thing for me. I experience it as just fine. I am not particularly glad of it, as I say. The reality of my life is that I was born in this place. I find it only as a help.

I can't say what it would have been like if I had been born a white Englishwoman. Actually, I think I *can* say it. It seems as if it would have been quite wonderful because whenever I was growing up and looked at white Englishwomen, they seemed to have a life denied me. This isn't to say if I had been born a white Englishwoman, I wouldn't have been perfectly miserable. They didn't seem perfectly miserable; they seemed rather privileged and had all the things I couldn't have. I think I just made the best of what I had. What I had was my mother, my father, my mother's family, my father's family, all of that complication, my history, which as far as I know, began on boats. I'm part African, part Carib Indian, and part—which is a very small part by now—Scot. All of them came to Antigua by boats. This is how my history begins.

AV: The critic and black studies scholar Henry Louis "Skip" Gates Jr. has stated about your work that "she never feels the necessity of claiming the existence of a black world or a female sensibility. She assumes them both. I think it's a distinct departure that she's making, and I think that more and more Black American writers will assume their world the way that she does. So that we can get beyond the large theme of racism and get to the deeper themes of how Black people love and cry and live and die. Which, after all, is what art is all about." I agree with Gates's comment, but is this a conscious attempt by you not to overtly claim you are a Black female writer? Also, do you mind that you are still stereotyped as a Black, female, Caribbean writer?

JK: No, I thought what Skip said was very revealing for me because I did not know that I had been doing that. I come from a place where most of the people are Black. Every important person in my life was a Black person, or a person who was mostly Black, or very deeply related to what we call a Black person. I just assumed that is the norm and it is the other people who would need describing. I assume most of the people who are important to me, and not last among them is my own self, are female. When I write about these people it would never occur to me to describe their race or their sex except as an aesthetic. I wouldn't say, "She has two eyes." I assume everyone has two eyes, and the only reason I would mention the eyes is if it were a superficial decision. It's not conscious at all that I leave out a people's race. Race is important, but the thing I know deeply is that when you say someone is White or Black—in my case I never say anyone is Black because I assume that to be the norm—because everybody has an idea of what that means. I never say people are white. I describe them. When you get to know people, you don't describe someone as "my wife that white woman." Or that man we just met [Kincaid is referring to a strange fellow who interrupted the taping of the interview for half an hour to pontificate his unusual views of the world], would you say, "He is a white man?" No, because what you would say is that he's a very intrusive person and that he was somewhat boorish, except we were sort of interested in his lunacy. So you look at him and immediately identify him as someone who is intrusive, and then from there you pick up on certain characteristics, but the least thing about him is that he's white.

To answer the second part of your question about being stereotyped, I think for the people who want to do it that it must be a very convenient way, but it really belittles the effort being made. When I sit at my typewriter, I'm not a woman, I'm not from the Caribbean, I'm not black. I'm just this sort of unhappy person struggling to make something, struggling to be free. Yet the freedom isn't a political one or a public one: it's a personal one. It's a struggle I realize that will go on until the day that I die.

I'm living rather an ideal life. I think we all want to live a long life in which we attempt to be free. It's a paradox because the freedom only comes when you can no longer think, which is in death. You don't want to die, but you want to be free, and that's the outcome of the freedom. Perhaps I should say this is only a very personal view. In the meantime, you struggle to make sense of the external from the things that have made you what you are and the things that you have been told are you: my history of colonialism, my history of slavery, and imagining if that hadn't happened what I would have been. Perhaps I would have been an unhappy woman in pre-European Africa. Who knows what I would have become? That's what I struggle to understand about myself.

It's not connected to the shell you see sitting at the typewriter. It's connected to the inner thing. Whatever I may say about being black, Caribbean, and female when I'm sitting down at the typewriter, I am not that. I think it's sort of limited and stupid to call anyone by these names. The truth is, would we say John Keats is a white man who was a poet from nineteenth-century England? No, we just say he is John Keats. You think of these people in terms of their lives, and so that's what I'm saying. When you think of me, think of my life. My life is not a quota or an action to affirm an idea of equality. My life is my life. If it helps people to get to something I've written I'm glad, but on the whole, I wish these terms would go away. Is my work any good? That is what I wish to know.

AV: Why was your childhood, which often serves as a basis for your stories, filled with sadness and anger, when most readers would expect to find growing up on an island to be happy and carefree?

JK: I can say to most readers: try living on a Caribbean paradise and see if they find it happy and carefree. The thing I've learned is that all of life in every stage is hard to live. (How much more interesting it would have been for the world, not to mention less painful, if the Europeans in the fifteenth century had decided that the trouble with the part of the world they were in should be worked out within their borders?) Life is hard whether you live on a Caribbean island or somewhere else. No one living in these places you might think of as a paradise thinks it is a paradise. They all want to leave. Even if someone could live the life of a tourist, no tourist goes to these places and wants to spend the rest of their life there. It was hard to grow up in a place like that, in particular because it doesn't have the comforts you think a place like that has. A person living in a place like that finds the sun hard to take. They find the nice days after a while hard to take. After a while it becomes a prison. Life is just extremely hard. I don't know of one person who lived in the West Indies as a child who thinks, "Oh, I always wish to remain a child in this wonderful atmosphere."

AV: In the magazine *W* you indicate you dearly loved the St. John's library in Antigua, which closed in 1974 as a result of an earthquake: "Antigua used to be a place of standards. There was a sort of decency that it just doesn't have anymore," you said. "I think the tragedy of Antigua for me, when I began to see it again, was the loss of the library." You seem to see this event as being somehow symbolic of the state of your country. Does it apply to other countries as well?

JK: I hate to speak for other countries that have been and are in the situation Antigua is in, which is a former colony that is now independent. The sad fact is they are all in the same boat. It is very hard to admit this, but they were all better off under colonial rule than they are now. This isn't to say that I want colonial rule back. I'm very glad to get rid of it. I'm only sad to observe that the main lesson we seem to have learned from colonial rule is all the corruption of it and none of the good things of it. We seem to have learned none of the good things about Europe. I don't say "Western civilization" because I think this is a new term that implies white people and white superiorities. I now suspect when people refer to the greatness of Western civilization that they really mean the greatness of the white people of the world. I'm not going to say that. What I am going to say is that we learned none of the good things from Europeans—such as their love of education, of their documenting the historical past, even if they lie about it, which they often do. Another great thing about the Europeans was their understanding of a community, even if they violate it sometimes—no, they violated it all the time. They understood the idea of a community even as they limited it only to people who looked exactly like them. So the French are excluded from the English idea of community and the Welsh are excluded and Scots are excluded and so on and so forth. Yet there are some great things Europeans had when they were among us, when they were ruling us, and one of them was education. The library in Antigua was a colonial institution and, had Antigua still been a colony when we had that earthquake, then the library would have been rebuilt and perhaps made better. Things like that are sad to admit, but we learned only the bad aspects. We have kept and refined all the bad aspects of colonial power.

In Zimbabwe they have on their books laws that were put in place by the whites to oppress the blacks. The blacks, when they got power, kept those laws on the books and now use them against each other. In all of these places they practice oppressive political ideas. There is always a ruling power who behaves like the colonial power. They treat the citizens in the worst colonial way, but the only difference is that the countries are independent. We have no one to rebel against. There isn't any dividing line. It's like people in our own family doing these terrible things to you. They look like you. They're not white. They're not from far away. Yet they are behaving in the same way the colonial powers did.

So I come from one kind of corruption, the moral corruption of Europe, and now I find myself in a new kind of corruption. My background is that I am a product of corruption.

AV: There is a litany of items in "Girl" (a story from *At the Bottom of the River*) about a mother telling her daughter about what to do and what not to do when it comes to being a nice young lady. Is this the way it was for you and other girls in Antigua?

JK: In a word, yes.

AV: Was that good or bad?

JK: I don't think it's the way I would tell my daughter, but as a mother I would tell her what I think would be best for her to be like. This mother in "Girl" was really just giving the girl an idea about the things she would need to be a self-possessed woman in the world.

AV: But you didn't take your mother's advice?

JK: No, because I had other ideas on how to be a self-possessed woman in the world. I didn't know that at the time. I only remember these things. What the mother in the story sees as aids to living in the world, the girl might see as extraordinary oppression, which is one of the things I came to see.

AV: Almost like she's Mother England.

JK: I was just going to say that. I've come to see that I've worked through the relationship of the mother and the girl to a relationship between Europe and the place that I'm from, which is to say a relationship between the powerful and the powerless. The girl is powerless, and the mother is powerful. The mother shows her how to be in the world, but at the back of her mind, she thinks she will never get it. She's deeply skeptical that this child could ever grow up to be a self-possessed woman and, in the end, she reveals her skepticism; yet even within the skepticism are, of course, dismissal and scorn. It's not unlike the relationship between the conqueror and the victim.

AV: What is the connection in the story "In the Night" between the *jablesse* (she-devil) and her night-soil father with the woman she wants to marry? Is the woman a jablesse?

JK: No. That story is really a portrait of night in Antigua. I don't remember it as being a story about a particular person. It's a portrait of a character within twenty-four hours.

AV: Why does the narrator skip from one sex to another in such stories as "In the Night" ("Now I am a girl, but one day I will marry a woman"), and "Wingless" ("I myself have humped girls under my mother's house")?

JK: In a way I can't answer that because I wouldn't want to explain it very much. I think when I was writing those stories, I really wanted to disregard certain boundaries, certain conventions. These were stories written in my youth. (I think of the time before I had children as my youth.) These are stories in which I had endless amounts of time to consider all sorts of things and endless amounts of silence and space and distance. I could play with forms and identities and do things then that I can't do now because I don't have the time to plumb that kind of depth. They were attempts to discard conventions, my own conventions, and conventions that exist within writing. I still try to forget everything that I've read and just write. That was what that was about, and it really doesn't bear close interpretation from me. The reader would have to do that.

AV: You depict the most ordinary events. In the book *At the Bottom of the River*, are you trying to show that the most ordinary events can become extraordinary?

JK: Oh, yes! I think there is no such thing as an ordinary event. I believe everything is of the deepest significance. If you could isolate an event, it would lead to profound things. For example, if you would trace the ancestry of everybody who has crossed this room you wouldn't be able to do anything else.

AV: A number of your stories such as "What I Have Been Doing Lately," "Blackness," "My Mother," and *Annie John* (where the girl is sick and hallucinates over some pictures she is trying to clean) incorporate a type of magical realism. Are these phantasmagoric scenes derived from Latin American writers such as Borges or García Márquez, or even possibly Lewis Carroll?

JK: If it went back to anyone, it would be Lewis Carroll. Borges is the kind of writer when I read I'm just absolutely in heaven. I wouldn't say the same thing is true of García Márquez. I like reading him, but I don't feel it's the most wonderful thing like when I read Borges. The truth is, I come from a place that's very unreal. It's the reason for its political malaise, because it will not just look at the thing in front of it and act on it. The place I come from goes off into fantasy all the time, so that every event is continually a spectacle and something you mull over, but not with any intention of changing it. It is just an entertainment. It's just some terrific thing you told yourself that happened today. I wouldn't say that I was influenced by these other writers you mentioned, because for me, it's only an accident. It's really the place I grew up in. I'm not really a very imaginative writer, but the reality of my background is fantastic.

AV: You were born in in 1949 as Elaine Potter Richardson, but in 1973 you adopted the pseudonym "Jamaica Kincaid." Was this name bestowed on you by George Trow of the *New Yorker*, and how was it chosen? You also stated that changing your name was a way of disguising yourself so you wouldn't have to be "the same person who had all these weights."

JK: No, by the time I met George Trow I had already changed my name. I wasn't that young. It's really more of the second question. I wanted to write. No one I knew had ever written. I thought serious writing was something people no longer did. By the time I discovered it was still being done, I didn't know how I could do it as the person who left home. I thought, and I think I would have been correct, I would have been judged pretentious. I would have been judged as someone stepping out of the things that had been established for me. I would have been laughed at. I didn't want anyone who knew me to know I was writing. I thought quite possibly my writing would be bad. The choosing of the name is something that is so private—because it also involved a lot of foolishness—that I can't even begin to tell you. It would involve remembering worlds of things that I remember quite well, but I'm no longer sure how to interpret what I was doing. I remember what I was doing, but I don't quite understand why I was doing it. So I'd rather not quite figure that out.

AV: If you don't want to answer the question directly, that's fine, but why "Jamaica" instead of "Antigua"?

JK: You see, you're trying to give it a logic that it did not have at the time. I was playing around with identities. When you're young you don't know how old you'll get to be and you feel every moment is *the* moment. In my case, there were many possibilities, and that is the one I settled on. I had no idea anyone would one day be asking me how it all came to be, or I would have made better sense of it at the time. I wanted to write, and I didn't know how. I thought if I changed my name and I wrote and it was very bad, then no one would know. I fully expected it to be bad, by the way, and to never be published, or heard from again. I thought they'd never get to laugh at it because they wouldn't know it was me. So I changed my name. It was done one of those nights when you're sitting up late with friends who were trying out identities. If you saw photographs of me then, you would see how easy it was to do that. It was around this time I had started to write. When I started to get published no one ever called me Elaine. I'd always been unhappy with my name. You can almost say I became a writer just so I could change my name.

AV: Too English?

JK: No, the name Elaine always seemed stupid. (I hope there are not many Elaines out there.) At the time I changed it, I didn't know there were African names, although I don't think I could have done that because at this time I have as much connection to Africa as you do. The connection I have to Africa is the color of my skin, and that doesn't seem enough to have changed it to an African name. My new name unconsciously had the significance I wanted it to have, since that is the area of the world I'm from. "Jamaica" is an English corruption of what Columbus called "Xaymaca." Kincaid just seemed to go together with Jamaica, but there were many combinations of names that could have been chosen one night when my friends and I were sitting around.

AV: You also stated that changing your name was a way of disguising yourself so that you wouldn't have to be "the same person who had all these weights."

JK: I could never lose the Elaine Potter Richardson identity, but I wanted to say things about the people in Antigua. I have met people, and they say I just can't talk about my family or friends in a bad way. This was a way to talk about things without people knowing it was me. I wanted to be able to be free of certain things. I wanted to speak truthfully about what I knew about myself without being myself. I supposed I had no idea it would have significance for anyone else.

AV: You left Antigua in 1966 when you were seventeen and moved to Westchester, New York. Why did you move, and was the decision yours alone?

JK: No, I left because of economic reasons. We thought I'd be able to help my family by going away, to work and perhaps get an education. I come from a very poor family who worked very hard. At the time, my father was getting older and couldn't work as much as he used to. Actually, my education was cut short because I was supposed to go and help my family. I didn't go on to study at the university. I got to a certain level at school and was taken out so that I could come to America to work and help my family.

AV: So you didn't want to go to New York?

JK: No. I would have preferred to stay in school and gone on to university, but I was sent away. I was so depressed about what was happening to me. I wasn't going to be the person they thought I was going to be, which was one of these very uppity, ridiculous, university-educated women. Those type of women come back to Antigua and become schoolteachers, and they are very impressive, very important people in the community. I wasn't going to be like that. Instead, I was going to be this supporter of my family and I was so miserable. Everyone said I was really very bright. I didn't want to go, and I was very depressed, but it wasn't really my decision.

AV: It's lucky you didn't become a librarian, because you wouldn't have a job in Antigua.

JK: You're right—I wouldn't have a job. I probably would have gone to Canada. That's another thing that happens. All of these educated people in the West Indies can't find work there, so they go to Canada and the United States. In Trinidad, every Saturday there are people from American hospitals recruiting nurses. Trinidad and places like that are robbed of their best nurses because nurses get paid better here. In my case, I ended up going to Westchester because that was where I was going to be a nursemaid and go to school.

AV: *Annie John* appears to be an autobiographical novel. You have also stated (*New York Times Magazine*) that "lying is the beginning of fiction." Do you think fiction works best when reality is mixed with fiction?

JK: Well, I certainly can't make a fast rule about it and say that about everything. It seems to be that those things are true for me so far, and I don't know what I'll do in the future. How I've written so far is to exploit my personal experiences. I have no idea of writing as an objective exercise. I only write about myself and about the people connected to me or the people I'm connected to.

I, for instance, could not write a marvelous novel as far as I know. I could not write even a very bad novel about someone living in Houston, Texas. I would not know how. I can only write about the things I know. I happen to be that sort of writer. The process of fiction, for me, is using reality and then reinventing reality, which is the most successful way to do what I do.

The part about "lying is the beginning of fiction" was true. I used to be accused when I was a little girl of having a strong imagination, and that was why I was a liar. I lied all the time. It was a way, I thought, of protecting my privacy. They tried to beat it out of me, sometimes literally, by giving me a spanking—no, a beating! (There is great cruelty to children in the West Indies.) I was always mistrusted. The only thing I was accused of was that I had a good memory. I never forget anything that happened. I would hear people telling something that happened, and they would leave out, in my opinion, the crucial parts. Every part was crucial. If someone left something out, then I would tell what happened and they'd look at me in amazement. My memory was considered an act of treachery, and I was asked not to have such a good memory. Essentially, I would be told I should just forget certain things that happened. It was considered one of my greatest faults, but I'd remember everything and then I would invent things. For instance, if something happened, such as a little smoke coming out of a building and the fire truck came, then I would say, "Oh, it was the biggest fire you ever saw, and hundreds of fire trucks had to come." I was incapable of just describing something as it really happened. I would remember that it had happened, and I might exaggerate the details, but other people would forget it happened. So that is essentially what my fiction is. It really happened, but the details become exaggerated.

AV: Antigua appears to be paradise on the outside, but an evil lurks, embodied in the basket of green figs balanced on Annie's mother's head. The basket has a snake hidden within. Is this biblical or a Conradian evil or something else altogether?

JK: It would be biblical, although these things are very unconscious, or subconscious. I did not know how much until very recently, when I began to just read my writing out loud and eventually just collected the images of my writing. I began to realize how my writing and my use of images are based on my own understanding of the world as good and evil, as influenced by two books in the Bible: Genesis and Revelation. If that's all any writer has been influenced by, it would be enough. My understanding of the world is influenced very much by those two books, which were my favorite books to read from the Bible. I used to read the Bible as a child just for fun. I really loved reading it, especially Revelation, which I could not get enough of. I used to make myself afraid just by reading it. Do you know that part where it is the end of the world and they turn into rocks? I took it literally.

It became very real to me. I'm very influenced by the first book of the Old Testament and the last book of the New Testament. Everything in between is just sort of picturesque, but the beginning and end are the real thing. I did not know how much of an influence those biblical images had on my writing and understanding of the world until very recently.

It also turns out there are recurring images of Lucifer, whom I apparently identify with, from *Paradise Lost*, which I did not know. I did not know how much I was rooting for the Devil.

AV: Would you also apply Lucifer's comment from *Paradise Lost*, "Better to reign in Hell than serve in Heav'n," to Antigua's colonial situation?

JK: Yes. It is better to reign and to have self-possession in Hell than to be a servant in Heaven. You know how people would say, "Better red than dead"? I'm someone who would never say that. I always say, "It's better to be dead than to live like this. It's better to risk dying than to live as a slave." Always I say that.

AV: Is Annie John's love for Gwen supposed to be a substitution for her mother's lost love? Or are these lesbian tendencies?

JK: No, they weren't meant to be. I think I am always surprised that people interpret it so literally. The relationship between Gwen and Annie is really a practicing relationship. It's about how things work. It's like learning to walk. Always there is the sense they would go on to lead heterosexual lives. Whatever happened between them, homosexuality would not be a serious thing, because it is just practicing. The stories in *At the Bottom of the River* about the relationships between women are not meant, at least in my mind, to be homosexual. They were meant not to observe the convention of men and women, because I was trying to do away with certain conventions. I don't know if it comes up any place else, but Americans rather like to have things very much defined or to have things very much be what they say they are. The question of sexuality in these stories is not meant to be dwelt on because that is not the main thrust of them.

AV: There is a scene in *Annie John* where the narrator sees her reflection in a window, yet doesn't recognize herself because she "had got so strange." Do you see yourself, both as a person and a writer, still changing, or have the changes become less noticeable with age?

JK: By nature, I'm the sort of person who is never the same. Sometimes it's disturbing to me, because I find myself in a moment I like very much and wish I could stay that way, but I don't. I change very much. I'm still changing, but I don't always like it because it is not always convenient.

AV: Annie John's request to make a new trunk indicates she wants to start her own life, while the recovery from her illness as the long rain stops indicates she has moved from adolescence to womanhood. Is this correct?

JK: I think it is, but again, at the time I was writing it, I wasn't conscious of these things as you point them out to me. If I were an objective reader, I'd be able to see it. I was writing these stories, and I was far less conscious of things than I am now. The sickness in the long rain actually happened when I was seven years old, with whooping cough, and I would get delirious. It's actually to that moment that I trace my fear of rodents. I was lying in my bed when I looked up, and around the edges of the ceiling that had this boarded mantel, I thought I saw hundreds of rats running around in a circle. I thought there were hundreds of them, but I think now there was only one. I was powerless to do anything. I put that incident into the teenage life of the girl and made it a period of transition. I exaggerated the details.

AV: In *A Small Place*, you criticize tourists who go to Antigua to "escape the reality of their lives," which implies tourists are an unthinking lot, and that tourists and their ancestors have profited from using Antigua. Isn't this a generalization that is both unfair and discriminatory?

JK: Not at all. If you think it's unfair and discriminatory try it the other way around. Imagine that your existence depended on people who are very different looking from you and whose difference seems to give them privileges that you cannot even imagine. Just imagine the situation in reverse. For example, in Vienna they depend mostly on tourism. You and the Viennese look alike, so that alienation just isn't there, but even if you're a tourist among people who look like you, they resent it. I can tell you there are differences in going to Vienna and going to Antigua. If you don't go to Vienna for fun, you can also go to experience all of the cultural benefits and gain a deeper understanding of the Western world. If you go to a place like Antigua, it's to have a rubbish-like experience. You want to forget who you are for a moment. You're not interested in these people. They have nothing of value you want to bring home. It's an escape, a moment to forget who you really are. If you think there isn't anything with it, then try living it, and you'll see how quickly you want to shoot every tourist you ever meet. It's deeply wrong.

AV: The Antigua you grew up in no longer exists, but it is the one you love. Still, you wrote a scathing diatribe against the English for trying to make Antigua English. Yet now the English are gone, and you hate Antigua even more. Why?

JK: The question isn't whether the current system doesn't work, so let's bring the old system back. The English were wrong when they were there, and it is wrong today. I think, dare I pat myself on the back, that it's very good I'm able to admit we've made a mess of things. I don't wish the British to come back. I wish the British to stay in Britain. I wish everyone would stay where they came from because when we go to other places—no matter if we say you go to extend your influence—you eventually exploit. Antigua is in terrible shape, and it should be changed into something better. It's not a question of degrees of morality, but simply just morality. Just because Antiguans behave like fools doesn't mean we should have other people who are also fools.

AV: You say that Antiguans who graduate from the Hotel Training School are nothing better than contemporary slaves who wait on tourists. Isn't this extending the metaphor a bit too far? After all, aren't they free to choose to work for a hotel and to have the right to earn income?

JK: Antigua used to have a teacher's training college of which we were all proud, but it seems it was a peculiar choice to change a teacher's college to a school for graduating hotel employees. First of all, have you ever heard of anything more ridiculous? I don't believe Italians or French go to training school to be waiters or even if there is such a thing as a training school, because it's something anyone can do. If you have to go to a training school, then there must be something desperately wrong. We're not talking about a scientist or a brain surgeon. We are talking about putting a pineapple on a table. If you need to go to school to learn how to do this, then what are we really talking about?

I can't see there is a sense of freedom because that seems to be the wrong word. It implies you are free to be a hotel waiter or to starve. I know how to set a table. I did that in Brownie meetings. These are things everyone knows how to do. If you don't know how to bend and kiss behinds, do you mean you are going to school for that?

I don't mean to take lightly the institution of slavery, but it seems to me the mentality of these small islands is very much related to slavery. These island rulers are pretentious, since they pretend their little islands are nations. Back home they talk about the nation of Antigua, but it's only a stupid little island. If they'd only do something ordinary and logical such as educating their citizens that would be fine, but you don't want them to pretend to be something they are not. The fact is, they don't even do the things that a small village in the US would try to do.

AV: You live in America, you are married to an American, and you are published by an American publisher; yet you continue to use English spellings (e.g., "colour" instead of the Americanized "color"). Why?

JK: I've lived in America longer than I've lived in Antigua. I lived in Antigua sixteen years, and I'm now forty-two. From the time I was seventeen to now, it has been twenty-five years I've lived in America.

When I talk about going home, my husband says, "What home are you talking about?" I think of Antigua as my home. I'm not an American citizen. I haven't become an American because I don't think America needs another writer. Antigua needs a writer more than it needs an American citizen. I have no intention of becoming an American citizen. My children are American, and they can say the Pledge of Allegiance just like my husband can, but they don't have to say it because they're Americans. No American has to say it.

AV: What has been Antigua's response to your book *A Small Place*? I can't imagine the government looks upon you favorably.

JK: I think about that all the time. I imagine that I'd be shot. I haven't been back since the book was published. I wanted to go this year, but I didn't want to be separated from my children. I booked a flight the day the war in Iraq started; yet I didn't know how it would turn out, and I decided not to go. Now I don't have the time. God knows if they would shoot me, but it's a criminal place. I wouldn't be surprised if they had henchmen who would do it, because politics in the West Indies is very tribal. People take their colors very seriously. They divide themselves into people who wear red and who wear blue.

My mother is a blue. I am nothing. When I was growing up, we were reds. Then my mother joined the party that broke away, and they are blue. She takes it so seriously: "No, I could never wear that." Even though she was visiting me in the United States, she brought her loyalties with her. This makes you think there isn't any hope for people in Antigua who think like this.

AV: The character Lucy appears to be similar to Annie John, except she is a few years older. Did you consider keeping the name "Annie John" for this character?

JK: I didn't consider it a continuation because I would never write like that. It's a continuation only in the sense it's about my life, which is the same life I'm writing about, but they weren't meant to be the same person at all. In any case, a key to Lucy is the name Lucifer, and so she couldn't be called Annie at all. It's a very shallow—though understandable—connection to make, because the reader isn't me observing what I'm doing. I'm not interested in making the thing whole. I'm interested in parts of things. When Annie left her mother, that was it. We're not going to hear from Annie again. We're not going to hear from Lucy again. You might very well hear about a woman's life in the metropolitan area of the world, whether it's London, New York, Toronto, or wherever. You might very well hear about how this life turned out, but to say it's a continuation of Lucy would be a mistake.

Very, very crucial to understanding Lucy is her name. I think most people in America have such a different background than I do. People in America, especially in universities, are so obsessed with race that they miss the crucial thing about Lucy. The great influences on that young woman's life are Genesis and Revelation, and strangely enough, *Jane Eyre.* I think all sorts of things escape American readers.

I suppose my writing is as mysterious to an American reader as someone like Zora Neal Hurston is to me. She's a woman who wrote in the twenties, part of the Harlem Renaissance, who had a very brilliant career and then died a maid in poverty. It's one of those stories which either you think is an American story or you think it is a racial story, but those are things that to really understand what I'm trying to do you'd have to know. Lucy is a very moralistic person, and she's very judgmental, because her view of the world is very much shaped by a nineteenth-century view.

AV: The scene in which Lucy tells her dream to Lewis and Mariah is uncomfortable, because the couple looks at the dream from a Freudian and sexual viewpoint, whereas Lucy interprets it as meaning she has accepted them into her life. Did you have something like this happen to you in real life?

JK: Well, that I will not say. The scene really explains itself because the people had become real to her. If you show up in someone's dream, it means they are finally real to you. It's a cultural gap. I tried to show that Lucy did not understand it; she only reports what happened in her dream. Of course, I understand it, but Lucy doesn't and isn't quite clear about it. Lucy doesn't know who Dr. Freud is, and it's said with a certain simplicity. I think it's the sort of thing I wouldn't have been able to write five years ago. I wouldn't have been able to separate the knowledge I have of Freud from the knowledge I did not have.

AV: There is a contrast between the island girl, Sylvie, who has the teeth bite mark on her cheek, and Mariah, who "looked blessed, no blemish or mark of any kind on her cheek or anywhere else." Lucy does not identify with pleasant-smelling Mariah; she prefers to have a powerful odor. Why is Lucy, as well as Annie John, so iconoclastic? She seems to rebel against most things that are good, yet she has no reason to act this way.

JK: I think it's that "reign in Hell, serve in Heaven" problem again. A person like Sylvie seems more self-possessed to her. Even in her embryonic consciousness-raising, she knows that it's better from a feeling of self-possession to be Sylvie rather than Mariah, spiritually speaking. There's something sad about Mariah and, ultimately, defeated. She's the victim among the conquerors, whereas Sylvie is the victor among the defeated.

Later on, Lucy develops sympathy and grows to love Mariah. Lucy is the sort of person who, no matter what happens to her, would never identify with the victors. Lucy is naïve, but she is not stupid.

Mariah is a lovely person. She didn't think the world would turn on her. What undoes Mariah is trusting in human nature, but this is not possible for Lucy, who trusts and mistrusts at once. It's not the sort of thing Mariah would understand, because she thinks love is all. Lucy thinks love is fine, but she doesn't look upon love as an absolute reality.

AV: Mariah shows Lucy the daffodils in the garden, but Lucy wants to kill the flowers. Why do so many of your characters have such negative, conflicting feelings?

JK: Let me answer that in a roundabout sort of way. My husband and I went to Paris last September on a boat. We sailed on the *QEII*, and after we arrived in Southhampton we spent a couple of days in

London. Every time I go to England, I almost have a nervous breakdown. I have such conflicting feelings of England. I love it, and I hate it. It's not possible for me to be a tourist. I realize I'm a visitor, but when I go to England, what happens is that I also confront my past.

AV: It's ironic the English were waiting on you.

JK: Yes, that's true, although there weren't many English waiting on me. They were Pakistani, Irish, and Africans, but not many English were waiting on me. We stayed in London and took a train to Dover, where we were going to catch a ferry. We were getting to Dover, and I couldn't believe what my eyes were seeing: the White Cliffs of Dover! I had yet another nervous breakdown that was quite like Lucy and those daffodils. I had heard so much about those white cliffs. I used to sing a hymn in church that was about longing to see the White Cliffs of Dover over and over again. Things like that permeate my memory, but these things have absolutely no value to me. I hardly know the names of any flowers growing in the West Indies, except the hibiscus, but I know the names of just about all the flowers in England, and I also can identify them. There is something very wrong here when I know the name of each flowering bush growing in England, but not in Antigua. I know the White Cliffs of Dover, and I've yearned for them. I could have lived a millennium without ever seeing them. There is something wrong there, just as it would have been false for a person like Lucy to love those daffodils. Daffodils do not grow in tropical climates. I know a poem about daffodils, but I did not know a poem about hibiscus.

AV: Was there resentment after seeing the White Cliffs of Dover?

JK: Yes, of course there is resentment.

AV: But aren't the White Cliffs really amazing?

JK: They *are* amazing. They really are amazing.

AV: Lucy identifies with the French painter Gauguin, who found his homeland to be a prison and wanted something different. The two are much alike, even though Gauguin escaped to the islands while Lucy left the islands. Do you feel much in common with Gauguin, whose painting *Poemes Barbares* is the cover picture for *Lucy*?

JK: I hesitate to say I identify with this man. I must say, as I was writing parts of *Lucy*, I was reading one of his journals called *The Intimate Journals of Paul Gauguin*. I found it a great comfort because he was so unrelenting of himself. He was very selfish and very determined; yet there are two things that struck me in that book. The first thing that struck me is his account of his friendship with van Gogh, which is the most hilarious yet cruel thing I've ever read. I never have laughed so much in jest. He describes van Gogh cutting off his ear, and you are just aghast because it's all very astonishing. The second thing was when he asked Strindberg to write an introduction to one of his shows. Strindberg wrote back a very long letter saying why he could not do it because he disliked Gauguin's work. So Gauguin used the letter as the introduction, even though the letter stated what was bad about his paintings. Gauguin wasn't afraid to use someone's negative view of his work. He wore it as a badge. I rather admire that.

I think the criticism I most value comes from people who do not like my writing. There's almost nothing that makes you feel more superior than the people who don't like you.

AV: The narrators or main characters of your fiction seem to have a cursory or dispassionate regard for sex (such as in the chapter titled "The Tongue" in *Lucy*). What was your viewpoint of sex as a young woman, and how has it changed as you've grown older?

JK: Good heavens, I don't think I could answer the first part of the question, although I must say Lucy rather enjoys it. What Lucy doesn't want is to be possessed again. She has just escaped a certain possession from her mother, and she doesn't want to be possessed again. I think at the end of the book she wishes she could be possessed and loved, but she can't at this point in her life. I suppose what she is saying is that she wishes time would pass quickly to allow herself to be consumed.

AV: Your writing style in *Lucy* is somewhat unusual in that you often start a passage, but before it is fully developed, you digress to a previous experience. For example, there is the party at Paul's where Peggy disapproves of Paul, but then you digress to the story of Myrna and Mr. Thomas on the island.

JK: It's not anything deliberate, but last night after my reading someone said they really admired the way I had done that scene. It sort of leads you to explain how something was written, but I've come to understand there is no such thing in writing as a technique. Quite often you invent what you're doing while you're doing it, and it would be quite wrong to apply that style to all my writing. I was not aware of any special thing when I did that. I did that in *Lucy*, but I have no intention of using it again. If it were to turn up again, it would be because I felt that was what was needed.

AV: With each book, your characters gain both insight and maturity with age, culminating with the ability to possibly love. Will your next book develop along these same lines, or do you plan to take off in a different direction?

JK: I really cannot say. For me, writing is a revelation. If I knew what it would be, then it would be of no interest for me to do it. When I sit down to write, I will reveal to myself what I already know. I already know all of this. I know how it works, but I haven't quite said it yet. The minute that I'm conscious of it, then it's of no interest. When I sit down to write it, it will become conscious to me. I will know it, and then I will move on. I don't know what will happen. I don't know how it will work.

AV: What are your thoughts about interviews? In what ways are they good or bad? Do interviews help you understand yourself and your writing by openly discussing your work?

JK: I forget interviews once they are done. The two or three times I've been interviewed, I have read what I've said when I edit it, but I'm shocked that I've said these things. I find that some of my responses sound very intelligent, or they may sound very stupid. I can't believe it's me. I just simply forget it. I never listen to myself on the radio. I've been on television once, but I would never watch myself! Doing this interview is like having a conversation, but later I will just forget it. It's of no help, and it's of no hindrance.

AV: In the past twenty years, your life has changed dramatically. Do you have a different perspective of the world now than you had back when you were an au pair?

JK: Yes, and it's not good. No, it's worse than I thought. The world is not a better place than when I was a servant. It's true if I'd gone to England, I would have remained a servant, and it was only by sheer chance that I came to America. I'm really glad I did come to America, which is a place that has allowed me to denounce it. I think it's to America's credit that it can spawn someone like me. I like living in America because it gives me the language and the idea to rearrange the world in what I'd think would be a just equation. I can't say that my perspective has changed. I think by now, I'm supposed to be a Republican. I'm supposed to be someone who says, "Yes, the system works." But actually, I'm someone who says, "I'm not sure that it works." I suppose if my perspective has changed it would be that I'm now a politically conscious person. To America's credit, I've become—at least verbally—a politically conscious person. I suspect that if I wasn't writing, being someone who has become politically conscious, then I would be throwing bombs. If I didn't have the pen, I would certainly be someone who would take up the sword.

Valeria Luiselli. Courtesy of Leonardo Cendamo.

The Social Fabric: An Interview with Valeria Luiselli

Valeria Luiselli was born in Mexico City, but spent many of her younger years in various countries as she traveled with her father, who was a diplomat and businessman. After earning a bachelor's degree in philosophy from the National Autonomous University of Mexico, she moved to New York City, where she studied dance, worked as a librettist for the New York City Ballet, and received her PhD in comparative literature at Columbia University.

Luiselli's first four books were written in Spanish, although she now writes in English. Her works of fiction and nonfiction include *Sidewalks, Faces in the Crowd, The Story of My Teeth,* and *Tell Me How It Ends: An Essay in 40 Questions,* all of which have earned critical accolades and awards. Her latest book, *Lost Children Archive,* a novel that brings the immigration crisis to heartbreaking life, was published this year to great acclaim and cemented her reputation as an essential writer of the twenty-first century. *Lost Children Archive* won the Rathbones Folio Prize and was longlisted for the Booker Prize and the Women's Prize for Fiction.

The following interview was conducted on February 26, 2019, at the Four Seasons Hotel in downtown Houston before her speaking engagement that evening for the Inprint Houston Reading Series. The digital taping of the interview was conducted in the farthest table of the breakfast/bar area to avoid noise of the hotel patrons, but even then there was Muzak as well as construction outside the window from where we sat. Even so, the interview went very well, and my impression of Luiselli was noticeably elevated due to her remarkable responses. I walked away very impressed.

Allan Vorda: You were born in Mexico City, but left Mexico at the age of two when your father moved to Wisconsin to complete his doctorate and became a diplomat. From there you lived in a number of countries. What effect did this have on you at such a young age, to be exposed to so many different cultures?

Valeria Luiselli: We left Mexico to move to Wisconsin, but we returned to Mexico after a few months. Then, shortly after the 1985 earthquake in Mexico, the three of us moved to Costa Rica. My father worked for an NGO there. We then moved to South Korea, where my father worked as a diplomat. He was later posted to South Africa, and I went with him. When my father and I moved to South Africa, my mother went to Chiapas. Later on I moved to India on my own, where I finished high school, in a boarding school.

It was in my early childhood in which linguistic dissonance became one of my main emotional concerns and a marker of my identity. I left Spanish as a language when I was five years old when we had moved to

South Korea. The language spoken in the streets was utterly foreign, and the language spoken in school—English—was also foreign. The process of being silenced, of non-communication, was a difficult one, but I also attribute my decision to become a writer to those childhood months. I learned to inhabit a solitary, luminal, and observant space. I learned how to be an observer, and to always remain situated between cultures and spaces, a little phantasmagorical, if you wish. I've always carried a feeling of being there and not being entirely there. I sometimes feel, having been eternally displaced, that the place I occupy is always an in-between. I learned how to read and write English when I was in South Korea. English became the language of my instruction, the language of my reading and writing, and the language in which I thought and expressed myself most coherently. Spanish was reduced, for many years, to a vacuum-packed language, a language spoken only at home.

When I moved to Mexico for a short while, as a teenager, between South Africa and India, I felt utterly foreign in my city and in my language. This is when I started to take a different interest in my writing. I started writing in Spanish and trying my mother tongue for the first time. When I wrote my first book, *Sidewalks,* it was set in Mexico City, and I decided to write it in Spanish. It was a decision to write myself into a language and culture and city that had never quite been my own. Linguistic identity, though, is a problem that I have not solved. My last two books were written in English, and I now write in English more than Spanish. I often wonder what long-term effects this new distancing from my mother tongue is going to have, but I hope all of it comes together in a way that is fertile for my writing. Maybe it's not a problem at all, and simply the precondition of my work as a writer.

AV: When you were in South Africa you met Nelson Mandela on two occasions. What do you remember about these encounters?

VL: I was a child when I met him, so I remember Mandela as a formidable storyteller. The first time I met him, I was part of a delegation of foreign children that had just arrived in South Africa, and we were invited to his home to meet him. Mandela had us sit down in his living room while he sat in his armchair, and he began telling us stories of his imprisonment. I remember a story where Mandela was in jail talking to a cockroach in order not to lose his sanity. I remember the impact the image made in my mind. I still think about that story: about the place of storytelling in circumstances of absolute isolation, as well as about language and communication in spaces of incarceration. I also remember Mandela's deep, deep gray eyes, and him asking me, I think the second time I saw him, what I wanted to do as an adult. I told him I wanted to be a prose writer, and he said, "Well, then you need to read a lot."

AV: During this time of travel your mother left the family to join the Zapatista movement in Mexico. I have to say I admire her decision to do what was important in her life. How did this tumultuous decision affect your family? Were you concerned for her safety, and did your parents ever reunite?

VL: She worked in a women's collective, a nonprofit that supported the Zapatistas, particularly Zapatista women and their children. I admire her decision now, but I think I *grew* to admire it. When I was ten years old, it was difficult to understand why she would choose politics over family, or her commitment to a community and a social transformation in southern Mexico over her kids and our own process as a family. It took me years to forgive and understand her decision. Now as an adult, I understand and I admire it. I think she has been an important influence in my life, in terms of how to remain free from the constraints of social expectations, remain connected to a community with whom you work, and knowing how to integrate that work into your life. She comes from a family of women who were very active in indigenous communities in Mexico. I also feel part of that lineage of women who have been strong, committed, and free.

AV: Does your mother speak Mixteco, as seen in the movie *Roma*—and did you like the movie *Roma*?

VL: *Roma*? I think it is a masterpiece. But no, my mom doesn't speak

Mixteco, which is a language mostly spoken in Oaxaca. My maternal family was originally from Pachuca, and my mother's grandmother spoke Otomi (Ñañú). Unfortunately, as happens in Mexico so often, Spanish erased Ñañú in my maternal family line. Part of assimilating to an urban middle class meant erasing your indigenous background as much as possible. There are still sixty-eight indigenous languages in Mexico—many of them in danger of disappearing forever.

AV: When you were nineteen you enrolled at the National Autonomous University of Mexico, where you received a bachelor's degree in philosophy. What philosophers influenced you, and did philosophy give you a different perspective when you started writing?

VL: I think philosophy gave me a different approach to reading. You can't skim philosophical texts. You have to read the texts over and over until it sinks in, whether it's a paragraph or a single sentence. It's like reading poetry. It's a different way of reading, and I'm happy I chose that path. I became a reader thanks to my professors and the texts I was exposed to in my late teens and early twenties. To be honest, I was more than influenced by philosophy—I was obsessed. I thought that anything that was not philosophy was trivial. I liked everything, from the pre-Socratic aphorisms that would make me sit down and think for a long time, to philosophers that wrote about the contemporary world, like Hannah Arendt and Walter Benjamin, to the more dry, analytic philosophers, like W. V. O. Quine or Gottlob Frege. I read Hume with a lot of interest, as well as Gadamer. I tried to like Heidegger, but there was a baroque-ness in the language to which I never quite connected. (Perhaps it was the way he was translated into Spanish.) Wittgenstein was one of the philosophers that I read the most. At the time we were reading Wittgenstein, we also had very rigorous classes in logic and set theory, the more mathematical side of philosophy. I preferred the sparseness of Wittgenstein. Unfortunately, we read very few women. I read Maria Zambrano, a Spanish philosopher who arrived in Mexico as an exile. She was the only Hispanic woman that I was reading as a philosopher. Rarely did teachers move away from the canon.

AV: Would you consider yourself religious or nonreligious?

VL: Unfortunately, I'm not religious at all. I think I have moments in my life where I can connect to spirituality. For instance, reading Simone Weil—it's hard for me to read her work because my brain has to perform a constant operation: I need to replace the words "god" with "spirit" or "reason" when I read her sentences, if I want to embrace her very lucid thoughts. Nevertheless, thanks to a writer like Weil, I think I have had moments of a deeper connection to a sense of spirituality. Weil also has one of the most lucid essays on pain.

AV: Your previous book, *Tell Me How It Ends: An Essay in 40 Questions* (Coffee House Press, 2017), can be seen as a prelude for *Lost Children Archive.* What was the inspiration for *Tell Me How It Ends*?

VL: It's interesting that *Tell Me How It Ends* will always be read as a prelude to *Lost Children Archive*. It came out several years before *Lost Children Archive,* and it may serve as an explanatory backdrop of the political crisis that is unfolding within the pages of *Lost Children Archive*. But I started writing *Lost Children Archive* first in the summer of 2014, during a road trip with my family, long before *Tell Me How It Ends*. When we returned to New York, I became more deeply involved with the crisis within the space of the immigration court in New York. I started screening and translating in court for children who had just been put on the priority docket. They had just been bumped up in priority for cases being addressed, which means they had less time to seek lawyers. They used to have one year, but now they only had twenty-one days to find a lawyer. Many volunteers had to help screen and find lawyers for the kids so they wouldn't get deported.

I became involved with this kind of work while I was writing the novel, and what happened is I started using the novel as a space in which to pour all my angst and fury and political frustration and emotional sense of stalemate. But I slowly started to realize I wasn't doing justice to the novel by trying to turn it into that kind of vehicle for my politics, and I wasn't doing justice to the subject matter itself, either, because I was trying to thread it into this fictional narrative. So

I stopped writing the novel. Then, John Freeman, whom I'd worked with as an editor in different projects, suggested I write a nonfiction piece on what I was witnessing in court. I kept saying no, I can't, because I don't understand immigration law well enough, I'm too caught up, I can't write this, etc. And as good editors do, he insisted and insisted, until I gave in. I'm now very thankful that he encouraged me to write that essay. I wrote the first version of *Tell Me How It Ends* as a short essay, and he published it in *Freeman's Journal*. Once I had done that, I was able to go back to the novel and not feel the responsibility of directly covering the crisis. I could focus on other issues and allow the novel to breathe with fictional lungs, so to speak.

AV: Some of the statistics you mention are shattering: 80 percent of migrant women and girls are raped, and 120,000 migrants since 2006 have disappeared. In which countries do the rapes take place? Of the missing 120,000 what do you think happened to them?

VL: Most of this takes place in Mexico, which is shattering and fills me with shame as a Mexican. Central American kids come out of horrific circumstances only to come into deeper horror in Mexico. They eventually make it into the United States, if they make it all the way, where there is still more horror awaiting them.

The train routes known as La Bestia became one of the most common modes of transportation for migrants moving across Mexico. Along the routes of La Bestia, drug lords, gang members, policemen, and military started abusing these migrants. The rapes and disappearances have a lot to do with the collusion between these different forces, with no accountability. People can disappear, and then reappear in a mass grave, and there is no one that is going to be held accountable. The trend in Mexico and the US has been toward criminalization and incarceration. The governments either violate a person's right to due process or they are incarcerated while they await due process—if it's going to happen at all. The difference in the US is that incarceration is part of the industrial prison complex, and it's profitable.

AV: In the *Columbia Magazine* (Winter 2018) you said, "I'm not interested in intertextuality as an outward, performative gesture, but as a method or procedure of composition." Can you elucidate on this and how it applies to *Lost Children Archive*?

VL: There are these concepts that come up again and again, mostly in interviews, when I talk about my writing. I'm often asked about intertextuality and autofiction and meta-literariness. I think my qualms with those labels are that they often serve as a dike to an otherwise potentially interesting flow of conversation. It's like they place a label and there is just no more to say about a book. Maybe a text is intertextual but how so? How does it incorporate other references and place different books within a constellation to create interesting tensions? Often, labels like those end a conversation rather than begin it.

Intertextuality, for me, is just the process by which I work. I write with books all around me. Often a sentence or image I'm working on might remind me of something I read ten years ago. So I go back to that book and try to unearth it, and it makes me think of something else, so I go to another book, and so on and so forth. All these things speak back into the book I'm writing. I'm interested in relationships, method, and how the method imprints itself in the final result. I'm interested in shortening the distance between the method and the result, and by this I mean allowing the method to leave fingerprints of itself in the final result. In my case, books are in conversation while I'm writing.

AV: *Lost Children Archive* tells the story of a family driving from New York City to Arizona to do the husband's sound recording project while the wife tries to find two missing Mexican migrant girls. Early on the daughter is swimming in a pool and the worried mother states, "a friend of mine calls this 'the rescue distance.'" Your reference to Samanta Schweblin's novel *Fever Dream* (originally called *Rescue Distance* in Spanish) is a good analogy. There is also a video of both of you being interviewed about literature and the importance of Juan Rulfo's *Pedro Paramo*. How much of an impact have such writers had on you?

VL: Rulfo is a writer that Schweblin and I have surely discussed as a major influence. *Pedro Paramo* is this tiny but monumental novel in the Spanish-speaking tradition that really broke with the linear conception of time and space, which is pervasive in most novels. Rulfo did something that was completely different, in a way that gave all his readers and following generations a sense of freedom. Yet to say one is influenced by *Pedro Paramo* is like being a musician who says he or she is influenced by Bach.

AV: What about Borges and Cortázar?

VL: They were very influential to my generation. That was our canon—Borges, Cortázar, García Márquez, Rulfo. . . . Most of us came of age reading very few women writers. We had to go out and actively find them. I would say the current Latin American generation of writers is primarily a female generation. While there are some great male writers, the ones who I admire, seek out, and read the most are women.

AV: "All I see in hindsight is the chaos of history repeated, over and over, reenacted, reinterpreted, the world, its fucked-up heart palpitating underneath us, failing, messing up again and again as it winds its way around a sun. And in the middle of it all, tribes, families, people, all beautiful things falling apart, debris, dust, erasure." This negative view of the world propels the mother to action: "I am not sure how I will do it, but the story I need to tell is the one of the children, who are missing, those whose voices can no longer be heard because they are, possibly forever, lost." Did you have an epiphany like this to write *Lost Children Archive*?

VL: Damn, I was in a dark place. I don't think one could feel otherwise in the context of what I was seeing. What we are seeing, all around us. Pockets of fascism and extreme right-wing politics sprouting across the globe, along with a growing intolerance to different points of view, even within the so-called left. And then surveillance, be it the NSA or the companies that rule our lives. And also, of course, the current global exodus of people in search for conditions that make life livable. Not since the end of World War II has there been a global exodus like the one in these past few years. And the response of countries to which people migrate is usually inhumane, even brutal. The USA, in particular: mass incarceration of asylum-seekers is now the normal procedure here.

In any case, I wrote this novel while being very angry and disappointed. I was thinking about ways of documenting and of telling stories that might restore in us a more compassionate, lucid, and reflective understanding of our way of being in the world. We've become voracious agents of mass consumption, entertainment, Netflix series, and health products. But we're losing touch with our fundamental human values. We are losing touch with a sense of community, and mutual responsibilities. I know it sounds a little naïve, but I really do think we need to slow down, and detach from some of these things that are sold to us as vehicles to happiness, but which do not really create any lasting, deeper bonds between us. What I do think creates more lasting and deeper bonds is sharing stories, communicating, talking to each other, listening, and understanding. And I do think literature has played and will continue to play a crucial role in keeping the social fabric together.

AV: There is an emotional scene in which the mother sees migrant children in New Mexico being put on a plane to fly back to their home country. Did you see something similar to this?

VL: No, I've never witnessed a deportation. I've seen people at airports in custody of border patrol or ICE; I've been in detention centers and in border-crossing points along the existing portions of the southern wall, but I've never seen a deportation like the one I described in the novel. I read about a deportation while I was driving through New Mexico, and it created an impact on me, but I didn't witness it. I think it probably happens often in my work that people read it as a memoir, or a blurring of the boundaries between fiction and nonfiction. I guess I am writing documentary fiction—fiction that comes from documenting, but is nonetheless fiction.

AV: When you start the "Deportations" chapter, you switch narrators from the mother to the son. Why did you do this, and was it difficult to write from a ten-year-old boy's perspective?

VL: It was difficult to write from a ten-year-old boy's perspective, but it was also a very liberating space. I don't write linearly. It's not like I wrote the woman's thread, then the boy's thread, and then the elegies. I wrote them all together. They all splintered from a common gravitational center and grew in different directions. Because it's a novel of echoes, there are echoes between different scenes and threads. I would often write a scene in one voice and then have an echo in another voice. The boy's voice, in that procedure, felt like a playground, kind of a sad playground at times. It would always get at me, but it was also freeing to have that rhythm to go back to from time to time.

AV: "Echo Canyon" covers about twenty pages in a Joycean stream-of-consciousness, even using Joyce's repetition of the word "yes" just like at the end of *Ulysses.* The chapter's climax is where the supposedly "real" boy and girl meet with the fictional *Elegy* children. It's like a parallel universe where reality meets unreality. Can you extrapolate a bit about what you are trying to achieve with this interesting literary concept?

VL: That was the hardest part of the novel to write, as you can imagine, because it required a difficult, delicate architecture. Not only is it a run-on sentence, but it changes narrators every time one of the narrators focuses on the sky above the valley; yet the children are moving toward each other, unknowingly. Every time a narrator looks at the sky in which thunderclouds and birds are gathering, it switches to the other narrator. Joyce of course was in my mind, but I was also thinking of Juan Rulfo, Jerzy Andrzejewski, and László Krasznahorkai.

I don't want to offer an interpretation of that passage, though, because when authors do that they kind of drown the possibility of other minds coming in and offering other interesting interpretations. Let me just say that that part of the novel—that is spoken by the boy into the recording machine, and then passed to the sister as a version of their story—is a culmination of all the stories the boy has been listening to: his mother talking about the crisis on the border; his father talking about the Apache wars; the books they are reading, among which are the elegies of lost children. It all comes together in the same way that books become part of our own experience without us necessarily having lived those experiences. Literature is like a prosthetic memory. There is a Borges story called "Shakespeare's Memory," in which a scholar receives a ring which supposedly will give him access to Shakespeare's memory. It will implant Shakespeare's memory in his own mind. The story follows what happens in his mind as Shakespeare's memory enters and mixes with his own. Ricardo Piglia, a brilliant Argentinean writer and scholar, interprets that story as an allegory about literary memory, about how we incorporate experiences that we have read, and how they become part of the webbing of our own lived experience.

Annabel Lyon. Courtesy of Phillip Chin.

The Golden Mean: An Interview with Annabel Lyon

Annabel Lyon was born in Brampton, Ontario, and when she was a year old her family moved to Coquitlam, British Columbia. Lyon received a BA in philosophy from Simon Fraser University and an MFA in creative writing from the University of British Columbia. Her first published book was a collection of stories titled *Oxygen*, followed by *The Best Thing for You*, which was a collection of three novellas. *The Golden Mean*, her first novel, was her reimagining the relationship of Alexander the Great and his teacher Aristotle. Her novel was nominated for the three highest Canadian literature awards, which resulted in her winning the Rogers Writers' Trust Fiction Prize. A sequel,

The Sweet Girl, which explores the life of Aristotle's daughter Pythias, was published in 2012. *Consent* is her most recent novel.

This interview was conducted January 2010.

Allan Vorda: What was the inspiration for writing *The Golden Mean*? Please describe the process of writing this novel and what a typical day of writing was like.

Annabel Lyon: I was a philosophy major as an undergraduate, and my two main areas of interest were ethics and ancient philosophy. *Aristotle's Ethics* was a book I returned to again and again; I found a lot of solace, and a lot of relevance, in it. The questions he was asking 2,300 years ago: What's a good life? How do you find a mean between extremes? What's a good citizen? These were questions that continue to be relevant and engaging today.

The novel took seven and a half years to write. I had two children along the way, so my writing day changed from having a lot of free time to squeezing in two hundred words while they napped. So there really was no "typical" day!

AV: Your novel is set around various times of Aristotle's life, but primarily around 342 BCE. How valuable was Plutarch's *Life of Alexander* for your research? Did you use research from such books as Paul Cartledge's *Alexander the Great* or *The Landmark Arrian*? What other books would you recommend for someone wanting to learn about Greek history?

AL: I referred to Plutarch very often. Since Arrian and Quintus Curtius (the major ancient biographers of Alexander) wrote mostly about his adult life, and my book ends just as he's coming to the throne, I didn't use them so much. The two texts I returned to mostly for more general history were Hammond and Griffith's *A History of Macedonia,*

Vol. II and *The Cambridge Ancient History, Volume VI, The Fourth Century BC.* Those are big chunky texts; at the other end of the spectrum is a slim little book called *Aristotle: A Very Short Introduction* by Jonathan Barnes. Very quick and entertaining for someone new to the subject.

AV: Aristotle is thirty-seven when he is given the fifteen-year-old girl Pythias as a gift from his employer Hermias. It seems throughout the novel there is an uneasy contest of wills and thoughts between them. Even though Aristotle is twenty-two years older than Pythias, he cannot always read her thoughts, and it seems that he is not even sure if she loves him. It also seems that Pythias is sometimes cold to Aristotle. How did you develop these characters, and what was their relationship like from the research you have gathered?

AL: Nothing is known about their relationship, not even how old they were when they married, so I had to speculate based on what was typical in Greek and Macedonian society at that time. There are different accounts of Pythias's relationship to Hermias—daughter, niece, ward, concubine—so I imagined she hadn't been treated particularly well before her marriage to Aristotle, that maybe she'd even suffered some kind of sexual abuse, and that this was always going to be an unspoken issue between them. This isn't explicit in the novel, but it helped me imagine a married life that was both kind and uneasy.

AV: There is no direct mention of Alexander, although he appears unnamed a few times, until page forty-seven. Then Alexander's father, King Philip, requests Aristotle become his tutor. This is certainly an odd couple relationship, not only due to their age difference (when Alexander is sixteen, Aristotle is forty-two), but that Alexander is a brash, headstrong youth who is used to getting his own way. Yet Aristotle subtly manages, through his brilliant intellect, to keep Alexander in place. Was writing the development of these two disparate personalities difficult for you as a writer?

AL: Alexander was particularly problematic. I knew I wanted to contradict the prevailing stereotype of him as a sexy, hot-blooded military genius (e.g., Colin Farrell in Oliver Stone's movie), so initially I thought I could get away with making him a bratty, arrogant, spoiled teenager and leave it at that. But the deeper I got into the character and the more research I did, the more I realized he was probably a very damaged person from very, very early in life: his parents loathed each other and manipulated him to hurt each other, and he was trained as a child soldier (historians tell us he was leading troops by the time he was sixteen). He became much darker than I expected when I began writing about him; in the end I came to understand him as someone suffering from post-traumatic stress disorder. The ancient historians bear this out: Plutarch, for instance, describes him suffering alcoholism, depressions, headaches, blind rages, etc.—all the hallmarks of PTSD.

AV: To continue this ongoing theme of relationships, perhaps the most interesting is Aritstotle's benign treatment of the mentally and physically challenged Arrhidaeus. He is the half-brother of Alexander which rumor contends that Olympias (Alexander's mother) poisoned Arrhidaeus so her son would one day become king. Please discuss the relationship of Aristotle and Arrhidaeus and how he later makes Alexander recognize "the golden mean" of their relationships.

AL: Arrhidaeus was a real historical character, Alexander's elder half-brother, and I couldn't resist giving Aristotle both boys to tutor. I grew up with an elder brother with a mental disability and so I felt like I could portray Arrhidaeus realistically and sympathetically. I wanted to believe that Aristotle, with his encyclopedic understanding of the world and his generous intellect, would see that a person like Arrhidaeus wasn't damaged or a mistake; rather, he was a human being with possibilities, just as Alexander was.

AV: Aristotle comes under the tutelage of the character Illaeus, who is homosexual. How did you develop the fascinating character of Illaeus, who is one of the few fictional characters in your novel, since he was a brilliant young man who never fully used his talent for creation? And why didn't he make an advance on the young Aristotle?

AL: Aristotle was sent to Athens to study under Plato at the age of seventeen; pretty precocious! So I imagined he must have shown a lot of promise even earlier than that, and that his parents might well have tried to find him a tutor earlier in his teens. So it became necessary to imagine such a tutor. My fictional Illaeus was a pedophile; he never made an advance on Aristotle because, as a teenager, he was already too old for Illaeus's taste. Pedophilia—men in sexual relationships with young boys—was perhaps not common, but certainly known in the ancient world.

AV: One of the other fictional characters is the slave Athea, who cusses a lot and thinks she knows everything. For example, she does things for Pythias to make her sexually attractive to Aristotle; Pythias subsequently becomes pregnant and Athea helps deliver the baby. Yet later on, when Pythias is dying, she refuses to be near her. (Athea had been exiled from her village as a Scythian healer because there was a young child Athea had been nursing who died.) This is one tough woman who appears to have issues with men and authority. How did you develop this character who is so singularly strange yet so intriguing?

AL: Your take on her is interesting! I don't see her as a know-it-all so much as a competent women with a gift for medicine who isn't allowed to practice her craft. What she flees from is Pythias's illness and death; I imagined she'd seen so much death in her life that she simply couldn't handle it anymore. It was important to me to create a strong female slave character to confront the two big blind spots that Aristotle had (to the contemporary mind, anyway): his misogyny and the fact that he was a slave owner. There's so much to admire in Aristotle, and yet he had these two horrendous aspects to his personality that as a modern woman I had to force myself to confront. I used the character of Athea to do that.

AV: Aristotle ponders the education of Alexander: "Such a needy little monster cub. Shall I continue to pose him riddles to make him a brighter monster, or shall I make him human?" Interesting introspection by Aristotle, but what was the right choice?

AL: As I mentioned earlier, I think the damage was done to Alexander very, very early indeed, and Aristotle probably came on the scene too late to really do anything about that. That's one of the tragedies of their relationship, for me.

AV: Aristotle states after the birth of their daughter: "I myself, though she's only a girl, undertake to supervise her education, which must begin, I will tell anyone who will listen, as early as possible. In the ideal state, the education of children will be the highest business of government." Comment on this passage, which not only applies to little Pythias and to Alexander, but should be a maxim for every civilized country.

AL: The second part of that quote is Aristotle's own words, and I think he's absolutely right; education ought to be one of the highest businesses of government. I was generous to him in the first part, though; in fact, Aristotle didn't particularly believe in the education of girls outside of those skills she'd need in the domestic sphere. He didn't believe in the equality of the sexes.

AV: There is a beautiful description by Aristotle of mother and child: "I understand that every household with a new baby goes as foolish fond, and I collect more quietly, and to keep myself, my own talismans: the spider's thread of milk from wife's breast to daughter's lip when they draw apart after a feeding; the abrupt drop of the baby's brows when something amuses her; the way, at times of great distress, she buries her entire face in her mother's breast, as though seeking oblivion there. Liberty and self-sufficiency: the house is like a ship." Can you add anything to this beautiful passage?

AL: This is a description of my own baby daughter, and one of my favorite passages in the book. I remember writing it, on a day when I was so tired and just wanted to sleep, but I was forcing myself to write two hundred words a day no matter what, so I wrote about the only thing on my brain at that time: my baby. She was probably around two months old when I wrote that. It's a little gift to myself, that I left it in the book.

AV: Interpret the passage of Alexander and Hephaestion, upon completion of a wrestling match after an apparent quarrel: Aristotle ruminates: "I'm aware of Hephaestion, who is lingering in the colonnade, toweling the golden sweat off himself and laughing with two older pages who likewise have hung back from the lesson. Extraordinary behavior, since lovely Hephaestion does not noticeably have a mind of his own. When he sees me looking at him, something in his face falters." You portray Hephaestion as feebleminded and perhaps flirting in front of Alexander. What are you trying to convey in this passage?

AL: Not really feebleminded, just very beautiful and sweet-natured and not as bright as his friend. It's not in his nature (as I imagine him, anyway) to be mean or manipulative, which is what he's trying to do in this scene.

AV: In *The Landmark Arrian* (edited by James Romm) Hephaestion's position is "not merited by his experience or military talents" and was "only a mediocre military officer." Nevertheless, Hephaestion was promoted by Alexander to head half of the prestigious Campanion cavalry. Then, in the later stages of their campaign, Alexander made Hephaestion "chiliarch" (i.e., commander of a thousand) and, upon his death, no one assumed this title. What was Hephaestion really like in your opinion as a soldier, and what was the extent of his relationship, possibly sexual at some time, with Alexander?

AL: I assumed (as historians and novelists have before me—for instance, the wonderful Mary Renault in *Fire from Heaven*)—that Alexander and Hephaestion were lovers. They certainly were intimate lifelong companions, and died within months of one another. I imagine he was stunning to look at, and competent but perhaps not brilliant as a soldier. Brave and loyal and utterly devoted to Alexander.

AV: You present a sublime analogy with Aristotle trying to teach Alexander about "the extremes as caricatures." Alexander interprets this to mean himself and Arrhidaeus. Please elucidate this subtle yet wonderful scene of tutor and student.

AL: In his *Ethics*, Aristotle presents the idea of the mean as the best form of human behavior. "Mean" doesn't mean "average" or "mediocre"; instead, Aristotle suggests we should strive to find a stable, rational middle ground between extreme behaviors (for example, cowardice on the one hand and rashness on the other; the mean would be bravery). I imagined Aristotle extending this to an understanding of people, of personalities; that a young man like Alexander could look at the extremes in people and try to embody the mean in himself, as an ideal of what a man could be.

AV: Aristotle experiences his first battle as a medic for Philip at a place called Chaeronea: "The trumpet sounds again and the medics stop moving, like children playing a game of statues. From far, far away, a shouted command, a long silence, another shout. A sound like the surf, and the head says, 'Stations.' He doesn't need to shout. I look at the ground, have the leisure to observe the kinky walk of a beetle in the dust. After a few minutes of listening to what sounds like a distant ocean, the young medic next to me pulls out a set of dice. 'Play?'" Please describe the genesis and meaning of this strange yet wonderful passage.

AL: I wanted to write a great ancient battle scene, but at the same time I was tickled by the idea of playing with the so-called "rules" for ancient tragedy, some of which Aristotle articulates in his *Poetics*, including keeping all the violence offstage. I decided I'd have Aristotle travel to the battle with the medics (since he'd have medical knowledge inherited from his own father, a physician), but then be stuck inside the tent treating the wounded rather than observing the battle itself. I wanted to give the battle scene itself a kind of dreamy quality, where perspective is all off—the battle sounds like gentle surf, his world becomes a beetle in the dust—to heighten the brutal reality of what comes after.

AV: There is also your description of Aristotle treating the wounded at Chaeronia, where Aristotle daydreams: "There is, too, the matter of purpose; can one say the soul is the purpose of the body? I feel a woolliness there, a gap in the teeth of my logic. Pythias has such a comb, of tortoiseshell, which she tries to use despite a gap the width of two fingers where the teeth have broken off." Can you comment on this metaphorical scene, where Aristotle temporarily loses touch with reality as he works as a medic with the wounded soldiers?

AL: I imagined Aristotle suffering the psychological effects of battle, as so many have, and distancing or detaching himself and losing himself in memory as a way of coping with the extreme violence around him. I really believe that PTSD is as old as soldiering itself; just because these were ancient men doesn't make them any less men, any less prone to suffering and compassion and revulsion and guilt, all those complex emotions that soldiers experience in Iraq and Afghanistan today.

AV: You write like a man. I mean this as a compliment, as you are basically narrating Aristotle's perspective. For example, you mention Aristotle, after talking to Plato, spends the evening with a young prostitute, before going to the Academy: "My hands still smelled of the girl, or I imagined they did. I plucked a large flower from an arrangement and shoved finger after finger down its white throat, reaming for scent." This is something D. H. Lawrence might have written. What do you recall about writing this beautiful passage, and how did you develop this style of writing?

AL: Thank you! In fact, I never really gave it much thought; partly because I don't think there are significant intellectual differences between men and women, and partly because I think the experience of sex (for instance, looking at this passage as an example) is pretty universal, and transcends gender. Also, I have a husband to proofread for me!

AV: There is a passage, at the end of Chapter Four, where Aristotle has just left Plato, who has given him a plate of food. Aristotle is thinking about the prostitute he has seen for months and earlier this day: "The girl had licked and bitten, licked and bitten, until I didn't know myself. I knew I had seen her for the last time. Giddy, I gave the plate away." Essentially, Aristotle has given up pleasure to pursue knowledge. Please elucidate on this scene.

AL: I think of it as moving on to another love: he moves from a very physical, carnal need for love of the girl to a more ambitious, more intellectual, and more risky love for his new teacher. Not a sexual love, this time, but risky because he stands both to gain and to lose much more: respect, fulfillment, admiration, a sense of purpose in the intellectual life. All these things will eventually become a greater solace to him than erotic love.

AV: At the beginning of Chapter Five, Pythias is dying: "I can't help thinking of her pain, also, as a rational being, one with whom she must argue to rescue herself, but as a poor reasoner she cannot. I see the perplexity in her face, the lines in the brow, as pain's logic bests her again and again." This speaks volumes about people facing death and not totally understanding their own mortality, as well as Aristotle's compassion.

AL: You've chosen one of the passages I'm most proud of in the book. His sense of women as something less than men is here, but it's tangled up with his love for his wife and his desperate unhappiness at the prospect of losing her. And that idea that pain is relentless; he knows this himself, without ever really being able to articulate it, from his own depression. The relentlessness of pain, and our helpless compassion for others in pain: two sides of a coin, an essential part of the human experience.

AV: One wonders if Aristotle has his head in the clouds. For example, he never notices his servant Herpyllis until Pythias is dying. All of a sudden he begins to notice how this woman has always made the rooms and cooked the meals so perfectly: "I'm noticing everything now." Shortly thereafter, Herpyllis raises her dress while working in the kitchen and smiles at him, but he is basically flummoxed by her flirtation. Later on she will become his companion. What does this say about Aristotle, who has previously been oblivious to this woman, yet with whom he will spend the rest of his life?

AL: It speaks to an essential selfishness in him, certainly, and his views on women, again: he has animal needs that need to be met, and when his mate is gone he doesn't waste time finding another. But the flip side of that is the idea that his love for his wife blinded him to other women around him: while she was alive, he literally couldn't see other women. He could only see her.

AV: You describe Philip's court at Aegeae in the last chapter. For your research, did you travel to Greece? And, finally, what can readers look forward to in your next book?

AL: I wasn't able to travel to Greece during the research because I was busy having babies and couldn't leave them (they're five and three now), so this is all book research. I did travel to Greece after the book was published to research the sequel, which will take place at the end of Aristotle's life and feature his teenage daughter, also named Pythias, who is only four in *The Golden Mean*. She'll be sixteen in the new book. I went to Athens, Sounion, Delphi, Chaeronea, and Chalcis, where Aristotle died. The novel will open with Aristotle's death and follow the first few months of Pythias's life alone, as she must make her own way in the world without men around to protect her. She'll try on a number of different roles—priestess, midwife, hetaira—before settling into the role the historical Aristotle imagined for her, as articulated in his will (a real historical document, included as an appendix to *The Golden Mean*): wife and mother. I'm interested in whether the same eerie links between past and present will appear in this novel as they did in *The Golden Mean*, or whether the life of a woman 2,300 years ago will prove infinitely more foreign. Certainly, my life as a twenty-first-century Canadian woman much more closely resembles a male life back then, and I'm finding imagining myself in a woman's body at that time, with all that entails—marriage in early teens, illiteracy, lack of a political voice, high likelihood of dying in childbirth, desperately needing male protection—a really interesting challenge.

Emily St. John Mandel. Courtesy of Sarah Shatz.

Too Good to Be True: An Interview with Emily St. John Mandel

Emily St. John Mandel was born in 1979 and raised on Denman Island off the west coast of British Columbia, Canada. Despite this she was technically born as an American with dual citizenship because her father, who was from California and a conscientious objector during the Vietnam War, moved to Canada, where he raised his family in a hippie culture, with homeschooling heavy on reading and very little math or science. When Mandel turned fifteen, she finally attended a local school and took college exams where she scored one hundred percent in English, but only one percent in math and science. At eighteen she left school to study ballet and contemporary dance at the School of Toronto Dance Theatre, but one day she picked up a free newspaper and read a book review, and her entire life changed: she began corresponding with the review's author and the pair struck up a romance and moved to New York City, where Mandel subsequently met the man who became her husband. "If I hadn't bent down that day and picked up that weekly newspaper, this entire life I've built might not have happened," she told *Publishers Weekly* in 2012.

Before she left Canada, she had already started writing her first novel, *Last Night in Montreal,* which in turn was followed by *The Singer's Gun* and *The Lola Quartet*—each of which might be termed detective-noir novels. From there was a sudden departure with *Station Eleven,* a dystopian science fiction novel that became a runaway bestseller, one with the unusual distinction of being nominated for both the National Book Award and the Hugo Award. Mandel's latest novel, *The Glass Hotel,* involves a Ponzi scheme inspired by the Bernie Madoff debacle, and so much more. *The Glass Hotel* is not just a total departure from *Station Eleven,* but a novel that shows Mandel cannot be confined to one genre and is willing to take chances to evolve as a writer. Her next novel, titled *Sea of Tranquility,* was published in April 2022.

This interview was conducted May 2020.

Allan Vorda: When I interviewed Jennifer Egan about her novel *Manhattan Beach,* I asked if she felt any pressure to follow up her Pulitzer Prize-winning *A Visit from the Goon Squad.* I'll ask you the same question: Did you feel any pressure writing *The Glass Hotel* after the enormous success you had with *Station Eleven*?

Emily St. John Mandel: Yes, absolutely. If you have the unbelievable good fortune to have written an immensely successful book, then with the book that follows, there's a sense of an invisible audience peering over your shoulder. I'm not complaining—we're talking about the least sympathetic problem in the world here—but it probably made the writing of *The Glass Hotel* a little slower than it might have been. I never had any kind of pressure from my agents or publishers, though, which I very much appreciated.

AV: It seems that anyone who interviews you now must ask the obligatory question about how *Station Eleven* deals with a pandemic flu. I almost prefer not to go there, but it seems inescapable. Do you have any thoughts you want to add about the pandemic coincidence of *Station Eleven* with COVID-19? And more importantly, how are you dealing with the virus in New York City?

ESJM: What quickly becomes clear, if you read about the history of pandemics, is that epidemiologists talk about pandemics in the same way seismologists talk about earthquakes, which is to say that no one's talking in terms of *if* there will ever again be another earthquake. There will always be another earthquake, and there will always be another pandemic. This isn't to minimize the horror of the present moment in any way. Pandemics are a part of human history, and this current moment is only shocking to us because we haven't had a major one in a hundred years.

I'm doing okay in New York City. A few of my friends have had the virus at this point, but none of those cases have been severe. We hear ambulances day and night, and the daily death tolls are staggering. A nuance that sometimes gets lost in talk of "flattening the curve" is that the flat top of the curve is a devastatingly high plateau. My four-year-old daughter expresses a lot of sadness about not being able to see her cousins and her friends, and creating a stable, calm environment for her while trying to get my own work done is a daily juggling act. But I feel profoundly grateful for my life here. We have groceries delivered once a week. Our house has a terrace on the roof, with a large-scale container garden that I've been building up for years now, so I've been gardening and working as much as I can and reading in the evenings after my daughter goes to bed.

AV: Jeevan says to Arthur Leander in *Station Eleven*: "You do give a lot of interviews" whereupon Arthur replies: "Too many. Don't write I said that." What are your thoughts about doing interviews, especially since book tours to promote your new novel have been cancelled?

ESJM: I'm aware at all times of how fortunate my situation is that people want to interview me. I have extremely talented publicists, and I know I get an extraordinary amount of press, for which I'm very grateful. But I can't help but see interviewing as an extremely fraught and high-risk activity at this point. I've had a few awful experiences where I was either badly misquoted or a few quotes were plucked out of context from a very long interview, and in the resulting piece I felt that I came across as an idiot. I'm grateful but wary; I guess that's how I'd summarize it at this point.

AV: Your characters and the worlds they live in are often on the dark side. What attracts you to write about this aspect of humanity?

ESJM: I think it makes for more interesting fiction.

AV: In the last several decades, Alice Munro, Margaret Atwood, Michael Ondaatje, William Gibson, Carol Shields, Rohinton Mistry, and yourself are among the Canadian writers who have found wide readerships and critical acclaim. Besides obvious talent, can you point to any reason why a country that doesn't have an overly large population has produced so many fine writers?

ESJM: I don't really have a theory on this one. It's a thing, but I don't know why it's a thing. I did come across an interesting idea twenty years ago that I've been thinking about ever since—I was sitting in a cafe, and the guy at the next table said "Canada's such an Apollonian society, so they produce these incredibly intense artists." Maybe there's something to that.

AV: After the dystopian approach of *Station Eleven,* what stimulated you to write a novel partly based on Bernie Madoff's Ponzi scheme?

ESJM: I was fascinated by the scale of the crime. The thing with that Ponzi scheme is that the returns could be graphed on a perfect 45° angle, like a child's drawing of a mountainside. Which is to say that it should have been apparent to any sophisticated investor that something was awry, and yet a great many very financially sophisticated people fell for the scam. Which means there was a fascinating kind of mass delusion at play—it was as if all of these people who should have known better decided en masse to believe in a fairy tale.

But more than that, I was fascinated by the staff. About six or seven of Madoff's staffers went to prison, because it's not like he was formatting all those fake account statements by himself. When Madoff was arrested, I was an administrative assistant at the Rockefeller University in New York City. I really liked my coworkers, and what I found myself thinking about was the camaraderie that you have with any group of committed people who work together, and then I couldn't help but think about how much more intense and wild that camaraderie would be if we were all showing up at work on Monday morning to perpetuate a massive crime.

AV: You were born on Vancouver Island, off the west coast of British Columbia, and I understand you grew up mostly on Denman Island, a much smaller island nearby. The setting for some of the scenes in *The Glass Hotel* is the far northern end of Vancouver Island. What characteristics of where you grew up were helpful in writing about this setting?

ESJM: Just the knowledge of it, I'd say. Writing about places you don't know very well is an invitation to receive several hundred emails telling you about all the details you got wrong.

AV: There is a passage where Vincent's mother, who wanted to write poetry, "somehow found herself sunk in the mundane difficulties of raising a child and running a household." I think so many writers who are parents will identify with this—how do you manage to write with all of the demands of motherhood and daily chores?

ESJM: I think this is an area where acknowledging privilege is important. There's a reason why my daughter's former nanny is the final name in the acknowledgments of *The Glass Hotel*: no one was more important than her in my ability to write that book. Writing while parenting is a problem that can be solved by spending an enormous amount of money on childcare, and that's how I did it. I try to be transparent about this, because I don't want parents who are struggling to get any writing done to feel like they're just not working hard enough. The success of *Station Eleven* allowed my husband and I to employ an almost-full-time nanny for three years, after which I helped her find a new job and my daughter started going to a preschool full time. Which was also expensive, but only about half as expensive as employing someone.

But now, in quarantine with no access to childcare, it's a whole different thing, and a different kind of privilege comes into play: I have a spouse who's able to work from home. My husband and I trade off on childcare throughout the day. It's difficult and exhausting, and neither of us has enough time, but we're making it work, and I believe we can keep going this way indefinitely. I've been thinking a lot about how much more difficult this time must be for single parents.

AV: *The Glass Hotel* starts with Vincent's apparent suicide plunge into the ocean, followed by the words "Sweep me up." The words not only allude to the last words spoken by Søren Kierkegaard and to the reader who is about to get swept up with your prose, but to Vincent as well, as we learn later: "She'd never had a clear vision of what she wanted her life to look like, she had always been directionless, but she did know that she wanted to be swept up, to be plucked from the crowd. . . ." Tell us how the character of Vincent came into existence. From a rebellious teenager to a photographer, trophy wife, and eventual recluse, she definitely experiences a lot of changes in her life.

ESJM: She began as a trophy wife. If you're going to write about a white-collar crime, you're writing about money, and the phenomenon of trophy wives is a tiny niche of the economy that I find interesting. The rest of her biography came about from imagining her character arc before and after her time with Alkaitis. I liked the idea of a character who was able to reinvent herself at will, which is a quality that I admire in real life.

AV: Mirella, who is married to the Saudi prince Faisal and seems like a sort of doppelgänger for Vincent, tells Vincent that cities, while different, are really the same because "money is its own country" and that while the scenery might be different, "my life felt more or less the same in Singapore as it did in London." Jonathan Alkaitis's extension of this is that "money is a country, and he had the keys to the kingdom." It's ironic that at the end, Alkaitis is in prison, and the only key is the one that locks him in his cell. Global economics seems like a challenging topic to tackle in a novel—does this subject come naturally to you, or did you have to learn a bit about finance to go where you needed to in the book?

ESJM: I did have to learn a bit about finance. But what's perhaps more relevant to those quotes of Mirella's is that I've lived in more than one socioeconomic class, and having money vs. not having money are such profoundly different states that moving from one to the other really is as profound as moving between countries.

AV: When Alkaitis's financial world collapses and he is sent to prison, his mind collapses into a non-consensual reality. The internal conversation Alkaitis has with himself is where he "likes to indulge in daydreams of a parallel version of events—a counterlife if you will." And you subtly explore how he constructs this counterlife: "Vincent isn't in the counterlife. He feels it's important to keep the two separate, memory vs. counterlife, but he's been finding the separation increasingly difficult. It's a permeable border." Alkaitis fantasizes he has escaped and is living in Dubai, but "it's more like a creeping sense of unreality, a sense of collapsing borders, reality seeping into the counterlife and the counterlife seeping into memory."

I think these "counterlife" segments, how you get into Alkaitis's mind, are brilliant pieces of writing, bordering on the Dostoyevskian. Can you reveal how you decided to write these parts of the novel, and how you were able to get in Alkaitis's head so effectively?

ESJM: Thank you. They were among my favorite parts of the book to write. Pretty early on, I realized that this book was going to be a ghost story, but what is a ghost story, actually? We tend to use that phrase in kind of a classical sense, as in the specter wafting down the corridor in the dilapidated old house or whatever, but it can be interesting to think about different ways of being haunted. Your counterlife is your counterfactual life: that's the life wherein you married a different person, or went to a different school, or emigrated instead of staying or vice versa. What if your life is being haunted by the ghosts of the lives you didn't live? I liked that idea. I appreciate what you said about getting into Alkaitis's head effectively. The answer to how I did it is the same as the answer to how I did anything in this book—I just revised it dozens of times over a period of years.

AV: Your description of Alkaitis's physical life in prison is very convincing as well. Did you visit any prisons, or do any other research to make these scenes so realistic?

ESJM: I'm glad that rang true. Prison life has been pretty well explicated in popular culture at this point—consider *Orange is the New Black, The Wire,* etc.—so I had some visual sense of what the inside of a prison looks like, and I'd also read a lot of essays and books that went into the rhythms of prison life in more detail. Not long before the deadline for my second pass proofs—which is to say, pretty much the absolute end of the editing process, when the book's already been typeset and your publisher really doesn't want you to make major changes—I had the opportunity to visit a men's medium security facility in the Midwest as part of a prison literature program. It was sad—I'd describe the atmosphere as heavy—and also interesting. The details of the yard in the book came from that visit. You walk through a prison yard and there's just a kind of aesthetic poverty about it, like there aren't enough colours in the landscape: blue sky, green grass, cement, beige and blue buildings, tan and grey uniforms, and that's it. When a bird lands, it's somehow shocking, because that's the only unregulated movement in the landscape.

AV: Earlier this year, Bernie Madoff asked to be let out of prison due to failing health. What are your overall thoughts of Madoff—and wouldn't it be interesting to see what he thinks of *The Glass Hotel* if he gets a copy to read?

ESJM: If you read Madoff's prison interviews, he just comes across as such a garden-variety sociopath and narcissist. The scale of his crime was extraordinary, but the man himself is so uninteresting. I have no respect for him, so I don't care what he thinks of my work.

AV: Neal Stephenson's character Enoch Root appears in different novels that span centuries. In a similar way, some of your characters from earlier novels reappear: Jonathan Alkaitis and the band Baltica (*The Lola Quartet; The Glass Hotel*), or Leon Prevant and Miranda (*Station Eleven; The Glass Hotel*). Ruth Franklin in *The Atlantic* argues that you are constructing a sort of multiverse that demonstrates the power to imagine simultaneous realities. Can you address this concept as it applies not only to your characters, but also to the various ghosts that permeate your novels? And tell us, when writing, are you consciously thinking about using certain characters in your future work?

ESJM: It depends on the character and the work. When I wrote *The Lola Quartet*, it wasn't clear to me that I would return to either Jonathan Alkaitis or Baltica. But with *Station Eleven*, I knew I wanted to use Miranda and Leon again in future works, which presented an obvious problem, because I had no interest in writing a sequel and that book's a bit of a dead end—a flu wipes out most of the world's population. But to Ruth Franklin's point, of course in fiction anything is possible, so I began laying the groundwork for the multiverse idea in that book. Toward the end of *Station Eleven*, two characters are playing a game they sometimes play, where they just riff on ideas about what alternate universes might look like. ("Imagine a universe where the flu never happened and the world didn't end.") This mirrors a passage in *The Glass Hotel* where Vincent is thinking about alternate realities, which is a kind of game she plays with herself sometimes, and she imagines a world where that terrifying new flu wasn't quite so swiftly contained. In both passages, I was trying to lay the groundwork so that I could reuse some of *Station Eleven*'s characters without necessarily placing them in the same universe as *Station Eleven.*

As it pertains to ghosts, the multiverse idea is probably expressed most strongly in the sections having to do with what Jonathan Alkaitis—the Ponzi schemer sentenced to life in prison—thinks of as his counterlife, the life where he fled to Dubai instead of waiting to be arrested. I wanted to create increasing ambiguity about the reality of that alternate life: at first it just seems like a daydream, but my hope was that as the book progressed, and as his grasp of reality weakened, the counterlife would begin to seem more and more real.

AV: Leon's accountant tells Leon about Alkaitis's Ponzi scheme: "'Leon, it wasn't real. None of it was real. Those returns. . . ' She didn't add *that I told you seemed almost too good to be true,* because she didn't have to." This seems to be the essence of a Ponzi scheme: that it is *too good to be true* and only a few, like Ella Kaspersky, see it for what it is. Any thoughts?

ESJM: There's a herd mentality that comes into play with con artists. Suppose your savings are invested in a Ponzi scheme. You might have an uneasy thought one day, as you peruse your account statements, like "Wow, these returns are really surprisingly high, I wonder if something's maybe amiss here." But then you look around, you see all of these other investors who seem untroubled, and it's easy to tell yourself that if anything were seriously wrong, someone else would have noticed and said something by now. People like Ella Kaspersky have the courage required to question things that a crowd of others are going along with.

AV: Oskar Novak states at his trial that "It's possible to both know and not know something." This appears to echo the Heisenberg Principle of Uncertainty, but I wondered if this oxymoronic statement by Oskar actually means something else.

ESJM: What I meant is that you can know intellectually that the returns on your investment are too good to be true, and yet choose *not* to know it, because those returns are so good and everyone else is going along with it. Or in Oskar's case, you can know that you're committing a crime that will ruin lives, and yet also choose not to know it, by means of self-justifications and denial.

AV: As I mentioned earlier, ghosts (and people who are invisible) crop up in all of your novels. In an interview with Hannah Beckerman in the *Guardian,* you stated: "The truth is that I'd always wanted to write a ghost story. It's a form that I feel I love." Can you extrapolate on this?

ESJM: I'm not sure that there's much more to say about it. I've always been drawn to ghost stories. I think I just like the idea of there being some mystery in the universe.

AV: You also seem to have a substantial degree of knowledge about shipping in your novels. How did this come about?

ESJM: Through the most boring way possible! I regret to say that I don't have a colorful past aboard a merchant vessel or anything like that. I just researched the subject. I read a book and a lot of articles and found YouTube channels belonging to merchant seamen.

AV: You have said you liked the structure of David Mitchell's brilliant novel *Cloud Atlas,* but couldn't make it work for *The Glass Hotel.* Can you say more about the process of restructuring and revision for *The Glass Hotel*?

ESJM: Sure, absolutely. For anyone who's unfamiliar with *Cloud Atlas,* it's got this wonderful symmetrical structure that moves forward and then backward in time. My copy's in a box somewhere, so I can't reference the exact time periods here, but if section A is set in, say, 1650, and section B is set in the 1800s, section C in 1950, etc., then the structure of the book could be mapped as A, B, C, D, E, D, C, B, A. I wanted to use that structure in *The Glass Hotel,* but the challenge with that structure is that in the second half you're committed to returning to those points of view and points in time that you laid out in the first part of the book, which makes it really hard to maintain narrative tension.

So I wrote a draft that used that structure, and it was apparent with the first round of editorial notes that it absolutely did not work. The book wasn't suspenseful enough. So I broke the book apart and submitted it again with a completely different structure, something less formal and less linear. But then there were issues around the dramatic peak of the book falling at the wrong point in the narrative—you want the dramatic peak of the book to be pretty close to the end, generally speaking, and mine was near the beginning—so I restructured it again for the third round of edits.

AV: You said after writing *Last Night in Montreal,* which has a wonderful ornate prose style, that you read Norman Mailer's *The Executioner's Song,* which made you pare down your style for your subsequent novel, *The Singer's Gun.* What can you discern about the evolution of your prose style? I imagine your prose will undergo further changes the more you read and the older you get.

ESJM: I think my prose has gotten looser with time. I'm a little less concerned with grammatical perfection than I used to be.

AV: *The Glass Hotel* has a mystical and inscrutable ending, vaguely reminiscent of Marilynne Robinson's *Housekeeping*. I thought it was a sublime way to wrap up the novel. Did you have this end in mind from the beginning?

ESJM: No, I came up with the ending pretty close to the end.

AV: Emily, thank you for this interview. It has been a sheer pleasure to immerse myself in your fiction.

ESJM: It was a pleasure speaking with you! Thanks for interviewing me.

Benjamin Moser. Courtesy of Beowulf Sheehan.

Writing Sontag's Life and Work: An Interview with Benjamin Moser

Benjamin Moser was born and raised in Houston. He graduated from Brown University and received his PhD from Utrecht University. Moser's first book was a biography of the Brazilian writer Clarice Lispector titled *Why This World: A Biography of Clarice Lispector* (Oxford University Press, 2012); he subsequently edited a series of translations of Lispector for New Directions, and has published translations in Dutch, French, Spanish, and Portuguese. Based on his biography of Lispector, he was invited to write a biography of Susan Sontag, which took seven years to complete. *Sontag: Her Life and Her Work* (Ecco, $39.99) is the fruit of this labor; the book is a revealing, in-depth portrait of one of the twentieth century's most powerful intellectuals. Moser's biography of Sontag won the 2020 Pulitzer Prize.

The following interview was conducted in October of 2019 at the ZaZa Hotel in Houston, while Moser was in town to give a talk about the book.

Allan Vorda: How is the tour going; what has been the reception of the book; and what is it like to be back home in Houston?

Benjamin Moser: The tour is great. This is the tenth city I've visited, and it's always great to be back in Houston, where I grew up. I'm lucky the reviews have been good. Sontag was so polemical I thought I would get more negative reception; I've received some, but I thought it would be 50/50, when in fact it's been more like 90/10. That's a great thing for a writer, especially when you know you're playing with fire with someone like Sontag. The opinions can be so ferocious—people hate her, people love her, people hate that you love her, etc. It was great to write about such a controversial person.

AV: You received your BA from Brown University and a PhD from Utrecht University. How did you wind up in the Netherlands to do your graduate work; what was your dissertation on; and why did you decide to become a biographer?

BM: Ending up in the Netherlands had nothing to do with my graduate work. I met a Dutch person when I was living in New York, and I moved to Holland because of that.

Typically, in America, you enter a graduate program and do your years of misery for a PhD, but I had already written *Why This World: A Biography of Clarice Lispector*, which became my first book. A Dutch friend of mine was writing a biography of a Dutch writer, and he was submitting it as his PhD at a Dutch university to the Dutch department. He suggested I submit *Why This World* to the Portuguese department. *Why This World* was never meant to be a dissertation, but it was long enough and substantial enough to be one; I had to do some bureaucratic stuff and I had to take some classes, but basically your dissertation is your PhD.

AV: Why did you choose to write biographies about Lispector and Sontag?

BM: Because of my work on *Why This World,* I was asked by Sontag's son, her agent, and her publisher to do her biography. I didn't really decide to become a biographer—basically, I had written one biography and I thought I was finished with biographies, but I realized I wasn't because it's an irresistible subject. It was a big honor to be asked to write about Sontag.

AV: Sontag moved to New York from California and began writing essays, yet at age thirty-two she ends up dining with Leonard Bernstein, Richard Avedon, William Styron, Sybil Burton, and Jacqueline Kennedy at a New York restaurant. Everyone looking at this table would have had to wonder who the hell is this beautiful young woman? How do you explain Sontag's fame that seemed to rise from out of nowhere?

BM: This is a hard question to answer. You think, okay, she's good looking, she's interesting, and she's smart, but there are a lot of good-looking, interesting, smart writers who never end up hanging out with Jackie Kennedy. Sontag enters the world as this nerdy grad student type. She spent several years writing a book on Freud with her husband, and then suddenly she becomes very famous. I think what put her over the boundary between well-regarded young writer and famous person was the essay "Notes on Camp," which was published right around the time Jackie Kennedy's husband was killed in Dallas.

"Notes on Camp" seemed to tap into something very subversive and very surprising. It basically had to do with the emergence of both women and homosexuals into a broader awareness. It was scandalous. It's hard to imagine. So much has changed since that time. Diane

Carroll just died and she was eighty-four years old—she was the first black person to ever be on television and not play a servant—so you can see how far we've come. To write about gay culture in public was completely shocking at that time, and it made Sontag seem dangerous, and sexy, and subversive. Suddenly, she was catapulted to this level of celebrity, which she occupied for the rest of her life.

AV: You state Sontag's "equation of sleep with death would never change," since she viewed sleeping as sloth and "tried to avoid it, and was often ashamed to reveal that she slept at all"; she became a chronic user of amphetamines in order to write longer. Sontag also stated: "My desire to write is connected with my homosexuality." Sontag had a lot of issues in her life, including a fractured relationship with her mother; a pathetic marriage; the use of drugs and alcohol; smoking two packs of cigarettes a day; lack of hygiene for days at a time; and her sexuality. Yet this was a *driven* woman. What do you think were the driving forces behind Sontag's desire to write and be famous?

BM: I don't think her drive existed despite these issues; I think the drive existed partly because of these issues. She was someone who was in flight from death in a certain way, as we all are. She was nervous about being gay, and she was always nervous that she was falling short in various ways. But I think that feeling motivated her. If she didn't have those qualities, she wouldn't have been the person that she became. If she had lived happily in Tucson or Los Angeles, she would not have been Susan Sontag.

AV: Philip Rieff was twenty-eight when he married the seventeen-year-old Sontag, after knowing her for one week. Briefly describe their marriage and the likelihood that Sontag, and not Rieff, should have been credited as the author of the book *Freud: The Mind of the Moralist.*

BM: This was something that everybody knew, because Sontag had always said it privately. But she gave up this book because she was trying to get divorced. Rieff was threatening to her. She had a child with him, and at the time you could easily get your child taken away from you if you were gay. She wanted to be rid of Rieff, so she said just take the book, let me have my kid, leave me alone. I don't think this is something she did immediately, but it's something she arrived at because she was sick of the whole situation.

She regretted it for the rest of her life. She would always talk about it. I worked on the Sontag biography for seven years, and I think she worked on Freud for eight or nine years. The thought of someone taking away a piece of work after all those years is maddening. So it doesn't surprise me that she was resentful.

AV: Since you have a Jewish background, as do your subjects Sontag and Lispector, did this prove helpful and give you a better insight into writing these biographies?

BM: On Lispector, definitely. For Sontag, not really. Sontag was an American Jew like I am—it wasn't a big issue for her. I think you can overstate these similarities, like I'm Jewish and she's Jewish. I'm gay and she's gay. I'm American and she's American. I think her Jewish background is pretty standard, and in New York it's not a disadvantage. It might have been a disadvantage if she were like Lispector, who came from a place of deathly anti-Semitism in Eastern Europe, but that wasn't the case for Sontag.

AV: Irene Fornés, a Cuban American playwright and director, became Sontag's lover in 1959. Despite having been married and having a son as well as a lengthy affair with Harriet Sohmers, you state that "Irene introduced her to the orgasm" at age twenty-six. Sontag wrote: "I feel for the first time the living possibility of being a writer. The coming of the orgasm is not the salvation but, more, the birth of my ego. For me to write I must find my ego." How important, both sexually and intellectually, was Irene Fornés in transforming Sontag's life?

BM: It's so funny: when I got to the UK to do some publicity, which was three weeks ago, people immediately asked me about the orgasm.

Everybody was really interested in this, and I thought it was fascinating because it's one of these things that you see has changed so much. Now there is so much more awareness of sex, but a lot of older women told me: "We really didn't know about this, no one told us!"

There was no sex education. It was unspeakable in the media. I think what the orgasm represented for Sontag is a possibility of freedom. She's locked into this marriage and this conservative society and all these ideas, and suddenly she has an orgasm with this incredibly sensual and sexual woman. This was really appealing to someone like Sontag, who had always been living in her own head.

Sexual liberation, if you want to put it that way, was extremely exciting, and in fact she starts writing more after that. She had already written the Freud book, but she starts writing with a lot more excitement. She starts looking for that thrill you get from certain forms of sex—and from certain forms of art.

AV: Another person who heavily affected Sontag's life was Roger Straus, of the Farrar, Straus, Giroux publishing firm: "He published every one of her books. He kept her alive, professionally, financially, and sometimes physically." Without Roger Straus, would Sontag have achieved the heights she reached?

BM: That's a good question, and it's hard to say. Straus provided unstinting support, and not a lot of writers have that. He loved her, and he saw her through some of her more reader-unfriendly phases. He would take care of her son when she was on vacation. He would pay her light bills. He protected her. She didn't have a father; her father died in China when she was five. So Straus was a father figure, and a lot of other writers were jealous of this. That sort of relationship is rare for a writer, and she found it at a young age; I think it was incredibly helpful.

AV: You state that "hidden in 'Notes on Camp'—not, it must be said, well hidden—is a still more aggressive contention. Camp, as Sontag posited it, was not about leveling: *au contraire.* It meant the establishment of a new hierarchy. The true 'aristocrats of taste,' she proclaimed, were homosexuals." How important was this essay, which was a bold statement of homosexual superiority?

BM: It was extremely aggressive, in a way we can't really imagine now. If you look at the letters to the editor, they were absolutely outraged. It's almost hilarious to read these letters; they were saying it's the death of America. What they meant was if gay people were allowed to exist without shame, then culture would collapse, moral value would collapse, and consequently the whole country would collapse. You can see how long and how obsessed the right wing has been with these things. Since we are both from Texas, we know the right wing is still at it.

"Notes on Camp" was very aggressive in a way I don't think Sontag thought it would be. I think she thought it was kind of prankish. It was almost a joke to her. But as Freud tells us, jokes reveal deeper truths, and the deeper truth she revealed was that there was a whole restless movement in America. There was a desire to not conform, not just live the life that your parents live. She gave permission for that, including a sexual acceptance for people, and it was very exciting.

AV: Can you tell us a bit about Paul Thek, whom Sontag said was "the most important person in my life"?

BM: Thek was a part of the movement in her life of which Fornés was also a part. Neither was educated, while everybody Sontag knew was a super-refined Jewish intellectual. I think Fornés had a fifth-grade education, and I don't think Paul graduated from high school. Yet they were both geniuses. They didn't need all the books. They could just create, and they gave Sontag permission to extend her curiosity into areas that wouldn't have been approved by academia, or by the official voices of the critical-intellectual patriarchy. She was absolutely turned on by him, including sexually. He was hot. This was something completely different from her professors at the University of Chicago.

AV: Sontag was derided for her essay "What's Happening in America," where she stated the "white race *is* the cancer of human history." What were the short-term and long-term effects of this statement in regard to Sontag's reputation?

BM: Long-term, zero. To my sadness and pain, I haven't had any right-wing haters for this book. I thought more right-wingers would come out and attack Sontag, but the right wing now has no intellectual component. It did; there was a completely legitimate conservative school of thought in America. For example, the culture was against expanding the canon of great books; it was a discussion that Sontag was a part of. But now? Does Donald Trump care about Aristotle? One suspects he does not.

"The white race *is* the cancer of humanity" is really a statement from and about the age of Vietnam. I think it was hard for people to imagine how maddening the Vietnam War was, until Trump came along. Even if you didn't like Obama, for example, whether from the right or the left, he seemed like a reasonable guy. And then all of a sudden the whole country gets flushed down the toilet. You see the reactions people have. I think Sontag's real contribution comes when she gives up radicalism, with statements like these that sound so over the top, and embraces liberalism, which is about progressive, democratic change. It's not about overthrowing the government. It's not about tanks in the streets. It's about what she does later in her life, like in Sarajevo.

AV: Your analogy between Trump and the Vietnam War is perfect. I grew up during the '60s, and every day you turned on the television there was horrible news, and people kept asking themselves when it was going to end. And now it's the same with Trump; every day there is breaking news, and you think when is this nightmare going to end.

BM: That analogy helps me understand Sontag. When I first started to research her, I thought it was kind of crazy of her to say things like that. But looking through that lens, I don't think she was crazy at all. It makes perfect sense.

AV: In the '60s, Sontag had affairs with Richard Goodwin (her first orgasm with a man), Robert Kennedy, and Warren Beatty; yet she had no real interest in these men. These affairs were merely "amusing" to her, but afterwards "it was back to the monastic cell." Is this how Sontag spent a good portion of her life, with brief affairs with both men and women?

BM: Her affairs with women were not brief. Her affairs with men were often with men who turned her on because they were so remarkable. The men you listed were fascinating people, but the sexual aspects were often one-night stands, or maybe two weeks, as was the case with Warren Beatty. Her emotional involvement was with women; there is not a word in her journals—and there are one hundred volumes of her journals—where she's tearing her hair out about a guy. It's all the women that she's emotionally attracted to.

Mostly, though, I think she did spend a lot of time in the monastic cell. She wouldn't have produced as much as she did otherwise. There was no way you could write those books if you were screwing around all day. You have to *work* to write all those books.

AV: Sontag's son said, "I don't think Susan ever loved anyone the way she loved Carlotta," in reference to Anna Carlotta del Pezzo, Duchess of Caianello. The painter Marilu Eustachio said of her milieu that everyone did something, but Carlotta "was the only one who did absolutely nothing." The poet Cavalli added: "I don't think she ever read a book in her life." And, when Eustachio reproached Carlotta for her languor, you state that Carlotta bristled: "So you think it's easy, doing nothing?" It seems unimaginable that Sontag, a noted workaholic, could be so in love with a woman like this.

BM: It's like a fantasy for Sontag. Carlotta was beautiful, aristocratic, and fascinating to Susan. There's a moment in the book where someone says, she's not the type of person who thinks, "Instead of being at this party in Capri, I should be writing a play." And that's exactly what Susan was like—always feeling like she should be doing something important. Of course, Carlotta's life was not enviable; she's what the British call a waster. Carlotta hung out and got drunk. But it was precisely this kind of indolence, taken to an extreme degree, that was attractive for someone like Sontag, who was always working so hard.

AV: Another person who affected Sontag's life was the actress and director known as Nicole Stéphane, but whose real name was Nicole-Mathilde-Stephanie de Rothschild, a member of Europe's greatest banking family.

BM: Nicole comes after Carlotta. She was connected with all these famous people. She was also a motherly figure for Sontag. I don't think they were really in love with each other, sexually. But Nicole adopted Susan and took care of her and made sure she bathed and made sure she got in the taxi on time. This was at a time that Susan was really falling apart, and Nicole gave her the strength to pull herself back together.

AV: If it were not for Sontag's son, David Rieff, needing a physical to enter Princeton, she would have never had her physical, in which "a metastasized cancer, stage 4" was discovered in her left breast. This fortuitous event gave Sontag almost another thirty years.

BM: Even with the discovery, she almost died—it was stage four, and it was forty years ago, when cancer treatment was a lot less effective than it is now. She survived by a miracle.

AV: In what ways did the poet Joseph Brodsky, with whom Sontag fell in love, change her life?

BM: He had come out of the Soviet Union, and he insisted how bad communism was, which she didn't really understand. I think she knew it intellectually, but she didn't know it emotionally until she met him.

And, of course, he was a great artist, and she was always extremely attracted to great artists. He bullied her, which is interesting, because she was known as a bully herself. When she met some of these stronger forces, she reacted in a completely opposite way, as a lot of bullies do when they meet a stone they can't move.

AV: You recount how in a Town Hall meeting, Sontag said, "Communism is in itself a variant, the most successful variant, of Fascism. Fascism with a human face." What was behind her shift from a radical stance to a liberal one?

BM: This is what Brodsky brought about, and it was also the result of Vietnam. Living in a very small, New York, left-wing, Jewish, intellectual world, Sontag didn't quite realize that communism wasn't really part of the conversation in the rest of the country. I think this was the moment where she became a real liberal. She stands up for someone like Salman Rushdie, working at PEN to protest the imprisonment of writers in Korea, and starts going to Sarajevo.

I think communism is attractive as an idea because it promises a complete elimination of injustice. But that's not what liberals believe. Liberals think maybe you can't improve everything, but you can open a kindergarten for underprivileged children and help twenty kids get a better education. This requires a bit of humility. The world needs to be changed, and we all know it. But it's easier said than done. So should you give up and do nothing? Or should you do your little something in your own little place?

AV: In your chapter "The Word Won't Go Away," you discuss how Sontag, who was gay, failed to address the AIDS epidemic. Why didn't she address the issue, and do you think she regretted her silence?

BM: That's a really tough question because of the speed with which these things have changed. My dad grew up in Houston, and he said when he was a kid it was unthinkable that a black guy and a white guy would eat at the same table. It was just something that did not exist. Gay rights were like this in a certain way, but the change was very radical and very fast.

Sontag grew up in a world in which lesbians were considered man-killing dykes, and gay men were guys who flashed little boys on the playground. There was no gay representation, no ideas, no discussion. It was totally taboo. If you were discovered to be gay, you could lose your home, you could lose your job, and you could lose your child, which almost happened to Sontag.

She was someone who was called upon by the community to make a huge change in her life, and she wasn't able to make the change that quickly, even though she was fifty at that time. Sontag always had relationships with women, but there was an internalized homophobia which kept her from playing a role in certain areas. This isn't to say she didn't play a role. The fact was she was gay and everyone knew she was gay, but she never talked about it. I can't tell you how many lesbians have told me how inspiring she was. She embodied the idea that you could be gay and be an intellectual and write and be respected. Being gay didn't have to mean the end of your life. This was really meaningful to a lot of people.

AV: Your comments make me think about Richard Dawkins's *The God Delusion,* in which he discusses a poll breaking down the chances of being elected president of the United States. At the bottom of the list is being black, gay, and an atheist. Since that short time ago we have had a black president, and Pete Buttigieg is running for president. Perhaps in our lifetime we will have a president who is an atheist, and remove that last prejudicial issue.

BM: I think Americans are sick of having religion shoved down their throats. I hope it won't even be a question in the future. No religion? Who cares? Let's talk about healthcare.

AV: How instrumental was the great photographer, Annie Leibovitz, in helping Sontag both emotionally and financially? Their long-lasting affair was bizarre in that Sontag would often ridicule Leibovitz in public, yet Leibovitz put up with the humiliation and gave Sontag a lot of money during their relationship.

BM: This was hard for me to understand, because I heard shocking stories about their relationship, none of which was a secret—it was all in public. Susan would say terrible things to Annie. Annie, on the other hand, was not a pushover. She has now been at the top of her profession for fifty years, and was someone who was powerful in her own right. It made me wonder how she could put up with Sontag's ridicule.

I finally talked to Annie after a couple years of trying to reach out to her. I was actually walking along the street in Paris when I got a phone call from one of her studios. Some woman said, "Annie wants to talk to you, can you come see her tomorrow?" I said, "Sure. Where?" They gave me an address in the West Village of New York. I got on a plane and I went the very next day.

I talked to Annie all day, and I really understood that despite all these negative stories, Annie is a tough cookie. She didn't really mind as much as other people thought she did. She can hold her own, and she really loved Susan.

AV: Sontag was a natural beauty, but you indicate she never took care of herself, which included not brushing her teeth or taking a shower for several days. It makes me wonder why people were attracted to her, especially the physical relationships. Why did Sontag have such little regard for her own hygiene?

BM: Sontag's sister said this was a problem even in elementary school. I think part of the attraction was it didn't look like she was trying hard. She was just different. It's a mystery as far as the hygiene goes, but she had star power that is hard to quantify.

AV: If Sontag didn't address the AIDS situation properly, she definitely exceeded expectations regarding the Serbian-Bosnian conflict. Do you think this was the best moment in her life?

BM: The other night when I was in Los Angeles for a reading, there was this old guy in the audience. I was so excited because it was Merrill Rodin, who went with Sontag to see Thomas Mann in 1949. They had this game called the Stravinsky game, in which you would ask yourself how many years would you give Stravinsky in exchange for you dropping dead right here on the spot. They concluded that they'd be willing to die in order to give Stravinsky four years of life.

So she always thought culture and art were worth dying for. She thought art made human life more than the sum of pain and suffering and misery. She found a place where she could put that idea into practice. This is the story of what she did in Sarajevo by putting on Beckett's *Waiting for Godot* in 1993.

I can tell you all those mixed feelings people might have had about her in New York, or Paris, or wherever—none of those mixed feelings existed in Sarajevo. People loved her for what she did. They named the square in front of the national theatre for her. She found the thing she was meant to do in her life, and that was to stand for culture and art and civilization and tolerance and antiracism and antiwar.

AV: Sontag had a lot of occasions that helped her to project "her own desire to be reinvented." In this she was a precursor to someone like Madonna. How was Sontag able to stay in the limelight for roughly fifty years? Do you think her prominence will diminish over time?

BM: It's interesting you mention Madonna, because reinvention is often a word that comes up with her. The thing is with Sontag, when you look at her life, and her process of going from one thing to the next, it's not a reinvention that comes about because she has a new album, which is the impression you get with Madonna. That's not to belittle Madonna; I think she's more interesting than that. But with Sontag she was always trying to find something to do with herself, and it often comes out of pain and longing and failure. She's propelling herself, and finding a way to get back on her feet and do something new. I think it's really American in a certain way, and really courageous. This is a woman who almost died of cancer twice. A woman who was always struggling, who was often unhappy, and who was nevertheless able to keep going and produce this incredible amount of work. One of my ambitions for this biography is that I want people to come back to her work. I realize this is probably romantic, but I really hope people will start reading Sontag.

AV: What plans do you have for your next book? Will it be another biography, or perhaps something else?

BM: I have no idea, but it's not going to be another biography. I really don't know what I'll do, but I think about it all the time. I'm waiting for the love of my life to come along and explain it all to me. It will happen, but for right now, I just have to let Sontag flow out of my system.

Steven Pinker. Courtesy of Rose Lincoln.

A New Enlightenment: An Interview with Steven Pinker

One of the most popular and widely read cognitive scientists of our era, Steven Pinker is the Johnstone Family Professor of Psychology at Harvard University, where he conducts research on cognition, language, and social relations. Pinker received his BA in psychology from McGill University in 1976 and his PhD in experimental psychology from Harvard University in 1979. He later did research at the Massachusetts Institute of Technology, where he taught from 1982 until 2003. He is the author of over a dozen books, including *How the Mind Works, The Better Angels of Our Nature, The Sense of Style,* and most recently *Enlightenment Now: The Case for Reason, Science, Humanism, and Progress.*

Pinker was named one of TIME's one hundred most influential people in the world in 2004, has been twice named to Foreign Policy's list of top global thinkers, and was elected to the National Academy of Sciences in 2016. He has won many awards both for his books and his research, and he chairs the Usage Panel of the American Heritage Dictionary. Known for his long curly locks as well as for his impressive intellect, Pinker was voted in 2001 as the first member of the Luxuriant Flowing Hair Club for Scientists.

The following interview took place at the ZaZa Hotel in Houston on March 9, 2018, with my son, Shawn Vorda, providing additional questions.

Allan Vorda: What was the genesis for writing *Enlightenment Now*?

Steven Pinker: One source was my coming across data sets that showed the world had improved in areas beyond those I had documented in *The Better Angels of Our Nature*. That book, which came out in 2011, was itself inspired by my surprise at data that showed many measures of violence had been in historical decline, such as crime, war, and violence against women and children. That surprise led me to the conviction that it was an underappreciated story waiting to be told, and it set the challenge to me as a psychologist to explain it. Why has there been so much violence throughout human history, and how have we managed to tame it? *Enlightenment Now* came from a similar epiphany, namely the realization that it wasn't just violence in which the human condition had improved, but measures of hunger, disease, child mortality, maternal mortality, literacy, work hours—pretty much every aspect of human flourishing has shown an improvement. Once again the vast majority of literate, educated people are unaware of these improvements, and once again they demand an explanation. I suggest that the overarching cause for this human progress consists of the ideals of the enlightenment: reason, science, humanism, and progress.

AV: Can you briefly describe these four major ideals?

SP: The commitment to reason amounts to our not trusting sources and claims to knowledge other than reason, such as dogma, sacred texts, authority, tradition, intuition, gut feelings. Every belief should be justified by reason. The companion value of science holds that the world is intelligible, that we can understand it by forming possible explanations and testing them empirically against the world. And the value of humanism is the commitment to human well-being and flourishing as the ultimate moral good, as opposed to the glory or preeminence of the nation, tribe, or faith, as opposed to obeying divine commandments, as opposed to achieving feats of heroic glory, as opposed to advancing some mystical force or struggle towards a messianic or utopian age.

Shawn Vorda: In Part II of *Enlightenment Now*, you explain how these ideals have led to progress in just about every single measure of human well-being. Bill Gates recently cited five of his favorite facts from this section, ranging from time spent doing laundry to a global increase in IQ. Gates also declared *Enlightenment Now* is now his favorite book of all time. Are there any facts regarding progress that you consider particularly promising?

SP: Certainly the rise of global literacy is promising. The fact that 90 percent of the people in the world under the age of twenty-five can read and write is unprecedented in human history. The decline of extreme poverty is also promising; the level of extreme poverty is less than 10 percent, and the UN has set as one of its sustainable development goals the elimination of extreme poverty everywhere by the year 2030. Lifespans continue to rise, and life expectancy at birth is increasing. Also the many technological innovations in the pipeline promise additional improvements in human well-being; these include energy technology, recycling technology, synthetic biology and rational drug design, genomics, and many others.

SV: Despite an increase in the literacy of the world, recent Pew results indicate an overall decrease in literary reading. Do you have any thoughts on these results? Have you considered producing your work through other media, such as podcasts or YouTube, where they might reach a wider audience?

SP: It seems these are happening at opposite ends of the literary spectrum. The increase in literacy pertains mainly to the children in the developing world who formerly could not read at all, as opposed to the literary elite who might be reading less fiction or literature. I have been struck by ideas I want to share, and how the world of non-text media has exploded. There are hundreds of podcasts, and YouTube videos seem to get greater circulation than text interviews and articles. People recognize me on the street because they've seen me in a YouTube video, and impressionistically that does seem to have increased. I suppose I would need numbers to know whether the increase in YouTube viewership came at the expense of people who would otherwise read, or if it consists of people who would otherwise be watching television programs or playing video games.

AV: In the chapter "Reason" you state: "People affirm or deny these beliefs to express not what they *know* but who they *are*." In a polarized political society it seems we have come to a point where a political party puts their agenda ahead of the best interests of America. Essentially, a person might identify himself by saying, "I am a Republican" instead of saying "I am an American." What can be done to limit this trend?

SP: I don't know what can be done, but certainly identifying it as a prime source of public irrationality would be the first step: especially if a larger community of people can think about what can be done about it. I don't have a prescription for turning around an entire society from the trends that have been following for the past twenty years. At least being aware of it would mean that some portion of the intellectual community, those that are not ideologically or tribally committed, are at least aware that all of us are vulnerable to it. Whether that can proliferate, go viral, or reach a tipping point, I don't know. But there have been inroads against other forms of irrationality. People don't believe in alchemy or unicorns or miasmas. There is an increasing number of people who are aware of the data revolution and insist on metapolls like 538.com, or sabermetrics in sports, or evidence-based policy and medicine. It is nowhere close to a consensus, but it has certainly penetrated the awareness of many elite professions. Political tribalism as a source of irrationality is a new idea, and I think it's largely unknown. I think if it becomes better known, it sets the stage for us to take measures against it.

SV: Also in "Reason," you discuss "The Most Depressing Discovery about the Brain, Ever" or "How Politics Makes Us Stupid." Can you briefly describe the studies related to these articles?

SP: These were studies done by the Yale legal scholar Dan Kahan, who was a big influence on that chapter. The studies presented people with data from a fictitious study in which the first impression of the data contradicted the actual message of the data. That is, if you looked at the absolute value of the numbers but didn't do a simple comparison of ratios, you could misinterpret the results. Kahan varied whether the content of these studies were politicized (the effect of a concealed carry law on violent crime) or politically neutral (the effectiveness of skin cream treating a rash). He post hoc divided his subjects into numerate, more numerate, and less numerate groups based on tests of mathematical ability. In the case of politically neutral content (the skin cream study), the more numerate subjects scored better than the less numerate subjects, regardless of left- or right-leaning tendencies. But when it came to political issues (the gun control study), each faction fell back on their primitive, innumerate impulses. The subjects were seduced by raw numbers and made mathematical errors if the results didn't agree with their ideology's favored position. It suggests that we're apt to ignore evidence when it presents a challenge to our favored position, and we're all too ready to accept evidence when it confirms it.

AV: Recent studies have shown that 23 percent of people are nonreligious and the numbers are increasing every year. Nevertheless, when there is a political discussion on cable TV networks, they often talk about the religious right and the evangelical vote, but they virtually never mention the nonreligious vote, which is almost a quarter of the populace. Why is this?

SP: In part it's because religious groups are organized and they form effective voting blocks. They're emboldened by their coalition and encouraged to vote in large numbers. Many of the so-called "nons"—people without a religious affiliation—are not necessarily rational, secular atheists; rather, they're people who have just dropped out of all institutions. They've not only dropped out of organized religion but also out of engagement with the entire political process. This is a regrettable development, because it's an example of how democratic politics is often pushed by the most energized interest groups, as opposed to the interests of the population as a whole. Perhaps it also speaks to the lack of political shrewdness of non-evangelical movements since they have not had the same success in mobilizing their forces and getting their faction to the polls. I also suspect a reason for the disengagement of so many center and left-wing voters is the left has joined in the Trumpist denunciation of mainstream institutions and his dystopian vision of American society. If you agree with Trump that the country is a cesspool of inequality, crime, police shootings, and racism, then you're apt to figure there is no difference in the major party candidates. So it doesn't matter if your president is Hillary Clinton or Donald Trump, because they're both presiding over equally dysfunctional systems. One of the reasons I think it is essential to take note of the progress that has occurred is so people don't become cynical or fatalistic about our existing institutions, or perhaps tempted towards radical or nihilistic alternatives.

AV: Every day we wake up to news that is generally depressing. Your book is the opposite, since it presents a very positive outlook for our species, especially over the last couple of centuries. This seems to go against the grain of the "modern apocalypse" in regard to concerns of overpopulation, resource shortage, pollution, and nuclear war. What is the greatest existential risk now facing us, and is there an existential risk that concerns you in the far future?

SP: I don't know that the risk is existential, but climate change certainly poses a serious risk of disruption and perhaps human misery. If climate change disrupts the growth of food, forces wide-scale migration, and results in catastrophic tipping points like the diversion of the Gulf Stream, there could be wrenching changes. I doubt they would be existential, but they don't have to be existential to cause great amounts of misery. The chance of nuclear war is something we should be concerned about, although I think the chance is small, but the consequence could be catastrophic. Again it's too easy to leap from something being horrific to something being an existential threat. In the most extreme nuclear winter scenario, the threat could be existential, but that would require the exchange of hundreds of weapons. A single nuclear exchange would be far short of an existential threat.

SV: In a recent event we attended in Houston, both Sam Harris and Geoffrey Miller expressed concerns over the existential threat of Artificial Intelligence. Miller was specifically concerned with an ongoing "arms race" between China and the US to develop AIs for defense systems. You explain in your book why you don't share concerns regarding AI, but you do mention concerns regarding nuclear war. If newly developed AI is linked to our defense systems, is that not slightly concerning?

SP: I don't think it's more concerning than the systems we have now. In fact we have AI in cruise missiles, and it's a cliché of computer science that once a system starts to work we no longer call it AI. AI is reserved for computational challenges at the frontier of knowledge. So there isn't even a clear line between AI and computer programming. There is a fantasy of a godlike artificial general intelligence that would be omnipotent, omniscient, and have the power to solve any problem instantly, and in some scenarios has a thirst for infinite power and influence. I think that's fanciful. There is no evidence that current AI is on such a trajectory. It's not clear that the concept of artificial general intelligence is even coherent, because intelligence requires knowledge in the domain in which one is reasoning. There is no reason to think that merely being intelligent is tantamount to seeking power and domination. The fear an AI system hooked up to vast infrastructure might be given a vague goal that would include collateral damage to humans is utterly fanciful, like giving an AI a task of curing cancer where it turns us all into guinea pigs for lethal experiments. I think if we were smart enough to design a system that could cure cancer, we would not be so stupid as to give it a blanket goal without programming in the various tradeoffs and considerations. Any system that is intelligent enough to accomplish anything of interest would be intelligent enough to consider all the tradeoffs and potential for collateral damage.

In general I think apocalyptic scenarios are accepted with too much credulity, whereas the reasons that apocalyptic scenarios don't occur are boring and people don't like to write about them. The previous apocalypse scenarios haven't happened. We have never run out of a resource, and population is likely to plateau in the second half of the twenty-first century. The apocalypse makes for too enticing theater to be evaluated rationally. The AI scenarios assume an utterly implausible handover of control to the systems, or an equally implausible megalomaniacal designer of the system, or a lack of control of the system despite the fact every interface with the real world has to be mediated with humans to make it happen.

SV: In "The Environment" chapter, you discuss the dangers of climate change and William Norhaus's concept of a Climate Casino: if there is an even chance the world will get worse and a 5 percent chance of catastrophe, it would be prudent to take preventative action even if the outcome is uncertain. However, you seem less concerned with issues regarding resources. Could the same logic of the Climate Casino also be applied to concerns with resources, or other concerns in general?

SP: Yes, it could be applied to other concerns in theory. When it comes to resources, I think the concern is misconceived, because the model in which we successfully extract more and more of a resource until it depletes violates the way resources actually are exploited. Namely, as the more plentiful deposits are consumed, it becomes more and more expensive to get at the remainder, and that incentivizes economies to develop more efficient ways to extract the resources that remain, to conserve existing resources, or to switch to some substitute. Long before a resource is exhausted, the world typically does find a substitute. To quote Jesse Ausubel: The reason the world switched from wood to coal at the advent of the industrial revolution is not that we ran out of wood, just like the reason we switched from coal to oil is not because we ran out of coal. It's because the new resources turned out to be more efficient with fewer negative side effects than the older one.

SV: In "Safety" you explain that we are safer in basically every aspect of life: in the workplace, from natural disasters, from homicide, etc. Gun control and safety is at the forefront of political discussions given the recent events in Florida. You briefly state "neither right-to-carry laws favored by the right, nor bans and restrictions favored by the left, have been shown to make much difference." Do you have any further thoughts regarding gun control?

SP: I'm in favor of tightening gun control. It should be regulated like any other kind of dangerous technology, the way we regulate cars. The interpretation of the Second Amendment which nullifies controlling guns like we control cars is erroneous. It's a tragic mistake the Supreme Court upheld that interpretation. I think it's unlikely stricter gun control would make much of a difference in homicide rate, though. There might be fewer mass shootings, but there are so many guns already out there. The US has such a well-developed culture of retaliation, intolerance of insults, and "culture of honor," as anthropologists call it, that whatever the number of guns we do have, we're still going to have a higher rate of violence than other European countries. I do think these regulations are worth implementing, and I think we need to acquire more knowledge about the effects of gun restrictions. The acquisition of such knowledge has been impeded by an absurd gag order on the Centers for Disease Control which prevents studies on gun violence. Being ignorant is always worse than being knowledgeable, and the policy of not studying something is always the worst conceivable policy.

AV: A common argument is with the increase of automation and AIs, there will be fewer jobs for humans. Can you explain your thoughts on this sentiment? Could there ever be a second Luddite revolution? Do you have any thoughts on universal basic income?

SP: I don't have a confident expectation with what will happen with growth of AI or automation. On one hand they will clearly eliminate many jobs, but that doesn't necessarily imply new jobs won't materialize to put idle hands to work. Every challenge for robots has turned out to be much harder than we originally anticipated. We don't even have cars that are allowed to drive automatically from point to point; there is some skepticism as to whether we're going to see them any time soon. We may have trucks and cars that can change lanes, slow down or speed up on the highway, but we will still put a human behind the wheel to get it to the last couple of miles of the loading dock. Driving is a relatively easy challenge compared to ones that require a lot of tactile feedback, such as laying bricks, changing a diaper, or emptying a dishwasher. Even these tasks turn out to be harder than we thought. I'm skeptical of scenarios in which AI will revolutionize life because the problems AI have been set to solve are really hard problems, harder than one might think. I think this is a near consensus from people who are actually working in AI, at least ones I know. It may be as some jobs go the way of telephone switchboard operators or wheelwrights, the gains from automation could be redirected to other fields. We could perform more healthcare needs, hire teachers that instruct in the developing world over the internet, or plant forests to suck CO^2 out of the atmosphere. We just don't know whether the economy will be supple enough to find new lines of work for the people that have been displaced from their old lines of work. Indeed, in the stats thus far, there hasn't been the leap in productivity unemployment one might expect from rapid advances in AI or automation.

We also know that economies can expand employment opportunities in response to the supply of workers. This is what happened in the 1970s, when massive numbers of women entered the workforce. Each woman that received a job did not necessarily take a job from a man; rather, the total number of jobs increased. For all we know this could happen again. If not, and if there is widespread unemployment or underemployment, it might increase pressure to adopt a UBI (Universal Basic Income) or at least a negative income tax. We already have one, the income tax credit, but it could be expanded to discourage Luddites. It would allow the economy to adapt dynamically to opportunities made available by technology and not be dragged backward by Luddites. That alone might be a reason to encourage that kind of income transfer, so the entire society can benefit from the obvious gains in productivity that AI promises, even if it hasn't delivered it so far. Many of the jobs rendered obsolete by robots aren't particularly desirable jobs anyway. It's kind of perverse to romanticize the job of a coal miner, or a forklift operator, or a truck driver—professions that not so long ago were the subject of woe and pity and concern.

AV: Since people are living longer, what impact do you think this will have on our health regulations and the possible legalization of euthanasia?

SP: It's possible that the ability of medical technology to keep people alive in a state that isn't worth living, that is in pain or disability, could increase pressure for physician-assisted suicide. I personally think this would be a tremendously humane development, assuming it came with obvious safeguards so you don't have daughters-in-law wanting to do in their mothers-in-law to accelerate their inheritances. States and countries that have adopted physician-assisted suicide, as far as I know, don't have an epidemic of sons- and daughters-in-law knocking off granny.

AV: In *Enlightenment Now*, you state C. P. Snow "never held the lunatic position that power should be transferred to the culture of scientists." Why not? Wouldn't it be interesting to see what scientists, engineers, and humanists could achieve if they were appointed to positions in the president's cabinet?

SP: I certainly think individual scientists who develop the expertise to run for office deserve our support, and I personally support a number of them. Not least to change some of the culture of the legislative process from the one that is second nature to lawyers, where the goal is to win, and replace it with one that is second nature to scientists, where the goal is to seek the truth. These are very different objectives in debate, and I don't think we're very well served by the lawyerly one. What I was referring to is the fear among many intellectuals that C. P. Snow's arguments and my arguments that suggest we should all think more scientifically is just a power competition among the elites. I certainly don't think just because someone is a scientist that their positions on all issues should be taken seriously. I list a number of crackpot opinions that are often popular among scientists—not scientists that actually have the discipline and knowledge to run for legislative office. For example: we should have mandatory licensing for parents who screw up their children and harm society; we should seek the ability to colonize other planets in case we foul the earth so much that it's unfit for human habitation; or the only way to prevent war is through a world government; or the only way to eliminate poverty and hunger in the developing world is to let them die of hunger or disease. I've heard all of these ideas from scientists now and again, and they're all cockamamie ideas that should not be indulged just because they're from scientists in some other field.

AV: They wouldn't necessarily have to run for office, but they could be appointed, so you wouldn't have people like Ben Carson saying things like the worse thing since slavery is Obamacare.

SP: On the other hand, he's a neurosurgeon. I agree scientists who engage with the political process would be both an asset to the cabinet or to Congress. I think a better example might be the contrast between Rick Perry as the Secretary of Energy, who is an utter ignoramus and buffoon, compared to Ernest Moniz or Stephen Chu. It's heartbreaking.

AV: Since the time of Freud, psychology has become an influential science, and it really seemed to take off in the 1960s. Its popularity with the masses may have tapered off, but there are expanding fields of psychology led by yourself and others such as your sister Susan Pinker, Jordan Peterson, Geoffrey Miller, and perhaps Gad Saad might also be included. What is your opinion about the importance of psychology in the world we live in today?

SP: I think psychology is tremendously important as a reminder of our limitations, our biases, our fallacies, and our illusions. Here I would point to cognitive psychologists like Daniel Kahneman, Richard Thaler, Tali Sharot, my colleague Dan Gilbert, and Dan Ariely, who have brought into the public sphere an awareness of our cognitive limitations. We should not be so fooled by our intuitions and gut feelings. An awareness of our moralistic biases is highly relevant to discounting our own moral outrage and trying to put our ethics on a more defensible basis. Here I would point to people like Jonathan Haidt and Joshua Greene—those are two examples, but similar to my discussion with scientists, it doesn't mean we should trust everything psychologists say. Rather, the field of psychological research should be integrated into our understanding of politics, persuasion and behavior change, and the judicial system, so that our best understanding of us as humans is brought to bear on the design of our institutions. I have to add this is an idea that very much came out of the Enlightenment—that there could be a science of human nature and that it should inform the design of our institutions. That was at the forefront of the design of the American democracy, in *The Federalist Papers*, and in comments by John Adams, Benjamin Franklin, and Thomas Paine. They all alluded to their own intuitive psychology and their observations of what makes us tick, in order to design instructions that would lead to greater well-being.

Richard Powers. Courtesy of Dean D. Dixon.

A Fugitive Language: Two Interviews with Richard Powers

Richard Powers was born in 1957 in Evanston, Illinois, and enrolled at the University of Illinois as a physics major before switching to English as his chosen field. Upon receiving his BA and MA, he moved to Boston, where he worked as a computer programmer and a night watchman in a museum, which inspired his first novel, *Three Farmers on Their Way to a Dance,* in 1985. After publishing a second novel he moved to the Netherlands, but eventually returned to the US to teach for many years (first at the University of Illinois, then Stanford University) before moving to the Smoky Mountains, where he now lives in nature as he pursues an ascetic lifestyle of reading and writing. Over the years, he has published thirteen novels, typically taking two to four years to write each one. Among his numerous literary awards, he has won the National Book Award for *The Echo Maker* and the Pulitzer Prize for *The Overstory*.

As with each of his novels, his latest book *Bewilderment* explores new territory; in this case, the relationship of a father (Theo) and his troubled nine-year-old son (Robin). The son undergoes a metamorphosis after participating in an experimental trial called Decoded Neurofeedback. The father, a university teacher and researcher, works on a project that entails creating imaginary planets to which he gives fictional names. Father and son take approximately a dozen visits to these simulated worlds, yet these Planet Seeker visits, in conjunction with the difficulties Theo encounters as a widower raising a son and the effects of Decoded Neurofeedback on Robin, raise the question of what is real and what is simulated. It is an amazing journey that has in-and-out-of-this-world experiences, but perhaps most importantly, Powers does an incredible job of showing the boundless love that a father has for his son. This interview took place over email in May of 2021.

Bewilderment

Allan Vorda: The epigraph for Daniel Keyes's 1959 novel *Flowers for Algernon,* taken from Plato, incorporates your title: "Anyone who has common sense will remember the bewilderments of the eye are two of the kinds, and arrive from two causes, either from coming out of the light or going into the light, which is true of the mind's eye, quite as much as of the bodily eye." Was *Algernon* an inspiration for *Bewilderment*?

Richard Powers: It's the touchstone intertext for my novel. Keyes wrote the short story the year after my birth, and the novel version appeared when I was nine—the same age as Robin through most of

Bewilderment. I read the story in the sixth grade, when I was eleven, and it settled into a permanent place in my imagination as one of those bedrock fables that helps to explain life.

The story itself is mentioned several times in the course of my novel, and on at least two occasions, it serves to further the plot. I even explicitly reference *Algernon*'s epigraph, from Plato's "Allegory of the Cave," and as you point out, those words serve as one of the sources of my title. But *Algernon* is also the inspiration for the science fiction invention that serves as the central plot of the entire novel. Daniel Keyes's story tells of a cognitively challenged man who, through a breakthrough in scientific technique, is granted intelligence far beyond ordinary human limits. A couple of years ago, when I read about a remarkable new technique called decoded neurofeedback, I instantly thought of using it to tell a similar fable. Suppose researchers perfected an empathy machine that could greatly magnify our ability to apprehend the world through our feelings? What might we humans learn to become? *Bewilderment* turns the *Algernon* fable on its head. In place of intellect, it deals in *emotional* intelligence. It tells the story of a little child, going into the light.

AV: *Bewilderment* is an extraordinary story of the heartfelt relationship between a father and his son. As someone who doesn't have any children, how were you able to capture the essence of the feelings of Theo and Robin?

RP: Well, I had a lot of experience being a child. And when I grew up, I began to suspect how my father had been a child once, too. I was also an older brother, with too much parental instinct for my own good. I have been an uncle several times over, and I've been a surrogate dad to more than one of my friends' children. I spent many years as a teacher, in constant contact with lives looking for guidance and direction. I've watched almost everyone I've ever loved struggle with the unsolvable mystery of how to raise another life. So my own life has been more than full of vicarious parenting.

Children can possess enormous amounts of innate emotional intelligence, but adult pragmatism and practicality tend to wear it down.

While finishing my previous novel, *The Overstory,* I read numerous accounts of the toll our growing environmental catastrophe is taking on the young. I kept running across a recent neologism: *solastalgia,* the emotional anguish caused by an apprehension of the dying planet. It occurred to me that we were raising a generation of troubled kids, born homesick for a place that they never knew. What would it be like to raise a child suffering from such an illness? I'd never seen a parenting story that addressed that question. So I wrote one.

AV: Early on we learn that nine-year-old Robin has issues with anger. Is his anger due to his mother's death? Is there a medical term for what is afflicting Robbie?

RP: So much of the book is concerned with the crudeness and insufficiency of our diagnoses, etiologies, and understandings of childhood neurodivergence. Robin's behavioral differences go way beyond anger issues. He's an uncanny child, intense and otherworldly, whose peculiarities prevent his successful integration into the social world. When I was a child (possessing many of these qualities myself), many of Robin's behaviors would have been diagnosed as "abnormal." Our tolerance for difference has grown in the years since then. But our understanding of the clinical underpinnings of such differences remains limited and primitive.

To lay blame for Robin's "condition" either on his mother's death or on some genetic disorder is already to fall into that limited thinking. There are medical terms for Robin, to be sure. But they are almost all crude and pathologizing. As Theo puts it: "I never believed the diagnoses the doctors settled on my son. When a condition gets three different names over as many decades, when it requires two subcategories to account for completely contradictory symptoms, when it goes from nonexistent to the country's most commonly diagnosed childhood disorder in the course of one generation, when two different physicians want to prescribe three different medications, there's something wrong."

We in the States still seem less interested in understanding "challenged" kids than in treating and altering them. Just a couple of days ago, Elon Musk announced on national television that he has Asperger's Syndrome. That announcement may go a ways toward helping parents understand that neurodivergence is much subtler and more wondrous than they may fear, and not always in need of a "treatment."

AV: There are several references to birds in *Bewilderment*. Theo's late wife, Alyssa, used to go birding with her friend Marty Collier. Her son is named after her favorite bird. Robin shows his dad an owl that lives in a nearby tree. Theo and Robin see three sandhill cranes (which recalls your novel *The Echo Maker*) flying north, to which Robbie says, "How would we ever know aliens? We can't even know birds." Do you have an interest in ornithology?

RP: I have been an avid (if still totally amateur) birder since before I published *The Echo Maker*. I'm a total autodidact, but I've been to some of the greatest birding spots on the continent: the Platte River, Southwest Texas, Cape May. I no longer keep life lists or day counts, which tend to commodify the experience too much for me. I can't always tell what I'm looking at (especially with warblers, in the spring and fall!). But the thrill never gets old, even in seeing "commoners." I saw a pair of scarlet tanagers the other day (early in May, in the Smokies) that were so bright I thought for a moment that two bits of orange and red emergency reflective tape had blown up into the trees. When I hear the pileated woodpecker and the barred owl who live right near my house, it's enough to make it a good day. A good bird sighting can match any artistic pleasure.

The Smokies are covered in such dense forests that birding here is usually more of a matter of hearing than seeing. While writing *Bewilderment,* I began studying and learning the songs of the hundreds of birds who come through the area. A bit of musical background has helped in this. I've also become a devoted supporter of American Bird Conservancy, which does astonishingly good work, on a very limited budget, to preserve habitat and protect birds—highly recommended for anyone who'd like to perpetuate and extend the joy that birds bring!

AV: Theo creates imaginary planets with different characteristics for his Planet Seeker project. How did you come up with names like Mios,

Nithar, and Zenia and the planets' different features? How do these discussions help bind the father-son relationship?

RP: I took great pleasure in shaping and naming these planets in the hope that these voyages to surreal places would intensify the domestic realism of the rest of the novel. The names of the planets are playful trips in etymology, and I tried to cast a wide linguistic net in naming them. All the names grow out of ancient roots and have some bearing on the allegorical nature of each place. As all good religions understand, the mystery of our ability to know ourselves is also the mystery of language. Childhood consists of struggling to come to terms with a bewildering array of names and words. Every word is another planet.

The voyages that Theo and Robin take to these imaginary places are both a form of shared play as well as an exercise in mutual empathy. For the son, the stories are pure escape and emotional adventure. For the father, they are exercises in the recovery of childhood mystery and his own love for speculative fiction. I am lucky to be pen pals with Kim Stanley Robinson, a towering figure in contemporary American speculative fiction, and I sent him a copy of the book in galleys. He remarked on being taken back to his own early pleasures in the genre of 1950s and 1960s "planetary romances," a tradition that he dates back to Melville and others' travel romances to remote islands. He cites Le Guin, Pangborn, Vance, Sturgeon, and Brunner as being great practitioners of the form. These are writers whose influence I have felt with real force—writers touched with wanderlust and desire to travel beyond the constraints of an increasingly domesticated Earth.

Other planets are, of course, always other people, and dreams of travel are filled with the fear of otherness and the desire for unachievable empathy. But Robinson also hit on the jackpot point—that all these travels to other planets are meditations on the unbelievable luck and incredible beauty of *this one*. As he put it to me, any alien father and son out there, dreaming up a place like Earth, would be tempted to laugh away the idea as way too rich and fecund and lucky to be anything but the wildest science fiction.

AV: The discussions Theo has with Robbie get into the Fermi Paradox. Robbie asks Theo how many galaxies there are in the universe, and Theo says: "A British team just published a paper saying there might be two trillion." This is mind-boggling. What are your thoughts about sentient life in the universe? Assuming there is sentient life and contact gets made in the future, doesn't it make you wonder how we Earthlings would respond, especially since there is so much xenophobia in the world today?

RP: The math for calculating the likelihood of intelligent alien life is so full of gaps and unknowns that it truly is anybody's guess. The denominator of habitable planets is growing rapidly, and it is already so large that it would seem to make the existence of intelligent aliens almost a certainty. But there are so many possible filters and bottlenecks that we can't entirely calculate, since we are in the untenable position of reasoning from a single case—our own. Nevertheless, the smart money is leaning toward "Yes." When I was young, it was almost taboo for serious scientists to talk about the possibility in public. Now, astrobiology is a respected career. My lay-person's hunch is that they are almost certainly out there, but at distances so great that we may never detect even indirect evidence and could never hope for direct communication.

As for how Earthlings would respond to any detection of life elsewhere: Now there is *the* classic SF question! And it has been answered in so many ways. Some writers point out that what Freud called "the narcissism of small differences" tends to gets tempered a bit when people are confronted with a much deeper outside difference. Some (I'm thinking of James Tiptree Jr.) seem to suggest that the desire for alien intimacy is the strongest urge we can feel. Others emphasize how resourceful and infinitely pliant a hatred of everything alien can be. Given human psychology, there may be a connection here!

I can't pretend to understand humans, and I have no great insight into their profound, primal contradiction. We are xenophobic, yes, and our tribal loyalties can make us hate just about anyone and anything that does not look enough like us. But we are also filled, especially as children, with what E. O. Wilson calls biophilia. Children are born scientists. They also tend toward pantheism, and they can see God crawling all over every inch of the backyard. I want to write stories that can help return us to that state of consciousness, books that can reenchant and "bewilder" people in the etymological sense: to make them a part of wildness again. The chief crisis of humanity is that we see this planet not as a finite, living system but as a bottomless commodity to exploit and an endless terrain to subdue. We desperately need stories that can alter that. The most bewildering fiction is a kind of empathy machine, training us to see our seemingly disparate selves as imbricated in an unfolding, experimental network that is trying to travel everywhere.

AV: There are a number of scenes in *Bewilderment* that refer to the president, which the reader can assume is Trump, making outrageous decisions. One example is the president's solution to stop forest fires in California by writing an executive order to cut down two hundred thousand acres of national forest. As a former physics student and an environmentalist who believes in science, what has it been like for you to have watched Trump with his anti-science approach to such things as global warming, conservation, and COVID-19?

RP: The president in *Bewilderment* isn't Trump per se, but he is a very close fictional double! He, too, has figured out that in the era of digitally leveraged politics he can sell fear, anger, hearsay, confusion, persecution, and paranoia much better and spread them much faster than humility, empathy, wonder, and science. The xenophobia, tribalism, and superstition whipped up during the four short years of the Trump administration have stunned and demoralized me. His outright rejection of empirical evidence in favor of wishful thinking destroyed not just the public's belief in scientifically demonstrated fact, but also demolished anything that looked like a shared trust in any kind of accountable process for determining facts in the absence of consensual belief. The trend of those years was terrible and obvious: evidence has given way to wishful thinking, and ideology has replaced all appeal to empirical data and measurement.

The destruction of national set-aside land over the last four years, the removal of protections to air and water, the reversal of all our hard-won progress on climate change, and the redoubled war on everything that isn't human tore the heart out of me. But the real tragedy of those years, one that will continue to harm humanity and all the rest of creation for a long time to come, was the massive resurgence of human exceptionalism that Trump fostered simply by preaching a sense of aggrieved entitlement. Trump's white nationalism and his toxic male paternalism are part of a larger, unbridled gospel of human separation from and domination over everything else alive.

Good scientific practice, with its self-restrained and tentative nature, is helpless in the face of swaggering self-assertion and grandiose privilege. Rational argument, statistics, and an appeal to facts do nothing in such a battle. But stories can sometimes sway a reader's heart, and the questions of children can sometimes shame adults into seeing themselves. That's why the story of a child coming into the light seemed to me the perfect antidote to Trump's America.

AV: There are numerous sentences throughout the novel that just sparkle. One example: "Rising from the leaf duff in a bowl-shaped opening off the path was the most elaborate mushroom I'd ever seen. It mounded up in a cream-colored hemisphere bigger than my two hands. A fluted ribbon of fungus rippled through itself to form a surface as convoluted as an Elizabethan ruff." Is there a method to this creative architecture? Do you think of some exquisite sentence and write it down to be used later, or does your Muse inspire you when you actually sit down to write?

RP: Thanks for the kind words. I'm grateful to hear that. Of all the elements of writing, I have always been mostly drawn to explorations of style. When I was younger, that sometimes meant striving to create lots of sentence-level effects through diction, register, and elaborate syntax. I often tried to create a style that called attention to itself. As I grew older, I became interested in simplicity and constraint, while still searching for a language that was distinctive and unpredictable. Often this has involved a more passive approach to sentence-making than in the past. Nowadays I like to take the sentences I'm working on out on the trail with me. I don't attack them with conscious attention, but rather, I let them percolate in the back of my mind as I walk, and I focus my attention on all the life around me in the woods. Before I've gone far—usually no more than a mile or two—the solution to the sentence or paragraph that I've been puzzling over will present itself to me, almost intact. Of course, the tiny bits of tinkering and adjustment continue when I get home, and those never stop, even after publication, I'm afraid.

AV: While discussing the Trappist planet, Robbie asks: "What about God, Dad?" Theo's response to his son is, "I mean, God isn't something you can prove or disprove. But from what I can see, we don't need any bigger miracle than evolution." Was there a point in your life that you came to a similar conclusion?

RP: I began falling away from traditional religion when I was a teen. The more I learned about the complexity of life and the shared features of biochemistry and genetics across all living things, the more spiritual power I found in the grand biogenetic synthesis. As Darwin suggested in the famous last lines of *The Origin of Species,* there is more miracle and greater potential for inspiration in the accreting discoveries of empirical science than there is in the Bronze Age story of a personal God, especially the anthropomorphized one we've inherited. If you're talking about the creation of meaning, nothing is more staggering or meaningful than a sense of what a few self-replicating molecules have been able to manage, shaped by natural selection and the other regulators of evolution.

Religions based on a soul-testing God who is intent on the salvation of separate souls (a God who seems remarkably indifferent to the fate of non-humans, by the way) have proved to be a disaster for the planet. Yet religion is likely to be the only thing strong enough to compel people to rejoin and rehabilitate the living planet. We need a different kind of religion now if we mean to stick around here for much longer. I'm looking for that in all kinds of places, from Taoism to Native American belief in Interbeing. We need the pantheism of children and the sense of awe expressed by the best natural scientists. We need to remember that "religion" derives from deep linguistic roots that mean, literally, "tying back together."

AV: "They share a lot, astronomy and childhood. Both are voyages across huge distances. Both search for facts beyond their grasp." On one hand, Theo is a scientist who appears to be living in the real world while trying to deal with the reality of being a widower and single parent. On the other hand, he also lives in a simulated world with his imaginary planets. What are the consequences of this duality for the father-son relationship?

RP: My goal in creating Theo Byrne was to make him broadly sympathetic but also wholly ambiguous and questionable. That's why the book is told in first person. First-person narrators are intrinsically unreliable, to some degree. They perform themselves for the reader, making the equivocal case for themselves even as they explore the limits to their own self-understanding. Theo seems aware of his ample faults, as a scientist, a friend, a husband, and a father, but readers are likely to have deeper insights into him that he himself has not yet been able to reach. That makes him something of a tragic character in the classic sense, I suppose.

And yet, for all his fallibility and the limits of his self-knowledge, I'd like to think that there is something redemptive to him. Philip Roth once said that we really begin to love a person when we see them trying to be game in the face of an impossible situation. As Theo became substantial for me, I couldn't help but love him. He knows he is thrashing about, that he is ill-equipped for the challenges of his life, especially after the death of his wife, Alyssa. But there is nothing—*nothing*—that he wouldn't do to try to protect and care for his son.

AV: To expand on the previous question, when Robbie begins experiments with Decoded Neurofeedback, he becomes so proficient that not only does his anger disappear, but he becomes incredibly intelligent. Do you think the roles of parent and child have been reversed to some extent? If so, to what betterment or detriment for each person?

RP: I suspect that everyone who has ever raised a child has, sooner or later, felt the roles of parent and child reversing. It's a dirty little secret of myopia known to every child, as well! Mark Twain has a very funny line: "When I was young I thought what a fool my father was. When I became a man I was surprised how much he had caught up in the meantime." The story of Robin's accelerated education is an only slightly fabulistic exemplar of the uncanny (but not uncommon) moments when parents feel reminded, humbled, or outright schooled by the wisdom of their children.

AV: The Buddhist prayer Aly says to Robbie at bedtime—"May all sentient beings be free from needless suffering"—does not get answered. In fact, each family member experiences "needless suffering," whether self-inflicted or not. Would you care to comment on the irony of this and the place of praying?

RP: It's a matter of debate whether Buddhism is theistic. In general, though, prayers in that faith are directed not so much outward as inward, toward a self in need of transformation and interconnection. Aly's prayer is derived from the Four Immeasurables, and to think on them is less a matter of petition than of practice. "Let *me* never cause needless suffering to another sentient being."

The first of Buddhism's Four Noble Truths is "the truth of suffering." All creatures *will* suffer, and much of that suffering will be needless. But suffering can be lessened through a change in consciousness. The bedtime refrain that Aly taught Theo and that Theo teaches Robin is an expression of will, that needless suffering should not be compounded. It's a way of strengthening identification with all things and helping to see ourselves in everything that isn't us. Just to say the words out loud is to start to change the consciousness of a culture that has not always admitted to how much needless suffering it inflicts. Prayer, like fiction at its best, is an empathy machine, a way toward that state of Interbeing where needless suffering diminishes.

AV: Making the analogy to Algernon, Robbie tells Theo that he is "still the same mouse, Dad. I just have help now." Robbie also says he has "three really smart, funny, and strong guys" walking with him, "just like they're helping to row the boat or something. My crew." What should the reader make of these imaginary friends?

RP: I think they should be just as bewildered by the words as Theo is! What's happening to Robbie at this point is a locked room mystery. In fact, that's true for the whole book. Theo never really knows what's going on inside his son's head. But when Robin starts training in Martin Currier's empathy machine, Theo's own capacity for empathy is really put to the test. How much of the improvement in Robin is being caused by the feedback? How much of the perceived benefit is only a matter of cueing? How much is Robin doing by himself, in the novelty of the experience and through the force of his own imagination?

Nabokov, in his great afterword to *Lolita,* talks about how he drew inspiration for the book from reading "a newspaper story about an ape in the Jardin des Plantes who, after months of coaxing by a scientist, produced the first drawing ever charcoaled by an animal: this sketch showed the bars of the poor creature's cage." We are each trapped inside our own heads, making art and saying sentences that bewilder other people. We will never know what it's like to be another person, let alone an ape or a bat. No empathy will ever be strong enough to give us anything else but the View from Here.

But here's the thing: when I read a book by someone from another time and place, maybe even someone who is long since dead, it's like I have company, a helper in my head—my "crew." I carry that feeling of having houseguests around with me, even after the act of silent communion and neurofeedback is over. The mystery is not what is in the other locked room. The great mystery is how the View from Here can sometimes become the view from anywhere.

AV: Robbie sees a young climate activist named Inga Alder on TV and, being inspired, decides to do his own protests at the states' and nations' capitols. Greta Thunberg, her seeming real-world counterpart, also has Asperger's, which she claims is a gift. What do you think about Thunberg, who dropped out of school to bring the world's attention to climate change, and her connection to Robbie?

RP: I'm never comfortable giving away my keys to open any *roman à clef,* but this one kind of gives away itself! Inga, like Thunberg, declares that her cognitive "challenge" is really her superpower. Robin himself immediately recognizes the affinity, the moment he first sees her and hears her talk on television. He says, "She's like me, Dad," and the words make Theo's skin pucker.

Thunberg is an astonishing and unique spokesperson for a new human consciousness. The need for humans to come back and live here, inside the webs of the living planet, has rarely been more powerfully articulated or advanced. There is no gainsaying her blunt willingness to confront the truth and to challenge our attempts at denial and self-deception. I believe that Thunberg's skills, her courage, her moral clarity, her powers of persuasion, and the truth of her vision are in no small part a function of her "superpower." It may well be the neurodivergent who lead the way in the transformation of human culture that we will need in order to preserve and extend this planet's experiment in self-awareness.

AV: There is a scene where Theo and Robbie are in the backyard at night which Theo recounts: "He propped his head on the pillow of my arm. For a long time, we just looked up at the stars—all the ones we could see and half the ones we couldn't." Then Robbie says: "Dad. I feel like I'm waking up. Like I'm inside everything. Look where we are! That tree. This grass!" This scene, which echoes the book cover, shows the love of father and son as they share this wonderful, magical moment in time. Was this scene from your own childhood or something else entirely?

RP: I remember many such moments of "oceanic consciousness" from my own childhood, and I have continued to experience them, although less frequently and intensely, as an adult. But this scene came about from my trying to inhabit Robin's consciousness as fully as I could. To show him at his zenith, as his ability to experience "Interbeing" reaches its peak, I read a great deal of spiritual and religious writing, especially in the Eastern tradition. The writer Charles Eisenstein was helpful throughout. I also turned to the best examples of "nature visionary" writing, both classic, like John Muir and Aldo Leopold, and contemporary, like Robert MacFarlane and Robin Wall Kimmerer.

AV: In many of your novels you explore various types of consciousness and how individuals think and express themselves. What are your thoughts about humans having implants in the future?

RP: To some extent, *Bewilderment* is itself wrestling with the question of technologically mediated consciousness. It does so through the fable of neurofeedback, of course, but, more fundamentally, it dramatizes Theo's dilemma of whether to medicate his child. Therapeutic drugs have helped countless people function better on this planet, but Theo is reluctant to experiment with them on such a young and still-forming brain. For him, the ways of going wrong in such an experiment outnumber the ways of going right. But more importantly, he isn't convinced that his struggling child needs to be cured of anything. How much should he try to "correct" his child, simply to conform to contemporary practice in raising children?

These questions of clinical treatment shade off into the increasingly real question of cognitive or emotional enhancement. (Think of the number of students out there taking ADD medication, not to treat a diagnosed condition, but to improve their academic performance.) I have no doubt that humans will get better and better at controlling and mediating mood, emotion, behavior, perception, and cognition through pharmacology and other kinds of neural intervention. But I also know so many kinds of neural interventions—music, love, hiking, poetry, sitting by the river, breathing in a cascade's negative ions—that I'd rather experiment with.

AV: It seems evident in the recent stages of your writing career that you are very concerned about our environment and the impact humans are having on it. Since moving to the Smoky Mountains, some readers might consider you as a modern-day Thoreau. What are your thoughts about the future of our environment, and are there any organizations that concerned citizens should consider supporting?

RP: There are so many! Those that concentrate on the reversal of habitat destruction are especially important to me, as that will be the key to slowing down the mass extinction that we are inflicting on the planet. The organizations Save the Redwoods, Old Growth Forest Network, the National Forest Foundation, and American Forests do good work in this country. I've already mentioned American Bird Conservancy, which is one of the most effective and efficient environmental organizations around. Wangari Maathai's Green Belt Movement is helping to transform Africa. Look for smaller, targeted, lean, and efficient organizations that are doing work close to your own heart.

Perhaps even more useful than sending cash to such outfits is committing yourself to hands-on efforts where you live. Rehabilitation begins at home, and to the extent that we are going to reintegrate in a sane way with the living planet, it will be through local efforts to understand and restore what life wants to do *nearby.* Why not start in your yard? Get rid of invasives, plant native species, give up your desire to control things with chemical inputs, and love what happens when local life comes rushing back in.

AV: Your books never seem to repeat themselves. This allows your readers to examine and reflect on life in ways they ordinarily would not. To paraphrase one of your sentences from *Bewilderment*, your novels let the reader "wormhole" into a different world, even if all of your novels are not "small, light, portable universes." If this question is not too impertinent, can you provide an example or two where you might have read a book and decided "I want to write this type of novel"?

RP: That's not at all impertinent to ask. I do this all the time! In fact, I have spent much of my life like Borges's "Pierre Menard, Author of the Quixote." (I really, really wish I could have written that story.) At one time or another, I have wished that I could rewrite, verbatim, works by Melville and Byatt and Proust and Pynchon and Stoppard and Mann and Le Guin and Mitchell and Whitehead. The list is long, and a certain kind of emulation-gone-astray has left genetic markers all over my thirteen novels. For *Bewilderment*, in addition to *Flowers* *for Algernon,* I took lots of inspiration from Alan Lightman's *Einstein's Dreams,* Italo Calvino's *Invisible Cities,* Olaf Stapledon's *Star Maker,* and so many others.

AV: On its surface, *Bewilderment* could be viewed as a straightforward novel about a father and son relationship, a mystery novel, or even touching upon the realms of science fiction. It also seems to have affinity with fabulist writers such as Calvino, Borges, and Barth. Do you welcome such comparisons and would you ever consider writing a science fiction novel?

RP: I have lived my whole literary life, both as a reader and a writer, straddling that gap between psychological realism, on the one hand, and formalist, fabulist, or more "experimental" writing on the other. Ordinarily, people seem to show devotion to one side of this dualism, and abhorrence for the other side. I love them both, and I've struggled for a third of a century to find ways of writing books that can triangulate between and combine what Zadie Smith famously called these "two paths for the novel." So it thrills me that you feel that "a straightforward novel about a father and son relationship" might also owe a debt to Borges, Calvino, and Barth! All three of those writers have had massive influence on me, and I had them all in mind at one time or another as I wrote *Bewilderment.* I wanted to hybridize modes and aesthetics in a way that showed how porous that species boundary really is.

But in this book, I had other motives for trying to fuse realism with fable, reasons having to do with the subject matter of *Bewilderment.* The novel, as a form, is one of the most complex and effective empathy machines that humans have yet come up with. It works best when it can excite all kinds of concurrent but sometimes incommensurable parts of the brain. The strange loop of fiction makes it possible for us readers to reflect on our own processes, even while we are immersed in the stream of them. And while reading, we begin to see how much of what we take to be inarguably real is, in fact, the result of fabulous maps and shorthand fables that we ourselves have created. Likewise, the primal fables that the best fiction serves up can come away reflecting the most practical and hard-headed realism.

You ask if I've ever considered writing science fiction. As I see it, *Bewilderment* is itself science fiction, in the purest sense. The entire book takes place on a counterfactual Earth, it invokes a dozen voyages to other planets, and it hinges on a plot involving a level of neural technology that doesn't yet exist. But the fact that it didn't feel like science fiction to you pleases me. Not that I'm unhappy with the label of science fiction writer. *Galatea 2.2* and *Plowing the Dark* both used science fiction, and *Generosity* was a finalist for the Arthur C. Clarke Award for science fiction. I'm always proud when SF writers like Kim Stanley Robinson and Carter Scholz claim my books as SF. My aim, though, is to absorb the science fiction elements into a texture of plausible realism and to tell a story where facts and fable fuse seamlessly in the reader's mind.

AV: When I saw you speak at Rice University for a reading of *The Overstory,* you were gracious enough to let your good friend Tayari Jones speak after you. I thoroughly enjoyed her novel *An American Marriage.* Are there any other novels by writers that you might suggest?

RP: Anthony Marra's *A Constellation of Vital Phenomena* was one of the most ambitious and achieved debut novels I've ever read. I really enjoyed *The Alaskan Laundry,* by Brendan Jones, who I worked with when I was at Stanford. I was lucky to read Sandro Veronesi's novel *The Hummingbird,* which made such a splash in Europe, in an early English galley. It is just now being published here. David Benioff's *City of Thieves* was very well done. Anything by the extraordinary writer Colum McCann will provide great rewards.

AV: I cannot put into words how much your writing has brought enjoyment into my life. Since you quoted a Buddhist saying in *Bewilderment,* I will leave you with another Buddhist saying: "What we think, we become." Thank you for your sublime novels and for doing this interview.

RP: Thank you for such kind words. Regarding your Buddhist saying, I used a similar quote, by Bernard of Clairvaux, as the refrain in my novel *Galatea 2.2*: "What we love, we shall come to resemble." When an idea pops up in two such different cultures and traditions, perhaps there is something to it! I'd also like to hope that what we read and think about, we will come to love.

Orfeo

Orfeo offers a montage of time capsules from the life of Peter Els, a seventy-year-old musician-composer who is on the run from the FBI in connection to bioterrorist activity. We see the people and events that have now brought him to national attention as he is dubbed the Bioterrorist Bach; apparently for putting his musical compositions into bacterium. As the title suggests, the story riffs on the Greek myth of Orpheus, the legendary musician who could enrapture the gods themselves, to produce an allegory of the possibilities of music and how it can shape and affect people's lives. Throughout, Powers meditates on a litany of composers (from classical to contemporary) as well as historical events, creating a wonderful composition of its own in the process. *Orfeo* is a beautiful book from a writer who has the gift of literature at his fingertips; all we have to do is listen.

This interview was conducted January 2014.

Allan Vorda: The title *Orfeo* is a reference to the Greek myth of Orpheus, a legendary musician who could charm all living things with his music. The myth recounts his playing music to soften the hearts of Hades and Persephone in order to let his dead wife Eurydice return to earth. How did you come up with the title *Orfeo*, especially since Peter Els's music doesn't always charm everyone, and he leaves his wife to pursue music?

Richard Powers: The Orpheus legend is one of the oldest and most important stories in Western literature. Make that world literature. It's a complex set of loosely linked stories, with Orpheus's descent into the underworld being the best-known and most important part of the legend. As far as I am aware, Orpheus is the only mortal who ever succeeded in beating death and persuading Hades to let one of his dead souls return to the world of the living. Orpheus's mastery of music and his ability to make even stones weep with the beauty of his playing makes him a perfect metaphor for music's mysterious ability to produce the profound human feelings from nothing but patterns of vibration. Reworkings of the legend pervade the arts, especially music, where everyone from Monteverdi (in the first ever opera) to Gluck to Offenbach to Stravinsky to songwriters like Andy Partridge and Nick Cave have taken a crack at it. In films, of course, there is the classic *Black Orpheus* and Cocteau's Orphic Trilogy. I wanted to try my hand at a twist on that very long tradition and to indicate, in the title, that this book functions as an allegory even as it tells a realistic contemporary tale. Since my story is concerned with one man's attempt to locate and reproduce the transcendent power of music, and since it also concerns a flight through the underworld of the contemporary culture of fear while attempting to resurrect a lost past, the legend was made to order. Nothing can compare to music in its power to raise the dead.

AV: Since you wrote your last novel, *Generosity*, you had teaching assignments in Germany and at Stanford University. Did these experiences contribute in any way with writing *Orfeo*? For example, your novel utilizes the Siege of Münster (Germany) as well as Peter's visit to Dr. L'Heureux (writer and former Stanford professor).

RP: My fascination with the Siege of Münster dates back to a visit I made to that city in the early 1980s. When I saw the iron cages still attached to the steeple of the St. Lambert's church, where the bodies of the leaders of the rebellion were kept after their deaths, a quaint centuries-old story suddenly came alive; one of the most incredible accounts of a group search for transcendence I'd ever heard. I used the event as an intertext in my novel *Operation Wandering Soul*, although it makes only a small cameo there. I always felt that the Münster Uprising would have made the greatest kind of contemporary opera, and since I was incapable of writing that opera myself, I had to get Peter Els to do it. The story is a kind of archetype for the millennial cult gone horribly wrong, a pattern that has recurred again and again over the centuries. Suffice it to say that Waco was far from being the last recap we'll see. People long so badly for heaven on earth that we're willing to go to hell to try to bring it off.

As for "Dr. L'Heureux" and the terrific Stanford novelist of the same name—well spotted! The use of the name is my Easter egg for a wonderful writer, who happened to supply me with the story on which Els's malady and diagnosis are based. During that same visiting stint at Stanford (where I now hold a permanent position), I had the extraordinary opportunity to work as an assistant in the lab of biochemist Aaron Straight. My weeks doing bench work on a large-scale genetic screen gave me a chance to see the field from within and helped me imagine my way into Peter Els's second career as a would-be DIY molecular engineer.

AV: You have used places where you have lived, especially Illinois, for settings in your novels. One place you haven't mentioned very much is Thailand, where you lived from age eleven to seventeen (1968-73). What was it like growing up there as an adolescent—did anyone you know claim to have seen a phi (ghost), and do you foresee writing a novel set in Thailand?

RP: In fact, there are similar small references to my experience growing up in Bangkok scattered here and there throughout most of the other novels. But the fourth of those books, *Operation Wandering Soul,* treats those experiences in depth, and one of my strongest memories of my years growing up there forms the foundation for the dramatic centerpiece of the childhood of Richard Kraft.

I moved to Bangkok when I was eleven and returned when I was sixteen. I left the north shore suburbs of Chicago and returned to the northern Illinois cornfields of DeKalb. In between, I lived another life altogether, one that would have been unimaginable to me without living through it. And when I came back to the States, I never again entirely fit in to life as lived here. Those years in Southeast Asia made me a permanent outsider, an observer in my own life. They started me in an itinerant life that has led me through many countries and lots of temporary addresses. It's pretty safe to say that that early dislocation and relocation to the other side of the world was the first step in my becoming a writer.

AV: *Intersections: Essays on Richard Powers* (Dalkey Archive Press, 2008, edited by Stephen J. Burn and Peter Dempsey) states "Powers has consistently constructed his books around interlocking narrative frames, splitting his novels into two or more story-lines. Rather than advancing toward some melodramatic convergence, these parallel lines typically uncover resonant symmetries in apparently dissimilar situations." In what ways do you agree or disagree with this statement?

RP: The Burn and Dempsey collection is filled with wonderful things, and I am deeply appreciative of the insights it contains. I do think it correctly identifies my interest in creating parallax and triangulations of plot using multiple narrative frames. But I think the way that my books deploy multiple narrative frames has been so different over the eleven novels that such a stripped-down description threatens to become a little misleading. The qualitatively distinct frames of *Three Farmers,* for instance, share almost nothing with the temporal shuttling between different moments of Peter Els's life in *Orfeo,* now appearing twenty-nine years later. There is a big difference in alternating between adjacent frames of equal importance (such as in *Gain*) and creating a kind of nested-Russian doll structure (as in *Prisoner's Dilemma*). I have seen reviewers and critics desperately trying to shoehorn the formal and structural devices of *Galatea* or *Time of Our Singing* into that formula, thereby missing as much of those books' structures as they succeeded in capturing, using the simple generalization.

AV: One of your early influences was Thomas Pynchon's *Gravity's Rainbow,* which you first read at age sixteen and which you have "reread portions of . . . every year." What is it about Pynchon that you admire, since your writing styles are dissimilar?

RP: More things than I can name. One of the many pleasures of Pynchon is that he doesn't have a single style, but manages to create a whole panharmonicon of voices and styles and tones and moods and registers, borrowing from high and low, sublime and ridiculous, combining the entire spectrum of what prose can do into a symphonic whole. I can't pretend to do even a fraction of what he manages, but he has inspired me to open up my own stops and try to vary my own style as much as possible, depending on the needs and purposes of any given scene. Pynchon is also the master of casting the reach of fiction far beyond the concerns of the merely personal and domestic, out into the vast world of human concerns, professions, researches, and industries. I learned from him that the sciences and math and engineering are actually the stuff of human passion and obsession, and that the erotics of knowledge can make for a story every bit as mystifying and thrilling as the old questions of who's up and who's down, who's in and who's out, and who gets to marry whom.

AV: *Orfeo*, your eleventh novel, is the journey of Peter Els and his lifelong obsession with music. It has been documented that your family would gather around an organ for sing-alongs, and that you and your four siblings "all sang and played instruments." What was your musical background like as a child, and who were your favorite composers or musicians?

RP: First above all, Bach. I loved him passionately from the earliest age. I had an old, scratchy set of the Brandenburgs that my choir director gave me, and I would listen to them again and again every night, sometimes all six of them at one go, before falling asleep. It made my brothers and sisters nuts. (This is the experience that forms the basis for young Peter Els's transcendent early bliss, listening to Mozart's *Jupiter*.)

The rest of music opened up to me out of that deep spring of Bach's endless invention. Interestingly, I had a real affinity for thorny twentieth-century music while I was still in my early teens, and I had to circle back to the Romantics and the warhorses of the nineteenth century when I was a bit older. And most embarrassing of all, it took me until well into adulthood before Beethoven opened up to me and I could hear him as the heart-crushing, restless revolutionary that he is. Late in life, I came to love early music, especially Renaissance vocal polyphony. A couple of years ago, I felt a period of sadness, thinking there was no more of Western concert music left for me to discover and thrill to. The beauty of writing *Orfeo* was that I could spend my days returning to the amazements of the music of my own lifetime, and to hear much of it for the first time.

AV: *Orfeo* chronicles the life of Peter Els from a child to age seventy, but the story is told in snapshots at various times in his life. One of the most important early life-changing events is when he meets Clara Reston. Els gives up a possible career in chemistry after Clara introduces him to Mahler's *Kindertotenlieder*: "the song began its chromatic wanderings, and Peter Els never heard music the same way again." It's ironic that Clara makes him fall in love with her and music, but then leaves him, yet Els has now become addicted to the possibilities of music, and his life will never be the same. Can you comment on how choices early in life can totally change the direction one takes? I believe you had your own career change as an undergraduate at the University of Illinois when you switched majors from physics to English Rhetoric.

RP: Oh, gee. Where to start on this one? Our beginnings never know our ends. There was a Clara in my life, who I commemorate in this fictional girl. People leave, you find them again decades later, and you discover that the influence that you thought had ended long ago goes on forever, a stranger thing, different, and luckier than you could have supposed. I always thought I would be a scientist. Then I was sure I would become a poet. Then I programmed computers for a living, thinking that it was simply a way to keep a roof over my head, never dreaming that, far from delaying my growth as a novelist, that experience would one day supply the bread and butter of three of my novels' plots. And then there is that closet full of songs and musical compositions that I have accumulated over the decades. If you had told me, when I was young, that I would one day, in my fifties, work in a biochemistry laboratory, in preparation for writing a book about a composer who trained in chemistry and who becomes, in his seventies, a DIY genetic engineer, I'd have said, *Tell me another one.*

AV: The major relationships in Peter's life include his wife Maddy Corr and his friend Richard Bonner. Of the two it is Bonner who exerts the most influence, though it is not always positive. It probably is too much of a stretch to liken the Els-Bonner relationship to the Humbert-Quilty Doppelgänger, but how did the character of Bonner evolve, since he is so different from any character you have created?

RP: Well, where do any of these troops and troops of people come from? Bonner has his precursors, both in my work (I'm thinking of Eddie Sr. in *Prisoner's Dilemma* and Philip Lentz in *Galatea*) and in my life. We find, in the memories of the big personalities that change us, the extremes hiding in our own temperaments. But all my characters—the principals, in any case—are composites of many lives and much aimless imagining.

AV: Wagner, Mozart, and Mahler influenced Peter in various ways. Did you have experiences similar to Peter's when you first heard Mahler's Fifth Symphony? It's amazing that Mahler could create such great music and then enter into a disastrous marriage, which seems to have greatly stifled his creativity.

RP: I was eighteen when I first heard Mahler's Fifth. "Clara" hated it; I thought it was the bee's knees. She later did a one-eighty, completely forgetting about her antipathy, and claiming that she'd always adored the piece. So it goes, with the gap between our experiencing and remembering selves.

Mahler, too, has been making cameos in my novels for a long time. But for me, it's the song cycles first and the symphonies second, as far as the force of their influence.

AV: Peter's love of the old classical composers gives way after being influenced by teachers such as Karol Kopacz and Matthew Mattison. Peter then turns to minimalist composers like John Cage, Philip Glass, Steve Reich, and Harry Partch. Do you have any special affinity for these minimalist composers, in particular, for Partch, who led a very strange life and composed some very strange music?

RP: I do have a little trouble with the label "minimalist." It runs the risk of obscuring more than it reveals. And I certainly wouldn't use it in reference to Cage or Partch, who were each up to very different things than the cycling, strobing, phase-shifting preoccupations that sometimes characterize Glass and Reich. My fascination with Partch dates back to my undergraduate days at the University of Illinois (where I have Peter Els go to graduate school). Partch had been in residence there, not too many years before I arrived, and one could still feel his ghostly presence. I think his whole menagerie of invented instruments played in my imagination as much as his microtonal subdividing of the octave into dozens of intervals.

But what these four composers do have in common—and what thrilled me about them and made me want to use them to inspire Peter Els—is their insistence that the language of music can be extended into whole new places. Strange places? What isn't strange, heard for the first time? All four of these composers were preoccupied with sonority, with the sound of sound itself. All four of them asked people to listen again to what they thought was noisy or banal or trivial, and to hear it as beautiful and new.

AV: You also devote attention to Olivier Messiaen and his *Quartet for the End of Time,* first played in a Nazi concentration camp in 1941. When did you first encounter Messiaen and why did you choose to incorporate it into *Orfeo*?

RP: The *Quartet* is one of those few avant-garde pieces that have entered into the canon of commonly performed concert music. I first heard it in the mid-1970s, performed by the very hip "supergroup," Tashi, who had formed for the express purpose of performing the Messiaen! I had to include it in the book because it is such an otherworldly thing, and the story of its creation is one of the most dramatic stories of twentieth-century music. As much as any other piece, it shows the capacity of the human creative spirit and reveals how making music can be a matter of life and death.

AV: You also refer to Steve Reich's *Proverb,* which utilizes Wittgenstein's proverb "How small a thought it takes to fill a whole life." Reich was a philosophy major at Cornell and studied Wittgenstein. I interviewed him a long time ago and asked him what he thought about contemporary musicians. He said: "When I was fourteen years old there was rock and roll—Fats Domino and Bill Haley—but frankly I thought it was stupid. I didn't like rock and roll. I was a snob and still am." This sounds a lot like Peter, who was forced to listen to rock and roll by his brother Paul. Is Reich's comment something with which you can identify, and did you have any similar experiences?

RP: Reich's comment made me laugh! I, too, was a musical snob as a kid, and I still am, I guess. Only it doesn't feel like snobbery; it just feels like a flavor of deep and different joy. I didn't hate rock and roll; I loved lots of it. I absolutely worshipped the Beatles and every band that succeeded in sounding the least bit like them. But a good song was a burst of adrenaline. Even the most interesting of them rarely survived repeated listening. I wanted a kind of music that could concentrate me, that could teach me how to concentrate. Music that would keep getting richer and deeper, the more I listened.

It's funny, that accusation of musical snobbery that lovers of "classical" music have to suffer. Rock is always considered the rebellion—the cutting loose from the staid, stiff conventions of concert music. But the reality was, when I was growing up—and this is ten times truer now—popular music was the triumphant, hegemonic, staid, conventional form, and it took a fair amount of courage and rebellion for a kid to hear the wildness in "serious" music.

For me, the real difference isn't between high music and low, adventuresome versus conventional, exciting versus dry. The big difference is between music that employs a high degree of repetition and music that depends on change and development. The first kind of music can pop up on your car radio and you can love it before you get to the end of the first chorus. The second, you have to live with for a while, before you can hear where it wants you to go. But for that, you need time and attention and effort, resources that are deeply endangered in the era when all music is available to anyone from anywhere all the time.

AV: Another major change in Peter's life is when he chooses music over his family of Maddy and Sara: "For nothing, for music, for a chance to make a little noise in this world. A noise that no one needed to hear." Later on, Peter tells Clara that "it's all your fault," but that he felt it was "as good a life as any." Then, after Peter sees Maddy in St. Louis, he tells her: "I never should have left you and Sara for music. Even to change the world." It seems Peter vacillates on whether he has made the right decision, but do you agree that Peter's choice of music was neither right nor wrong?

RP: Right or wrong? I'm not sure it's a question of morality. It's a question of trying to know with precision what it is that we're really after in life and to predict accurately how best to get it. And we are all notoriously bad at that. I think Peter is filled with all kinds of feelings about his choices by the end of his life—as many feelings as he has tried to locate and capture in the mystery of music: horror, shame, pride, perseverance, regret, recommitment. Do I judge him? Naw. I love the guy. I've been there.

AV: For all of Peter's efforts to create music, he is troubled by the loss of his relationship with his daughter Sara, thinking "he'll never make anything to compare to her for pure wonder" and that Sara is "my only decent composition." It's ironic that Peter compares his daughter to a composition, but ends up making music that isn't always satisfying.

RP: More than that: he's forced to admit that this "composition" came about largely in his absence, and that whoever his daughter is, she is only his doing to a very small degree. And yet: he feels, for her, a pride that nothing else he has ever made can give him. I never had any children but my books. Regret? Sometimes. But then I start to think of the next book, the perfect one that I might still write. . . .

AV: Peter's life-altering decisions are wonderfully exhibited later in the novel when Peter, who is on the run from the authorities, stops at a café and sees "a bat, hunting by echo-map, flying in paths so skittish they seem random," and then hearing Reich's *Proverb* "electrifies Els:

one simple veer that changes everything." What was the inspiration for this scene?

RP: I honestly don't know. I seem to have dragged that up from some dream world. I set the scene in a favorite café that I frequented when I was an undergraduate and still filled with the excitement of discovering new music. But I gave the scene that soundtrack from Reich, a piece I didn't discover until I was well underway writing the book!

AV: In the fall of 2009, at the age of sixty-eight, Peter has an epiphany while walking his dog Fidelio. It is based on his love of music over everything else ("Music to abandon a wife and child by") when he hears on the radio soundtracks extracted from DNA: "But the real art would be to reverse the process, to inscribe a piece for safekeeping into the genetic material of a bacterium." Is this possible? How did you come up with this idea, which eventually turns a gentle composer into the fugitive Bioterrorist Bach?

RP: It is indeed possible, and shortly after I submitted the manuscript to my publishers for final production, I read a news article announcing that scientists had succeeded in doing it. A little bit of Googling will turn up the account. There are many more similar stories on their way into the world, I am sure.

The first use of a similar technique that I know about was by the bio-artist Eduardo Kac. Way back in 1999, he encoded the line from Genesis, "Let man have dominion over the fish in the sea, and over the fowl of the air, and over every living thing that moves upon the Earth," and inserted it into a bacterium.

But the idea of telling a story about an artist whose work would alert the authorities in Patriot Act America came from the arrest of the bio-artist Steve Kurtz, back in 2004. Kurtz's work, using genetically modified organisms, appeared in museums all over the country. Nevertheless, it was four years before the government accepted the obvious and dropped charges against him.

AV: There are several references to God throughout *Orfeo*. There is the epigram that states: "But I was like a kid who confuses his grandfather with God" and Partch's comment to "bless the giver. And she shall be multiply blessed . . ." Sara says to Peter: "I thought you were God." Partch's comments are his own, and I can understand Sara's comment, but the one that bothers me is when Jen, Peter's much younger platonic-girlfriend-student, asks what he thinks about a piece of music she has just played. Peter's response: *"I have two words for you,* he intones. *And one of them is* Holy. . ." Assuming this means the Holy Ghost, why would Peter make this statement when he apparently gave up religion as a young man when he was seeing Clara: "She only had to smile at his churchgoing, and from one Sunday to the next, he quit his family's faith."

RP: Well, the second word he has in mind isn't "Ghost," but something much more scatological! He is happily astonished by his student's composition, and he is praising her as playfully as he can. So I suppose that renders a bit of your question moot. But it's true: the quest for a transcendent music is, throughout the book, shown to have religious overtones. The link between religious and musical awe is a strong one, as evidenced by the fact that half the greatest music in the world is religious. Peter is after a kind of atheist's salvation through art.

AV: Peter's picaresque journey ends when he meets Sara in California to patch up their relationship. This reconciliation occurs just before he runs outside holding a "bud vial high, like a conductor readying his baton to cue something luckier than anyone supposes. Downbeat of a little infinity. And at last you will hear how this piece goes." Essentially, Peter was an innocent man whose guilt and fate were fabricated by the legal authorities and the media; his only real guilt was his self-inflicted psychological guilt from hurting the ones he loved. One can only think that Peter deserves a better coda.

RP: I would like to think that this is a complex, rich, somewhat mysterious ending. But I feel pretty certain that I would only diminish it by spelling out my own interpretation of it. I have no doubt that people will hear that piece in lots of different ways. That, too, is the beauty of art: you can't control what people will think of or do with it.

AV: Can you briefly discuss what your next novel will be about, and if there are any plans for your books to be made into movies? I would think that *Generosity* and *The Echo Maker* would be interesting to see on film.

RP: I have become obsessed with trees, a massive part of the world and of human history that has been almost invisible to me until now. Seeing trees, and starting a story about them, has changed the way I see everything. I am savoring the idea of spending the next several years in their company.

AV: As they say in Thailand, Khob khun krab!

RP: Allan—Mai pen rai krab! And thank *you*, for the chance to do as expansive an interview as I've done in a while.

Marilynne Robinson. Courtesy of Alex Soth Magnum.

A Life of Perished Things: An Interview with Marilynne Robinson

Marilynne Robinson was born in 1944 and raised in northern Idaho, where her family has lived for several generations. She graduated from Brown University in 1966 and received her PhD in American literature in 1977 from the University of Washington. Robinson has taught at several universities (including the University of Kent, Amherst, where David Foster Wallace was a student), but mostly at the University of Iowa Writers' Workshop until she retired in 2016.

Housekeeping was published in 1982, when she was thirty-eight. It was nominated for the Pulitzer Prize, won the Hemingway Foundation Award for Best First Novel, and later was made into a feature movie. *Mother Country* was published in 1988 and was a finalist for the National Book Award in nonfiction. Her second novel did not appear until twenty-two years later. *Gilead* won the 2005 Pulitzer Prize.

Robinson then wrote *Home*, winner of the Orange Prize for Fiction in 2009, and *Lila*, winner of the National Book Critics Circle Award. *Jack*, the fourth of the Ames family saga, was published in 2020.

This interview was conducted by phone on March 15, 1993, from her office at the University of Iowa. Throughout the interview her voice was mirthful and her laughter engaging. Not only did she convey a vast understanding of the process of writing, but she was incredibly well-versed on a range of subjects from history to contemporary social and environmental issues.

Allan Vorda: Do you look upon the writing of fiction as a way to exorcize pain, to give memory some type of permanence, or something else altogether?

Marilynne Robinson: Something else altogether. I've always had trouble describing to people what I think fiction actually is, but I think it's not more securely anchored in biographical or psychological experiences than something like a painting or sculpture would be. I think of fictions as freestanding objects that exist for their own value. I really hesitate to say I have written or would write fiction to satisfy some other purpose other than simply my interest in writing fiction.

AV: You mentioned in an interview with Kay Bonetti [Audio Prose Library] that while you were working on your dissertation a professor said he would like to see some of your fiction. Since there was nothing from your undergraduate days you wanted to show him, you went to the library and fell asleep. Then you woke up and proceeded to write that whole passage in *Housekeeping* about the grandfather who subsequently dies when the train plummets into Fingerbone Lake. This passage seems to have been the germ for the whole novel—yet it's almost like you dreamed it. What are your recollections of this fantastic story within a story?

MR: It's actually fairly much as you described it. I had this story in mind more or less whole that day in the library. I don't know why. I didn't, at that point, think of it as part of a novel. I think it was related to many other things that preoccupied me at that time. It seems like it was something I was simply inventing out of whole cloth for perfectly accidental reasons; and yet there it was. I do remember I was very engaged by the writing of it when it occurred.

AV: You studied creative writing at Brown University with John Hawkes as your teacher. What was this experience like, and did Hawkes influence your writing style?

MR: John Hawkes was a wonderful editor of my writing. He made me aware very quickly of when I was writing well and when I was not writing well. It helped to sensitize me very effectively, I think, to what the possibilities of my writing style were. He didn't allude to his own writing when he taught. The similarities some people find between our styles were more the consequence of his teaching influence bonding to my writing than my looking at his.

AV: What writers influenced you, and which ones do you admire?

MR: I suppose I have been influenced by practically everything I've read. The writers I most consciously respond to are the nineteenth-century American writers like Melville, Dickinson, Poe, and Twain. I've always found that to be a very rich period, but it seems to me it ended before it was completed in a way. I was very interested in taking up what seemed to be philosophical or theosophical or aesthetic issues which they brought up, but too few people carried forward. I have also been influenced by such writers as Wallace Stevens and William Faulkner.

AV: You said the nineteenth century ended before it was completed, but aren't writers like you still carrying on that tradition? It seems writers like you or Ron Hansen or Kazuo Ishiguro are writing more in the vein of nineteenth-century or early twentieth-century stylists rather than that of the more contemporary twentieth-century writers or even the twenty-first century, which looms around the corner.

MR: I think it takes a lot of looking backward to decide which is the real style of the twenty-first or the twentieth century. I think people like Hemingway are very much descendants of the kind of writing that interests me. Also, I think people feel some nervous obligation to come up with what they take to be a contemporary style, but whether it lasts or amounts to anything is another question.

AV: You stated in the interview with Bonetti that while "working on my dissertation I began to feel as though I had lost the option of being a fiction writer." Why? Was there something about being in that ivory tower of academic research that made you feel more an observer than a participant?

MR: I never experienced it as an ivory tower. I feel I'm much more in an ivory tower when I'm writing fiction, as a matter of fact. The prevailing wisdom of the time was that you do one thing or you do the other. I think it has been fairly unusual for people to get academic PhDs and to write fiction. The idea was, if you developed one style of writing or one habit of mind, then it more or less precluded the other.

AV: You said in an interview with the *Iowa Review* that "I've probably thought of Poe at least once a day every day since I was ten years old. I've never quite understood this incredible affinity. It's probably unhealthy." Aunt Sylvie in *Housekeeping* can be viewed as an extension of the lonely, morbid world of Poe, but how do you see your writing style compared with Poe's? For example, *Housekeeping* explores that dark and lonely world, but the spiritual tone of the book is positive and optimistic compared with Poe.

MR: As I said when I was talking to Kay Bonetti, I don't really understand my affinity with Poe. One thing I see in Poe is a very deep intelligence. His prose is very elegant and carefully wrought. I think Poe is a philosophic writer. It's hard to explain precisely what I mean by that, because I've spent a lot of time trying to explain it to myself. If you read his essay "Eureka," you can see how his mind is working and how seriously he undertakes prose.

I don't think of Sylvie as morbid at all. I wouldn't ever use that word to characterize her. I don't think of Poe as being as nearly as morbid or pessimistic as everything thinks. I don't even think "pessimism" is exactly the word that I would apply to Poe. One of the things that struck me about Poe when I was young was that he was probably the only writer in literature who admired women for being good at mathematics. The things he found attractive and fascinating were the mastery of obscure languages and things that were somewhat esoteric. And in the oddest way, I think it was a liberating idea for me when I was a young girl.

AV: You said that "Poe really feels as though he's writing to himself." Do you think this holds true for you and other serious writers?

MR: I think to the degree writers are serious there is a greater tendency for them to write to themselves, because they are trying to compose their own thoughts. They are trying to find out what is in their minds, which is the great mystery. Finding out who you are, what is in your head, and what kind of companion you are to yourself in the course of life. One of the things that is interesting about writing is that it does give you some access to that, and it's quite surprising to find what's there.

AV: You also mention that the characteristic mode of thought of most classic American writers is "based on the assumption that the only way to understand the world is metaphorical, and all metaphors are inadequate, and that you press them far enough and you're delivered into something that requires a new articulation." Can you elaborate on this, since you certainly make use of metaphors, and could you also clarify the meaning of a "new articulation"?

MR: I think, to a certain extent, what I mean is a new metaphor or a larger or a more refined metaphor. To the extent that the system is working well for you or the method is working for you, you are discovering things that are authentic discoveries rather than repeating or rephrasing things you have acquired out of other people's thinking. It bears a very strong comparison with methods of speculative science. It bears a strong comparison with almost any kind of ambitious thinking that people do. The important thing for me is that metaphor is not ornamental. It's methodological. It has something to do with the way in which truth is inaccessible and the way in which truth is also accessible. That is the means by which in its own highly bracketed and conditional way it is accessible.

AV: You once stated that "I don't think I could have written *Housekeeping* if I hadn't had children." Why? Is there a connection between your children and the characters in the novel?

MR: No. I just wouldn't have known all the sorts of strange emotional dynamics of having your identity invested in another person. I wouldn't have known the disparity between how you perceive yourself and how you are perceived by people that are very dear to you.

AV: You have also said that *Housekeeping* is not autobiographical as far as characters, but your hometown of Sandpoint, Idaho, was used as a setting for Fingerbone. Could *Housekeeping* have been written using the sod-houses of Nebraska in the Great Plains where your grandfather grew up, or is the Northwest setting crucial to the story?

MR: The importance of water is so great in *Housekeeping*. A lot of the book is a meditation on that lake and the memories that accompany it. I think without that lake it would necessarily have been a different book.

AV: Do you think where one grows up determines how one writes? For example, you grew up in the Northwest, your grandfather was from the Midwest, and you were educated at Brown University in the Northeast.

MR: I have no idea. I think writers are so singular that it's very hard to say. You can't look at a landscape which has been written about as if you were seeing it for the first time. How we understand landscapes has an enormous amount to do with who has written about them, yet we think of it in the opposite order. We think Mississippi created Faulkner, although you could make as good of a case that for all purposes Faulkner created Mississippi.

I think the writers that really influenced me were the New Englanders. When I grew up in Idaho, I read *Moby-Dick* and looked at Lake Pend Oreille or *Walden*. Even though the scale of the landscape is much bigger in one case and much smaller in the other, I appropriated what I wanted out of both of them and felt perfectly at ease doing it, having not seen either the Atlantic Ocean or Massachusetts. What I took from them had to do with my own particular setting in life and the accidental overlap of what they did and what I felt would be interesting to do.

AV: Early in the novel Ruth has a dream of walking on the lake, with the dead people reaching up for her in conjunction with her grandmother's obituary. Is this a foreshadowing of what is to happen at the end of the novel?

MR: I didn't know what was going to happen at the end of the novel until I wrote it. The book ends in the way it does because of the subject it has. The subject pulls the book into its own shape and so at every point this is also true.

AV: Throughout the novel Ruthie and Lucille never seem to agree—whether it has to do with colors (e.g., the color of Sylvie's hair or the car their mother drove into Fingerbone Lake) or if their mother's death was intentional or not. Lucille is correct about the colors, whereas Ruthie is correct about their mother's death. Was this done intentionally to show that neither girl is always correct, thereby creating a certain ambivalence?

MR: I suppose what I had in mind more than anything else is that memory is unreliable. I don't want to sound tricky or anything, but it is Ruthie who's telling the story, which has something to do with what we take to be true.

AV: Right after Sylvie comes to stay with the sisters, Ruthie notices the similarity between Sylvie and her mother, so much so that "Sylvie began to blur the memory of my mother, and then to displace it." Shortly thereafter you write, "Memories are by their nature fragmented, isolated, and arbitrary as glimpses one has at night through lighted windows." These statements seem to recall Borges's comment in "Pierre Menard" that "error tries to tarnish memory." How do you conceive of time as it applies to both thought and relationships, since it seems totally anomalous in *Housekeeping*?

MR: I don't know what memory is, since memory appropriates things to itself and recreates itself constantly. I wouldn't say error tarnishes memory, but that memory is fluxile.

AV: In your essay "The First and Second Epistles General of Peter" you write, "The wrenching of time out of undifferentiated sequence is among the most brilliant accomplishments of the creators of biblical literature. For clearly there is a given-ness in things. Events do not occur in shapely forms as if they were the abstract of all possibility, or as if occasions were logical or Platonic structures that felt the pressure of chance and the tension of probability, and that energy flows toward event the way lightning pours through a fault in the atmosphere." In what ways is this statement, from both a biblical and literary context, applicable to your concept of time in *Housekeeping*?

MR: That's a tough question, since I don't have the text of what I said about Peter in front of me. I think to the extent that I can be, I am influenced by contemporary thinking about time.

I have a great deal of respect for the new cosmology because there is no reason to have a particular loyalty for any earlier cosmology. The things we know about time apparently are true and descriptive and have to saturate our experience along with everything else. It seems to me that's very interesting in terms of memory and experience, because we have no reason to believe that outside ourselves in the cosmos there are point-by-point linearities, or any of these kinds of things. To the extent we try to impose sequence and linearity on memory, we are falsifying them. It seems to me the ways of thinking about time that are available to us scientifically, and obviously were available to very early writers in the Bible, that these are very pregnant ways of conceiving. They should be very much attended to and should not be considered secondary to or criticized by old notions of time and experience.

AV: Regarding the theme of time, there also seems to be a longing for some type of permanence, as shown when Ruthie and Lucille are making the snow lady statue: "Her shape became a posture. And while in any particular she seemed crude and lopsided, altogether her figure suggested a woman standing in a cold wind. It seemed we had conjured a presence." But despite her hope that "the lady would stand long enough to freeze," that statue falls apart. Is this statue supposed to symbolize Sylvie, who will become just another substitute mother figure, and what are your recollections about creating this scene?

MR: I don't really recall creating this scene in particular. It's hard to explain to people that writing fiction is a lot like painting. I came to that moment, and I thought what is implied here is, simply, a snow woman. It seemed to me necessary out of the prose. I think there are lots of things it connects with: it connects with the arrival of Sylvie; it connects with the image of Lot's wife; it connects with all kinds of other things. And of course, the image of Lot's wife was suggested to me by the snow woman rather than the other way around. There is also the woman in the fallen house that she imagines, when she says she would have built a figure of snow, but those things are picking up on that image and doing it again. There is not a one-to-one relationship among these things. The snow woman exists fully in her own right. It just seemed to me a good thing to have in that place.

AV: Can you comment about the flooding of Fingerbone, and the inherent symbolism, biblical and otherwise? For example, you state: "So Fingerbone, or such relics of it as showed above the mirroring waters, seemed fragments of the quotidian held up to our wondering attention, offered somehow as proof of their own significance."

MR: Floods are full of suggestion for me. The particular passage that you read had to do with an image that was in my mind of the flotsam that would be visible, thinking of the flood as a sort of silver tray with bits of flotsam on it. It seemed to me when reality was transformed in a radical way, that the value of everything was also transformed. Thus, rather than seeing things as ordinary, you see them suddenly in terms of the pathos of their temporality and impermanence. The cross itself would have been thought of as something crude or disgraceful or whatever. But by the transformation, by the reevaluation, that came from the crucifixion, even a fragment of it, if it were an authentic fragment, would be transformed into something utterly different. That's the kind of transformation of the value, of worth, that was suggested to me.

AV: *Housekeeping* abounds with biblical allusions and metaphors—yet there are no blatant religious scenes where characters attend church or discuss the existence of God or one's mortality. Was this a conscious attempt not to have such scenes? And isn't *Housekeeping* essentially a parable illustrating a moral or religious theme in a contemporary setting?

MR: I would hesitate to call it a parable because I think parables tend to be misinterpreted. What parables *are* is misinterpreted. I don't think they seem the same way to me that they do to anybody else. If I were to refer to *Housekeeping* as a parable, I think people would completely and systematically misunderstand what I meant by it. I don't think people in general come anywhere near articulating in spoken language what they in fact think, not because they aren't honest, but because most of the deepest kinds of experience it never occurs to people to articulate. The most essential issues of the novel are experienced at the level of consciousness and not in dialogue, just because that's the way the world seems.

AV: Was this a conscious attempt not to mention such scenes overtly?

MR: It never occurred to me to mention them. I hope the novel implies that something of the same scale and seriousness that goes on in Ruth's mind also goes on in the minds of all the people around her. That's the nature of the human landscape. I do think people have very profound lives of which they say virtually nothing.

AV: What about Sylvie's "housekeeping," the obsessive-compulsive nature and forgetfulness of her cleaning? This concept of house-keeping, from a psychological point of view, certainly depicts Sylvie as mentally unstable, but the sisters initially regard her behavior as merely eccentric. Why?

MR: I'm not crazy about psychological questions. This book is not about reality. I'm very uneasy making judgments about sanity and insanity in the real world. And I certainly wouldn't want to bring them into my book.

AV: The critic Paula Geyh, in her article "Burning Down the House," states that "Sylvie mistakes accumulation for housekeeping—she understands the connection of housekeeping to the accrual of property, but not to the process of sorting and excluding, and so the parlor is filled with newspapers and cans stacked to the ceiling." Geyh later states the "Floor and couch are littered with the dismembered remains of birds brought in by thirteen or fourteen cats, indicating a confusion of the boundaries between the outside and the inside, between natural and social space." Housekeeping in your novel entails both material and spiritual boundaries. Can you discuss your thoughts on these boundaries and the general role of the woman as housekeeper?

MR: I tried in *Housekeeping* to speak fairly respectfully of the whole phenomenon of housekeeping. The grandmother, in particular, is a sort of artist in that form. I don't intend to create oppositions. In a way, Sylvie's housekeeping is a sort of variant of other people's housekeeping, in the sense that what is really accomplished in terms of accumulating things that matter and stabilizing environments and so on, is on a range between unsuccessful and even less successful. It's not as if anybody succeeds at this. It's just that Sylvie's failures are more obvious.

AV: There is a minor passage that discusses Sylvie's strange relationships with Edith (who dies in the boxcar) and Alma. What is the significance of this passage?

MR: It's like the snow woman. I remember thinking the passage was transforming a moment which could be viewed in many other ways. I was thinking of Lincoln's funeral train, and of her spirit standing above her, which was her breath rising in the air. I wanted to establish dramatic and heroic suggestions which would transform the West, to put her life and death into another frame.

AV: Eventually, a split occurs between Lucille and Sylvie, based on their respective approaches to life. This is highlighted by Lucille's abhorrence of deterioration, while Sylvie finds "fresh surprise" in the process and feels "the life of perished things." Doesn't this reflect Lucille's commitment to living in the everyday world, whereas Sylvie acknowledges the impermanence of the physical world, with death providing the release from it?

MR: I think that throughout the book I've tried to criticize the distinction between the material world and the spiritual world. It's not a distinction I habitually make myself.

AV: There is the analogy of the sister's house and Sylvie's housekeeping to the lake where things are "massed and accumulated, as they do in combs or in the eaves and unswept corners of a house." Things become lost, misplaced, or forgotten, only to be discovered in a corner of the house or the flotsam of the lake. Does this indicate that, despite the fragmentary nature of things, there is some permanence or meaning of life?

MR: At that point the book is just pointing out analogies; how to interpret them is another question. On the one hand, at the physical level, insofar as the things matter to us, insofar as where they are constellated into objects and people, obviously there is no permanence. Or at least permanence as we perceive it. That's simply a datum. It doesn't mean there is a discontinuity between things to which we wish to attach permanence and the larger forces by which they are subsumed.

AV: Lucille dreams she is a baby and Sylvie is suffocating her with blankets, while Ruthie dreams she is waiting for her mother to return. Ruthie believes her dream is no less valid than Lucille's. Ruthie also believes we are deceived by appearances, so there is no difference between reality or dreams. Is this essentially true?

MR: I think, given the fact that all experience is internal, is mental experience, it's not possible to make secure distinctions about what's real and what's not real. Dreams obviously have an enormous potency and meaning and reality. I'm sort of tinkering with that. I think if there is one thing I'm doing in this book it's criticizing distinctions that seem more misleading than descriptive.

AV: The eventual split that occurs between Ruthie and Lucille is perhaps best expressed in the issue of education. Lucille eventually rejects Sylvie's tutelage and returns to high school and tells Mr. French her "attitude has changed," but Ruthie rejects the standard education system in favor of Sylvie's teachings. Do you think Ruthie is conscious of her decision to pursue a different type of education, or is it merely her closeness to Sylvie that draws her in that direction?

MR: I would hate to characterize her motives. Obviously, she is very attracted to Sylvie. There are many other things which make Lucille's choices unattractive or unavailable to Ruth, emotionally and otherwise. I would really hesitate to characterize her because the book is a fiction, and Ruth's place in it is to express the active or kinetic space between the differences that Sylvie and Lucille represent.

AV: Perhaps the most important passage in the novel occurs when Ruthie and Sylvie take their boat trip to the remote valley. Can you comment on that strange conversation in the boat when Ruthie inquires about the children in the woods: "Have you ever seen any of them?" and Sylvie replies, "I think I have"?

MR: Nope.

AV: Ruthie feels the presence of the children as Sylvie did, but neither really sees any children when they are in the valley during their boat trip. Is the boat trip supposed to be a symbolic journey from earth to heaven, with the unseen children meant to represent the lost souls of the children? Or do the unseen children represent something else?

MR: It's not a journey from earth to heaven. I don't even submit to *that* distinction. It's very hard for me to say what those children represent. There is no direct equivalent for them in my mind. They are very highly charged for me with all kinds of things.

AV: There is that strange scene where Ruthie and Sylvie are sitting in the boat with the train going over them on the bridge, while underneath them at the bottom of the lake lies the train that Ruthie's grandfather died in. Is this supposed to represent a connection between the dead and the living?

MR: Certainly, Sylvie is there because the train did go into the lake. The obsessions of the family are constellated around specific events, and that is a connection between the living and the dead.

AV: Ruthie also likens Sylvie to her mother, Helen, and calls out both their names to get a response from the person in the boat. Can you comment on this passage? Also, what is the inaudible statement Sylvie makes but when asked by Ruthie as to what she said she says "Nothing"?

MR: I can't expound on the first question. Regarding the second question, the comment was inaudible so how can I know what she said?

AV: The Indian woman on the train responds to Sylvie's comment that Ruthie is a good girl by saying, "Like you always said." Who is this Indian woman supposed to be, since this is the only time she appears in the novel?

MR: Just herself. I think the most straightforward implication of the comment is certainly that Sylvie has not given up her transient ways.

AV: Ruthie states that she and Lucille were once "almost a single consciousness," but later they grow apart. Then Sylvie says about Ruthie, "She's like another sister to me. She's her mother all over again." Then at the end of the novel, when the house is burning, Ruthie says about Sylvie and herself, "I think that night we were almost a single person." This shows Ruthie has completely separated from Lucille and now identifies with Sylvie (and therefore, with her mother, Helen). Does this change in Ruthie indicate a spiritual transformation?

MR: I don't consider Ruth to be the only changing figure in an otherwise static situation. There's a lot of spiritual transformation.

AV: Sylvie is certainly not physically threatening to the community of Fingerbone; yet she is a threatening figure to them because she has a different concept of reality, as evidenced by her actions. Can you shed some light on why Fingerbone feels threatened, and conversely, why Sylvie doesn't feel threatened by their concept of reality?

MR: I think Sylvie feels somewhat threatened. But my intention, again, is never to establish hard distinctions. I think I've spent a fair amount of time drawing attention to the fact that Sylvie's sense of reality is very, very similar to the sense of reality of Fingerbone. She simply responds differently. The reason they feel alarmed about her is they understand perfectly well what she is thinking. She is *not* alien to them.

AV: There is such good characterization at work in *Housekeeping*, since in the world of the book the reader tends to identify with Ruthie and Sylvie, while in the real world most of us would probably side with Lucille and the residents of Fingerbone as to what is normal. Do you agree?

MR: I don't think I would apply the category of "normal" to the people of Fingerbone as I represent them. I don't like loading situations, and I think people tend to villainize Fingerbone, which bothers me because I never intended it to be that way. The anxiety Fingerbone has about Ruthie is whether she is safe and minimally well, which are perfectly legitimate concerns for people to have, especially in the circumstances as things play themselves out. I don't think there is any suggestion in the novel, anywhere, that these people have some notion of conforming her to some elaborate, pre-existing idea of what is appropriate. They simply don't want her floating around on a glacial lake in the middle of the night in a leaking boat. It's not a monstrous anxiety that they are entertaining here.

AV: Toward the end of the novel the house is described as being "like a brain," at which point Sylvie and Ruthie try to burn the house (just as Sylvie burned the newspapers) in order to erase their memory. Thus, leaving the burning house seems to mean not only an end to housekeeping, but an end to their earthly existence. This seems to be confirmed by their running down the railroad tracks and disappearing into the night. Is this symbolically and metaphorically correct?

MR: It's not articulated in a way that makes one have to translate it. It is not as if it were symbolical or metaphorical. It means what it means. It is what it is. I don't acknowledge the need to translate out of the text into something that in effect would seem to be more clearly or more efficiently what the text says. Sometimes it has to be done out of necessity by critics or whatever, but I don't have to do it.

I don't want to imply that I'm simply leaving latitude for other people to make more authoritative interpretations than I'm willing to make. To my mind, and I thought about this considerably during the course of writing, the last scenes in the novel don't translate directly into any other kind of statement. That's what I wanted. In other words, I'm not trying to say something else in veiled language. I wrote those scenes for themselves. I don't want people to feel they have utter interpretive latitude, but I'm asking them to respond to these things as complex utterances and not try to eke them out into explanatory statements.

I think the person who said every art aspires to the condition of music was correct. I was trying to do what music does by having a great burden of implication without being reducible into a statement or program or idea.

AV: You could have concluded the novel as the movie version does, with Sylvie and Ruthie disappearing into the darkness as they run down the railroad tracks. So how did you derive that strange ending where Ruthie is still narrating the story as if she and Sylvie are still alive? And is this only in Lucille's memory?

MR: At the point where I was at that place in the novel it seemed right to me. It seemed to conclude what had come before it.

AV: The critic Allyson Booth states in a footnote to her essay "To Caption Absent Bodies: Marilynne Robinson's *Housekeeping*" that "Ruth's text as a whole serves as a postscript to her own obituary." Doesn't this beg the question of how a deceased character can narrate her own story?

MR: That question again comes from the idea that fictions are impostures of a kind that attempt to produce something someone will mistake for reality. Fiction can do whatever it wants to do. There's no reason why I couldn't tell a story from the point of view of someone who wasn't born yet. People have done every kind of thing. It's a free country, the fictional country, very free indeed. You can do what you can get away with.

AV: What is your opinion of the criticism of your work? For example, critics such as Joan Kirkby and Paula Geyh cannot agree whether Ruth and Sylvie are still alive at the end of the novel. Does this give you a certain pleasure that critics come to different conclusions? Additionally, do critics sometimes point out certain motifs or elements of which you were previously unaware?

MR: Critics sometimes do point out things I never noticed before, and that's very funny. I heard a critical paper, by some strange accident, that pointed out neatly interlocking thematic things which I had never noticed. Maybe they are there. Maybe it was my subconscious doing all the bright stuff. And then there's the other side of that coin, which is that often things you really dislike are attributed to your work. Then the critics say you didn't do it consciously, and it was your subconscious that was doing it. This is a kind of thing that makes one gnash one's teeth.

AV: Does that give you a certain pleasure that critics come to different conclusions?

MR: It's very rare that I read criticism of *Housekeeping*. I probably have read two or three articles that people have handed me. Of course, anybody is flattered to be of interest to other people, but in terms of reading criticism, I don't read it.

AV: What did you think of the movie version of *Housekeeping*?

MR: I liked the movie very much and thought Bill Forsythe did a great job directing. I thought Christine Lahti was excellent as Sylvie and that the actresses who played the girls [Sara Walker and Andrea Burchill] were very good.

I know that a lot of choices about the film were made in terms of how things would look on film, which is a very special problem. For example, Bill Forsythe's choice about where to end the film simply had to do with the difficulties of translating the ending I had written into visual equivalents. The book was not exactly what most people would think of as being a filmable book. Forsythe had to make a lot of choices that responded to that fact. I don't take exception to any of the choices he made. I think he did a marvelous job and made fairly recalcitrant material into a lovely film.

AV: What was your feeling about seeing your fiction translated into another medium? Isn't it strange to see your memory and creative process not only put into words, but almost put into real life?

MR: It is strange. It's one of those experiences that little in life prepares you for, but on the other hand it always seemed to me to be Forsythe's film. Forsythe made a wonderful film, and I was very lucky. There are very few books that are made into films that come near being that satisfactory as film. It also seemed the movie was a sort of companion to my book rather than being something to be judged as a translation of my book. It didn't seem like my book being projected onto the screen. It seemed like something I was very familiar with but nevertheless was Forsythe's creation.

AV: There is a passage about Cain and Abel where you discuss the sense that someone's absence can become their presence. This can be construed on the physical level between the two sisters, but can't it also be viewed metaphorically and/or spiritually? For example, it could reflect the philosophy of Paul Tillich, who spoke of God's dynamic absence as also being a dynamic presence.

MR: I don't know if I have read that particular work of Tillich's, but I have been very interested in theology for a very long time, even before I wrote *Housekeeping*. I think part of the reason American literature of the nineteenth century seized on my imagination is because it is saturated with theology. Those frames of reference are very much in my mind. I don't think it's fair to exclude any respectable and interesting theological idea that was available to me at that time.

AV: People change as they get older due to their experiences. Has your philosophical or theological thinking changed since you were in college or since you wrote *Housekeeping*?

MR: Yes, of course. It's my sense of reality that's changed. It's like when I was writing that piece about the epistles of St. Peter. I was struck by so many things in the epistles that I would never have been so sensitive to at an earlier age. I think my sense of reality, in regard to what the world is and what its prospects are, has been severely chastened. This is the area of greatest transformation.

AV: Essentially the Bible is used as a reference text for *Housekeep-*

ing, and the interpretation of language is certainly important in both books. Do you think, however, that *Housekeeping* loses some of its value when interpreted by readers who are not religious or who do not believe in an afterlife?

MR: I have no way of knowing. There's no way of anticipating who will respond to what you write. I don't know what people's thinking is or where it comes from. I would never try to calculate or judge anybody's receptivity to anything I write.

AV: What part of the Bible influenced you the most in relation to *Housekeeping*? Do you see your writing as an extension of the Bible?

MR: It would be very hard to say. I think it's obvious that I have always been very struck by the Old Testament. I have always been very struck by the New Testament. I wouldn't presume to extend it, but I would consider myself to be in the company of commentators.

AV: Do you subscribe to the premise of John Gardner's *On Moral Fiction*? Do you think fiction should have a moral point of view?

MR: I have never read that book. Everybody brings it up. I think I am in line with Old and New Testament traditions when I say that people who are too willing to assume they know what morality is are probably in trouble. Openness and inquiry and graciousness of spirit are probably the things most to be cultivated.

I don't want to be dismissive of John Gardner any more than he wishes to be dismissive of other people. I do think things which are fundamentally generous in spirit are often taken to be immoral or amoral because they hesitate to disapprove. I really think everything has to be looked at in its own light.

AV: What do you think of Tom Wolfe's essay "Stalking the Billion-Footed Beast," which promotes writers of nonfiction and writers of the realist mode?

MR: I haven't read that either. People come up with these manifestos, and I'm sure they have some kind of value in the sense that they articulate positions. Realism is certainly the most artificial convention of all. It's fine too, just like the rest of them are fine. Every book has to be judged on its own merits. There is no reason to favor one kind of writing over another.

AV: There was a critic who made a comment about E. M. Forster when he was still alive that his reputation continued to grow with each book he didn't write. Do you see yourself in that light because you've written only one book of fiction? Why haven't you written more?

MR: I don't know. I guess I should be glad that E. M. Forster and I share this beatified state. I care about the writing of fiction, but not to the exclusion of learning. I spend a lot of time reading history. It's all important. I don't write unconsidered things. I do take my writing, and this is an understatement, seriously. I don't want to write as if just writing by itself were sufficient. Fiction is, however, the most important thing in my life. That's why I don't write all the time.

AV: In *Housekeeping*, there are no male characters of any real importance. In fact, if male characters had been used it most likely would have interfered with the storytelling and the relationships of the women. Were you aware of the lack of male characters when you wrote the book? Has there been any criticism or praise for a novel almost exclusively about women?

MR: People mention that *Housekeeping* is a story about women. I didn't intend to leave men out originally, but at a certain point I realized there were not going to be male characters, and I thought that's fine.

AV: *Mother Country* seems to have both a satiric and an ironic title, which condemns the British for allowing massive radioactive pollution from the Sellafield plant. How did you choose the title for your book?

MR: I don't know how those things come to mind. In both books,

Housekeeping and *Mother Country*, there was just a certain point in writing the book where the title seemed to appear. I think that *Mother Country* comes from the fact that, when I was a child in first grade in Idaho, the first lesson in social studies was one sentence that said, "England is our mother country." I thought this was an odd piece of colonialism to be inflicted upon the children of Idaho.

AV: In the introduction to *Mother Country*, you state you are "angry to the depths of my soul that the earth has been so injured." What brought this problem to your attention, and how did *Mother Country* evolve into a book?

MR: I was living in England in 1983, and I read about it in the newspapers and saw it on television. It was perfectly available to me at that time, basic facts and information. When I came back to the United States, I wrote an article which was published by *Harper's*, and on the basis of that article I was asked to write a book. Most of the research I did was in libraries in New England—the point being that any reader who wanted to reproduce what I had done, to find out what my sources were and how reliable my interpretations of them were—could reconstruct it. It also makes the point that everything I wrote, although it's completely unknown at the level of general information, could be known without ever leaving a good library in the United States.

AV: You state in *Mother Country* that "a fiction writer has to braid events into a plausible sequence" where "news is simply a series of reported incidents." Was it difficult making the transition from fiction to nonfiction, and which genre is more satisfying?

MR: I had written a dissertation before, which was on Shakespeare. It made me very grateful for my academic background, which taught me how to do research and to write nonfiction.

Writing fiction and nonfiction are very, very different things. In both cases you have an enormous problem of trying to break out of received ideas. Aside from that, it's just a different problem. For example, with nonfiction you might be trying to show some kind of sophisticated loyalty to information, whereas with fiction you're trying to generate the thing out of whole cloth, and those are very different kinds of problems.

AV: Do you find one genre more satisfying than the other?

MR: I like writing nonfiction, although I didn't like writing *Mother Country* because the subject matter wasn't pleasant. I'm happy writing nonfiction because I find things complementary. I have the illusion when I write nonfiction that things are less susceptible to misinterpretation.

AV: The Poor Laws in England, which were enforced for over five hundred years, had a Catch-22 effect by not letting people move to find work, even when no work was available locally. A similar Catch-22 is in effect with the Sellafield plant, which produces plutonium for profit while polluting the land and killing her people. This begs the question of whose interests are most important to the British government. Do you think the only way for Britain to prevent such problems is to abolish their system of socialism in favor of a more democratic system such as the United States has?

MR: The word "socialism" is problematic because Americans use it in two senses. They use socialism as it's presented in theory by people like Marx and Proudhon, where the idea is there will be some kind of mutual commitment to collective well-being. Then you have actual historical regimes that call themselves socialist, like Russia and Britain. There's no evidence in history that they have attempted to promote collective well-being. What they have actually done is make a contemporary version of feudalism and call it socialism. Americans have made the odd mistake of interpreting Marx in terms of the practice of the Soviet Union or other regimes that were equally bizarre. But if you look at Marx himself, he's not describing anything that remotely resembles the Soviet Union or Britain or anything else. He wouldn't use the word socialism because he disliked British socialism so much. It was exactly what he did not intend as an example of his doctrine.

Britain should be vastly more democratic than it is, but I don't think the opposition between socialism and democracy is appropriate. It's more like the difference between feudalism and democracy, what is going on there.

AV: *Mother Country* could be viewed as the nonfictional counterpart to Martin Amis's fiction in *Einstein's Monsters*. Strangely enough, an American attacks the British for nuclear pollution while a Briton attacks the Americans for promulgating the threat of nuclear holocaust. Do you see any irony in the fact that Americans and British are holding mirrors up for each other, but not looking at themselves?

MR: I don't think you can generalize from my book. I would be very interested to hear of another American book that criticizes British nuclear policy problems. There are many British books that criticize American nuclear policy. It's characteristic that Americans think anything bad that happens, happens in America, whereas the British think anything bad that happens, happens in America. And we seem to be predisposed to value their opinions. One reason that these very, very bad plants at Sellafield and elsewhere in Britain continue to operate is the fact they are there. Because we are so preoccupied with ourselves, Americans are not even aware that the British test their nuclear weapons in Nevada. Americans are typically not aware the British *have had* nuclear weapons for a very long time and *won't* subject them to arms control. We have acted as if the United States and the Soviet Union are the only players in nuclear issues. This is a sad eccentricity of ours, this selective immunity to information.

AV: You said in an interview with Kay Bonetti that the audience for *Mother Country* was the United States, because our country was the best hope to exert a positive influence on Britain to stop their nuclear pollution. Since your book has been available for several years, has there been any response from America and has there been any attempt to close the Sellafield plant by the British?

MR: It's hard for me to know. I get a certain number of letters from people, and the fact that *Mother Country* sold fairly well shows that

I've had some success in putting this information out. The British always are fussing about this plant. One day you hear they have a particularly high occurrence of cancer in the eyes of children around the Sellafield plant, but then an official comes out and says this is a coincidence. Then there is a particularly high incidence of bone cancer in children, and you have another excuse. There is always this sort of bubbling public relations problem that is associated with all the illness this plant causes. Then you might hear some murmurs of concern that maybe we shouldn't be doing this, but of course this goes on for twenty or thirty years and will go on forever as far as I can tell. The plant itself is expanding, and in the middle of the 1980s it was the largest construction project in Europe. Now of course a lot of the construction is done, which means all that gear they were putting in is now up and operating, so it's an expanding problem.

AV: I think you alluded in your book to the fact that there have been a lot of out-of-court settlements made with people who contracted cancer around Sellafield. It also seems that Ireland and other European countries would file lawsuits. Wouldn't all of these legal expenditures force the plant to shut down?

MR: The question always comes down to the amount of legal recourse people actually have. I described that part where out-of-court payments are made and this is set up so they will not have to go to court, supposedly. The government owns the plant, and they regulate the way in which it deals with its victims. There is no free-standing legal apparatus that can effectively oppose the government. As far as the Irish and many other European countries—they have had resolutions passed against the Sellafield plant but by the European Parliament—these things amount to nothing. They do nothing but ease public relation problems.

AV: It's ironic, because the British are not only polluting the Irish but part of their own country, not just in England, but in Northern Ireland.

MR: There's no question about it. The pollution is phenomenal because it has gone on for so long and on such a large scale.

AV: In your essay "Hearing Silence: Western Myth Reconsidered" you say, "A central myth of ours, if it were rendered as narrative, would sound like this: One is born and in passage through childhood suffers some grave harm. Subsequent good fortune is meaningless because of this injury, while subsequent misfortune is highly significant as the consequence of this injury. The work of one's life is to discover and name the harm one has suffered." First of all, to what degree of importance do you think great writing is a product of one's misfortune? Secondly, with all the harm that humanity has inflicted and endured, doesn't this imply great writing would be the product of malevolent times and that peaceful times would not spawn any writers of merit?

MR: The passage you quoted was intended very ironically. I would call it a mean little myth and say it is incompatible with art. The relationship of injury to art is that great art is fundamentally generous. The object of that generosity is often the overcoming of injury. The tendency of people to dwell on models of victimization, which makes them judge other people simplistically and harshly, is something I abhor.

AV: In what way does your short story "Connie Bronson" reflect the statement, "One is born and in passage through childhood suffers some grave harm?" Is Connie Bronson based on a real person and incident in your life?

MR: As a matter of fact, she is based on somebody I knew in grade school when I was a little girl in Idaho. I visited her house once. How can you tell what will matter to you or how important these things will be later in life? But there's a certain discomfort everybody feels with themselves, physically and so forth, and probably never more so than in childhood. "Connie Bronson" was written many years ago and actually predates *Housekeeping*, whereas "Hearing Silence" was written a year ago. I think "Connie Bronson" could be fairly described as a bit of juvenilia, if I could use that unkind language to talk about my own production.

AV: In "Hearing Silence" you also state, "Reading James Galvin's book,

The Meadow, I was movingly reminded of the West of my memory. It occurred to me how intrinsic a part silence is of Western culture and experience, and how vulnerable they are to misinterpretation for that reason." Can you elaborate on this statement within the context of the essay as well as your fiction?

MR: It seems to me that if there is anything writing aspires to beyond the condition of music, it's probably the condition of silence. It's a hard thing to talk about. Silence as a positive aesthetic is something I'm very aware of. I think that silence might be a music rather than an absence of sound, in the same way that space is a texture or filament of fabric and not an absence.

AV: In some ways, "Hearing Silence" is a continuation of *Mother Country*; that is, it deals with a country being blind to her own faults. For example, you state, "Americans are still so profoundly in awe of what they take to be their cultural origins that they cannot really criticize them." This implies a moral weakness and lack of courage in the collective consciousness of our country. What has caused this, and how can we correct such intangibles?

MR: I'm afraid we don't do better than we do because we are human. I think we are very human in that even our best intuitions are not available to us all the time or at the right time. Every culture is riddled with oddness and error, and we are too. What I particularly wanted to do in that book was to make Americans less immune to information and able to read a newspaper in a foreign country. I have no evidence that I accomplished my goals. My hopes were basically modest. I don't think the United States will be able to solve the human tragedy for ourselves or for anybody else.

James Romm. Courtesy of Tanya Marcuse.

Alexander the Great: An Interview with James Romm

James Romm is the James H. Ottaway Jr. Professor of Classics at Bard College. He has received fellowships from the Guggenheim Foundation and the National Endowment for the Humanities. His books include *The Edges of the Earth in Ancient Thought, Ghost on the Throne: The Death of Alexander the Great and the War for Crown and Empire,* and *The Landmark Arrian: The Campaigns of Alexander.* Romm's monumental effort of editing Arrian's original text with detailed footnotes and maps has created, according to the Editor's Preface: "the fullest, clearest description of the Alexander campaign available to English readers for a very long time, perhaps ever."

The following interview was conducted November 2010.

Allan Vorda: How did you get involved in this massive undertaking of editing Arrian's *Anabasis Alexandrou*? What type of research was done and how long did this enterprise take to complete under the title of *The Landmark Arrian*?

James Romm: It took about five years, but the last year was the equivalent of three normal ones. The research involved goes back even further, as I have been studying Alexander for at least a decade.

AV: Arrian states the war against the Persians was "not sprung from enmity but was a lawful struggle for the sovereignty of Asia." Isn't this statement somewhat incongruous as far as it being lawful and that there was enmity due to previous wars with Persia?

JR: I have to correct you and point out that the statement is Alexander's, not Arrian's. But yes, it's a hard statement to understand. Alexander seems to be making a distinction between a purely political struggle, where normal rules of engagement apply, and a grudge match where anything goes. But he elsewhere does express hatred of Darius and a sense of personal grievance. So there's some inconsistency.

AV: Upon the defeat of the Persians at Issus, Darius's mother prostrates herself in front of Hephaistion (as he appeared the taller), thinking he is Alexander. When she learns of her mistake, she apologizes, whereupon Alexander tells her there is no error as "Hephaistion, too, is Alexander." What do you make of this scene and Alexander's comment?

JR: I don't understand this comment, and I don't think anyone does. Maybe Arrian himself did not understand it.

AV: You state that some historians believe Darius's wife bore Alexander a child in 331 BCE. What can you add to this rumor and that Alexander later married the queen's daughter?

JR: We have the testimony of one source that the queen died in childbirth. Whose child was she bearing? It could have been Alexander's, but there's no hard evidence. I don't think it would have bothered Alexander to be involved first with the mother and later with the daughter.

AV: You mention the defection of the Phoenicians and their navy from the Persians to Alexander. How critical was this in the war?

JR: Extremely critical, in the battle for Tyre in particular. The mole which Alexander constructed to reach Tyre from land did not allow him to bring his siege weapons to bear against the walls. The defection of the Phoenician ships gave him control of the sea and allowed him to bring ship-mounted engines right up to the walls. That was the turning point in the seven-month siege.

AV: Arrian states in the battle of Tyre that eight thousand Tyrians were killed and thirty thousand captured and sold. Other reports state Alexander crucified two thousand males. What do you make of this and Alexander's cruelty?

JR: I think Arrian omitted mention of an episode that showed Alexander in a poor light. He does this on numerous occasions. We cannot be certain the crucifixions occurred, but it seems likely that some of the episodes Arrian omits were factual, and this may be one of them. Certainly, Alexander was capable of cruelty and acts of collective punishment when his will was thwarted.

AV: Arrian's list of Darius's troops at Gaugamela includes one million soldiers, forty thousand cavalry, two hundred scythe-bearing chariots, and fifteen elephants. The Macedonians have seventy-five thousand troops, and yet win at Gaugamela. Surely, this must be a gross exaggeration.

JR: All troop counts of Alexander's enemies in the *Anabasis* are exaggerated, but the fault lies more with Arrian's sources than with Arrian. That said, the Persians were capable of putting huge numbers of troops in the field. They outnumbered the Macedonians at Gaugamela several times over, but many of their infantry lacked adequate training and equipment.

AV: It seems Arrian glorifies Alexander and the Macedonians "in heroic poses." This constant glorification runs counter to Homer's *Iliad* that showcased many Persians as noble and brave. Why didn't Arrian temper his comments to be more realistic?

JR: The *Iliad* is a more compelling story because it's a fight between two noble adversaries. But few storytellers are as talented as Homer. The superhero narrative, which focuses on the glory and virtue of one leader at the expense of the other, is easier on both the author and the audience. Also, the Roman world in which Arrian lived was more unipolar than that of Alexander. His attitudes toward the barbarian world, and the East, were partly the product of his times.

AV: Discuss what is referred to as the "profound economic impact," the wealth that Alexander obtained from two centuries of Persian taxation. What happened to all of this wealth after Alexander's death?

JR: Much of it was drawn on by his successors to fund their wars against one another. The wastage was terrible. This story is told in more detail in a forthcoming book of mine, *Ghost on the Throne: The Death of Alexander the Great and the War for Crown and Empire*, appearing about a year from now.

AV: During various encounters of the Macedonians with foreign troops who had different languages, there is no mention of how they were able to communicate during meetings, surrenders, and truces. What do you know about how the Macedonians were able to communicate with their enemies or these "barbarians," as Arrian refers to them?

JR: Arrian does refer at various points to the need for interpreters. No Macedonians learned the language of their subjects except Peukestas, who taught himself Persian. Alexander had Greek taught to the Persians he expected to become part of his imperial regime.

AV: Arrian does not refer to vulgate sources about thirteen days of sexual congress that Alexander allegedly had with an Amazon queen named Thalestris, who wanted to have his child. Plutarch rejects this as a fiction. What do you think?

JR: I agree with Plutarch. Arrian was quite sensible to omit this story.

AV: During Alexander's campaign, which lasted approximately ten years, there had to be a sizeable number of troops killed or severely wounded. How did Alexander replenish his troops?

JR: Alexander sent back home for reinforcements on several occasions. But his losses in battle were very small compared to the other drain on his manpower, the posting of garrison forces to retain conquered territory.

AV: There is mention of Alexander's barbarous treatment of Bessos, who betrayed Darius. Reportedly, Alexander had Bessos's nose and the tips of his ears cut off before being executed. Please comment on another example of Alexander's cruelty and how factual it is.

JR: Even Arrian records this mutilation, so there is no reason to doubt it. As I said above, Alexander was capable of great cruelty against those who resisted him with determination.

AV: During the episode of Bessos, it appears that Alexander's drinking was getting out of hand. Shortly thereafter, Alexander kills Kleitos (whose sister nursed Alexander as a boy) in a drunken rage. What are your thoughts on this episode, in which Arrian deplores Kleitos's behavior and ultimately praises Alexander for his subsequent grief?

JR: Arrian wants to exculpate Alexander wherever possible. He obviously can't excuse the murder of Kleitos, but he manages to assign equal blame to Kleitos and to Alexander, and then to praise Alexander for his remorse. It's a pretty generous treatment, but he does ultimately chalk the episode as a black mark against Alexander, not least because the king was drinking to excess.

AV: After Alexander defeats the Sogdians and their leader, Oxyartes, he marries the beautiful Rhoxane. She is the virgin daughter of Oxyartes and considered the most beautiful woman, other than Darius's wife, in Asia. Tell us about Rhoxane, the child she bore Alexander, and her ultimate fate.

JR: This is another story that is told in detail in my forthcoming *Ghost on the Throne.* It's a tragic tale. Rhoxane was in her early teens when Alexander married her, perhaps about twenty when she was pregnant with his only legitimate child. Eventually she gave birth to a boy, Alexander IV, who immediately became one of two crowned heads of state, sharing the kingship with his uncle, Philip III. For thirteen years thereafter Rhoxane and her son were pawns in the power struggle for control of the empire, controlled by no fewer than five of the successors at various times. Eventually, mother and son became prisoners of Kassandros, who kept them in seclusion for six years before having them secretly assassinated. None of the successors at that point wanted a legitimate monarch to assume power.

AV: Arrian states: "Of course, one must not examine ancient tales about the divine too minutely. For stories that strike a listener as incredible because they violate our sense of what is probable begin to seem credible when an element of the divine is added." Despite the allusion to Alexander's divinity, this statement could easily apply to Arrian's over-the-top tributes to Alexander's greatness as violating the reader's sense as to what is actually credible.

JR: Arrian speaks here of tales that rely on the divine as an explanation, and, to his credit, he mostly avoids this in his own narrative. He does believe that the gods were somehow involved in Alexander's success, but never attributes any historical event to their influence. The closest he comes is the statement that some god induced Darius to change his ground before the battle of Issos, because it had been foretold that Persia would fall. But even here Arrian says "perhaps." He's no Thucydides, but within the context of ancient historiography, he's fairly rigorous about excluding supernatural factors.

AV: Koinos makes an impassioned speech to Alexander that the troops are tired and want to go home, to which Alexander eventually agrees. What was the state of Alexander's army at this point in time, as they had already reached the Hyphasis River in India?

JR: Both their gear and their morale were in pretty bad shape. They had marched for months through monsoon rains and tropical heat. One of our sources reports that, when they received new armor and clothing in India, they burned the ones they had. But the biggest factor motivating the mutiny was their fear of war elephants; they knew that if they went on eastward toward the Ganges, they would have to fight a lot more of these.

AV: Shortly after this episode, Koinos "died of a disease." Is there any knowledge of Koinos's age or the disease from which he died? This seems highly suspicious.

JR: Some modern scholars have speculated that Koinos was poisoned, but we have no evidence of this. No ancient source suspects foul play, even the ones that want to believe the worst about Alexander.

AV: During the battle with the Mallois at the Hydraotes River, Alexander jumps into the Indian citadel and single-handedly fights the Indians. Alexander is severely wounded by an arrow: "While his blood remained warm, Alexander defended himself, though he was in a bad way; but when a huge rush of blood gushed from the wound along with a hiss of air, he was overcome with vertigo and faintness and collapsed." His life is saved by a handful of his men including Peukestas, who covers him with his shield. Please recount your thoughts on this battle, Alexander's rashness to fight alone, and the wound he received.

JR: The episode at the Malloi town is one of the hardest to understand, in terms of Alexander's thoughts and motivations. There are different versions of it, and it's hard to know exactly what happened. My best guess is that Alexander meant to shame his troops, who were fighting less vigorously than he wanted, by going first or even alone into combat. He expected in this case that they would immediately follow him up the wall and into the town, but the scaling ladders broke under their weight, causing a lengthy delay in which he was left virtually unaided. Alexander would not have jumped into the town had he known he would be stranded there for more than a minute or two. He was not delusional.

AV: An Indian sage supposedly foretells Alexander's death: "King Alexander, each man can have only so much land as this on which we are standing. You are human like the rest of us, except in your restlessness and arrogance you travel so far from home, making trouble for yourself and others. Well, you will soon be dead and will have as much land as will suffice to bury your corpse." Do you think this really happened or is this just Arrian introducing the foreshadowing element of the Fates into the story?

JR: This is one of several episodes in the ancient sources where Indian sages express their dismay at Alexander and his whole value system. It is the kind of scene the ancient world loved to elaborate on and fictionalize, but there is probably some kernel of truth in it. Strabo, another important source for Alexander's invasion of India, preserves a fairly credible report by Onesikritos, a Greek officer, of his visit to an Indian religious academy, and it contains exchanges very much like the one you mention.

AV: Alexander declares himself a god. Is this a true description by Arrian and, if so, what do you make of this?

JR: I think you have misinterpreted the speech Alexander makes here. He tells his rebellious troops that they ought to just go home and abandon him and tell their countrymen they did so, and then says sarcastically that "such a report will be holy in the sight of god." He doesn't refer to himself when he says "god," and never, in Arrian's account, makes claims to his own divinity.

AV: Alexander's lifelong friend and companion, Hephaestion, dies at an early age at Ecbatana, probably due to malaria. Alexander is devastated by his death. Please comment on their relationship, which some have speculated was homosexual at some point, and his abilities as a soldier, since Alexander had given him the title of chiliarch.

JR: There is no doubt that they had a very close friendship and that Alexander trusted Hephaestion more fully than his other officers. He promoted Hephaestion to high commands despite the man's shortcomings as a soldier, which created considerable ill will among his more soldierly officers. But there is simply no evidence of a sexual relationship. There may have been one, and Alexander almost certainly had sexual intimacy with other males, but the relationship portrayed in Oliver Stone's movie is based on pure speculation.

AV: Alexander dies in Babylon at the age of thirty-two, a few months after Hephaestion. There has been much speculation on the cause of his death. Some claim it was poison or malaria, but it is suggested it was due to typhoid fever. Please extrapolate why there has been so much controversy over his death.

JR: Appendix O is the work of Eugene Borza, based on a medical panel he attended some years ago that examined the evidence presented by Arrian. There are various questions that other scholars might ask to complicate the issue. Is Arrian's account credible? Should it be relied on for a medical diagnosis? Might it have been falsified by those who had a vested interest in portraying Alexander's death as natural, rather than the result of poisoning? These are very knotty issues, and, to many historians, insoluble. The second appendix that addresses the death of Alexander, by Brian Bosworth, raises some of these problems and poses a kind of counterweight to Borza's view.

AV: Arrian speculates about Alexander's early death that "perhaps it was better for him to depart at the high point of his fame." What do you think would have happened if Alexander had lived for another thirty years? Do you think he would have gone on to conquer Libya, Carthage, and perhaps early Rome?

JR: He certainly intended to take on Carthage, and quite likely would have succeeded. After that, the rest of the Mediterranean, including Rome, would have been easy pickings. The face of the world would have been entirely different had Alexander survived to carry out the plans he had at the time of his death.

AV: Arrian's primary sources for writing about Alexander were Ptolemy and Aristobulos. Based on these sources and the fact that Arrian was writing about Alexander four hundred years after his death, then how credible and objective can Arrian's work be?

JR: The narratives of Ptolemy and Aristobulos were lost after Arrian read and used them, but we can judge by his history that they were fairly good eyewitness accounts, though tending strongly toward a positive view of Alexander. The alternative source used by other historians—Kleitarkhos—was not as reliable and may not have been an eyewitness; but Kleitarkhos also does not have a vested interest in making Alexander look good. Any responsible investigation must use all the available sources, but Arrian is the best of these. He is certainly not objective, but he does not go so far in the direction of eulogy as to lose our trust.

AV: Finally, what is your overall opinion of Arrian's writing and the life of Alexander?

JR: Alexander's story is the ultimate case of truth stranger than fiction. The circumstances that put such an incredibly talented, ambitious, and charismatic man in control of an immensely powerful army, at a moment in history when world supremacy was up for grabs, seems like the premise of a myth or a fantasy novel, not a historical narrative. The more I learn about the era, the more I am awestruck at the immensity of change over a very short period of time. Possibly the world has never before or since seen such rapid and far-reaching transformations.

Arrian's writing is imbued with the same sense of awe that I am describing, but it is focused on the single figure of Alexander rather than the larger era of which he was a part. A more responsible historian would have said more about Alexander's father, Philip, who set the stage for his conquests; about Alexander's adversary, Darius III; and about the Greek city-states, still powerful enough during the Macedonian invasion of Asia to bring it to a halt, had they acted in concert. Arrian is a biographer as much as a historian, and prefers to keep his eye on Alexander at all times. The result is a compelling story of an individual, but one misses the sense of the wider world that was in the throes of cataclysmic change.

Samanta Schweblin. Courtesy of Ludwig Suhrkamp.

Discovery in Darkness: An Interview with Samanta Schweblin

Samanta Schweblin was born in Argentina in 1978 and graduated from the University of Buenos Aires. In 2001 Schweblin published her first book, *The Nucleus of Disturbances*; this was followed by *Mouthful of Birds* (2009), *Rescue Distance* (2014), and a collection of stories called *Seven Empty Houses* (2015). All of her books were originally published in her native Spanish, but since then have been published in twenty languages. At the invitation of the German government, she moved to Berlin for a writing residency; there, she finished *Rescue Distance,* which recently was published in an arresting English translation (by Megan McDowell) with the revised title of *Fever Dream.* It was later nominated for the Man International Booker Prize, which also nominated *Mouthful of Birds* for its English translation. Her most recent novel, *Little Eyes*, was published in 2020.

Fever Dream is a short novel involving a deathbed conversation between a woman named Amanda and a young boy named David. The story itself is like a fever dream that moves in and out of both time and reality. Something in the rural countryside, possibly water or pesticides, is making the people very ill. When David was sick, his mother, Carla, took him to a woman "in the green house" who healed him by "transmigration"—moving some of the illness to another person. David's focus now is to make Amanda understand the "exact moment," while Amanda's focus is to maintain a "rescue distance" from her daughter to try and prevent her from getting ill.

Since Samanta was living in Berlin, she requested the questions be sent to her in Spanish. Even though Samanta's English is better than adequate, I contacted my good friend, Liliana Avila, to transcribe my questions to Spanish and to add questions of her own. Once Liliana received the answers from Samanta, she then translated Samanta's answers from Spanish to English. The result below is a window into a truly unique Latin American writer at work today.

This interview was conducted during November 2017. I later had the pleasure of meeting her when she gave a reading of *Fever Dream* at Rice University along with Aminatta Forna. During my research, I previously had seen pictures as well as a video of Schweblin, but when I got my book signed I was really struck by her looks and how sweet she was in person. Totally unpretentious and genuine.

Allan Vorda: You were born in Buenos Aires in 1978. What was it like growing up there and what was your educational background?

Samanta Schweblin: I was born in Buenos Aires but grew up in Hurlingham, a neighborhood that at that time bordered with more rural areas. The route, for example, that is very present in my books, I took it every morning to go to school. In the same block one could have a pharmacy with its large neon sign, and on the other corner a chicken coop and horses tied to a light pole. I think that something of this area where the countryside and the city come together has been very marked in my texts. It was a very free childhood; I could leave home alone since I was little, and I had gangs of friends. These are unthinkable things for a ten-year-old to do now in Buenos Aires, with the violent and insecure place that the city has become.

My literary training began on my seventeenth birthday, when I began attending literary workshops in the capital. I also enjoyed the fifty-minute trip to the city by train, the personal feeling of independence that let me go alone with that excuse. Then, I did the film career, which was also a great push for writing, because I specialized in the area of the screenplay. I kept going to literary workshops until I was thirty.

AV: Since you were born in Argentina, the country of the great Jorge Luis Borges, did his writing have any influence on you? What about other South American writers such as the Brazilian Machado de Assis, the Columbian Gabriel García Márquez, and any other writers?

SS: Of course. I always say that I fell in love with literature by reading the Americans. Borges has always fascinated me, but from the intellectual side, not so much from the emotional, which I believe is the one that penetrates deeper in my inspirations. I was fascinated by Juan Rulfo, Adolfo Bioy Casares, Julio Cortázar, María Luisa Bombal, Alfonsina Storni, Antonio Di Benedetto. It is a tradition that I have learned a lot, and to which I owe my fascination for the strange, the unusual, and the dark.

Liliana Avila: All of your previous works until *Fever Dream* have been published in Spanish. Before we get into *Fever Dream*, perhaps you can discuss a couple of stories from *Siete Casas Vacias* (*Seven Empty Houses*). What inspired you to write this book? What do you want to convey to the reader?

SS: Several things. The loneliness and isolation that lead us to language, and how many times we fail to communicate what connects us. But I did not want a dense, dark book at all. Or maybe dark, but not a sad and painful darkness; rather the darkness to which one looks to discover new things. These characters have dragged their problems for a long time, and precisely because of the extreme situation to which they have come, each one discovers something like a "healthy location" that allows them to escape, or to heal themselves, or to think in a different way.

LA: In the first house, mother and daughter are lost in a neighborhood. Then they enter a house that they damaged a little bit with their car. Why does the mother not seem to care about this, yet is distracted admiring a sugar container? Why was the sugar container the point of her attention in all of the chaos?

SS: I think that's part of what the story is about. These are decisions that I take from the intuitive, and I find it's difficult to think from a more rational place. But perhaps, as readers, following these two women with this interrogation ringing behind our backs forces us to look at what happens with a different attention.

LA: It seems to me that in every house you try to reflect a situation of stress, such as when the inhabitants run naked through the house. This seems to be a daily situation. Why does the family see this as normal?

SS: The idea was to play a little with social and cultural boundaries. I think we live in a world where "the normal" is just a cut that each society creates for itself, but leaves out a number of situations, thoughts, and events as part of what we catalog as normal. In this story, for example, it is considered acceptable for children to play nude. It is also considered acceptable that two old men—possibly with Alzheimer's—run naked through the garden. But it is not considered acceptable that both couples play naked together. When the narrator sees his children and their parents playing naked, it seems to be the freest, most beautiful and sincere event that he has seen in a long time, but from the gaze of the rest of the family the situation is out of control, and the danger is imminent. Where is the limit then?

AV: What was the genesis for writing *Fever Dream,* which was originally called *Rescue Distance* (*Distancia de Rescate*)?

SS: *Rescue Distance* began as a tale of which I wrote dozens of versions, but it just did not work. It was in one of those many drafts that David's voice appeared. When David spoke, he ordered everything. During my writing process, David asked Amanda "what's important?" This is a question that is repeated throughout the book and that somehow I was also asking myself. Forcing me not to split, to advance as fast as possible but also attentive to every detail. I discovered that it was a story that needed a different time signature; I needed introspection, review, and the search that only an intense dialogue between two people could give me.

For me, even in the most subtle and introspective story, it's all about tension: this is the thread that ties a reader to story, something in the rhythm and in the argument that hypnotizes and pushes us to read with great attention. As a reader, I love the storytellers who play with this, and as a writer it is something I always look for. I think I have learned to develop some of this in my stories, but *Fever Dream* was quite a challenge because I did not know if I would be able to keep that thread tense beyond the ten or twenty pages to which I was accustomed to working as a storyteller.

AV: The novel is set in a clinic where Amanda lies dying and conversing with a young boy named David. It seems in their conversations that the boy is more knowledgeable about the events they are recounting. Why is this?

SS: David is a boy who is only eight or nine years old. But at four years old he underwent a strong intoxication that almost took his life. Helped by a "healer" to which his mother took him (or perhaps by his own efforts to survive—I like to keep both possibilities open), David was able to survive. But something changes in him; he has been too close to death, maybe even touched it, and it is as if something of that darkness had been growing all that time in him. Now he is still a child, but seems to bring from that closeness with death some vital information, a knowledge that no one who has not travelled that route can have. That is why he is able to help Amanda, because the path she is making toward death is the same path he has made a few years back.

AV: And where did the idea of transmigration come from?

SS: That was my invention. As the healer explains, if you can migrate part of one body to another, you can also divide intoxication, and then, divided now into two bodies, intoxication loses strength, and could be neutralized. But the "healer," "the woman of the green house," is not an invention. In my childhood, I met many women like her, even in Argentina where I always lived in the city. And in the field these figures are even stronger. Our health system leaves us exposed to the most humble workers—especially those who work around the soybean areas—and these women are a great incentive, sometimes the only one they can access.

AV: Nina answers her mother, Amanda, in plural to what David says, "I like that. About the plural." This seems to suggest the plurality of existence between David and Amanda.

SS: That's right. It is a very subtle nod for the most attentive readers. But there is a sort of circularity in history, or perhaps a certain fatality in the destinies of these characters, which makes the idea of "the plural" already in Nina even long before their migration is made.

AV: Amanda says to David, "I think about you, or about the other David, the first David without his finger." Who is this other David?

SS: Amanda says this by recalling the strong sentence of Carla, David's mother, who in her first conversation in the garden of Amanda's house confesses that this David is no longer her son. The previous

David was an angel, but the transmigration has not left anything of that child, and now it's a "monster."

AV: David wants Amanda to focus on the "exact moment," which he says is: "It's something in the body. But it's almost imperceptible, we have to pay attention." Why is this so important for David? Also, since Amanda is dying, why can't Amanda have the woman in the green house do transmigration on her?

SS: David and Amanda try to understand together what has happened. That's why we thoroughly review Amanda's last days over and over, trying to see each step in more detail. The exact moment is when the disaster begins to unravel, the moment when the rescue distance is cut off forever. Amanda cannot do the transmigration because she is in the emergency room, very far from the green house. Besides, Amanda does not believe in those things. And finally, the woman in the green house is at that moment attending Nina—which Amanda discovers with desperation, in her own delirium of death.

AV: The story goes back and forth in time, which parallels the fever dream where Amanda has a hard time remembering everything. What made you think of using this device, and was it difficult to write scenes like this?

SS: It was a difficult structure to handle, not only for the three times, but also because there are three voices narrating each of those times: David, Amanda, and Carla (through Amanda's memory). I knew I was building a complex text, but I didn't want it to be complicated. I accepted its complexity, but I needed it not to be confusing at any time. So it was a very hard job of correcting, rewriting, and rereading.

AV: Amanda says there is "a can of peas of a brand I don't buy." Amanda later states, "the can has an alarming presence. This is important, right?" To which David replies, "This is very important." Can you tell us anything about this bizarre scene?

SS: Well, it's a dream, so there's no strong logic here. But I wanted to play with the symbolic: the idea of a mother who finds inside her house a product she would never choose to feed her family. The whole story is crossed by a landscape and a town that suffers the dire consequences of living near soybean fields, genetically modified soybeans, fumigated by strong agro-chemicals. This lethal combination leads to the tables of many families a dangerous diet. It's a type of food that a well-informed mother would never choose for her children.

AV: At one point Amanda recalls Nina saying, "I'm David." To which David replies to Amanda, "Is this a joke? Are you making this up?" And Amanda says, "No, David. It's a dream, a nightmare." Amanda later says to David that if Nina "won't talk to me in your voice, there will be no perplexing can of peas on the table." Now it appears that Amanda knows what is going on and David is not aware of the transmigration between him and Nina. Can you explain this?

SS: I do not think Amanda knows more than David knows. It is simply a reflection of Amanda, the idea that as long as she is able to feel the weight of her daughter in her hands, then she will have the certainty that what happens is not a dream. Perhaps the dream frightened her too much, and she does not want to confuse sleep with reality again. She is frightened and needs to escape, so she concentrates on the real, the concrete, and the only certainty she has at that moment is the weight of her daughter in her arms.

AV: There are numerous cases of deformed and dead children who have drunk the water. Why doesn't the water bother Carla and her husband? Why haven't the local people and authorities done anything to fix the water problem?

SS: There are many things at stake in that question. To begin with, at least in my imagination, it is not clear to people that poisoning comes from water (in fact, this is the case in many communities in rural Argentina). But in relation to these pesticides that the big companies use to fumigate—and that later contaminate the waters—it also happens that a great part of these communities work in those fields, and they cannot or do not want to denounce them.

AV: You are now living in Berlin—what made you move from Argentina and how long do you plan to stay in Germany? Will you continue to write in Spanish?

SS: I moved by an invitation from the German government, a one-year residence for foreign artists. In fact, it was during that year that I finished writing *Fever Dream.* But then, once the stay was over, I was invited to give some creative writing workshops, and soon I was already working, with new friends and, above all, in love with the city. It was very easy to stay. I feel comfortable and at the same time strategically isolated for writing. I think I'll be here for a couple of years. But I will always write in Spanish; it is the language in which I think and in which I read.

AV: What can your readers look forward to with your next work of fiction?

SS: I'm afraid to answer this question, because I do not want to limit my next steps in any way. But I'm sure I'll continue to write, and I'm sure I'll also be very attentive to how tension is built and maintained in a story. I think this curiosity is the heart of all my texts, and it's something vital that I also seek in everything I read.

Hubert Selby Jr. Courtesy of Catheryn Kilgarriff.

Examining the Disease: An Interview with Hubert Selby Jr.

Hubert "Cubby" Selby Jr., the son of an engineer, was born on July 23, 1928, in Brooklyn, New York. He attended Peter Stuyvesant High School for one year before shipping out with the merchant marines. During the late 1940s, while working as a merchant seaman, he contracted tuberculosis from cows on board that had bovine tuberculosis, and spent the next three and a half years in the hospital. During an operation, doctors removed several of his ribs, whereupon one lung collapsed and the other was partially removed. For the rest of his life he suffered from chronic pulmonary problems. Due to chronic pain, for decades he was addicted to various drugs, including morphine and heroin. He held various jobs, which included working as an insurance analyst and as a freelance copywriter for the *National Enquirer.* Selby eventually moved to California and kicked his drug habits. For the last twenty years of his life he taught creative writing at the University of Southern California.

Selby's published books include *Last Exit to Brooklyn* (a collection of six semirelated stories), *The Room, The Demon, Requiem for a Dream, Song of the Silent Snow* (short stories), *The Willow Tree,* and *Waiting Period.*

The first time I encountered Selby, I was in graduate school doing research on another writer. While perusing some microfiche, I ran across a story in the *Provincetown Review* titled "Tralala." I recall the initial shock of reading his extremely graphic prose and the feeling that each word of his stream-of-consciousness style was catapulting the reader to read even faster. When I finished "Tralala" and the horrific ending that befalls the "protagonist," my heart was racing.

Immediately thereafter I purchased *Last Exit to Brooklyn* and *The Room.* Reading these books confirmed that Selby has his own inimitable style. In fact, critics sometimes found it frustrating because there did not seem to be a group of writers with whom he could be lumped. Selby wrote about morally depraved people who live in an unforgiving underworld that had been rarely portrayed in literature at that time.

Fifteen years had elapsed when I noticed in the newspaper that *Last Exit to Brooklyn* was being made into a movie (starring Jennifer Jason Leigh in an engaging performance as Tralala) that was to be released first in Europe before making it to America. Reading this newspaper clipping spurred my interest in Selby again, whereupon I contacted his agent and tracked him down in West Hollywood.

The interview with Hubert Selby was conducted on November 18, 1989. Mr. Selby spoke by phone from his home in West Hollywood. He was very adamant about getting his point across and expressed disappointment that his fiction has not received the credit that it should have. For many years he had been working off-and-on a book titled *Seeds of Pain, Seeds of Love,* but he died in 2004 before completing it.

Allan Vorda: You were born, raised, and educated in Brooklyn. What effect did this environment have on your writing?

Hubert Selby Jr.: There is really no way of knowing for sure if any writer's environment has an effect on your writing. There is no way of determining that because you can't do a controlled experiment. I think one of the biggest influences of being born and raised in a city like New York is that it gave me a universal appreciation. A lot of people in Europe consider me European. I didn't understand why until I moved to Los Angeles. I can see why Los Angeles is really an American city, whereas New York is very international. I think growing up in New York is the best gift you can have living in this country.

My mind was opened to a lot of things I wouldn't have otherwise known. I believe the biggest influence of growing up in New York was that it made me very responsive to speech and the music that is in speech. I write by ear, and the music of speech fascinates me. I don't think you have that in the rest of the country. You don't have the incredible diversity of music you have in the speech of New York. It doesn't make any difference if someone's ethnic background is Greek, Italian, or Jewish, whereas if they live outside New York they would all sound flat, like the Midwest. In New York, you couldn't begin to describe the different flavors of speech. Consequently, I think the music of New York speech has been a big influence on my writing.

AV: How did you develop your writing style, which sometimes resembles a stream-of-consciousness paper from a creative writing class?

HS: That I wouldn't know, never having gone to school, praise God. It's hard to say exactly. We are never really aware of as much as we believe we are aware of, because self-deception is part of the human condition. I think my writing style, as I've said, is a product of my fascination with speech and the music of speech. I am not too concerned with the physical environment but with what goes on *inside* a person.

This is really important to me, because it is what goes on in our heads that creates the world we live in. So the stream-of-consciousness just comes naturally.

I have of course read Joyce and have been influenced by him. I think every writer who has read Joyce has been influenced one way or another by his work. But it's the interior dialogue that we have with ourselves that really fascinates me and how it is reflected in our physical world. Maybe that is why my writing at times looks like it is a stream-of-consciousness.

AV: I understand you contracted tuberculosis and spent three years in the hospital, had some of your ribs cut out, lung problems, and asthma. How has illness and a sense of your own mortality affected your writing and your outlook on life?

HS: You spend three and a half years in bed, and it affects your life, and everything that affects your life affects your work. I also believe you don't understand life until you die or come close to dying. That may have a lot to do with the nature of my writing. Lying in bed also gives you a greater opportunity than usual to look inside yourself and find out exactly what's going on. I had never read a book until then. That's where it all started: reading, and then a desire to write.

AV: Did you find it difficult to get your stories published in the beginning? Is it still hard to get published?

HS: I never really tried to get published. I knew people who suggested I send it here or there. I followed their advice and got published in the *Black Mountain Review* and *Provincetown Review*. The same thing happened with the books. I don't know whether I have more trouble getting published today or not. In this country, not too many people want to have anything to do with me. That could be translated into having a problem getting published.

AV: Why do you suppose a lot of people don't want to have anything to do with you? Because of the fiction? Because it's not commercial?

HS: I have to assume they are frightened by something. For example, I recently read an article in the *Smithsonian*. It was about writers who are associated with Brooklyn, and they listed writers like Tom Wolfe and Henry Miller, but I was not on the list. You can hate a writer, but how can you not include my name with a list of writers associated with Brooklyn? That's the attitude of the literary establishment toward me in this country.

AV: What writers have influenced you?

HS: There are a lot of writers I admire, but as to who influenced me, it's hard to say. One of the reasons it's difficult is that when I started reading, I read everybody at once, which was a great advantage because I didn't have to work under the influence of any writer. For example, I didn't have to write like Hemingway, but later on Steinbeck, Faulkner, and Hemingway certainly influenced me and to a lesser degree, Mickey Spillane. There also seems to me a very close kinship to Celine in my work. I remember reading *Thais* by Anatole France. It just knocked me over, and I'm sure that had a tremendous influence on me. William Saroyan, I remember, also knocked me out.

Obviously, James Joyce and especially William Carlos Williams. I have no way of knowing how much Williams influenced me, but he did, not the least of which is his use of the American language and his insistence on its rhythms. Isaac Babel was a tremendous influence. I also like Gilbert Sorrentino, Richie Price, Michael Stevens, and Joseph Ferrandino, who wrote a book about Vietnam called *Firefight*. I adore the work of Joseph Heller. Unfortunately, I don't get to read as much as I'd like, so I'm not too familiar with all the writing that is going on.

AV: Are the recurring character names in *Last Exit* and your subsequent fiction based on real people? If so, did they know they were being written about? Any knowledge of their whereabouts thirty years later?

HS: These people were real in the sense that they're not totally fictionalized people. I create real people in my books, but there was no

Harry Black or Tralala. Actually, there was someone named Tralala, but I never saw her or met her. I just overheard a conversation between two guys in the Greek's saying, "remember that time Tralala put her tits on the bar?" Later on someone said something about finding Tralala naked in the lot. I don't even know if Tralala was her real name or a nickname.

AV: What about Tony and Vinnie?

HS: They're based on hundreds of Tonys and Vinnies I've known in my life, but the interesting thing you were asking about thirty years later is that there were three guys from that neighborhood around the army base that came down to the movie set. We had a reunion where we discussed the old days in the '50s and '60s. Each of them had read all or part of the book, and they all had the same reaction: "This never happened!" or "This ain't the way it was!" In a sense, it's all based on reality and in my experience as it goes through my imagination, but there is no Harry Black or Tralala or any specific person it was based on.

AV: Many of your characters are intrinsically angry—angry at everybody in particular and society in general. Do they embody your own sense of personal rage?

HS: Yes. During that time, anger was the only thing I was aware of, but I had no idea how much I loved these people I was creating. I became really aware of it watching the film *Last Exit to Brooklyn* being made and looking at the finished product. I do remember it took me six years to write *Last Exit*, and it was a real struggle. I remember when I would finally finish a piece and the people would end up in the terrible places they end up, then I would quite often pass out. I think by the time I had finished "Tralala," I spent two weeks in bed. I really got involved with my characters, and I lived and died with them. I was enraged at everything, and to the best of my ability, I directed all my rage and anger toward God, because that was the son of a bitch who did this to me.

AV: Is it your aim for the readers to incorporate the anger in your fiction, albeit unconsciously, into the real world of their own lives?

HS: I don't know if what you mean by "incorporate into the real world" means to go out and be angry with someone you weren't angry with before. I've never heard of that happening. The people who talked to me about *Last Exit* all use the same word regarding their reaction to the book, and that's "compassion."

This was not a conscious intention of mine as I wrote *Last Exit,* but one of the results of the book, from what everyone tells me, is they feel compassion for these people, and they end up loving people whom they previously felt were unlovable. It's a great thing to happen, and I think the same thing happened with the film.

AV: Do you see your writing as an extension of the Angry Young Men writers, such as Sillitoe and Osborne, in England in the '50s?

HS: I don't believe so. I haven't read them extensively. They were socially conscious people making a social statement. I am not.

AV: In *City of Words: American Fiction 1950-80,* Tony Tanner says: "A good way to describe what Selby is doing is to say that he is trying to depict a human version of what the ecologist John Calhoun called a 'behavioral sink.' In a 'behavior sink' all normal patterns of behavior are disrupted, and the unusual stress leads to all forms of perversion, violence, and breakdown." Is this an accurate assessment?

HS: I don't think in those terms. I'm not trying to depict a human version of anything. I am doing the best I can to create real people. Now maybe these people fall into this category as this man perceives it. My intent, however, is to put the reader through an *emotional experience* and not have him just read stories. I have to write from the inside out. Now if in doing that, it ends up these people fall into what this guy categorizes as a "behavioral sink," then maybe it is true, but it was never my intent.

AV: One of the major problems your characters experience is a lack of communication, and whatever communication there is seems to occur in a sea of obscenities and anger. Why do your characters persist in such impossible relationships?

HS: I think that's what this guy is referring to when he says a "behavior sink." My characters live in a fictional hell because that is the way the world is. You defend by attacking. We do that as individuals and as couples because we don't communicate with ourselves. If we are not communicating properly with ourselves, how are we going to do it with another human being? If we can't do it as individuals and couples, how can we possibly do it as a nation? It's easy to look at what the politicians have done in the last twenty years and see how communication is so faulty that it's destroying the world. It's very easy to see this, but not quite so easy to see it within ourselves and how I miscommunicate with myself. That's the thing that fascinates me. We believe what is true is false and what is false is true. I don't really go out to hurt you or hurt me, but I believe I'm doing something that's going to make me feel better.

AV: Some of your characters—who evoke some of the most sadistic, cruel, and lowest standards of human behavior—get their comeuppance at the end (e.g., Tralala in her story and Harry Black in "Strike"). Do you believe your characters, as well as people in real life, deserve to be punished?

HS: I don't believe in punishment. Punishment is a religious concept that has nothing to do with the reality of my being. When I'm communicating with myself, I know I am not guilty. I know sin does not exist. Therefore, there is no need for punishment. I absolutely do not believe in punishment. I guess it's called karma. I don't know anything about it, but I do know there is a cause for every effect. It seems our world, especially religious people, really believes in punishment. (I've been a member of Amnesty International and of the Urgent Action Network, for whom I've been writing to heads of state for a long time.) The response of people is that they really believe in punishment. They do not believe in the correction of errors because they believe in sin. So they must punish people. Look at Jerry Falwell or the Ayatollah Khomeini and see what they believe in, see what they propose. They want punishment. No, I don't believe in punishment. I believe in the correction of mistakes. It's my mistakes that I can correct. It's my duty and obligation to be willing to do that.

AV: How did you choose the title *Last Exit to Brooklyn?*

HS: The title comes from a sign on the Belt Parkway as it goes from Brooklyn into Queens. There is an exit sign which says "Last Exit to Brooklyn." There is also another sign at the other end just before you go into the Brooklyn Battery Tunnel that says "Last Exit to Brooklyn Street."

AV: "The Queen is Dead" is a pathetic story of a hip queer looking for love, but all Georgette finds is sarcasm, hate, and violence. Typically, the reader would be sympathetic to the narrator, but do you think most readers are when Georgette is a weak-willed, speed-freak transvestite?

HS: It depends upon how well readers communicate with themselves. If they insist upon denying that there is a bit of Georgette in them, just as Vinnie and Harry do. They weren't willing to accept that Georgette exists within you and me. Perhaps my attitude is a little different, but I can see the terrible hunger for acceptance in motivating and perverting Georgette's behavior.

AV: What was the basis for writing "The Queen is Dead," and how were you able to write from the mental perspective of a drag queen?

HS: I don't see how it's so difficult. Look at how many male writers have written great female literary characters. That's something very personal with Georgie and myself. I didn't know it at the time, but I identified with Georgie from the inside. I realize now that Georgie felt like an outcast.

AV: So Georgette was based on an actual person?

HS: There was a real kid named Georgie. Georgie must have felt like an outcast who was totally alienated. He was hysterical in his defense—and his defense was his hysteria. And the more he fed that with stimulants, the more hysterical and wack and flighty he became. I've always felt like an outcast who was alienated all my life. Georgie and I had that point of identification, although this was totally unconscious. I had a tremendous sympathy for Georgie. I felt like my life was fucking ruined and a disaster. So I had this empathy, sympathy, and compassion going for Georgie.

I wrote the first part of that story, which is one of the first things I ever wrote, from the beginning up until Georgie gets stabbed and they take him home. Originally, the story was called "Love's Labours Lost." A year or two later I met someone from the old neighborhood, and they said Georgie had been found dead in the street, evidently an OD. He was only about twenty years old when he died. I was very, very moved by that information—so much so that I finished the story. I guess I felt Georgie needed more than to be just a death in the street. He needed a memorial. So I finished the story, which in turn led to my writing the entire book. Thus, in a very real way, Georgie is responsible for the book *Last Exit to Brooklyn.*

AV: Portions of *Last Exit to Brooklyn* were copyrighted as early as 1957—yet drugs are mentioned frequently in your writing. What was your exposure to drugs (long before it became fashionable in the '60s), and do you write under the influence of drugs and alcohol?

HS: I never write under the influence of anything. I tried it briefly. The last part of the "Queen is Dead," where Georgette is dying of an OD, I tried sipping beer a couple of times and I tried a little Demerol, but I just couldn't do it, and that is the only time I tried to write under the influence.

When I was in the hospital, I had a lot of drugs such as morphine, Demerol, codeine, and various sleeping pills. I also used heroin. I also drank every opportunity I could, so I had that point of reference, but I never wrote under the influence.

AV: The story "And Baby Makes Three" centers on an uncaring society of parents—to wit, Suzy, who two weeks after having a baby, doesn't give it a second thought while she parties until it's time to leave: "So she hunted around and found the kid and cut out." Why do most of your characters who have kids treat them so badly?

HS: I don't know the exact root of that, except I've felt victimized and alienated all my life. I've come to terms with that, and I realize feelings aren't necessarily facts. I was always very sensitive. There seemed to be a lot of that stuff when I was a kid—kids being battered and banged around. I don't know why I've always been so fascinated by that. I used to give things away to kids because I thought they didn't have anything. I have no idea why.

It has always pissed me off when parents have kids and then treat them so badly. I mean, for Christ's sake, the kid's response should be, "I didn't ask to be born. What the fuck are you on my back for?" I'm sure every kid has had the same experiences I've had. You can't reach a doorknob by yourself. You can't get a glass of water. You are totally dependent on the adult world. Yet, the attitude of the adult world is, "Get out of the way, kid, you bug me."

AV: The first three sentences of "Tralala" say a lot about the title character: "Tralala was 15 the first time she was laid. There was no real passion. Just diversion." Most readers would expect a girl's first sexual encounter to be special, but Tralala, in the world of Selby, is incapable of feeling. How did you create Tralala?

HS: I suspect we all feel the same way. One way or another, most of us are trying to defend against our feelings. We don't want to feel them, we don't want to interpret them, and we don't want to feel guilty. We want to try and project that guilt on someone else. I think we start at an early age to protect ourselves from our feelings.

I believe a story is given to me, and it is up to me to understand the essence of that story. It's a responsibility. It took me two and a half years to write "Tralala," which is only about twenty pages long. Most of that time was spent trying to understand the story. When I finally did understand what my responsibility was, then the story just flowed. This is what I was supposed to do with the story: to reflect the psychodynamics of an individual to the rhythm, beat, and tension of a prose line. I understand this to be my task. You previously mentioned that "Tralala" starts with a very tight, short kind of beat and then the line gradually opens up more and more until she reaches the apex of her life, where the line is almost a normal line, and then the line starts to fall apart. You expect it to disappear any second, but it keeps going on until the end. It never ends. It just stops.

AV: Tralala also is capable of great cruelty. For example, after Tony and Al have beaten up a seaman, Tralala, for no reason at all, "stomped on his face until both eyes were bleeding his nose was split and broken then kicked him a few times in the balls." Why?

HS: I'll tell you what Buddha would say. "Don't ask why. Why is not important."

AV: Tralala gets her comeuppance in the end after she has been gangbanged countless times: ". . . so they continued to fuck her as she lay unconscious on the seat in the lot. . . (the kids) tore her clothes to small scraps put out a few cigarettes on her nipples pissed on her jerked off on her jammed a broomstick up her snatch . . . Tralala lying naked covered with blood urine and semen and a small blot forming on the seat between her legs as blood seeped from her crotch." Please comment on what may be the most vividly disgusting passage in the annals of literature.

HS: I guess Christians would say Tralala collected the wages of sin. The Hindus would talk about karmic law. Maybe it's more important for us to see the results to understand some of the spiritual principles underlined.

Tralala does get her comeuppance in the end, even though she was raped. A rape doesn't occur if you're insisting on it, but she didn't know what she was insisting on—again, this miscommunication with one's self. She didn't start out to get herself gangbanged, but she made a conscious decision to inflict pain on Annie and Ruthie. She resented them and tried to ruin their good thing with Jack and Fred. Tralala was projecting that anger on them, but her anger finally caught up with her. That's the law of the universe.

AV: The story "Strike" shows Harry Black as another pathetic character incapable of goodness, who only feels good when other people are miserable. Harry isn't happy until he makes love to the transvestite Alberta. Why are love and happiness often equated in perverted scenes for most of your characters? Is there anything normal in Selby's world of fiction?

HS: First of all, to get the record straight, we can't pervert our concept of love. For instance, we have these great church leaders in this country and other countries, such as Iran, who say people should be murdered. That's not love to me, yet they claim to be teaching love in the name of God. Now the perversion of it is something we live with and deal with all the time. I believe *Last Exit to Brooklyn* is a microcosm of our world from the beginning of time and will continue till the end of time. I see that perversion of love everywhere. I think it's really dramatized in the book and magnified many times. I also see that perversion permeating in what the US has done politically in Nicaragua, El Salvador, Vietnam, and elsewhere.

AV: Harry Black, who is seemingly incapable of crying, starts to cry when he is brutally beaten after he tries to have sex with ten-year-old Joey. Harry's last words are, "God You Suck Cock." It seems incongruous that Harry is now capable of feeling but blames God for the condition of the world.

HS: Anger is an attempt to make somebody else feel guilty. Ultimately, Harry's last act is to accuse God of this problem. It is very simple and very logical.

AV: It seems you have a low opinion of religion.

HS: I don't believe in organized religion. I don't believe it is possible to seek spiritual principles and to make spiritual progress within an orthodox, organized religion. I'm certainly not in accord with what organized religion has done since the beginning of religion. Certainly, more people have been murdered in the name of God than under any other guise.

I no longer resent them or blame them. I understand that I must love them as much as I love my children; otherwise, I am doing what I accuse them of doing. That's one of the laws of the universe. I try not to use the word "God" because there is such a misconception around that word. I do believe in a power of infinity and unconditional love, simply because that power has revealed itself to me from within me. Now I attempt on a daily basis to commune with this power and to live according to the spiritual principles that it dictates. That is my life.

AV: *Last Exit to Brooklyn* has finally been made into a move twenty-five years after the novel was published. What are your thoughts about the movie?

HS: It was received very well in Europe where it opened on the twelfth of October 1989 in Munich. It is scheduled to open in the US around March or April of 1990. I think the film is really great because it does justice to my fictional work. This may be one of the few times it has been done. We did not change the dark, oppressive nature of the book and thus remained faithful to the basic spirit of the book. The film consisted of an American cast and crew and was shot on location in Brooklyn, but the producer and director are German. Tralala was played by Jennifer Jason Leigh, Harry Black is played by Stephen Lang, Vinnie is played by Peter Dobson, and Joe is played by Burt Young. It's a real ensemble where no one character or personality prevails. I played the driver of the car that kills Georgette.

AV: What was your basis for *The Room?* Didn't you spend some time in jail?

HS: I did spend a couple months in jail, but the basis for *The Room* is variations on a musical theme. You have a theme of the prisoner's reality, which includes such variations as his memory of it and his projections. You might call it an enigma variation. I wrote a story in jail called "The Sound," and that is where the concept for the novel started. It was published in my most recent book, which is a collection of stories entitled *Song of the Silent Snow.*

The reason I was in jail was for possession of narcotics. Heroin. The actual charge was driving while under the influence. The drugs were an extension of all the addictive medication I had when I was in the hospital. I haven't had any drugs now for more than twenty years.

AV: The unnamed prisoner in *The Room* is the antithesis of the prisoner in Camus's novel *The Stranger.* Whereas Camus's Meursault is ambivalent and fatalistic, your prisoner is filled with anger but has no way to release it. How were you able to sustain this anger and transfer it to the page?

HS: I know enough about anger to be able to remember the experience of it. You pay a price for it, I can tell you. I tried to write from the inside out. I wanted to put the reader through an emotional experience, which means I must experience every emotion I'm writing in order to get it down to the point that the reader will experience it. I've spent a lot of time inside my head, and I understand the rage and frustration of being confined, not just in jail, but also the three and a half years in the hospital due to tuberculosis.

AV: *The Room* is written in such a manner that it is sometimes difficult to distinguish reality from the prisoner's fantasy.

HS: Initially, the reader may have a problem, but I believe once you get in the rhythm of the writing it becomes pretty obvious. I think the rhythm reveals everything so the reader can easily distinguish reality from fantasy.

AV: What was the reason for indenting the paragraphs more so than normal?

HS: Some of them are dropped paragraphs, but all my typography is musical notation. If it's indented more than usual and not a dropped paragraph, it's because I want that extra dotted note there.

AV: What was the stimulus for the brutal rape of Mrs. Haagstromm? Also, the original rape scene is part of the prisoner's fantasy, but later it appears to be part of the court testimony.

HS: The rape of Mrs. Haagstromm is a product of the prisoner's fantasy, where he attempts to destroy the prosecution and the cops. The rape scene is a product of his imagination, to prove the authorities are really guilty and not him.

AV: How did you select Mrs. Haagstromm's name?

HS: I don't know. If you notice, the other names are like Hollywood soap opera names, whereas Haagstromm seemed to be a perfect name for a perfect person. It seemed totally appropriate.

AV: Mrs. Haagstromm, an innocent rape victim, seems to dramatically contrast with Tralala. However, as you stated in an interview in the *Review of Contemporary Fiction*: "We all cause everything that happens to us, whether we recognize it or not." Does this apply to Mrs. Haagstromm?

HS: Everything that happens to us happens as a result of a decision we make, but she didn't necessarily make that decision, because she was a figment of the prisoner's imagination.

AV: It seems the prisoner becomes just as vindictive and sadistic as the two cops when he fantasizes about getting even with them. Essentially, the prisoner and the cops have the same mentality, don't they?

HS: Yes. Experiments have proven, since the book was written, that this is true.

AV: Discuss the scene where the prisoner fantasizes about having sex in church with Mary and the interplay of sex with the "Our Father."

HS: It just flowed perfectly and naturally from his psyche. It seems to be the most, as I'm thinking about it now, simple way again of accusing God of his problems. This guy is saying essentially the same thing as Harry Black: "Fuck God!"

AV: *The Room* also recalls the writing of Jean Genet's *Our Lady of the Flowers,* where the main character is in jail and draws an outline of his penis on a letter to his girlfriend. Please comment on Genet and such scenes in *The Room:* "It was as if that's all there was to him. As if that was all there was to be seen. Just a limp, sticky, scraping penis floundering around between his legs. And he had to walk behind it, slowly moving one leg and then the other, and follow it where it led him. It wasn't a part of him. He was a part of it."

HS: That was where he couldn't think above his navel, but I don't think Genet influenced that in any way. That's an awareness that you come to when you spend a lot of time locked up. I spent four years of my life locked up, both in the hospital and jail, and you become aware of where your mind goes.

AV: *The Room* ends with the prisoner basically imprisoned in his own mind. The novel seems to have come full circle to the beginning, where the prisoner talked about astronomers and time: "And where did it get them? So they figured out where Mars would be in ten thousand years. Big deal! Krist, what a stupid waste of time. And where did it get them? Where? After they figure all that shit out they're either dead or still sitting on their ass looking at the goddamn sky. Right back where they started from. You always end up where you started from."

HS: Whether you look at it realistically or metaphysically, you end up from where you started. You have to get back to the beginning where you created the mistakes.

AV: Is the prisoner insane at the end?

HS: I don't think so. Not insane in the worldly sense, but we all are insane because we have all taught ourselves that what is true is false and what is false is true. I believe that's a form of insanity, perhaps not in this world, but metaphysically. What the prisoner is saying at the end of the book is that he is really a prisoner of guilt. Specifically, most of his guilt is sexual guilt because everything in his head is due to sexual repression. He is interpreting all of life sexually and using it viscerally and vindictively. There is no love in that book, but there is a lot of sex and violence. Sex is used as a power tool, but never as an expression of love. The guy is obviously feeling guilt. Whether or not he actually did something is immaterial, because he has found himself guilty. At the end of the novel they open his cell door and tell him to come out, but he says no since he has judged himself, like mankind, to be guilty even though we are born innocent.

AV: With the novel *The Demon* you have a character, Harry White, who is initially the opposite of the character Harry Black in "Strike." Yet he chooses evil. Why do your characters, most who fail from a lack of mental control over their physical impulses, consistently choose evil when the alternative is the more obvious path to a satisfying life?

HS: For one thing, they don't *choose* evil. I don't think anyone deliberately chooses evil. If you will notice, the epitaph of that book says, "A man obsessed is a man possessed by a demon." We are dealing with obsessions of the mind, and the one basic quality about an obsession is that an obsession can never be satisfied. If your obsession is whiskey, there isn't enough whiskey in the world to satisfy you. An obsession can never be satisfied. What Harry attempts to do is to get free of the basic one point, I think he uses plants, and for a while, he directs all his energies to becoming a successful businessman. All these things work, but only for a while. As far as he is capable, he loves his wife and his family, but since he must satisfy his obsessions, then he has to surrender to it.

AV: It is unfortunate that John Gardner died so young because it would be interesting to have the two of you discuss his book *On Moral Fiction*. Do you think both of you are attacking the same problem from different poles? Also, what do you think of Gardner's book?

HS: That is something I'd love to discuss. The object, goal, and concern when I write are the perfection of my art. I try to write the best story I can write—how my personality is always involved with my sense of morality. I think you can see where one of my basic obsessions in life is love, the perversion of love, and the lack of love. You can also interpret what Gardner says as meaning we should be moral propagandists. I certainly don't believe that. I don't want to try and prove a point. If there is any point to be proven, the people that I create will prove and make that point. I believe the primary concern and responsibility of the artist is to be free of the human ego. So I don't think I have any business being in the book.

AV: There is a statement from John O'Brien's interview in the *Review of Contemporary Fiction* that says he believes Selby "can write so much about sex without being erotic." I think however, many readers find your scenes with Tralala or the rape of Mrs. Haagstromm very erotic, if not perverse.

HS: I don't think of my writing as being erotic. I guess if you associate sex with violence and look at it as a power play or manipulation, then I guess maybe it is erotic for some people.

AV: Sex in your fiction is often an act of desperation. Do you think this is basically true of sex in general?

HS: Yes. I think sex, when performed as an act of desperation, is a very basic instinct and it is an instinct for survival. Ironically, sex as an act of desperation often leads to reproduction and more desperation.

There is a lovely scene in a story by Faulkner called "Pylon," which is set in the old barnstorming days of pilots flying back in the '30s. It's about a guy who is supposed to do a parachute jump with his girlfriend. She is climbing out on the wing, but she has never done it before, and she becomes frightened. She starts to crawl back into the cockpit where the guy is flying, and she grabs his fly and tries to rip his fly open. I think that is an instinctual thing with us when our lives are threatened. We reach for our crotch.

AV: Regarding sex as an act of desperation, the one possible exception I see in your work is the story "Landsend" where Abraham is almost fucked to death by Lucy. It concludes with Abraham and Lucy grinding away, both of them very content.

HS: Even though Abraham and Lucy have a good time fucking all night doesn't mean there isn't desperation. Look at Abraham's whole day and what is the focus of his entire being. It is all sex and thinking about this fine, brown-skinned girl. It seems to me there is a great deal of desperation there. For example, when he comes home he is exhausted, but after he hangs up his clothes and puts on his hairnet it's not because he's going to work the next day. And how about his wife? She's certainly bitching about the desperation because she's reaching for his crotch after fantasizing earlier about finding another cock. Desperation manifests itself in their lives through sex.

AV: *Requiem for a Dream* shows the addiction of four characters, with three of them hooked on heroin. While the novel can be approached as a microcosm of society, in hindsight, it seems virtually prophetic, with so many people addicted to crack cocaine and the overwhelming impact on society in terms of addiction, crime, and violence.

HS: We are all dealing with mental obsessions, and in this case, the "Great American Dream": if you can make it on the outside, then everything is going to be fine. It's not true. I don't care how limited or how infinite your dream may be. Success is an inside job because life is an inside job. (Perhaps I'm too involved with America, but it seems like we are more involved with façade than any other country because the influences of Madison Avenue and Hollywood are so persuasive and so powerful.) I think it becomes pretty obvious, whether it's Sara or Marion, regardless of what values we may have adopted. We still have this obsession to look for anything that will quiet the raging in our heads.

AV: "A Penny for Your Thoughts" (from *Song of the Silent Snow*) shows Harry fantasizing about the girl Marie. This story is representative of a lot of your fiction in that your characters prefer to fantasize about doing something rather than actually doing it.

HS: It seems to me there are a couple of things involved. First of all, in fantasy *I'm the boss*. Nothing else really impinges itself or can interfere with my fantasy. Whatever I want to do, I can do. Fantasy is safe. I don't have to take any chance of failure. However, if I try to bring this life to life in the outside world, then I'm taking the chance of failure. We are also dealing with a very basic spiritual, metaphysical, psychological type of love. Remember, it was Jesus who said: if you go to bed with a married woman, you are committing adultery, and *even if you think it*, you've committed it. Now that's a very interesting thing. I don't believe he was just making some kind of judgement, but was explaining the nature of life with that remark because we do create the world we live in with our thoughts. When I am continually fantasizing about doing something, my inner self says, "Hey, this is real!" The mind, however, doesn't know the difference between reality or fantasy. We also don't have to put a lot of energy into it. There is no need to go out and actually do it; yet the incentive, the energy, and the need to act are gone.

AV: Finally, in the interview with O'Brien you stated your books "are trying to examine the disease . . . And the disease . . . is the lack of love." You then say your first four books only dealt with the problem, but that notes for forthcoming books would "incorporate the problem as well as the answer." Are you currently working on a new novel, and what can the reader look forward to from Hubert Selby Jr.?

HS: Yes, I'm working on a new novel called *Seeds of Pain, Seeds of Love*. I'm three hundred pages into it. This is a creative effort to not only examine the problem, but to get from the problem to the answer. There is a little touch of that in some of the stories of *Song of Silent Snow,* especially the title story, which is one of the last stories I've written. I hope this novel will succeed in the attempt to expand on the answer to the disease.

Yet this book is much different. My first four books examined the disease from a pathological perspective. I haven't been in any of my books. There is a difference now when I'm talking about the answer in this book, because most of the facts are facts from my life. I guess it could be considered autobiographical. Of course, you give a writer a fact and God only knows where you are going to end up. The basic facts are from my life, and in addition to that, this book is written in the first person singular. Whether it will be totally that way or not, I don't know. It will be recognizable as being written by me because I seem to have a very distinctive style or voice. I guess I'm one of those people who is more distinctive than others because of the nature and energy of my feelings as it is translated to my writing through my imagination. Hopefully, the seeds of my imagination will be productive.

Dan Simmons. Courtesy of Cliff Grassmick.

The Fifth Heart: An Interview with Dan Simmons

As one of America's best and most prolific writers, Dan Simmons has written in so many different genres that he is hard to classify. Simmons's fiction has delved into horror, science fiction, mystery, and historical fiction, with him winning the World Fantasy Award (*Song of Kali*), the Bram Stoker Award (*Carrion Comfort*), International Horror Guild Award (*A Winter Haunting*), the Locus Award (*Hyperion, The Fall of Hyperion, The Rise of Endymion,* and *Ilium*), and the Hugo Award (*Hyperion*). His works are permeated with literary references including Homer, Shakespeare, Proust, Keats, Chaucer, Dante, and Nabokov; one would be remiss not to mention Hemingway, who is a central character in Simmons's superb historical fiction novel *The Crook Factory.* Simmons's latest historical novel is titled

Omega Canyon.

Simmons's twelfth novel, *The Fifth Heart,* opens in 1893 in Paris with Henry James ready to jump into the Seine to commit suicide—only to be saved by the fictional character Sherlock Holmes. The plot revolves around Holmes enticing James to help him solve the possible murder of Marion "Clover" Adams. Clover, the wife of Henry Adams, apparently committed suicide by drinking chemicals from her photography studio. James has a somewhat cantankerous relationship with Holmes, but always ends up following him into a myriad of suspenseful scenes. The reader also encounters a litany of famous historical characters that weave in and out of Simmons's narrative. Although it has been researched to the *nth* degree, *The Fifth Heart* never fails to keep the reader's interest until the final page.

The interview was conducted April 2015.

Allan Vorda: You are noteworthy for writing in different genres. *The Fifth Heart* falls into the historical fiction category that you successfully delved into with such books as *The Crook Factory, The Terror,* and *Drood.* What is it about historical fiction that makes you want to write in this particular genre?

Dan Simmons: I've been accused not only of writing in different genres, but in creating my own genre with these "historical-novels-with-a-twist" I've been doing for some years now. (The "with-a-twist" in *The Fifth Heart* includes pairing Sherlock Holmes with Henry James . . . even while Holmes has logically worked out that he is a fictional character.)

What I enjoy most about writing these history-based novels are the weeks, months, and years of preparation in reading history tomes, books from the chosen era (including old novels), many biographies, and as much original source material as I can find. An era or event that I'd been interested in before and already knew something about becomes far more interesting as the age opens up through an accumulation of details and period-era sights and insights, even while the historical characters I've chosen to include in my novel become far more complex after serious examination.

Robert Frost was famous for saying that writing poetry in blank verse "was like playing tennis without a net." Well, my net in these history-based novels is that the actual historical personages have to be where they actually were at any given historical time (Henry James slightly excepted here, since spring of 1893 is one of the few misty regions in his incredibly well-documented life), and when they vent opinions or say something interesting, the comments have to be documented as having actually been made by that person (albeit, possibly in a different situation).

As for my preference to write across (and out of) genres, I read fiction in a wide variety of genres (and non-genres, unless one classifies "Literature" as a genre) and can't imagine anything more boring than restricting my reading to one kind of book. (The majority of my reading for pleasure is actually in nonfiction—usually not related to anything I'm writing.)

AV: The use of metafiction is increasingly common among contemporary writers; an example of this would be your use of *The Canterbury Tales* as a literary device in *Hyperion*. Do you consider *The Fifth Heart* a work of metafiction, or do you dislike the term metafiction as it applies to your writing?

DS: I think "metafiction" is an academic's word rather than a writer's description of his or her own work. Few real masters of the ironic folds of fiction some call "metafiction" seem to like the term. John Fowles adamantly didn't care for it, even though he was a brilliant author of the-writer-being-visible-in-the-work-of-fiction type of novel. In *The French Lieutenant's Woman,* for instance, the plot has moved to the point where the Victorian-era protagonist Charles will either win the one woman he truly loves or he will lose her forever. As the denouement hangs in the balance, Charles falls asleep in his railway carriage room and a stranger in period dress and with a full beard enters the compartment, looks intently at the sleeping Charles for a long moment, flips a coin, and leaves.

We readers know instinctively that the "stranger" was the 1969-era author John Fowles, stepping physically into his own novel, and that the coin toss was to determine—or to make the reader think he, the author, was determining right then—which ending to the novel he'd write.

Rather than the self-conscious and incomplete label "metafiction," this is just fiction. And fun.

A reminder that in the first real novel ever written, Cervantes's *Don Quixote,* in Volume II the same characters who'd appeared in Volume I of the novel fifteen years earlier all were aware of being characters in Cervantes's book and changed their behavior at times (and in one case the character's name) to conform better to expectations created by Volume I of the tale.

So "metafiction" ain't a new or postmodern phenomenon or technique. It's been there literally since the beginning of the literary art form called "the novel." I personally think it's a recognition, by the author, of his or her readers' intelligence. After all, even in the most "realistic" novel, the writer and reader are working together in a constant conspiracy to make fictional characters seem "real." It's the love of the Sherlock Holmes and Dr. Watson characters, with all of their shortcomings and frequently shocking inconsistencies, that has made the Holmes stories and novellas classics, not the often weak or actively spavined plots of the "cases."

AV: You have Sherlock Homes masquerading as fictional Norwegian explorer Jan Sigerson as well as other characters—essentially, a fictional character using the mask of another fictional character. This recalls the many masks used by Henry Burlingame in John Barth's *The Sot-Weed Factor.* Are there any writers or works you used as a model for creating a Holmes who doesn't know if he is real or fictional?

DS: "Sigerson" was Sherlock Holmes's invention in the Canon—via Watson and/or Arthur Conan Doyle, if you will—when, after Holmes returns to London and Watson after his three-year absence, he rather improbably tells Watson that if he's read of the amazing adventures of an explorer named "Sigerson," then he's heard part of what the detective has been up to.

Holmes's rationale for brutally fooling Watson, his closest friend, into thinking he, Holmes, had died at Reichenbach Falls—i.e., he was hiding out from second-banana villain Sebastian Moran and his minions for three full years—was weak to the point of pure absurdity. Holmes's entire explanation to Watson of where he'd been and what he'd been doing—as detailed in "The Adventure of the Empty House" (which was a weak and unconvincing story in its own right)—was an insult to Watson's (and the reader's) intelligence.

So, no, I didn't need a fictional model—Barthian or otherwise—for shaping Holmes as a fictional character who has come to the conclusion that he is a fictional character. And Sherlock would not have been the brilliant, busily ratiocinating detective we all admire if he had not worked out this rather obvious fact sooner or later.

AV: When characters are speaking in a novel it often ends up with a simple "he said." I see you employ a variety of different words such "groused James," "chuckled the detective," "snapped James," "persisted Holmes," "Holmes was muttering," "murmured James." Is there any secret in trying to discover a variety of new verbs to express statements made by your characters?

DS: In more than six hundred pages of *The Fifth Heart*, these are about the only speech signifiers other than "he (or she) said." Even most of the questions are tagged "he said."

We're just lucky that I didn't devolve into using Barnyardisms so common to amateurs' manuscripts: "he cackled," "she crowed," "he snorted," "she barked," and my favorite, from my dear friend Harlan Ellison: "Good morning," he pole vaulted.

AV: During your book reading in Houston this March you stated you read voraciously in doing research for your writing. For *The Fifth Heart*, would such books include *The Five of Hearts* by Patricia O'Toole, *Clover Adams* by Natalie Dykstra, *The Education of Henry*

Adams by Henry Adams, *Henry Adams and the Making of America* by Garry Wills, *The Education of Mrs. Henry Adams* by Eugenia Kaledin, *The Rise of Theodore Roosevelt* by Edmund Morris, *The Devil in the White City* by Erik Larson, *Team of Rivals* by Doris Kearns Goodwin, and the works of Henry James and Sir Arthur Conan Doyle? Any other books that were instrumental in your research?

DS: When my publisher finally asked me to send along my "Acknowledgments" page, it was actually a reference bibliography, single-spaced, that ran to more than fourteen manuscript pages and which included many of the works you cite above (though not *The Education of Mrs. Henry Adams* because I hadn't heard about it until I'd finished *The Fifth Heart*). But also less well-known books and collections such as the collected letters—a lifetime's worth—between Henry James and John (and sometimes Clover) Adams.

AV: I interviewed Greg Bear in 1989 and he said he had over twelve thousand books in his personal library. Perhaps I will interview a writer someday and he will say his library consists solely of a Kindle, but can you describe what your library is like?

DS: Eclectic. Boasting about the size of one's library is . . . well . . . rather like boasting about the size of anything one has. Rather uncool. Since I had so many years where I read important books—fiction and nonfiction—from the local library since I couldn't afford to buy hardcovers, many of the most important and formative books in my past aren't in the library that fills my rather large office here and spills over into the formal library room next door (and up to our mountain home as well). Many I do have. For instance, I have most of a wall of books about Abraham Lincoln—but I've never used any of that five decades of "research" in anything I've written. Maybe I never will.

AV: You provide insights from both Henry James and Sherlock Holmes, but it seems you get into the mind of Henry James more so than Sherlock Holmes. Would you agree with this statement and, if so, why?

DS: Henry James's thoughts (and point of view) were more expressive than Holmes's, well researched by the many biographies *of* the man and essays *by* the man, and his powers of trained observation of other people were as great—or greater—than the Great Detective's. As James himself put it: "A writer is a person on whom nothing is lost." That certainly describes Henry James. Who wouldn't choose such a man and mind as one's primary p-o-v character?

AV: Throughout the book James seems like he cannot stand Holmes, and often responds sarcastically to him—yet he invariably does what Holmes suggests. Holmes, for his part, seems almost oblivious to James's less-than-polite responses. Why did you build their relationship in this way, and why does Holmes put up with James?

DS: In *The Fifth Heart,* Holmes enjoys James and James's often barbed comments. Dr. John Watson was a boon companion to the detective, but he was a sycophant from time to time. A man of Sherlock's sharpness would have enjoyed Henry James's often sharp-edged and multileveled banter.

AV: Sherlock Holmes has a morphine addiction in the Conan Doyle stories, but you have Holmes using Bayer's new "heroic" drug, heroin. Can you comment on Holmes's addiction? It certainly makes for some interesting scenes, such as when he is shooting up right before fighting the gang that includes Culpepper and Murtrick.

DS: One British reviewer, in a rather thoughtful review about the real goals behind *The Fifth Heart,* did describe Holmes's desperate (and successful) fight with that gang just after he—Holmes—had shot up with the new "heroic" drug (so-called because as far as its inventor, Mr. Bayer, could see, it had no negative side-effects whatsoever . . . especially not addiction)—anyway, the reviewer described Holmes in that scene as "the most physically active junkie in history." I enjoyed that and laughed aloud.

AV: Henry James is a very secret person, but Holmes "already knew the secret-of-secrets that James would die to protect." There are also several scenes depicting James being uncomfortable yet fascinated when encountering naked or scantily clad men. Is there any evidence in real life that Henry James was homosexual?

DS: Biographers—back to Leon Edel, who in his massive and detailed five-volume biography of James and in his dozens of other edited tomes, such as James's lifetime of correspondence—knew that Henry James's emotional and erotic energies were focused on other men, but Edel, writing in the 1950s when he began his lifetime's work of being James's "definitive" biographer, didn't know what to do with the information then. So he hinted about it in various too-clever-by-half and literary ways. Now James is taught in most universities as a "gay writer," which would have horrified James for a variety of reasons, most of them aesthetic and motivation-directed.

But I'm convinced that the covey of recent biographies and even novels—such as Colm Tobín's *The Master*—which state flatly that James experienced *homosexual contact* with other men—are simply misguided. It doesn't jibe with the facts of James's circumscribed and incredibly controlled life and behavior. (Especially the sloppy biographical assertion that quickly became "fact" for Tobín and too many eager others that James experienced physical lovemaking with Oliver Wendell Holmes Jr., just after that other Holmes had returned, wounded and a hero, from the Civil War. It just doesn't pass the Henry James-reality test.)

What we do know is that as James got older, he seemed more "explicit" in expressing his love and affection to various younger men, although the "explicitness" was primarily in phrases of being hugged and even held that even the most masculine and heterosexual male writers of the Victorian era might (and did) use in letters to their close male friends.

Part of my enjoyment in writing *The Fifth Heart* was in pairing two of the most secretive and personally unrevealing men in Europe—with both of them being expert at sniffing out other people's deepest secrets. Perhaps that's one reason James sounded so frequently sharp or sarcastic toward the detective. Sherlock Holmes made him uneasy, even while Holmes chose James as the person he'd unburden himself to about some of the more shocking secrets of his own youth and upbringing.

AV: The title of the novel refers to the five people that are part of a club that has highbrow conversations; one of them is the mountaineer-author Clarence King, who you mention has his own "secrets within secrets" as Holmes follows him to Harlem. King has a limited role in the novel, but was his secret actually true?

DS: Yes.

AV: King recounts a story about trying to get to Long's Peak, which is one of the "fourteeners" along the Front Range where you live. I have climbed a dozen of these mountains, but I'm wondering if you have ever climbed any of the fourteen-thousand-foot-plus mountains in Colorado?

DS: Yes, I've "climbed"—as in walked and scrambled up—some of Colorado's "fourteeners." I convinced my wife Karen to move with me from western New York to Colorado in 1974 because it was too long a commute for me from Buffalo, NY, to the Adirondacks. And I wanted to *see* mountains out the windows of my home. We've never been disappointed with those views here, and we've never taken them for granted.

AV: The novel is essentially about Holmes (with Henry James filling in for his Dr. Watson) trying to determine if the death of Clover Adams (wife of Henry Adams) was a suicide or murder. You have your own version, but do you think Clover actually committed suicide?

DS: All evidence suggested that Clover committed suicide while in a deep depression after her father's death. Her brother also ended his own life, as did some of her immediate ancestors. Depression, for the Hoopers—Clover's (real name "Marion") maiden name—was a family curse.

AV: There are a number of scathing comments in the book, particularly from Henry James's point of view, in regard to America's culture. For example, "Holmes knew that his man belonged to several rather elite (for Americans) clubs." Do you think these comments are deserved for the country in the late nineteenth century?

DS: These "disparaging" comments reflect Henry James's written opinions—in essays and novels—at this time and earlier in his life. When he was young and just "liberated" to live in England and explore Europe to his heart's content, he argued that America could never really be "literary" or "a serious country" because it had too little history: no castles, no Roman ruins, no shards of Etruscan vases underfoot, no royal families whose histories went back centuries, and so forth. Later in his life, about a decade after the 1893 that is the target year for *The Fifth Heart*, James returned to America and scorned it for its tall buildings, commercial heart (or lack of), its loud hustle and bustle, and for its many immigrants in New York—especially the Jews—who had infested the nation and cities of his youth "like so many vermin." *Not* an especially enlightened view by our hero. (Henry Adams, the great historian and a hero to many of us would-be wannabe intellectuals, also evinced a verbalized and mean-spirited anti-Semitism, which I give opportunity for the reader to hear and see in *The Fifth Heart*.)

AV: In the chapter "The Constant Red Glow in the Darkness" you mention a secret chamber where Henry Adams could spy on people at Clover's gravesite with the wonderful Saint-Gaudens's sculpture. Did Adams actually have such a place or is this your own invention?

DS: I encourage readers to visit the actual Saint-Gaudens memorial sculpture to Clover in Rock Creek Cemetery, Washington, DC, and to see if they can find the secret entrance to Henry Adams's secret viewing-and-listening-place there. Adams often told his friends stories of people's shocked reaction to the powerful, powerful sculpture (which offers mourners no hint or hope of resurrection or other standard Victorian condolences). Would strangers have said that in front of Adams if he were sitting on a bench in the hedge-enclosed space in front of the sculpture at Clover's gravesite? Good luck to readers in checking this out for themselves.

AV: You write about Henry James reflecting on his life as a writer: "How different all that had been from his decades of disciplined isolation while writing his scores of stories and overflowing shelf of novels. But all that labor to what purpose?" Did you see some of yourself in Henry James when you wrote this?

DS: No, I simply wanted to let readers see James's very real disappointment—extra sharp in the 1890s—that he had not yet become *Maitre,* "the Master" in literature, a goal he had been working toward for so many years.

AV: Henry James is on the "El" in Chicago and sees everyone reading *Maggie: A Girl of the Streets.* Did Stephen Crane actually pay people to read his novel in public in order to influence others to buy his novel, and did he use the pseudonym of Johnston Smith?

DS: Yes, Crane actually paid men to ride the "El" while "reading" copies of his new book. (His *Maggie: A Girl of the Streets* came out in 1893, the year in which *The Fifth Heart* is set.) The El-gimmick was a form of the kind of irritating self-promotion that is the hallmark of so many infinitely lesser would-be writers online today. The only difference is that Stephen Crane was a genius. But the book didn't sell, Crane got the remaindered copies back, and near the end of his life, even in his final illness, he *faux*-bragged that "I have an incredible library of some four thousand volumes . . . only three thousand ninety-six of which are unsold copies of my own book."

Crane died at age twenty-nine and spent much of his final illness in a ramshackle, chaotic-with-visitors, run-down coast house in England not far from Henry James's tidy little country home in Rye. Even James noticed, when he visited once or twice, that the dying Crane was being lovingly tended to by a Florida whore of Crane's wide acquaintance. Crane wrote *The Red Badge of Courage* in 1894 when he was just turning twenty-three, almost thirty years after the Civil

War had ended and before he'd seen any hint of actual combat. (He amended that by accompanying Teddy Roosevelt's Rough Riders and other Americans soldiers to Cuba in the Spanish-American War as one of the earliest "war correspondents," and always choosing to be in the thick of the shooting and dying. He was a very good war correspondent, setting the bar quite high for future generations of combat reporters like Ernie Pyle.) If Crane could write that well—that penetratingly—at such an early age, what further masterpieces could he have produced if he'd been allowed by the Fates to accumulate another twenty or thirty years of human experience and literary maturation?

AV: You are currently writing your thirtieth book, titled *Omega Canyon*. Can you divulge what this novel is about?

DS: *Omega Canyon* is a WWII-era thriller, part of which is set on the Los Alamos mesa in 1944-45 (other parts are set all over Europe) . . . although complex in structure, it should be significantly shorter than most of my recent novels . . . and I'm enjoying the hell out of writing it.

Neal Stephenson. Courtesy of Brady Hall.

The Spatial Lattice of Consciousness: An Interview with Neal Stephenson

Born in Maryland, Neal Stephenson is the son of a professor of electrical engineering and the grandson of a physics professor. The family moved to Illinois and later to Ames, Iowa, where Neal graduated from high school. He received a BA in 1981 from Boston University, with a major in geography and a minor in physics. Stephenson first made his splash in the literary scene with the publication of the cyberpunk SF novel *Snow Crash* in 1992. Since then he has published a number of books, usually of substantial length, in the areas of speculative and historical fiction; these include *The Diamond Age*, *Cryptonomicon*, *The Baroque Cycle* (*Quicksilver*, *The Confusion*, and *The System of the World), Anathem, Reamde, Seveneves,* and *Fall,* with *Termination Shock* being published the latter part of 2021. Stephenson has won numerous awards including the Hugo, Locus SF Award (five times), the Clarke Award, and the Prometheus Award (twice). He lives in Seattle, Washington.

This interview was conducted on June 18, 2019, in the lobby of a downtown Houston hotel. We sat across a table from one another next to the bar that was closed. Stephenson is one of the leading science fiction writers whose novels tend to be considerably lengthy, invariably approaching one thousand pages. His novels often explore different time periods, and occasionally characters will reappear in other novels; one was even apparently killed off only to reappear later on. Stephenson's novels are thought-provoking to say the least, covering a wide range of topics, backed up with a lot of science. It should also be noted that some of his passages are flat-out hilarious. His appearance might be imposing to some due to his shaven head, goatee, and serious demeanor. Yet appearances can be deceiving, as during the interview he was engaging and congenial as well as being a brilliant interviewee. This was reconfirmed later that evening as he gave a reading from *Fall* and then took questions before a full house at the Christ Church Cathedral.

Allan Vorda: In *Fall,* Dodge Forthrast becomes brain-dead after surgery, whereupon he is placed in a cryonic state until future technology can restore his consciousness. What was the genesis for writing such a novel?

Neal Stephenson: The idea of uploading the brain is something people in the tech world have been talking about for a while, and of course, people have always thought about what happens after we die. Is there an afterlife? Is there something more? Since it's a topic of universal interest, it seemed like a good premise for a novel. I have also been interested in Milton's *Paradise Lost* lately, and I've been looking for a way to do something with it. I came at it from various angles over time, and finally decided *Fall* was a good way to approach it.

AV: This also raises the mind-body problem. As you write, "The mind couldn't be separated from the body. The whole nervous system, all the way down to the toes, had to be studied and understood as a whole—and you couldn't even stop there, since the functions of that system were modulated by chemicals produced in places like the gut and transmitted through the blood. The bacteria living in your tummy—which weren't even *part* of you, being completely distinct biological organisms—were effectively part of your brain." Do you agree the mind is dependent on the body? If so, would you qualify whether your *consciousness* is *you*?

NS: There is a kind of naïve idea about this distinction between the mind and the body that hasn't been taken seriously by people who think about it a lot. The idea is that you could just take the brain out of the skull, then keep it alive somehow, yet still have the same person. Everything you've just read in that passage is not based on my own ideas, but ideas that have been explored by philosophers, neurologists, psychologists, and so on.

From my point of view as a storyteller, I'm looking for ways to relate an interesting yarn. In the beginning of the novel, when the characters are beginning to scan the brains and put them up as digital simulations on the internet, they are coming at it from that naïve point of view, in which the brain is the only thing that matters. That has some unintended consequences as the situation develops, which eventually get rectified as people come up with a more sophisticated and nuanced view of what it means to be human. The questions you're raising are explicitly discussed by characters in the book, which they're working out among themselves as the situation develops.

AV: From a religious standpoint, various philosophers argue the soul can be separated from the body. The metaphysical existence of a soul is debatable, but throughout *Fall* you refer to the consciousnesses in cyberspace as "souls." Why did you choose that term?

NS: Because it's short—it only has four letters and it's a term that people would use. I'm trying to depict realistic characters, and I'm trying to use terminology they would adopt, even if it is not the terminology I would use. It's my job to think about what fictional characters would do and say, and not just what I would do and say.

The word "soul" has all kinds of religious significance, but it's also used in other kinds of settings. When people talk about an airplane that has crashed or a ship that has gone down, for example, they'll frequently say, "It was lost with 152 souls on board."

I wouldn't read too much into my use of the term. When the characters use it, what they're getting at is a rebooted consciousness: this digital simulation which has the complexity of the brain on which it was based. It has some of the personality and memories, and it acts and behaves as if it had the full complexity of a living human. When we talk about a human being, it implies a physical body. When we talk about a soul, it seems to be a more precise term for what we're denoting.

AV: At one point in *Fall,* El Shepherd wants to destroy the less developed souls who are wasting his money to keep the Process going. El states these "new fruit fly processes have to be terminated." Corvallis Kawasaki counters by saying these souls "are based on human connectomes." Can you comment on this moral question of what constitutes life, and who has the right to decide who lives or dies? Not insignificantly, this is being debated right now in our country regarding abortion.

NS: The fruit fly reference is to new animals that are being booted up by Spring; she feels the Bitworld isn't complete until it has birds and bees and other lesser creatures in addition to humans. Spring is trying to create those animals to more fully realize the world in which they're living. I think both El and Corvallis agree that souls, based on a human connectome, should not be terminated. What they're arguing about is this new phenomenon of less complicated creatures that have emerged due to the creative efforts of Spring within the story.

AV: "The mass of people are so stupid, so gullible, because they *want* to be misled. There's no way to make them not want it." A lot of fake news is disseminated by the internet, or what you refer to in *Fall* as the Miasma. Do you see any solution to preventing all of the disinformation we see? How do we preserve free speech?

NS: I'm not too worried about free speech. The constitutional guarantee of free speech refers to governmental activities, and basically says the government doesn't have the power to restrict people's exercise of free speech. It doesn't say anything about private companies and their activities. Platforms like Facebook, YouTube, and Twitter have been gamed by hostile state actors who are actively using them as part of a disinformation campaign, and to engage in a kind of non-shooting war with the United States. That is all completely obvious and out in the open at this point, and by failing to prevent this from happening, social media platforms are failing in their responsibility as corporate citizens. It appears they're trying to clean up their act and get better at this, but I don't think they're doing it fast enough. I question whether or not they have the ability to ever completely succeed at it, given their whole corporate valuation and revenue model is based on running these systems algorithmically, without any humans in the room.

I can't remember who is quoted in that line and I'm not sure it matters, but to answer the question on disinformation: I don't see a solution. I think it's a terrible problem, and we're in a terrible situation because of it. It will be very challenging for the responsible companies to change their ways. The only way I can see forward is for people to get more skeptical about what they see, which is difficult, because a lot of people are happy to swallow inaccurate information that aligns with what they feel. Along with skepticism, part of the solution might be that these platforms will fade away over time and be replaced by new ones. Maybe in ten years, we will be using different platforms that have been invented in the wake of the situation of today.

AV: This is a peripheral question, but nowadays a writer can Google a topic and get information immediately, whereas before the internet writers had to scour journals and microfiche in the library to find what they needed. It was almost like being a detective—time-consuming, yet often fun and rewarding. Have we lost something if writers no longer have to spend time in the library, or does it not really matter?

NS: I think it does matter, because serendipity is a valuable side effect of using old-school libraries. When you're walking down a shelf of books, looking for one particular volume you think is relevant, you may see other books surrounding it that are useful in ways you didn't expect. You can get the same results when flipping through an old paper card catalog or microfiche. One of the things digital information storage systems have not done well is reproducing that kind of serendipitous discovery. Balanced against that is the fact it's much easier to find things on the internet; you don't have to physically go to the library to do research, so everything just goes much faster.

I try to develop skills in how I use the internet to help make up for that a little bit. Rather than doing one search on one set of search terms, I'll try to create some serendipity on my own by trying a bunch of related search terms, and then searching outward from the first hit to make sure I'm not missing anything.

AV: The Forthrast homestead is located in northwest Iowa, a borderless, undefined territory called Ameristan that is populated by uneducated, gun-hoarding cults; one group in Iowa is building a two-hundred-foot-tall flaming cross, and another in Nebraska actually crucifies people. Yet you also suggest that Jake Forthrast, a survivalist from Idaho, can actually change into a reasonable human being, and your depiction of city-dwellers isn't without criticism. What is your opinion on how people in rural areas differ in thinking from people in cities?

NS: The situation that exists, not only in rural areas but all over the country, is that there is a divide. We tend to refer to it as red state versus blue state, but it's not really correct to think of it in terms of states—it's more finely detailed than that; the boundary is a very complicated fractal that can exist even between neighborhoods.

In the case of the novel, this is the same situation. Some areas are strictly blue-state; for example, in the town of northwest Iowa, there are dentists and doctors and all the people have learned to live in the modern world productively; they have money and education and they know how to do things. On the other side, past this invisible boundary, there are the have-nots who are suffering because they've fallen under the grip of algorithmically generated memes that are coming into their eyes and ears all the time, making it impossible to make sense of what is objectively real. This is an exaggeration of the situation which exists today. The purpose of the book is to provide a kind of glimpse into the future, a cautionary tale to make people consider the consequences if we keep going down this road. I try to depict some characters, such as Jake, who are trying to make connections, to address these difficult situations and find ways to work with it.

AV: Your book *Cryptonomicon* might be the only work of fiction to mention the Reimann zeta function, and *Fall* also invokes some mathematical statements such as "the plot of the integral." The majority of your readers probably don't know the meaning of mathematical or technical terms. In what way does this add to your writing?

NS: Based on my interactions with readers at my readings, I think this may be a pessimistic view. I'll allow a fair number of people won't necessarily understand these terms with absolute precision, but that's not what I'm thinking about when I'm writing this stuff. I'm in the business of writing stories about fictional characters, some of whom are well-versed in technology, mathematics, engineering, computers, etc. My strategy is to show them doing and saying things people like this actually do and say. Some readers may not totally understand some of the jargon, but that's how real life is. I'm hoping the result is to make the book seem more like real life, and in that way help the reader suspend their disbelief, and find the whole thing realistic and plausible.

AV: In *Fall,* Time Slip Ratio refers to the differences between

Meatspace (real world) and Bitworld (cyberspace) time. Enoch Root is a recurring character in your novels who is essentially immortal and never seems to age. If we consider the hypothesis that all reality is a computer simulation, then can Meatspace in the novel also be a simulation, and is Enoch Root from a reality outside this simulation? This could provide an explanation of Enoch Root's ostensible immortality due to Time Slip Ratio.

NS: What you just described is something I'm hinting at in the book, so I would say that you correctly pieced it together in a way that makes sense. I'm reluctant to say, "Yes, that's it," because the heart of this is not to just baldly describe the state of things. It is a natural question that arises: If you posit we can simulate reality with our computers, then the next question you have to ask is, could our world be a simulation on someone else's computer? Then it turtles all the way down.

AV: If given the option to upload your consciousness, would you do it?

NS: I'm quite skeptical of this kind of thing myself. I would have to know a lot more about the process and how it's supposed to work before making such a decision. This book isn't so much me advocating that process as just saying, "Let's suppose this would work to some degree and use that as a basis for a yarn." I want to tell a story and see where the story takes us.

AV: Do you play video games? If so, which ones, and does this add or detract from your writing?

NS: I used to play them more in the past. I like solo games, and the trend in the last decade has been towards multiplayer games. This is driven by economic considerations: game publishers get more bang for their buck if they can get customers to entertain each other. I would rather be on my own. My time spent playing video games has gone down, but I've played a little bit of *Red Dead Redemption 2*, and a little bit of *Anthem* recently. I'm probably more apt to play board games than video games at this point.

AV: *Fall* incorporates straight fiction, science fiction, and fantasy. Was it difficult to plot out three distinct genres?

NS: I don't see genre that much while I'm writing. Those are distinctions that are drawn by people outside who want to classify books. There is nothing wrong with those distinctions—by assigning genre labels to different books, we make it easier for readers to find books they're going to like, to find each other, and to form communities. So I have nothing against it, but those distinctions are all invisible when I'm actually doing the work. I don't have any mental sense of shifting gears; it's all an organic whole to me, and so there are no hurdles or difficulties associated with moving from one to the other.

AV: As a writer, you received a lot of recognition for writing science fiction, but do you feel that you've been stereotyped as an SF writer? Do you think this prevents critics from considering you for awards such as the National Book Award or the Pulitzer Prize?

NS: Probably to some degree, although I'm not particularly worried about it. There is an odd mentality around genres versus so-called literary fiction that I've been observing for some time, although more as a kind of anthropologist than a participant. I wrote about this a long time ago in a *Slashdot* interview, explaining what I call *Beowulf* versus Dante writers: *Beowulf* and *The Divine Comedy* are both great works of literature, but *The Divine Comedy* was written by a person who had a patron, whereas *Beowulf* probably just bubbled up from some guy telling stories in a bar. The same situation occurs today; you have some people working in a more literary area, where typically they're not supporting themselves through writing—they're employed by a university or something that effectively acts as their patron while they work on their art. Then you have writers who are making their living at it, and they sell a whole lot more books. Occasionally, you have someone who can do both, which is a marvelous thing.

I'm completely uninterested in drawing value judgments between those two styles. Consequently, I'm not a big fan of people who live in one camp and look down their nose at people in the other. It's quite possible I'm in a weird place and I'm not going to be winning a lot of awards, but I really don't care. I've been amazingly fortunate in my career. There are a lot of writers who make more money than I do, and a lot of writers who make less. My position has given me the ability to write full time and have a good standard of living, so I consider myself lucky. Whether I win awards or literary acclaim means nothing to me.

Robert Stone. Courtesy of Nancy Crampton.

The Apostle of the Strung-Out: An Interview with Robert Stone

Robert Stone was born in Brooklyn in 1937 to a father he never knew and a mother who was institutionalized for schizophrenia. He received a traditional Catholic high school education, which despite his spirit of rebellion, gave him a grounding in the fundamentals of English and a love of literature. Stone enlisted in the navy for three years, after which he returned to New York and attended NYU and worked as a copy boy for the *New York Daily News.*

His first novel, *Hall of Mirrors,* is set in New Orleans and won the Faulkner Award. It was also made into the movie *WUSA,* starring Paul Newman. Stone received a Stegner Fellowship from Stanford University, which is where he met Ken Kesey and was subsequently exposed to various drugs, including LSD. Later on, dealing with writer's block while living in England, he decided to go to Vietnam as a journalist to cover the war and get inspiration for his second novel. This resulted in the highly praised novel *Dog Soldiers*. The novel won the National Book Award for its portrayal of the drug culture and the moral effects Vietnam had on those who returned to the United States. The author's screenplay of *Dog Soldiers* was made into the movie *Who'll Stop the Rain?* starring Nick Nolte and Tuesday Weld. *A Flag for Sunrise,* a socio-political novel, depicts America's involvement in Central America, while *Children of Light,* primarily set in Mexico, metaphorically showcases the malaise of the Hollywood film industry. His last four novels were *Outerbridge Reach, Damascus Gate, Bay of Souls,* and *Death of the Black-Haired Girl.* He also published a memoir titled *Prime Green: Remembering the Sixties.*

Robert Stone's novels invariably explore the darker side of mankind. As the critic A. Alvarez has stated, "In just four novels in almost twenty years Robert Stone has established a world and style and tone of voice of great originality and authority. It is a world without grace or comfort, bleak, dangerous, and continually threatening."

Robert Stone died at age seventy-seven in Key West, Florida, in 2015.

The following interview took place on September 18, 1990, at the Wyndham Warwick Hotel in Houston, Texas, and was conducted shortly before Stone was to read at the Museum of Fine Arts. I recall going to his hotel room and being received by a distinguished-looking man in his fifty-fifth year. On the basis of my reading and research, I thought Stone to be more street-smart and tough-edged, due to his upbringing, but in the course of the interview he was polite and quite reserved. I was continually amazed at how gracefully and deliberately he spoke. It was obvious that words mattered, both written and spoken—and those words should be precise in their usage.

I also sensed he was a writer with something to prove. Other writers might have been satisfied to win the National Book Award or have their novels made into movies, but I don't believe he was terribly pleased by the criticism and lack of attention that met the publication of his fourth novel, *Children of Light,* possibly based on critics who expected another social commentary as he had written with *Dog*

Soldiers and *A Flag for Sunrise.* When I pressed him to discuss his work-in-progress, *Outerbridge Reach,* he resisted. Coincidentally, it was around this time that his voice started to weaken and crack as we approached the end of the interview. He decided it was best to stop so that he would not lose his voice before his speaking engagement that evening.

During the thirty-plus years since this interview was conducted, and having recently read Madison Smartt Bell's definitive biography of Stone titled *Child of Light,* I now feel extremely lucky to have been in his presence. Definitely one of America's great writers of the twentieth century.

Allan Vorda: When did you decide to become a writer?

Robert Stone: I wanted to be a writer from an early age. I had dropped out of high school and joined the navy when I was seventeen, and I think by the time I was eighteen or nineteen I knew I wanted to be a writer. I had always liked to write on some level, but I think what made me really decide to become a professional writer was the experience I had in the navy during the late 1950s.

AV: Did your experience working as a journalist for the *New York Daily News* help you prepare to write fiction?

RS: I don't think there is any direct connection, but rather a lot of indirect connections. I started as a copy boy and also wrote sports captions, but I didn't do anything of any particular complication. I certainly didn't learn anything about writing while working at the *Daily News,* but I did have experiences in New York that were useful to me in the long run. I would like to add that I am not one of those people who think news writing is good training for a writer. I think the opposite.

AV: You stated in *Modern Fiction Studies* that you prefer fiction to journalism. Would you comment on this?

RS: I think I may have said that you don't have to be in a position to let the facts get in the way of the truth. In fiction you order the illusion of continuity to suit a certain scheme when you have to deal with actual occurrences which are much more random and pointless. You then find yourself in the position of imposing a meaning. You might express it as discovering a meaning, but it is in fact imposing a meaning, and in this you're limited. You have this responsibility to be accurate, which in a way costs you in terms of essential truths. It's hard to be both perceptive and absolutely accurate. Fiction is something where you create the illusion of life, the illusion of continuity, and the illusion of cause and effect. That seems to be a freer way of working, and I find it more rewarding.

AV: Receiving the Stegner Fellowship in 1982 must have been a critical point in your life, because you moved to California and became involved with Ken Kesey and the Merry Pranksters. What was it like with Kesey, Cassady, Babbs, Mountain Girl, Owsley, and the rest of the Pranksters?

RS: I knew all those people, and I even rode on the bus with them—although not all the way across the country. I don't think anybody rode all the way across the country if they could help it. I've even used Cassady as a model for characters. It seems Cassady's fate in America is to be used as a model in so many different people's work. I used him after a fashion in a short story I wrote called "Porque No Tiene, Porque Le Falta," which is about a bunch of crazy American druggies in Mexico. It was in *The Best American Short Stories* of 1970, which was originally published in *New American Review #6.* The title is from the lyrics of a song called "La Cucaracha" that goes like this: "La Cucaracha, La Cucaracha/Ya no puede caminar/Porque no tiene, porque le falta/ Marijuana par fumar."

AV: Is Holliwell from *A Flag for Sunrise* based on Cassady or Kesey?

RS: No, Holliwell was certainly not anything like Cassady. Cassady was a guy of tremendous streetwiseness, but absolutely no education or cultivation except for what he picked up from Ginsberg or Kerouac or what he read in paperback books. He wasn't dumb, but he certainly wasn't intellectually sophisticated. Holliwell was a professor.

AV: What was your opinion of Cassady? You probably saw him a few years before he died in Mexico, didn't you?

RS: I saw him at his worst. I first met him in 1962 or 1963. He died in 1968, just before his forty-fourth birthday. He was a walking cautionary tale about speed. If you wanted to think of one hundred reasons not to take speed, then Cassady could provide you with at least eighty of them.

AV: You have also stated in *Modern Fiction Studies* that Dieter (from *Dog Soldiers*) is not based on Kesey, yet Dieter tells Marge that what he had experienced was something profound, "but rather difficult to verbalize." This seems to echo Tom Wolfe's *The Electric Kool-Aid Acid Test* where it says: "They made a point of not putting it into words. That in itself was one of the unspoken rules." Perhaps you can comment on this since Kesey, Wolfe, and you certainly make use of words.

RS: The thing is, that cult of ineffability that Wolfe is talking about is true of the Pranksters and of Cassady, but it is also true of just about every single other romantic avant-garde movement for the last one hundred and fifty years. This harks back to the first German romantics and the idea of what can't be verbalized and that which is entirely intuitive. The '60s were an American expression of an intellectual and artistic tradition that really is very old. The only thing unique about them was their American aspect. Dieter is just a person of that time who is a kind of spiritual adventurer, part-charlatan, part-genuine mystic. He doesn't resemble Kesey in personality or style of speech or even in action. He presided over a strange scene, but you can probably find eight hundred guys who presided over strange scenes in that period. He has things in common with Kesey inasmuch as they both were "gurus," as they used to say at that time, but they aren't alike.

AV: It's interesting that people such as Kesey or Kerouac or Cassady are often revered, but their real lives are not what most people imagine. For example, Jack Kerouac wrote *On the Road*, which is considered the bible of personal freedom and expression; yet Kerouac disavowed his status as the "Father of the Beats" or the "Grandfather of the Hippies." He became an alcoholic who was closer to being a redneck than a beatnik when he died in 1969. I don't know what kind of commentary this should elicit about the writer and the perpetration of the romantic myth.

RS: In the case of Kerouac, he was an extremely romantic, extremely sentimental, extremely sensitive individual. He was an inheritor in the tradition of Whitman and of the expanding American continent, which was a kind of mysticism of the land. It's hard to remember, if you weren't around or if you are not a certain age, the kind of ridicule Kerouac was subject to in his own lifetime. He was very famous and influential, but he was constantly mocked for his writing that came out of the '50s. All the big publications and the national news magazines, in a way that would simply not occur today, treated him like a complete joke, like a boob, like a comedian, like a clown. This hurt him. He wasn't being taken seriously by anybody, whether it was the news media or even the literary establishment; yet at the same time they were taking Ginsberg seriously. Kerouac was brutalized by the American media. He looked very strapping and strong, but his health had always been bad. He was insecure and he didn't have much self-confidence. He was tremendously hurt by the kind of mockery the news media subjected him to and he succumbed to drink. The rest of the story involves drugs when he became an anti-Semite and ultra right-winger. I think this was alcoholic anger and a combination of spoiled romanticism whereby his early youthful enthusiasm was disappointed. He had a lot of quirks and psychological flaws and he was stingy. He couldn't stand to give you a cigarette. He was very badly wounded by criticism and driven to alcoholism. The worse he felt, the more he drank; and the more he drank, the worse he felt. It became a vicious circle.

AV: I can see where you might identify with Kerouac—for example, by his upbringing and the fact that he was close to his mother. He also traveled extensively. I know your childhood was atypical. [Stone's parents never married; he never knew his father, who deserted the family. His mother lost her elementary school teaching job because of schizophrenia. He lived in various rooming houses and welfare hotels where his mother worked as a chambermaid. Raised a Catholic and educated by the Marist Brothers, he quit school before graduation after disgracing himself by drinking too much beer and being "militantly atheistic."] Is Kerouac someone with whom you identified?

RS: I don't know if I identified with him, even though I was a teenager and a young sailor when he was a famous novelist. I admired him a lot and liked his work, but I find it pretty unreadable to tell you the truth. I loved *On the Road,* although I'm not even sure why. I think because it just reached everyone who had that romance about the American possibility and the American road. In a way, I don't think we're alike either as writers or as people. Our backgrounds in some ways are similar, and we are certainly touched by the same artistic, bohemian tradition that we shared, but not too much else.

AV: There is a kind of Kafkaesque atmosphere in bits of your writing that borders on the unreal or surreal. Is this grounded in your experiences with drugs?

RS: I'm trying to replicate a state of mind, very often with the state of mind being a mixture of subjective things and objective things. I'm a realist as a writer in a very limited way. I'm trying to accurately portray emotional and psychological states, so they can be recognized. I think you have to go beyond the level of naturalism in order to do that. The only way you can make words evoke psychological and emotional states effectively is by creating an altered state of consciousness. My way of doing that is to write a lot of prose that is close to blank verse and is evocative in the same ways poetry is. I'm certainly not a naturalist or a conventional artist. I'm after another kind of reality: the kind of reality that is subjectively experienced from the inside.

AV: "Robert Stone is the apostle of the strung-out," according to Jean Strouse during her review of *Children of Light* in the *New York Times Book Review.* Your characters are among the most difficult for a reader to identify with of any contemporary writer, with the possible exception of Hubert Selby Jr. For example, Geraldine in *A Hall of Mirrors* seems to have the same mentality as Tralala in Selby's *Last Exit to Brooklyn,* as evidenced when Geraldine thinks to herself: "It would be hard to tell somebody, she thought, how you could come to hate a day like this. Because it was beautiful, by God, it was as beautiful as you could ever want. She felt a sudden urge to find the darkest end of the darkest rankest bar on Decatur Street and drink herself sodden."

Since many readers would have a hard time understanding or identifying with or even sympathizing with characters like Geraldine, what do you expect your readers to learn from them? Do you see any correlation between Selby's characters and your characters, since you both are from Brooklyn?

RS: There is not a writer I feel less in common with than Selby. His characters, it seems to me, have absolutely no inner life of any kind. What's going on with Geraldine in that particular scene is the fact that she is really moved by how nice a day it is and her capacity, her enjoyment of life, is considerable. It's her loss of happiness that she is lamenting, because things haven't gone her way. She is unhappy. What the narrator is trying to convey is the force of her unhappiness. I can't even imagine associating the word "unhappy" or something as relatively uncomplicated a thing as unhappiness with a Selby character. I mean Geraldine has an inner life, she has an interiority, she has a mind, she has emotions, and she is capable of love. I've never read a character of Selby's who had any of these things or who had an inner life at all. You can't identify with Selby's characters, it seems to me, because there isn't a hell of a lot to them. It's like identifying with Raymond Chandler's characters where the other people are all mono-dimensional. So if people can't identify with my characters, there's nothing I can do.

AV: I didn't say readers can't identify with your characters, but that it may be hard to identify with them.

RS: I really think that what my characters go through is what most people go through at one time or another. It seems to me most people feel the way Geraldine feels in that one particular scene. People often feel betrayed by love. They feel let down or as though they are letting other people down. They have trouble with drugs and alcohol, but none of these things in my experience is uncommon. If people don't identify with these characters and feel anything for them, then all I can say is they ought to.

AV: There is also a line from *A Hall of Mirrors*: "It's a great life if you don't weaken." This recalls the same line that appears in Alan Sillitoe's *Saturday Night and Sunday Morning.* Was this line taken from that novel?

RS: That line is taken from a contemporary country song by Roy Acuff, which goes something like this: "It's a great life if you don't weaken, but who wants to be strong?" I think it was on the juke boxes when I was in the navy around 1960.

AV: I wonder if that song predates Sillitoe's book, which was published in 1958.

RS: I doubt if Sillitoe, being in England, would have heard that song, but I think that's probably a common phrase thrown around.

AV: What about your literary influences?

RS: I was influenced by Hemingway as a young reader. Hemingway made discoveries that were almost technical about how prose works, and I've used those, as so many others have. Very much Joseph

Conrad, a writer I tremendously admire, and a writer who is tremendously influential now. Conrad shows what a novel is supposed to be and how it can be made to work in novels like *Victory* and *Under Western Eyes. Victory* is one of my absolute favorites. John Dos Passos and F. Scott Fitzgerald are writers I read with great pleasure when I was young. I also admire Flaubert and Evelyn Waugh. My literary influences are really quite conventional in a literary way.

AV: You provided the text for the Vietnam photo textbook called *Images of War.* My wife, who is from Vietnam, was looking at the book and almost became sick because the graphic photos brought back so many bad memories. How did you manage to write the text?

RS: I have done a number of texts for books of photography, including one for James Nachtwey's book, which is called *Deeds of War: Photographs 1981 to 1988.* It's one of the best books of photographs I've ever seen. I think people ask to me to write texts for the photo textbooks of Vietnam because I've written about Vietnam and I worked there in 1971. I wasn't there a terribly long time, but I've had certain adventures which to me were very important and they always stayed with me.

AV: I've read you spent less than two months in Vietnam; yet the texts you wrote were very insightful. What was your experience in Vietnam, and how did it shape your outlook?

RS: I spent a short time in Vietnam, but each day was different. It shaped my outlook on the United States in many complicated ways that keep changing. The idea of a mistake of that dimension was a very funny thing to see. If you were brought up as a kid during the war, you were used to an America which was always successful—and not just always successful, but totally and always in the right. Concerning the rights and wrongs of Vietnam, one can always go back and forth endlessly; certainly, it was a miscalculation, in spite of whatever else it may have been. This was pretty easy to see. You didn't have to be terribly astute: the size of the thing, the tremendous dimensions, the number of people, the number of installations, and the amount of material—you knew right away this was all wrong. It was all misapplied. It was a mistake. This gigantic ten thousand-mile mistake was very jarring to see. I never saw a single act that I found to be utterly inhuman. It was a sustained war, being very different from what most people imagined. We have the impression that the war fought in Europe during World War II was fought in a completely different way from Vietnam. The common belief is that civilians in Europe were universally spared and never got blown up or never got burned with jelly gasoline. In fact, this happened all the time. An enormous number of French, Dutch, German, and even Danish civilians were killed by Allied forces. I didn't see any atrocities or egregious acts of cruelty. What I did see was this ongoing process, this kind of blinker vision, go-ahead, can-do spirit. It told me something about the American can-do spirit and the idea about America which refuses to make choices and refuses to admit to the limits of its power. This is still going on today. I react to this, not because I think it's essentially morally wrong, although it often puts us there. I react to it as an American, as a patriot, as a taxpayer. This was a revelation to me. What I saw in Vietnam was this hubris, this overconfidence, this refusal to think in human terms about an enemy or about a situation. A war is an utterly human situation. Yet we treated it entirely as a technical problem. It was, in fact, a conflict between human beings, and we made it everything but that. This may not be answering your question, but in another way it is. We just absolutely declined to realize this was a hassle between human beings. We treated it as though it were an entirely technical problem, as if we were trying to build a skyscraper, when we're actually involved in a contest of wills with people we never tried to understand.

Let me give you an example. Frances Fitzgerald tells the story about her father, Desmond Fitzgerald, who is a CIA man. One day he had the job of briefing Robert McNamara, who was Secretary of Defense. The CIA always had to brief McNamara a couple of times a week, and you always had to bring your visual aids, because McNamara wanted everything quantified. The guys in the Pentagon, the Kennedy whiz kids who went on to work for Johnson, they had it worked out *statistically* with graphs. There was no way the war could be lost. No possible rate of attrition could keep the United States from prevailing. It was all on the charts.

Then one day, Desmond Fitzgerald went over for the briefing and he didn't bring any charts or any numbers at all. McNamara sat through his briefing and then said to Mr. Fitzgerald, "Where are your visual aids? Where are the figures?" And Fitzgerald said, in effect, "Well look, sometimes you just have to get out in the hills and walk around, ride the buses, get to the fruit market, listen to what people are saying, pick up on the gossip, and try to find out what's going on. Sometimes that's much more important than anything you could put on a chart." McNamara said, "Thank you very much, Mr. Fitzgerald," and then he said to his deputy, "I never want to see that man in this office again." *He wanted numbers.* He was a numbers man. The military establishment continues to be technically oriented, in a way that almost makes it unable to think. They can reason mechanically, but they can't exactly think.

AV: It's almost like the US military mind is like that of a robot.

RS: It's a robotic consciousness. It's a nonverbal and almost a nonhuman consciousness, which is not to say that these people are somehow like robots or that they are not human. The intelligence they have created is robotic and nonhuman. There is no way we can figure out exactly how much the Iranians hate us. We say Iran's motives have to be economically determined or that they won't cooperate with the Iraqis. We have no way of making the machine think. There are elements in Iran that hate us so much that they will endure any amount of deprivation in order to hurt us. We can't do that kind of thinking. We can figure out exactly how to hurt them economically and militarily, but we can't do the other stuff. This is one of the reasons why we couldn't function in Vietnam. We had no declared ends, except we were trying to fight a political war in utterly nonpolitical ways because our guys were all apolitical technocrats. They didn't want to pay any attention to the political dimension of it. The only dimension they had was one-dimensional.

AV: Too bad we didn't learn from the French, who were probably laughing at us the whole time.

RS: The French were laughing at us because they never believed we were trying to help them, and they didn't want us to succeed where they failed.

AV: Incidentally, on page 141 of *Images of War,* there is a picture of a man in a wheelchair who looks like Ron Kovic, who wrote the book *Born on the Fourth of July* that was later made into a movie of the same name. Is that Ron Kovic?

RS: My first response is to say no, but after looking at the photo it might be.

AV: Do you think winning the National Book Award for *Dog Soldiers* in 1975 increased expectations from critics and therefore increased the pressure on you as a writer? Do you think there was any harm in winning that prize so early in your career?

RS: The pressure is always going to be there, and the expectations ought to be high. You should always be trying to learn. No matter what you are doing, you should always be trying to do it better. I have no regrets about the award. I want the critics' expectations to be high. I don't expect to be let off easy, and I don't want to be let off easy by the critics. Not that I think the critics are always right or that they are always perceptive.

AV: You used a passage from Conrad's *Heart of Darkness* as an epigraph to open *Dog Soldiers,* and you have already said Conrad was an influence. Why has this book of Conrad's been such a popular literary yardstick for Vietnam stories? For example, the movie *Apocalypse Now* was loosely based on *Heart of Darkness,* even though Conrad was writing about Africa.

RS: Conrad was a chronicler of late imperial ironies. Vietnam was a situation he would have immediately understood. People in Vietnam were in a Conradian situation. They were in the same kind of trouble as Kurtz was or Baron Axel Heyst was in *Victory.* There are great similarities between late imperial England that Conrad was writing about and the American condition at the time of the Vietnam War.

AV: Correct me if I'm wrong, but your style recalls language used by such writers as Somerset Maugham and Oscar Wilde. For example, in *Dog Soldiers* you state: "In Converse's view, the idea of a Korean soldier reading a *Zap* comic was worth the loss of the case." Or, when Ian Percy is preaching to Converse, he says: "Why don't you go watch some other place die? They've got corpses by the river-full in Bangle Desh. Why not go there?" Whereupon Converse replies, "It's dry." How did you acquire this style of subtle wit and sarcasm?

RS: It's my natural style.

AV: There are several references to Satan throughout *Dog Soldiers* as well as references to angelic images, including the missionary lady who tells Converse that people who don't believe in Satan "are in for an unpleasant surprise." Do you think Satan, metaphorically speaking, lived in Vietnam?

RS: I think Satan is everywhere there are people. This is an aspect of people who are weak and short-sighted and enraged. This is where Satan is, wherever that is going on, and that is always going on somewhere.

The view I have of the world—which is reflected in *Dog Soldiers* and probably in all my books—is essentially a religious one in structure. It doesn't necessarily attach to any body or creed, but the world to me is structured in a kind of religious way. The metaphor of religion that is embodied in the tradition of Christianity is a very useful one for addressing the moral problems of the world. My schema, my parameters for dealing with the world and people, is essentially a religious one, and the terms in which I tend to think are religious terms.

AV: Converse changes Descartes's argument to "I am afraid, therefore I am." Yet the fear in *Dog Soldiers* seems to be sublimated by too much death and too many drugs.

RS: Converse has a very hard time of it. What he is about is perception. He is a subject of fear who is in very frightening circumstances. What I'm saying is that, only that, and really nothing more. I'm not making any broad philosophical point. I'm just saying this is a guy who found himself pursuing a couple of exotic impulses in a very frightening situation.

AV: Drugs play a significant role throughout much of your fiction. What role did drugs play in your formative years as a writer?

RS: I never became addicted to drugs. I don't think drugs particularly interfered with my life. Obviously, around the electric scene described in *The Electric Kool-Aid Acid Test,* drugs were taken. I don't know how different my writing would be without drugs. I certainly don't write in a state of intoxication of any kind. I do not take drugs or drink in order to write. I don't write stoned in any way.

AV: Yet you wrote a very convincing and powerful scene at the end of *Dog Soldiers,* after Hicks has shot up with heroin and is walking along the railroad tracks and the landscape around him is almost surreal. How did you write this scene so convincingly?

RS: It's really more about heat and pain than it is about drugs. If you know something about drugs, you ought to know something about how drugs work to write that scene. The reason he shot up with heroin was to kill the pain after being severely wounded.

AV: Do you feel any affinity with William Burroughs and such books as *Junkie* and *Naked Lunch*?

RS: Affinity is not exactly the word. What I admire in those works of Burroughs is their humor. I think that humor is essentially a humane and moral impulse. I admire the fact that Burroughs goes into this world of utter freakishness—a kind of nonhuman, brutal, and amoral world of freakishness—and introduces a certain humor which I think is humane and wholesome. But other than that, affinity is not quite the word. There is a lot in Burroughs I have no affinity for, but I do like his black humor.

AV: Do you know that the cyberpunk science fiction writers such as William Gibson consider both you and Burroughs as distinct influences for their genre?

RS: I hadn't heard that before, but I'm glad to hear it.

AV: There is an interesting passage that describes Hicks making love to Converse's wife:

> *Because of his nature and circumstances, the most satisfying part of Hick's sexual life had come to be masturbation—he preferred it to prostitutes because it was more sanitary and took less time. He did not take it lightly when, rarely, one woman pleased him, and his deepest pleasures were intellectual and emotional. He became a hoarder, careful and slow to the point of obsessiveness, a thinker.*
>
> *He eased toward the light, his strength in his tongue, stroking the sweet-sour depths and surfaces. When he was ready he went in, striking for the deepest darkest part of her the limits of himself could reach, then eased up, stirring, stroking from inside. She came and spoke to him; he thought she said, "Find thee."*

I found these two paragraphs very expressive, and yet Hicks is trying to intellectualize sex, which is pretty hard to do. Phrases such as "stroking the sweet-sour depths" are so wonderfully descriptive.

RS: I think what one is trying to do in art is to provide recognition. You are trying to create an experience for your audience, but you create an experience by leading them to recognition of something they already know. That makes the process—of reading, or looking at the picture, or whatever they're doing—a living, active process. So this "stroking the sweet-sour depths" passage is meant to lead people to recognition because everybody knows what that means. All I am trying to do is lead people to the recognition of something they already know. It just lights up the moment, and they know exactly where the character is.

AV: What about the words "Find thee"?

RS: It's from a line that's in the "Wreck of the Deutschland" by Gerard Manley Hopkins. I think the line goes, "Feel thy finger and find thee."

AV: There are interesting passages about existence in *Dog Soldiers*. The first passage is from Converse's insight on fragmentation bombing in Vietnam: "One insight was that the ordinary physical world through which one shuffled heedless and half-assed toward non-entity was capable of composing itself at any time and without notice, into a massive instrument of agonizing death. Existence was a trap; the testy patience of things as they are might be exhausted at any moment."

Can you comment on your views of existence or existentialism? Also, does being removed from war make one less cognizant of one's mortality?

RS: I think being away from danger and from pressure—or maybe it works the other way around when you see a lot of physical annihilation close at hand—your own mortality occurs to you more vividly and more pertinently. As far as philosophical views go, I think the great existential novelist is Dostoyevsky.

The fact that we have to impose meaning on a seemingly random and meaningless universe is something I share with most people. I think most people believe this in one form or another. I do believe in a moral dimension. I believe that nothing is free. I believe you always have to pay off one end or the other. I think there is a traditionally historical philosophy at the core of my system of beliefs. I think existentialism has become so much a truism that you can hardly speak of existentialism because we are all existentialists now.

AV: I find the dichotomy between the two: the intelligent world is probably viewing things from an existentialist viewpoint about the meaning of life, if there is any, and yet we are still living in a religious house. It is interesting how you manage to combine those two elements.

RS: I think it was Paul Tillich who spoke about God as a dynamic absence: If God is not, it doesn't necessarily change the way things are. Instead of a dynamic presence there is a dynamic absence. You don't necessarily have to have an extra-personal God to have a religious framework. You can have a religious framework that doesn't have God in it. In this case it can become an absolutely dynamic and highly significant absence or a kind of vacuum that blends absurdity to the human action. Those two things don't contradict each other. You don't have to be a Deist to see things in a religious framework.

AV: There is frequent mention throughout your fiction of moral issues. For example, in *Dog Soldiers* there is a conversation: "Aren't there some funny moral areas here?" Jody asks, and Margie responds, "I guess it depends on your sense of humor." Do you subscribe to John Gardner's premise from his book *On Moral Fiction* that fiction should have a moral point of view?

RS: I think it has to. We can't help having one. That's the nature of language, because you are always making choices, you are always presenting options. Fiction has an inescapable moral connection. There is just no way around it. You are always presenting things in a favorable or unfavorable light. You are always making judgments.

AV: Would you align yourself with such writers as John Gardner and John Fowles rather than William Gass, John Barth, and Thomas Pynchon?

RS: Yes.

AV: Tom Wolfe has recently written a controversial essay called "Stalking the Billion-Footed Beast." What are thoughts about Wolfe's essay, which many critics have found to be self-serving?

RS: I have a lot of admiration for Tom Wolfe. I think he's a very good writer. When he was a young writer, the realism-naturalism character appeared to be passé, while writers like Barth, Hawkes, Gass, and Coover—who I wouldn't put in quite the same category—were popular and whose characters or fiction often evoked a kind of nonrealism.

I think American realism, although not traditional realism, has made a tremendous comeback. Wolfe writes as though he is still going against the prevailing grain in writing a realistic novel, but that simply is not so nowadays. It was when he began to write in the early '60s, when *Giles Goat-Boy* and *The Sot-Weed Factor* were the big important books of the time, but those days are long gone. We've had an entire generation of young realist writers like Raymond Carver and Tobias Wolff and many others too numerous to mention.

AV: You mentioned two novels by Barth that some critics consider classics. Yet you are saying those books are no longer as important as they were.

RS: I don't mean to say those works are no longer important. I'm just saying they are not the dominant mode now. Tom Wolfe is somehow writing that these fabulist works of fiction are still the dominant mode in American fiction, which isn't the case. The dominant mode in fiction is realist writers like Bobbie Ann Mason, Margaret Atwood, and Richard Ford, and so forth. Tom Wolfe is not rebelling against the dominant mode anymore. Maybe he was in the past, but he is not now.

AV: Can you explain the following items from *Dog Soldiers*: the name Antheil; "Stone the gash"; Those Who Are; and A.M.D.G.?

RS: There was an American composer in Paris in the 1920s named

George Antheil who was a prolific composer. He wrote *Ballet Mecanique* and later went on to write movies. I like the name "Antheil" because it suggests fascism and insects. "Stone the gash" means to get a woman high. "Gash" is an extremely vulgar term for a woman. "Those Who Are" is an old Greek Homeric term. Hicks has the Greek letters tattooed on his arm and it has to do with Hicks's sense of who he is and a kind of secret society. A.M.D.G. is the motto of the Jesuits. *Ad majorem Dei gloriam* are the Latin words which translate to "to the greater glory of God." Those letters are inscribed over the gateway to Dieter's ranch.

AV: You wrote the screenplays for *WUSA* starring Paul Newman, based on *A Hall of Mirrors,* and also *Who'll Stop the Rain?* starring Nick Nolte, based on *Dog Soldiers.* Yet you have expressed reservations about the finished product.

RS: I think you lose a lot when you make a book into a movie, because you lose the open-endedness and you cut off possibilities. With literature, there are many possibilities where words can cast a certain shadow, whereas with film, you are absolutely limited to only one order of appearances. So the imagination can't run free. It's determined by what the eyes see.

There is also the tendency in which movies tend to resist moral ambiguities which are the principal subjects of my work. Movies don't like my ambiguities. Movies really compel you to decide if this is a good person or a bad person. It's almost the nature of motion-picture photography. You are always leading people to essentially simple judgments, and it's very hard to portray a lot of ambiguity.

AV: I think one exception would be Hitchcock's *Psycho,* where the audience is trying to identify with this woman who has embezzled some money and halfway through the movie she is murdered. I think the reader of *Dog Soldiers* experiences the same thing by trying to identify with Converse, but halfway through the novel Converse's wife takes off with the so-called paranoid psychopath Hicks. Perhaps if Hitchcock were still alive, he could have done justice to your novel.

RS: You can't have two things to deal with at once about a character in a movie. It's hard to get people in a movie to think that something is awful and funny at the same time. I'm not saying movies can't handle this, but it is much harder for a film to achieve.

AV: Such characters as Rheinhardt, Converse, Hicks, Holliwell, and Walker in your novels seem to share a fundamental inability to face reality, with their perceptions further distorted by drugs or alcohol.

RS: I don't think they are unable to "face reality." I think in fact their specialty is perception. They are constantly identifying and defining the nature of the action of reality in an extremely intense and perceptive way. It's not these men can't face reality; it's that they confront it all too well. They confront it all too vigorously and intensely all the time.

AV: Can you see any of these characters, who are using drugs or alcohol, where they might progress to the point of facing reality?

RS: It depends what you mean by "facing reality." What does it mean to face reality? Does it mean not thinking about how things are? There are very few people I know who have moved to a situation where they "face reality." As in the psycho-babble phrase, one can "take control of their lives" and can make their lives less chaotic. The trouble with my characters is that they are adventurers. They are pursuing sensation. They are pursuing more life. They are also victims of spite. These people are not so much avoiding reality as they are reacting with spite to the dissatisfactions of life which they experience. Ahab, in *Moby-Dick,* is acting in a tremendously spiteful way.

One can say this character's behavior is adolescent or immature, but it is also universally human. My characters are not missing some point, because they actually understand the situation correctly. It's their actions they cannot bring to bear because there is no completely satisfying moral ground for them to stand on. They have all lived examined lives. They all have highly developed moral sensibilities. They act against their own better instincts out of the necessities of the moment. They let each other down because of the situations they have gotten themselves into. They are not missing some point, as I have said, because they are involved in life in a very real way. The world they are seeing is quite clear. It does exist.

AV: Despite being on opposite sides of the law, Hicks and Danskin don't appear to be much different. In fact, I would say Hicks is a much better person—much more moral, and substantially saner than Danskin.

RS: That is the intention. Danskin is a smart, articulate psychopath. He is a true psychopath who has poor instincts. Hicks, despite what Converse thinks, is not a psychopath, while having very good instincts.

AV: What about the process of an interview? Does it help you when you try to verbalize your thoughts about fiction?

RS: Yes, it really does.

AV: The interview also allows the reader to get a better understanding of the writer.

RS: People don't understand that a writer is an illusionist, a performer. You don't expect an actor to be as crazy as his performance, and writing is performance. It is art. It is storytelling. Very few writers are the kind of creatures one might encounter in their books.

AV: Several critics were not very receptive to *Children of Light* because they said you were essentially reworking old themes, but in different settings.

RS: It seems to me *Children of Light* and *A Flag for Sunrise* are very different books. I can't imagine someone reading *Children of Light* and saying this is like *A Flag for Sunrise.* I don't know what they mean by that. If they mean heterosexual love and people's capacity for not coming through for each other, then those things are similar. I think the styles in the books are very different.

AV: What can readers expect in your latest novel, *Outerbridge Reach?*

RS: It has a lot of sailing in it. I don't want to say too much, but readers have a right to insight and poetry. That's what I'm trying to do.

Acknowledgments

First of all, I would like to thank Wipanan Chaichanta, which means Beautiful Infinity in Thai, and to those directly and indirectly related to my family: Le-My Vorda, Pat Vorda, Brian Redmond, Patty Robinson, Alana Vorda, Marianne Thai, Shawn Vorda, Melanie Savoie, and Tristan Vorda.

Others, in no uncertain order, who have affected either my life or my writing in some manner: Michael Skau, Jamie Sullivan, Duane Franklet, Shirley King, Josh Baker, Eric Pace, Rajiv Ramchandran, Jerome Guynn, Leigh Anderson, Lon Dentlinger, Kim Herzinger, Liliana Avila, Nina Shanu, Jennifer Otalor, Bich Hoang, John Peebles, Vicki Borst, Narisara Chaichanta, Diane Vorda, all my relatives in Chicago, Klaus Schulze, Roky Erickson, Arthur Lee, Mark Burgess, Neal Skok, everyone in the Montrose Book Club, and the most fun person in the world, you miserable toad, Chuck Brackett.

I cannot fail to mention Eric Lorberer, editor of *Rain Taxi,* who brilliantly edited a good number of these interviews, and Shawn Vorda who transcribed and edited.

Finally, many thanks to indexer Jay Knarr and to Daniel E. Williams, Molly Spain, Kathy Walton, Rebecca Allen, and James Lehr of TCU Press, who made thirty-five years of interviews come to life.

Index

About the Author

Allan Vorda was born in Evanston, Illinois, and raised in Omaha before moving to Houston. He received degrees in English from Creighton University (BA) and the University of Nebraska at Omaha (MA). Previous publications include *Face to Face: Interviews with Contemporary Writers* (Rice University Press) and *Psychedelic Psounds: Interviews from A to Z with 60s Psychedelic and Garage Bands* (Borderline Productions/UK).